WORKPLACE LEADERSHIP

WORKPLACE LEADERSHIP

First Edition

Edited by **Robin Lindbeck and Vince Nix**

cognella®
SAN DIEGO

Bassim Hamadeh, CEO and Publisher
John Remington, Executive Editor
Gem Rabanera, Senior Project Editor
Jeanine Rees, Production Editor
Jessica Delia, Graphic Designer
JoHannah McDonald, Licensing Coordinator
Natalie Piccotti, Director of Marketing
Kassie Graves, Senior Vice President, Editorial
Alia Bales, Director, Project Editorial and Production

Printed in the United States of America.

cognella® ACADEMIC PUBLISHING
320 South Cedros Ave., Ste. 400, Solana Beach, CA 92075

Brief Contents

Detailed Contents

Introduction

By Robin Lindbeck and Julia Barrett

Why Workplace Leadership?

Organizations want to be effective—effective in reaching their goals and effective in creating an environment that enables their employees to be effective. It is generally accepted that the effectiveness of a leader in a business environment will have an impact on business results (Goleman, Boyatzis, & McKee, 2002; Citaku & Ramadani, 2020). In a 2021 study of over 15,000 leaders and 2100 HR professionals in 1700 organizations worldwide, CEOs listed *developing next gen leaders* as their top challenge, with CEOs in 2023 listing *attracting top talent and developing next gen leaders* as their top two challenges (DDI, 2021; DDI, 2023). Clearly, developing workplace leadership—the ability to guide, inspire, and influence others toward achieving common goals and objectives within a work environment—is critical for organizations.

What Is Leadership?

Leadership, and the quest to understand leadership, has been around for thousands of years. "From its infancy, the study of history has been the study of leaders—what they did and why they did it" (Bass, 2008, p. 3). Leadership can be found at all levels of organizations and practiced by individuals with and without formal leadership positions.

Leadership Versus Management

Although both leadership and management display many of the same skills such as influence, working in groups, and goal attainment, historically it has been the overall purpose of function that distinguishes leadership from management (Northouse, 2019). Management is about stability—about producing order and consistency as opposed to leadership, which must focus on adaptability—producing change and movement and that "management is about coping with complexity ... [and] leadership is about coping with change" (Kotter, 1999, p. 52). Leaders identify the need for change and adaptability, set direction and create a vision, align people toward that direction, and motivate them to move in the new direction. Managers, on the other hand, execute the day-to-day operational responsibilities necessary within the new direction, organize and staff to achieve the new direction, and control and solve problems to achieve the new direction (Kotter, 1999; Bass, 2008; Kouzes & Posner, 2017). Each set of responsibilities is important to the achievement of the goals and organizational success.

In the current working environment, the distinction between leadership and management responsibilities may be clear, but the distinction between the leader and manager *role* is not as clear. An individual leader or manager will likely find themselves with a combination of both leadership and management responsibilities to fulfill their role and achieve the goals of the organization.

Definition of Leadership

There have been many conceptions of leadership over the years, with numerous researchers contributing to the ever-growing body of research on the topic. Whether defined as "establishing direction, aligning people and motivating and inspiring [them]" (Kotter, 1999, p. 6), being "patient, persistent, consistent, and persuasive [with] unshakeable commitment to the rights of the individual" (Phillips, 1992, p. 3), or "reciprocal process of mobilizing by person with certain motives and values, various economic, political, and other resources, in a context of competition and conflict, in order to realize goals independently or mutually held by both leaders and followers" (Burns, 1978, p. 425), there exist in the literature a wide variety of definitions of leadership. Northouse (2019) summarizes the range of definitions and perspectives for the purpose of creating a common definition, concluding that "(a) leadership is a process, (b) leadership involves influence, (c) leadership occurs within a group context, and (d) leadership involves goal attainment" (p. 3). Given that, he suggests the following definition of leadership: "Leadership is a process whereby an individual influences a group of individuals to achieve a common goal" (p. 5).

About This Book

The purpose of this book is to provide a foundation in leadership and to help you improve your leadership skills. This book is divided into four parts.

Part 1

This section provides a foundation for understanding leadership by providing an overview of leadership theories and discussing ethical leadership.

Parts 2–4

Parts 2–4 focus on common leadership competencies. Workplace competencies, conceptualized by Boyatzis (1982), refer to the features required to perform work, including the skills, knowledge, and motivation needed to work effectively in a particular position, such as leadership. Many organizations have used competencies to define and clarify the knowledge and skills required for specific jobs, and for specific leadership roles within their organizations. Parts 2–4 present some of the common competencies required for leaders in the workplace. Each of these practical chapters focuses on an individual competency and defines the competency, describes how to use this competency in the workplace, and ends with opportunities for you to practice applying the competency. Parts 2–4 organize these leadership competencies into three groups: leadership competencies needed to lead yourself, to lead others, and to lead the organization.

References

Bass, B. M. (2008). *The Bass handbook of leadership: Theory, research, and managerial applications* (4th ed.). Free Press.

Burns, J. M. (1978). *Leadership*. Harper Torchbooks.

Boyatzis, R. E. (1982). *The competent manager: A model for effective performance*. Wiley.

Citaku, F., & Ramadani, H. (2020). Leadership competency model-drenica: Generalizability of leadership competencies. *International Journal of Organizational Leadership, 9*, 156–162.

DDI. (2023). *Global Leadership Forecast 2023*. https://www.ddiworld.com/global-leadership-forecast-2023

DDI. (2021). *Global Leadership Forecast 2021*. https://www.ddiworld.com/global-leadership-forecast-2021

Goleman, D., Boyatzis, R. E., & McKee, A. (2002). *Primal leadership.* Harvard Business School.
Kotter, J. P. (1999). *What leaders really do.* Harvard Business School.
Kouzes, J. M., & Posner, B. Z. (2017). *The leadership challenge* (6th ed.). Jossey-Bass.
Northouse, P. G. (2019). *Leadership* (8th ed.). Sage.
Phillips, D. T. (1992). *Lincoln on leadership.* Warner.

UNIT I

INTRODUCTION TO LEADERSHIP

CHAPTER 1

Leadership Theories

By Ajit P. Bhattarai

Nothing is as practical as a good theory.

—Kurt Lewin

Learning Objectives

After reading this chapter, students will be able to:

1. List and describe person/leader-centric theories
2. List and describe contingency or situational theories
3. List and describe relations-centered theories
4. List and describe emerging leadership approaches

Let us start this chapter by inserting ourselves into the following conversation between two friends:

Norman: *Tough disciplinarians who run a tight ship always become successful leaders.*

Frank: *How do you know that?*

Norman: *I have worked with numerous leaders in my career. Most of the successful ones were always tough disciplinarians.*

Frank: *That's your opinion!*

Norman: *No, that's my theory!*

Frank: *How can that be a theory?*

Norman: *Because I have seen it enough times, and most of the time, I have been correct.*

Frank: *So, if you see something happening enough times, can you say that you have a theory about what is happening?*

Norman: *Well. ...*

Frank: *I think that's your opinion.*

Norman: *You keep saying it's my opinion, not a theory. What does that mean? In one of my classes, I read that "a theory simply explains what a phenomenon is and how it works" (Torraco, 1997, p. 115). So how am I incorrect?*

Frank: *What you read is true. Let me try to explain it. Further, what you claim might well be a theory, but it is informal.*

Norman: *What do you mean, informal? Then how does it become formal? And how does a theory differ from an opinion?*

Frank: *What Torraco notes is true. However, you must do many things before saying a "theory simply explains." First, you need to observe certain things repeatedly. I know you have observed numerous leaders in your career. But did you systematically observe them? What did you observe? Were you observing the same thing all the time? How did you observe? Did you keep detailed records of what you were observing?*

Norman: *Umm ... no.*

Frank: *You said leaders are tough disciplinarians. But what do you mean by tough disciplinarians? Were all the leaders you worked with tough in exactly the same way? Can you give a precise definition of what a tough disciplinarian might mean? Unless you can do so, you might not be comparing apples with apples. Further, will your friends who worked with the same leaders also describe them as tough disciplinarians?*

Norman: *Maybe.*

Norman: *You also said, successful leaders. What do you mean by successful? Were the leaders you talked about successful in a similar way? Did you measure their success in a similar manner? Further, would your colleagues agree with your definition of successful?*

Frank: *That's a hard no.*

Norman: *Okay. Your statement, "tough disciplinarians who run a tight ship always become successful leaders" is a cause-effect statement. Let me explain this a bit. Did you mean to say that one needs to be a tough disciplinarian to be a successful leader?*

Frank: *I guess so.*

Norman: *So, being a "tough disciplinarian" is the cause and "successful leaders" is the result. But how sure are you about this? Could there be other factors or variables in play? Let's say there were other factors. What impact did these other factors have on somebody becoming a successful leader? How would you know about them, and how would you measure them?*

Frank: *Well ... this is getting complicated!*

Norman: *Yes!! What I am trying to say is that certain things need to be done for something to be acknowledged as a theory. A formal study (or a series of research studies) is consciously designed and conducted. In these studies, assumptions are tested, relationships are explored, and answers are sought to see if the findings of the complex phenomenon being studied can be generalized to similar situations.*

Frank: *I see! This makes sense.*

Norman: *One last thing, theories are continuously tested and, if needed, reformulated based on newer findings from research studies.*

In this chapter, we will focus on leadership theories. But before we do that, we need to answer a few questions: What is a theory? What are leadership theories? Why study leadership theories?

What Is a Theory?

In the above conversation, Norman is trying to explain what theory means. His answers contain many commonly accepted thoughts about what is meant by theory. However, "the term theory can mean different things to different people in the social sciences, but most of the time it refers to a logical idea or conjecture about how a particular corner of the world works" (Remler & Ryzin, 2015, p. 26). According to Remler and Ryzin, a theory

1. identifies key variables,
2. tells the story of how variable(s) interact and cause certain things to happen (causation),
3. explains the difference in the results (variation)
4. generates testable hypotheses, i.e., "predictions of what will happen if our theory is correct" (p. 28).

Dugan (2017) further notes that a "theory strings together often-abstract propositions and hypotheses in an attempt to make meaning or explain complex phenomena" (p. 10).

Why Do We Need Theories?

Since "a theory simply explains what a phenomenon is and how it works" (Torraco, 1997, p. 115), "there is nothing as practical as a good theory" (Lewin, 1943, p. 119). Theories provide insights into how something is happening. When we know how different variables and constructs interact to impact a result, we can potentially know where and what action we can take to either continue the status quo or change it.

What Is the Difference Between Terms Like Theories, Models, and Frameworks?

Similar to how *theory* is understood differently, related terms like *models, frameworks*, etc., are defined and understood differently. Since leadership is variously described in terms of theories, models, etc., a working knowledge of these terms can be availed from Dugan's (2017) definitions listed in Table 1.1.

TABLE 1.1 **Definitions of Theories, Models, Taxonomies, and Frameworks**

Classifications	Definition
Informal Theory	Untested personal propositions about the nature of a phenomenon; frequently subconscious; delimited to one's worldview (p. 12)
Formal Theory	Empirically tested propositions that offer explanatory and descriptive insights into a phenomenon
Models	Descriptive representation, often visual, of a phenomenon; frequently derived from or seen as the application of theory; may or may not be empirically tested
Taxonomies	System of classification offering a useful organizational heuristic; may or may not be empirically derived
Frameworks	Abstract representation of ideas, frequently conceptual or philosophical; typically not been empirically tested

Note: From Leadership Theory: Cultivating Critical Perspectives by J. P. Dugan, 2017, p. 12, Jossey-Bass. Copyright 2017 by John Wiley & Sons, Inc. Reprinted with permission

What Are Leadership Theories, and Why Study Them?

Since what leaders do *or do not do* deeply impacts an organization's success or failure, it is pertinent that we understand what it entails to be a leader and what leaders need to do and not do while leading their followers. Bass (2008) notes that "theories of leadership attempt to explain its emergence or its nature and its consequences" (p. 91). Scholars in various fields study things like what makes an effective leader, how leaders influence their followers, etc., and develop theories and models that describe leadership. Not surprisingly, given that leadership is a complex process, it is understood differently by various sets of people, sometimes in conflicting ways (Dugan, 2017).

Leadership theories can be viewed from multiple perspectives and broadly be grouped into the following four categories:

1. Person-centric theories
2. Contingency or situational theories
3. Contemporary/relations-centered theories
4. Emerging leadership approaches

Person-centric Theories

Person-centric theories look at leaders' various traits and behaviors to describe what leadership is and what leaders do while leading.

Trait Approach

Nancy is a born leader. She was always destined to be a leader.

These are common phrases that represent trait theories. Trait theories of leadership, like the *great man* theory, are some of the earliest approaches used to explain leaders (van Zyl and Hofmeyr, 2021). For example, the *great man* theory can describe commonalities among historical figures like Mahatma Gandhi, Napoleon Bonaparte, Winston Churchill, et al. Based on the commonalities, one can then postulate that to be an influential leader, one must have the same common traits that Gandhi, Bonaparte, Churchill, et al. possessed.

Trait theories argue that leaders are born with innate characteristics, attributes, or traits that do not change over time. These innate characteristics (e.g., gender, ethnicity, familial ties, etc.) are what differentiate leaders from non-leaders. Researchers investigating trait theories study what makes some people great leaders. However, even after more than a century of research, researchers have yet to agree on a set of traits consistent among successful leaders in different situations (Northouse, 2022), with scholars like Stogdill (1948) noting that "leadership is not a matter of passive status, or of the mere possession of some combination of traits" (p. 66). While traits like intelligence, self-confidence, determination, integrity, and sociability are often listed as some key traits that leaders possess, the presence of such traits does not irrefutably prove that it is the mere presence of these skills that differentiates leaders and non-leaders.

While trait theories have been extensively critiqued, organizations worldwide have found them helpful in identifying potential leaders in the workforce. Thus, contrary to the earlier focus on traits like gender, ethnicity, familial ties, etc., that were thought of as necessities in a leader, the current emphasis on traits like possessing charisma and being visionary is more predictive of effective leaders. While some leaders naturally have traits like charisma, extraversion, self-confidence, etc., these personality traits can be potentially developed through various developmental interventions.

TABLE 1.2 **Benefits and Challenges—Trait Theories**

Benefits of Trait Theories	Challenges of Trait Theories
• Trait theories have provided certain characteristics that most successful leaders possess. This can allow organizations to have an early indication that certain employees might be suitable for leadership development programs. • When desired traits are clearly identified, trait theories can help leaders assess themselves and understand their weaknesses and strengths as leaders and take corrective actions.	• Biological traits cannot be taught. • There is no universally agreed-upon list of traits that leaders should possess. • Most traits can be subjectively described differently. • The presence or absence of certain traits in a leader does not guarantee successful and effective leadership.

Reflection Questions:

1. Think of a leader you had in the past (this could be a work leader, a coach, or a famous person you admire). What traits did the leader possess? How did those traits help the leader be effective?
2. Think of a role in which you are a leader, or a role you really want in the future. What traits help (and hinder) your effectiveness as a leader? What is one thing you can do to improve your effectiveness?

Behavioral Approaches

While leading projects, George is known to be considerate toward his employees, sometimes at the expense of the quality of work. This is in contrast to Harry, who is well known as a disciplined taskmaster in the organization.

Given how the Trait Approaches did not explain much about how leaders behaved, scholars began to study the behaviors of successful leaders. Behavioral approaches focus on what leaders do and how they act while leading their followers (Northouse, 2022).

Starting in the late 1940s, scholars at Ohio State University and the University of Michigan began studying leaders' behaviors through large-scale questionnaire studies. What we now know about leader behaviors mainly comes from these two seminal studies, followed by the work of Blake and Mouton that started in the 1960s. These theories can help us make some sense of how leaders like George and Harry lead in different ways by focusing on two dimensions:

1. the level of the leaders' focus on the work being done (task/goal); and
2. the extent that the leaders maintain the relationship with their employees during the task.

Ohio State University and the University of Michigan Studies

In the Ohio State studies (Halpin & Winer, 1957; Fleishman, 1957), the first dimension was labeled as "initiating structures" and the second dimension "consideration," while in the University of Michigan studies (Kahn, 1956), they were known as "production orientation" and "employee orientation," respectively.

Initiating structures (Ohio State) and production orientation (University of Michigan) are *task-related behaviors*. These involve giving directions to the employees to do their jobs, helping them improve performance, and structuring their jobs. Consideration (Ohio State) and employee orientation (UM) are *people-oriented behaviors*. They encompass showing genuine concern for employees' well-being and taking the needed action toward that end.

TABLE 1.3 **Comparison Between Ohio State and the University of Michigan Studies**

	Ohio State studies	University of Michigan studies	Notes
Task-related behaviors	Initiating structures	Production orientation	Giving directions to the employees to do their jobs, helping them improve performance, and structuring their jobs. The leader provides specific instructions, sets clear deadlines, clearly mentions what standards need to be met, etc.
People-oriented behaviors	Consideration	Employee orientation	Showing genuine concern for employees' well-being and taking the needed action toward that end. The leader is friendly and easily approachable and provides words of support, encouragement, and appreciation. The leader also takes actions that show their care toward the employees.

The managerial grid or leadership grid, initially formulated by Robert Blake and Jane Mouton in the 1960s (Blake & Mouton, 1964) and its various revisions (e.g., Blake & Mouton, 1985), is a globally popular model used to understand managerial behaviors (Northouse, 2022). It is similar to both the Ohio State and University of Michigan studies as it also focuses on two factors: *concern for production* and *concern for people*. These two factors are measured on a two-dimensional scale, and each axis on the grid has a scale (1–9): 1 represents a low concern for the axis item, and 9 means a high concern for the axis item. Based on the two factors *concern for production* and *concern for people*, five leadership styles are presented in the grid: impoverished management, country-club management, middle-of-the-road management, authority-compliance management, and team management.

1. Impoverished management (1, 1): The leader has low concern for both production and people. The leader might not have a full grasp of the work being done, be resistant to changes, and is generally not result-oriented. The leader is also not responsive to the follower's needs, can be labeled indifferent, and be seen as ineffective. Leaders who practice impoverished management are generally not liked.
2. Country-club management (1, 9): The leader has low concern for the work at hand but is highly concerned about maintaining a positive and friendly relationship with employees. The leader wants to create a pleasant work environment and wants to be liked by the followers.
3. Middle-of-the-road management (5, 5): The leader has a moderate concern for both production and people. The leader strives to manage a positive workplace but does not go overboard; the leader focuses on the work but is not a hard taskmaster and does not push people to achieve more. The leader might look complacent and can come across as someone who compromises and is an average performer.
4. Authority-compliance management (9, 1): The leader has a high concern for production (task) but low concern for people. The leader is acutely focused on the task but is not overly concerned about people and can come across as authoritarian.
5. Team management (9, 9): The opposite of impoverished management, with the leader having high concern for both the task and the people doing the task. The leader is focused on not only increasing productivity but also ensuring the followers remain motivated, empowered, and are continuously growing in the workplace. The leader can be seen as effective and has the follower's trust.

Per behavioral theories, effective leaders engage in balanced task and relationship behaviors with followers. In some situations, the focus on the task might be high, while in other situations, the focus on relationships will be higher.

TABLE 1.4 **Benefits and Challenges—Behavioral Theories**

Benefits of Behavioral Theories	Challenges of Behavioral Theories
• An advantage of behavioral theories over trait theories is that behavioral approaches can be taught to existing and future leaders. This means that most people can be potentially developed as leaders. • Leaders can be taught when to focus on relationships and tasks. • Leaders can be taught how they can apply different leadership styles in different situations. • After learning about behavioral theories of leadership, leaders can become more flexible in responding to situations.	• The theories do not consider how a dynamic environment can impact leadership. • Successful leaders with one leadership style in one organization might not succeed in another organization in a similar situation. • It takes time to learn the various theories. • Personal biases might hinder the adoption of certain leadership styles. • The theories do not provide specific guidelines on what to do in specific circumstances. • Even when the leader exhibits the *team management style (9, 9)*, there might not be good results or satisfied employees due to factors not in the leader's control.

Reflection Questions:

1. For each of the five leadership styles, what can be the possible impacts (both positive and negative) on organizational results, employee morale, and employee satisfaction?
2. For each of the five leadership styles, what might leaders do to improve organizational results and boost both the morale and satisfaction of the followers?
3. List and describe five situations where each of the five leadership styles just covered might be most appropriate.
4. Think of a leader you had in the past (this could be a work leader, a coach, or a person you admire). What styles did the leader use? How did each of the leadership styles affect performance? If you were in the leader's position, what style(s) could you have used also, or instead? Why?

Contingency/Situational Theories

The second broad category of leadership theory has been variously labeled as contingency and situational leadership theories. The thrust of these theories is to explore how leaders must consider the changing situations (environment) around them while leading.

The Fiedler Contingency Model

Kate, the new country lead of an IT company, has noted that Team 1 on the West Coast regularly exceeds its targets, but the corresponding Team 2 on the East Coast is struggling. Her investigations revealed that both teams engage in highly technical but very straightforward operations and are led by seasoned managers who have the authority to terminate employees not meeting the standards and approve bonuses and promotions for those exceeding the benchmarks. She also noticed that both teams had documented cases of poor manager-employee relationships. Struggling to make sense of this, she started consulting with other colleagues to identify the reasons for the struggles of Team 2. During her discussions, Megan, one of her Human Resource Development managers with a recent Leadership Certificate, suggested that they look at the leadership style of both managers leading Team 1 and 2 and that Fiedler's Contingency Model of Leadership might possibly explain the differences. The subsequent review showed that while the manager of Team 2 was a highly competent and hitherto successful leader, he was a very hard taskmaster. Megan also reported that in contrast to the Team 2 manager, Team 1's manager was more people focused. Based on the review and upon reading more about Fiedler's Contingency Model, Kate, the country lead, decided to replace the Team 2 manager with another manager who was more people focused.

This model (Fiedler, 1964) postulates that the optimal leadership style is situation dependent and was developed by Frederick Fiedler in the 1960s. The model has two interrelated parts:

1. Identifying the leadership style of the individual; and
2. Identifying the situation where a particular leadership style is most suited.

1) Identifying the leadership style.
Frederick Fiedler developed the "least preferred coworker (LPC)" scale, which asks respondents to think about their least preferred coworker. The LPC is used to ascertain whether the respondent describes their coworker in favorable or unfavorable terms. While thinking of the least preferred coworker, the LPC scale asks the respondent to rate 18 items such as "Disagreeable-Agreeable," "Inconsiderate-Considerate," and "Boring-Interesting" on an 8-point scale (Fiedler, 1978).

The LPC score is calculated by adding the respondent's chosen numbers from the scale. Respondents who describe their coworkers in favorable terms have a high LPC score and are classified as relationship oriented. Respondents who describe their coworkers in unfavorable terms have a low LPC score and are classified as task oriented. The respondent can then be placed in organizational situations that fit their relationship or task-oriented leadership style.

2) Identifying the situation where a particular leadership style is most suited.
Fiedler (1978) notes that the following three organizational situational factors can affect whether a leadership style is effective or not.

1. *Status of leader-member relations.* The status of *leader-member relations* (leader-follower relations) can either be *good* or *poor.* Some examples of the relations are the level of trust, respect, and confidence in the leader.
2. *Task structure.* The tasks that the followers do can be highly structured or the tasks can be unstructured. The *task structure* can be either *high* or *low.*
3. *Position power.* The *position power* of the leader can either be *strong* or *weak.* Some examples of position power are the leader's level of authority in things like hiring, promotion, firing, etc.

The model argues that a leadership style (inherent to the person) can be favorable or unfavorable, depending on the three situational factors. Some organizational situations might benefit from a task-based leadership style, while other situations might require relationship-oriented leadership styles. The model has eight different organizational situations based on the interrelationship between leader-member relations, task structure, and position power (Mitchell et al., 1970).

1. Situation 1: The leader-member relations are good (i.e., there is a high level of trust, confidence, and respect between the leader and followers), task structure is structured (i.e., the work is highly structured with clear policies and procedures in place), and position power is strong (i.e., the leader has the authority to take various personnel decisions like hiring, promotion, benefits increments, etc.) (Robbins & Judge, 2021).
2. Situation 2: The leader-member relations are good, the task structure is structured, and position power is weak.
3. Situation 3: The leader-member relations are good, the task structure is unstructured, and position power is strong.
4. Situation 4: The leader-member relations are good, the task structure is unstructured, and position power is weak.
5. Situation 5: The leader-member relations are poor, the task structure is structured, and position power is strong.
6. Situation 6: The leader-member relations are poor, the task structure is structured, and position power is weak.
7. Situation 7: The leader-member relations are poor, the task structure is unstructured, and position power is strong.
8. Situation 8: In contrast to Situation 1, the leader-member relations are poor (i.e., there is a low level of trust, confidence, and respect between the leader and followers), the task structure is low (i.e., the work is unstructured with clear policies and procedures potentially not being in place), and position power is weak (i.e., the leader does not have any authority to take various personnel decisions like hiring, promotion, benefits increments, etc.) (Robbins & Judge, 2021).

The Fiedler Contingency Model argues that relationship-oriented leaders (i.e., leaders with a high LPC score) are suited to lead in situations 4, 5, and 6. In contrast, task-oriented leaders (i.e., leaders with a low LPC score) are suited to lead in situations 1, 2, 3, 7, and 8 (Robbins & Judge, 2021).

TABLE 1.5 **Benefits and Challenges—The Fiedler Contingency Model**

Benefits of the Fiedler Contingency Model	Challenges of the Fiedler Contingency Model
• This model is intuitively appealing. • The model tells which leaders will be successful in which situations. Organizations can thus strategically appoint leaders in situations where they will likely succeed. • The model acknowledges the importance of followers and builds on the logic that leaders can compensate for followers' limited ability and motivation. • It is easy to measure.	• One fundamental assumption of this theory is that the leader's orientation, akin to personality, is fixed (Robbins & Judge, 2021). • Since the leadership orientation is fixed, it cannot be changed. The option left for organizations is to change the leader with someone who has needed leadership orientation. This might not be feasible in all situations. • There is limited guidance on where a leader with average LPC scores can be placed. • Choosing the 1–8 options in the questionnaire is a self-reported action, and the resultant LPC score might be subjectively exaggerated.

Reflection Questions:

1. Think of an organization in your life experiences that needed (or needs) strong leadership. Which leadership style (high or low LPC) would be most suited? While formulating your answer, answer the following questions:
    a. Was the trust level high or low (member relations)?
    b. Were the things that needed to be done clearly understood, how it was done, and what the standards were (task structure)?
    c. What level of authority did the leader have (position power)?

Situational Leadership Model

In her early days in the company, Mary was regularly provided with explicit instructions on how things were to be done by her manager, Rose. However, after a few months, when Mary started mastering elements of her work, Rose, while still giving regular directives, started becoming more of a workplace coach who provided support to help develop Mary holistically. For example, rather than giving the correct answer for a problem, Rose would ask Mary to recommend solutions that she thought were correct. They would then review the options jointly with Rose, only correcting when absolutely needed. They would also frequently go over things that immediately impacted Mary's work; Rose began to consciously involve Mary in issues that just did not narrowly focus on Mary's job responsibilities. After some time, when Rose started noticing Mary did not need frequent directions on the work being done, Rose began to focus more on developing her overall skills for higher responsibility rather than continue providing job-related directions. For example, Rose would solicit Mary's feedback while making decisions, etc. By the end of the year, when Mary had completely mastered her work and could work independently, Rose started delegating some additional work with higher responsibility.

In 1969 Paul Hersey and Ken Blanchard published an article titled "Life-cycle Theory of Leadership" (Hersey & Blanchard, 1969), where they discussed "the relationship between an effective style of leadership and the level of maturity of one's followers" (p. 29). Over the years, Hersey and Blanchard's work has gone through various revisions, and "now, most people refer to the life-cycle behavioral model as 'situational leadership'" (Hersey & Blanchard, 1996, p. 42).

The core premise of this model is that leaders must adapt their leadership styles based on their follower's readiness (competency, motivation, and developmental) levels. Depending on the follower's readiness, the leader may need to demonstrate directive behaviors such as providing explicit instructions and guidance, setting goals and standards, conducting regular assessments, and providing corrective feedback. In other cases, the leader may need to demonstrate supportive behaviors such as collaborative dialogue and problem-solving, using words of encouragement and praise, and involving the follower in decision-making. Furthermore, in some cases, the leader might need to engage in both directive and supportive behaviors.

In the Situational Leadership Model, the follower's readiness levels are determined by their *competence* and *commitment* (Dugan, 2017). Depending on the readiness level, followers are classified into belonging to one of *four development levels*: D1, D2, D3, and D4 (Blanchard et al., 1993). The leader uses a unique leadership style when working with followers at each of the four levels.

1. **Development Level 1 (D1):** At this level, the leader is dealing with an "enthusiastic beginner" (Blanchard et al., 2013, p. 32), i.e., a new(er) follower who generally has low technical skills (*low competence level*) but is normally highly motivated (*high commitment level*). Since the followers are new(er), the leader engages in *directing behavior* (*high directive—low supportive behavior*) to ensure that the followers become more competent (Blanchard et al., 2013). To make the followers competent in their jobs, the leader provides precise instructions, measurable and specific goals, hands-on demonstration, close supervision, etc. (Blanchard et al., 2013; Dugan, 2017). Communication is generally one-way from the leader to the follower (Bellou & Gkorezis, 2016). Further, only a small amount of time is used to provide socioemotional support (praising performance, sharing information, listening, two-way communication, etc.) (Northouse, 2022).
2. **Development Level 2 (D2):** Once the follower has started to learn and master some aspects of the job, at some point, the follower might feel they "haven't made as much progress as expected" (Blanchard et al., 2013, p. 33). This might lead the follower to become "frustrated and may even be ready to quit" (p. 33). Such a follower is labeled a "disillusioned learner" (p. 33) and is assumed to be at the D2 development level. Since the *competency level is still low* and the follower does not retain the same level of commitment and motivation as they had at the D1 level, the leader adopts the *coaching behavior* (*high directive—high supportive behavior*) to ensure the follower further improves competency and also remains committed (Blanchard et al., 2013). Similar to the D1 level, the leader continues to provide precise instructions, measurable and specific goals, hands-on demonstration, close supervision, etc. However, the frequency of such instructions and close supervision are generally fewer than in the *directing* style. Further, in contrast to the one-way communication in the D1 level, the communication is two-way since the leader starts soliciting the follower's input (Blanchard et al., 2013). The leader also starts providing regular socioemotional support to the follower to ensure the follower remains committed (Northouse, 2022).
3. **Development Level 3 (D3):** At this level, the follower demonstrates *moderate to high competence* in their job with *variable levels of commitment* (Blanchard et al., 2013). Followers at the D3 level are known as "capable but cautious contributors" (Blanchard et al., 2013, p. 33), and the leader engages in *supporting behavior* (*high supportive—low directive behavior*). The follower is independently allowed to make decisions on issues that are structured. However, the leader is still available to provide input, especially in cases of problems (Blanchard et al., 2013). Further, since the leader wishes to increase the follower's commitment, they continue to solicit the follower's input and feedback and readily provide recognition and praise.
4. **Development Level 4 (D4):** At this level, the follower has mastered all the know-how of the job (*high competence*) and is highly motivated to get the job done (*high commitment*), and is known as a "self-reliant achiever" (Blanchard et al., 2013, p. 34). The leader thus engages in *delegating behavior* (*low supportive—low directive behavior*). The leader delegates the complete responsibility of the job to the follower and rarely intervenes. The follower can do the job in the way they want. The follower is also highly motivated, given the trust shown in their ability.

TABLE 1.6 **Benefits and Challenges—The Situational Leadership Model**

Benefits of the Situational Leadership Model	Challenges of the Situational Leadership Model
• A leader has the option to be flexible. Based on the follower's requirement, the leader can change style and provide the required leadership style. • There are four styles that leaders can use. • Leaders can make followers feel valued. • Leaders can help mentor and develop future leaders.	• The leader's supportive behavior can focus narrowly on the job and impede the overall growth of the follower. • The leader might not have the skills to correctly assess the development level the follower is in. This might lead to incorrect styles being used. • The leader might be mentoring in a manner that will help the follower or the organization.

Reflection Questions:

1. Assume that you are a leader in a manufacturing plant and a new machine operator is assigned to your unit. (Alternatively, assume you are a leader of a student club and a new student is assigned to a committee that you chair.)
   a. How can you find the information you need to rate the readiness of this follower to operate the machine (competence and commitment)?
   b. You determined the follower has limited experience with this type of machine but is very excited to start this new position. How would you evaluate their readiness (competence and commitment)?
   c. Which leadership style will you use with this follower? What might you be doing to use this leadership style?
   d. It is six months later, and this follower is doing a great job on their machine and just received a promotion to lead a small team of trainees. What is their readiness for this new job? Which leadership style will you use? Why?

Path-Goal Theory

Harry believes his work effort will lead to a higher-than-expected sales margin this fiscal year. He expects that this increased margin will naturally lead to his increased yearly bonus. He is expecting to use this bonus toward the down payment for a house he has been dreaming of for the last few years.

Sally, Harry's manager, knows what Harry desires (a house) and how important the house is to Harry. She therefore engages in leadership behavior that motivates Harry to put in the required effort to meet and exceed the clearly defined goals (sales margin). In addition to motivating him, Sally also provides regular guidance and support in carrying out steps to meet the goals. Finally, she also actively acts to remove the roadblocks in Harry's path to meet the goals.

In the above example, Sally is demonstrating leadership behavior that is articulated in the *path-goal theory of leadership* (House, 1996). The central thesis of the theory is that "... leaders, to be effective, engage in behaviors that complement employees' environments and abilities in a manner that compensates for deficiencies and is instrumental to employee satisfaction and individual and work unit performance" (House, 1996, p. 323). This theory argues that leaders can take specific steps (demonstrate certain behaviors) to motivate followers to continue being productive and efficient. Thus, the leader:

1. clearly defines the goals
2. clarifies how the goals can be achieved
3. provides support when needed; and
4. removes roadblocks that followers encounter in their path while trying to accomplish their goals.

Additionally, the theory posits that to motivate a follower, a leader can engage in four leadership styles: directive, supportive, participative, and achievement oriented. The leader chooses an appropriate leadership style based on *follower characteristics* and *task characteristics* and what motivates them (Northouse, 2022).

1. **Directive leadership style:** When the task is ambiguous and/or complex *(task characteristics)*, and the follower has a lower ability to get the job and needs an external push to get the job done *(follower characteristics)*, the leader engages in the *directive leadership style*. In this style, the leader provides explicit instructions on what needs to be done, how it needs to be done, by when it needs to be done, and how the performance will be measured (Northouse, 2022). The focus is on providing clarity to the follower by making the task less ambiguous and providing guidance and structure (Northouse, 2022).
2. **Supportive leadership style:** When the follower is engaged in work that is dangerous and/or repetitive *(task characteristics)* and/or boring, and/or puts them under stress *(follower characteristics)* and wants "a friendly and psychologically supportive work environment" (House, 1996, p. 326), the leader engages in the *supportive leadership style*. In this style, the leader is friendly and approachable, provides emotional support and words of encouragement to the follower, and also provides confidence and a feeling of respect to the follower (Northouse, 2022). The leader's support is a source of satisfaction and motivation and a reliever of stress.
3. **Participative leadership style:** When the tasks are unclear and unstructured *(task characteristics)* but the follower has a high level of ability and can work autonomously *(follower characteristics)*, the leader engages in the *participative leadership style* (Northouse, 2022). Since the follower wants to feel in control and believes their contribution will matter, the leader involves the follower in the decision-making process: solicits opinions and suggestions and uses the feedback to make decisions.
4. **Achievement-oriented leadership style:** When the tasks are challenging, complex, and lack clarity *(task characteristics)* and the follower has high expectations and wants to demonstrate mastery and success in meeting the goals, the leader engages in the *achievement-oriented leadership style* (Northouse, 2022). The leader provides the follower with set goals with high expectations and challenges and also states their confidence in the follower's ability. The followers are provided an opportunity to work at the highest level.

TABLE 1.7 **Benefits and Challenges—Path-Goal theory**

Benefits of the Path-Goal Theory	Challenges of the Path-Goal Theory
• The theory is practical. • Leaders can motivate followers through their behaviors. • The theory lets leaders understand how and when different leadership behaviors are appropriate. • Shows how the relationship between the job, follower characteristics, and leader behavior can impact motivation and performance.	• The theory is complex and challenging to understand and master. • Leaders are expected to act rationally. • It might not be possible to constantly change leadership behavior in the workplace. Leaders might not have the ability to constantly change their behavior. • The theory does not take things like gender, culture, etc., into context.

Reflection Questions:

1. Which leadership style would you use in each of the following situations and why?
    a. Newly recruited data engineer: this newly recruited engineer was previously employed by a software company whose software you used. The engineer is well versed in the software and will be working on the software itself as a data engineer.

   b. Newly recruited data engineer: this engineer was hired straight out of college. Has rudimentary knowledge about the software being used but is relatively well versed in some other software systems.

2. Think of a leader you have worked for previously. Did the leader use all of the four behaviors? Did the leader have a preferred style? If you could go back in time, what advice would you give this leader? List and discuss specific situations where the behaviors would have been appropriate.
3. Discuss which leadership style will be effective in each of the following scenarios:
   a. The task is ambiguous but is also "intrinsically satisfying or environmental conditions are not stressful" (House, 1996, p. 341). Provide an example of such a task and how a leader can lead in such a scenario.
   b. The follower has a high level of knowledge and ability about the job, but the job is repetitive and/or boring and/or puts them under stress. Provide an example of such a task and how a leader can lead in such a scenario.
   c. The tasks are not ambiguous, and the follower desires direct instructions and wants to defer to the leaders. Provide an example of such a task and how a leader can lead in such a scenario.
   d. The follower needs constant guidance, second-guesses themselves, and the job is unclear. Provide an example of such a task and how a leader can lead in such a scenario.

Relations-Centered Theories

These theories move away from the narrow focus on the traits and behavior of leaders to the relationship and process that leaders create and engage with their followers while leading them.

Leader-Member Exchange Theory

Both Bobby and Alex are efficient in what they do. They require minimum guidance to meet and sometimes exceed what is expected from them through their formal job descriptions. However, there are some differences in how they go about their jobs and maintain their relationship with their manager. For example, Bobby comes to the office on time, does what is expected from her, and goes home on time. Her interaction with the manager is to the extent that is required to complete the job. On the other hand, while Alex also does what is expected from her, she is in regular conversations with her manager to see how she could add more value to the workplace and engage in additional work beyond what is written in the job description. Due to her being proactive, Alex and her manager have developed a higher level of trust in the workplace.

According to the Leader-Member Exchange Theory (LMX), Bobby is in the leader's *out-group* and has a *relatively low-quality LMX relationship* with her manager. While the manager does not dislike Bobby, there is a lower level of respect, liking, and trust. The relationship exists within the confines of the job description, and Bobby is only rewarded or punished solely based on her performance. In contrast to Bobby, Alex is part of the leader's *in-group* and has a *high-quality LMX relationship* with her leader. Members of an in-group strive to work beyond what is mentioned in the job description. Both the employee and the manager engage in mutually beneficial interactions, promote each other's ability to succeed, and generally develop loyal bonds among themselves (Wendt et al., 2009).

The LMX theory conceptualizes leadership as a dyadic process where both the leader and the employees are engaged (Graen & Uhl-Bien, 1995). The heightened engagement can potentially lead to higher motivation, lower turnover, increased organizational commitments, and improved performance at both the individual and the organizational levels.

TABLE 1.8 Comparison Between High- and Low-Quality LMX Relations

	High-quality LMX relationships	Low-quality LMX relationships
Group status	In-group	Out-group
Trust	High levels of trust	A lower level of trust
Respect	Higher level of respect	A lower level of respect
Liking each other	Higher level of liking	While the follower and the leader might not dislike each other, there is a lower level of liking.
Reciprocal influence	High	Low
Scope of relationship	Both the follower and the leader engage in mutually beneficial interactions and communication, promote each other's ability to succeed, and generally develop loyal bonds among themselves.	Relationships are confined to the job description.
Scope of work	Work can exceed the requirements in the job description. Followers want to do more than what is mentioned in the job description.	Work confined to the job description.
Impact in the workplace	• Preferential treatment compared to out-group members. • Innovative ways to work might come about. • Followers can be entrusted with additional responsibilities.	• Rewards and punishment are bounded by performance outlined in the job description.

LMX theory provides leaders incentives to initiate and engage in a mutually beneficial relationship with all of their employees, even those labeled as out-group members. However, the leader needs to be mindful of the potential for discrimination against out-group members and the formation of sycophantic cliques in the workplace amongst in-group members. Leaders can take steps to initiate and maintain high-quality LMX relationships with all their followers and minimize the number of followers in the *out-group* so that they do not practice favoritism.

TABLE 1.9 Benefits and Challenges—High-Quality LMX Relationships

Benefits of high-quality LMX relationships	Challenges of high-quality LMX relationships
• Innovative ways to work might come about due to the mutually beneficial relationship • Followers can receive additional roles and responsibilities • Followers are highly motivated and are more committed • Feeling of belongingness in the organization	• Favoritism and discrimination can creep in • Followers who are highly competent but are socially shy may lose out on opportunities to others who are less competent but have good relationships with the leader

Reflection Questions:

1. Think of an organization you have worked for previously. Did some of the leaders and followers have high-quality LMX relationships and low-quality LMX relationships? Describe the behaviors that demonstrated both of these relationships.
2. How can low-quality LMX relationships impact employee motivation and work performance?
3. Suppose you are transferred to a new unit in your organization. Over a period of time, you notice you have developed a low-quality LMX relationship with one of the employees who is highly competent but does not go beyond the job description.
    a. How will you ensure you do not discriminate against this employee when making decisions relating to raises, promotions, etc.?
    b. What steps will you take so that you can potentially develop a high-quality LMX relationship with this employee?

Transformational Leadership

In the 2011 movie Moneyball, *Brad Pitt plays Billy Beane, the general manager of the Oakland Athletics (Oakland A's), a Major League Baseball team.* Moneyball *is based on the actual story of how, against stiff internal opposition, Beane used an evidence-based quantitative analytic approach to successfully find undervalued players. These undervalued players were subsequently instrumental in the Oakland Athletics winning 20 straight games.*

Apple introduced the iPod in 2001. With this product, Steve Jobs fundamentally changed how we listen to music. Throughout his life, Jobs radically changed our perspectives on what electronic products should and can be.

Mohandas Karamchand Gandhi, popularly known by his surname Gandhi, was a wiry Indian lawyer who inspired a generation in what is now India, Pakistan, and Bangladesh to engage in satyagraha*—a form of civil disobedience that ultimately led to the independence of India and Pakistan from the British Empire.*

When a caterpillar emerges from a cocoon as a butterfly, it is said to have been transformed—changed from one form to another, which it was not previously. Leaders (e.g., Beane, Jobs, Gandhi, et al.) who inspire organizations or a large number of people to do or produce or become something new that is qualitatively different from what was being done previously are engaging in transformational leadership. Transformational leaders have charisma and vision, but it is not enough in itself for a leader to become transformational (Northouse, 2022). The leaders use their charisma and their power to motivate and persuade followers to voluntarily transcend their narrow interests and focus on wider organizational or societal-level goals (Bass, 1985). In organizations, this style includes encouraging creativity in followers, regularly recognizing follower accomplishments, building long-lasting trust-based relationships, and ultimately inspiring a shared and collective vision (Northouse, 2022).

A better understanding of transformational leadership can be had by discussing it alongside *transactional leadership*. According to Robbins and Judge (2021), transactional leaders are those "who guide or motivate their followers in the direction of established goals by clarifying the role and task requirements, allocating rewards and punishment where needed, and (passively or actively) intervening when the situation calls for it" (p. 227). The majority of theories we have discussed until now can be loosely termed transactional, since they focus on a *give-and-take* between the leader and the follower.

Transformation leadership is a process where a leader, while engaging with her empowered followers, creates holistic connections that result in heightened motivation, synergistic results that exceed what is expected from the followers, and positive changes in both the follower and the leader herself (Northouse, 2022). Furthermore, in contrast to a transactional leader who provides contingent rewards, takes only corrective actions, and can avoid making decisions, a transformational leader provides intrinsic and inspirational motivation, instills a sense of pride and trust among followers, and creates personal and meaningful connections with employees while engaging in thoughtful decision-making. Bass (1990) notes the following characteristics of transformational and transactional leaders (p. 22):

TABLE 1.10 **Characteristics of Transformational and Transactional Leaders**

Transformational Leaders
Charisma: Provides vision and sense of mission, instills pride, gains respect and trust.
Inspiration: Communicates high expectations, uses symbols to focus efforts, expresses important purposes in simple ways.
Intellectual Stimulation: Promotes intelligence, rationality, and careful problem solving.
Individualized Consideration: Gives personal attention, treats each employee individually, coaches, advises.
Transactional Leadership
Contingent Reward: Contracts exchange of rewards for effort, promises rewards for good performance, recognizes accomplishments.
Management by Exception (active): Watches and searches for deviations from rules and standards, takes corrective action.
Management by Exception (passive): Intervenes only if standards are not met.
Laissez-Faire: Abdicates responsibilities, avoids making decisions.

Note. From "From Transactional to Transformational Leadership: Learning to Share the Vision," by B. M. Bass, 1990, *Organizational Dynamics, 18*(3), p. 22.

However, it should be noted that transformational and transactional leadership should not be considered as oppositional. Rather, transformational builds on transactional leadership, which in itself is also essential in organizations (Robbins & Judge, 2021).

TABLE 1.11 **Benefits and Challenges—Transformational Leadership**

Benefits of Transformational leadership	**Challenges of Transformational leadership**
• Leader-follower relationships become more effective. • Followers can have high levels of satisfaction and motivation. • A high level of trust in the leader and the followers become empowered. • Leader effectiveness can increase. • Possibility of increased team performance.	• The theory lacks some conceptual clarity. For instance, it is not clear how the four characteristics interact with each other, which results in transformational leadership. • It is not how much the followers will develop as leaders when exposed to transformational leadership. • The theory does not explicitly discuss what a transformational leader needs to do.

Reflection Questions:

1. Think of a leader you have previously worked for. Did the leader exhibit transactional or transformational leadership behavior? Provide some examples to support your answers.
2. What are the short-term and long-term benefits and disadvantages of using the transactional leadership approach?
3. What are the short-term and long-term benefits and disadvantages of using the transformational leadership approach?

Emerging Leadership Approaches

Over the past half-century, additional models portending to describe alternative leadership approaches have been emerging. These emerging approaches (e.g., authentic and servant leadership) also combine what is known from earlier leadership theories focused on traits, behavior, situations, etc. Given that many of these emerging approaches strongly argue for ethical leadership practices, we start this section by discussing ethical leadership.

Ethical Leadership

In a TEDx talk, Liz Theophille, chief technology officer of Novartis, shares an amazing story. A few years ago, while working in another organization, she was tasked with consolidating three complex data centers in France, England, and Germany. This ultimately led to a decision to lay off close to 400 staff with whom she had worked closely. Even though the HR Department could have handled the process without Liz needing to be involved, Liz insisted on being directly involved in explaining what was happening to each employee being fired. Liz notes that the process whereby only the HR Department provides the termination letter "is a very inhumane, cowardly, and faceless way to manage employees that worked for the company for such a long time." Liz subsequently sat down with each employee and explained the reasons for the consolidation. However, during the process, Liz realized that she needed to do something else for her to be credible when she still had a job but was telling others that they would not have a job. She subsequently decided to leave the organization once the consolidation was complete, even though she was being promoted. Liz's dilemma of firing others while still retaining a cushy job and her subsequent resignation empathizing with her laid-off colleagues, evidenced a strong moral conviction on how organizations should treat their employees.

Grace (1990, 1998; Spalding Minor, 1998) defined ethical leadership[1] as a social behavior, maintained that "leaders" were originally chosen from within a society *because* they were seen as ethical individuals, and developed the "4-V Model." He maintained that from the beginning, leadership meant *being ethical* but after the 1900s, managerialism had eroded the ethical elements of leadership. Grace's model focused on *values, vision,* and *voice,* and the central construct of his model was *virtue.* Grace maintained that virtue was synonymous with the *common good.*

TABLE 1.12 Benefits and Challenges—Ethical Leadership

Benefits of Ethical Leadership	Challenges of Ethical Leadership
• Increases trust in leaders of communities and organizations. • Provides templates for followers on how they can treat each other and how leaders are expected to behave.	• Since the common good can be an intensely contextual construct, it might be challenging to engage in behavior that is considered ethical by everyone all the time, particularly as perceived out-groups. • It can be quite challenging to behave ethically across contextual circumstances.

1. Editors' note: We share the notion of the importance of ethics to leadership; our book includes a chapter on this subject *because* we believe ethical leadership *is* leadership. One can also corroborate Grace's 4-V Model structure with pervasive strategy constructs of values and vision, as described in this volume.

Reflection Questions:

1. As a leader, what are some ethical practices that you will follow? Please discuss the importance of these practices. How will these practices benefit the organization?
2. As a leader, what are some unethical practices that you will not follow? Why do you think these practices are unethical? How can these unethical practices harm the organization?

Servant Leadership

> *Years ago TD Industries won the contract for building the Dallas Convention Center. Bruce Arapis, a former vice president, was scheduled to serve as the senior project superintendent and the contract was awarded partly due to the Customer's confidence in Bruce. Bruce was delayed two months completing a previous job. In his absence, David Hollowell served as project superintendent.*
>
> *Once Bruce was free to join the Dallas job, he saw that David's performance in leading the team was outstanding. Together, with the approval of the Client, they decided that it would be in the best interest of the project for David to continue in the lead position and for Bruce to go into the field and head up the installation of the ductwork. In giving up the leadership role on this contract, Bruce renounced not only the personal recognition that he would receive as senior project superintendent but also the nice bonus that accompanies this position. Not long after this event, David took a similar action, stepping aside to give Mike Wilson an opportunity to expand his experience and leadership.*
>
> *When Bruce went to another job at Texas Stadium, David pitched in by arranging for extra staff to work overtime as needed. David also helped to assemble roof curbs on his personal time to meet the fast-track schedule for the football season. The project came in on time and beat the original budget.* (McGee-Cooper & Trammell, 2001, pp. 10–11)

In the above real-life anecdote, Bruce was practicing aspects of servant leadership. Eschewing the supposedly natural tendency of leaders to take charge, he allowed David the opportunity to develop and reap the benefits. While Bruce forewent immediate recognition and monetary benefits, he was able to inspire David to engage in servant leadership practices. McGee-Cooper and Trammell (2001) further discuss how servant leadership can also be practiced at an organizational level:

> Over 50 years, TD Industries has evolved into what the company calls a "leaderful" culture. In this organization, leadership is not about having others report to you as a supervisor. TD seeks to help each Employee/Partner to view him- or herself as a valued leader. From this position, each person must take responsibility for nurturing others, initiating ideas, asking for help, collaborating, calling others to action, challenging assumptions, offering suggestions for continuous improvement, and so on. Within this broad definition of leadership, each person becomes infinitely valued and valuable. (p. 10)

In the 1970s, Robert Greenleaf started theorizing about a leadership approach that focuses on how leaders serve others. He noted that

> The servant-leader is servant first. ... It begins with the natural feeling that one wants to serve *first*. Then conscious choice brings one to aspire to lead ... The best test, and difficult to administer, is: do those served grow as persons; do they, *while being served*, become healthier, wiser, freer, more autonomous, more likely themselves to become servants? *And*, what is the effect on the least privileged in society; will he benefit, or, at least, will he not be further deprived? (Greenleaf, 1970, p. 7)

Servant leaders use these various characteristics to constantly help the followers develop their fullest capabilities over the leader's own interest. This requires demonstrating strong moral and ethical behavior in how a leader first serves and then leads her followers. These leaders aim to serve not only their immediate followers but the organization as a whole, including building and nurturing the community at large. While servant leaders are generally altruistic in nature and have the best interest of their followers in mind while serving their followers, "servant-leaders are not micro managers" (Mayer, 2010, p. 150).

Spears (2010) "identified a set of 10 characteristics of the servant-leader that [he] view[s] as being of critical importance. These characteristics are central to the development of servant-leaders" (pp. 4–5). The characteristics of servant-leaders are:

1. listening
2. empathy
3. healing
4. awareness
5. persuasion
6. conceptualization
7. foresight
8. stewardship
9. commitment to the growth of people
10. building community.

Servant leadership focuses on how a leader simultaneously influences and follows her followers. In this theory, the focus is both on the leader (traits) and her behavior in prioritizing her followers by empathizing, nurturing, and empowering them. Spears (2010) notes that servant leaders are generally

1. excellent listeners with empathy
2. possess high levels of situational awareness and foresight; and
3. can also persuade and steward a diverse group of followers.

TABLE 1.13 **Benefits and Challenges—Servant Leadership**

Benefits of Servant Leadership	Challenges of Servant Leadership
• Altruism is at the core of servant leadership. • The followers are the central focus of most of what the leader does, including sharing control and influence. • The advancement of the follower is a key concern for the leader.	• Might not be applicable in all organizational contexts. • Can be misunderstood as micromanagement leading to resistance and resentment from followers. • Implementing servant leadership can be challenging since not everything that a leader needs to do is completely clear.

Reflection Questions:

1. List and discuss a few organizational contexts where servant leadership might be appropriate.
2. Organizations sometimes need to lay off people. During this painful process, how do you think organizations that practice servant leadership engage with layoff compared with organizations following traditional leadership practices? Also, discuss what servant leaders themselves do during the layoff period in the organization.

Adaptive Leadership[2]

Company A perennially advertises itself as a family and female-friendly workplace and claims that it regularly involves the staff members while reviewing its policies to make everyone feel included. As part of its regular review, the company's benefits team is about to make some significant decisions relating to maternity leave. However, the benefits team is composed solely of cis-gendered males. One of the production managers, Sher, who supervises numerous cis-gendered females and is not a part of the company's benefits team, feels the company's "espoused and actualized values" (Dugan, 2017, p. 266) do not reconcile. He thus approaches the company's Board of Directors to ensure that the company's benefits team has a fair representation of staff members whom the new provisions in maternity leave policies will directly impact. Sher strongly advocates for a fair number of females to be represented in the company's benefits team at a minimum when the benefits team discusses issues relating to females. Sher (the manager) fears that his direct approach might and will ruffle some feathers and that he might be victimized later. However, he strongly feels that as a leader, he needs to engage in this difficult conversation with the organization.

Heifetz et al. (2009) describe adaptive leadership as "the practice of mobilizing people to tackle tough challenges and thrive" (p. 14). Adaptive leadership focuses on "how leaders encourage people to adapt—to face and deal with problems, challenges, and changes" (Northouse, 2022, p. 285). The key term in this theory is the word *adapt*, which in turn means taking a *pragmatic approach* to leadership (Dugan, 2017).

Heifetz and Laurie (2001) note that "adaptive work is required when our deeply held beliefs are challenged, when the values that made us successful become less relevant, and when legitimate yet competing perspectives emerge" (p. 4). When leaders undertake adaptive work, they make specific changes in how they lead:

- The leader resists providing solutions that the followers simply follow.
- Rather than simply providing solutions, the leader starts asking tough questions.
- "Rather than protecting people from outside threats, leaders should allow them to feel the pinch of reality in order to stimulate them to adapt" (Heifetz & Laurie, 2001, p. 4).
- "Instead of orienting people to their current roles, leaders must disorient them so that new relationships can develop" (Heifetz & Laurie, 2001, p. 4).
- "Instead of quelling conflict, leaders have to draw the issues out" (Heifetz & Laurie, 2001, p. 4).
- "Instead of maintaining norms, leaders have to challenge 'the way we do business' and help others distinguish immutable values from historical practices that must go" (Heifetz & Laurie, 2001, p. 4).

When leaders practice the above behaviors, which go against how leaders might be expected to lead in a particular situation, the followers can be disoriented. Furthermore, the leader shifts the responsibility of coming up with solutions to problems to the "collective intelligence of employees at all levels, who need to use one another as resources, often across boundaries, and learn their way to those solutions" (Heifetz & Laurie, 2001, p. 4). The discussion until now makes a few points quite clear:

- assertions made by adaptive leadership run counter to most other leadership theories
- both the leader and the follower will be disoriented since they are not following their typical roles; and
- following premises of theory is challenging.

---

2. Compared to previous sections in this chapter, this section on adaptive leadership is considerably long. This length does not indicate that this approach is better than other theories, models, or approaches. Nor does the length signify any particular affinity of the author with this approach. The only reason this section is comparatively long is that adaptive leadership is premised on multiple ideas and the lack of elaboration of any of the interrelated terms makes it very difficult to comprehend this approach.

Heifetz and Laurie (2001) list and discuss six principles that can be followed when faced with challenges of engaging in adaptive work:

1. Getting on the balcony
2. Identifying the adaptive challenge
3. Regulating distress
4. Maintaining disciplined attention
5. Giving the work back to people; and
6. Protecting voices of leadership from below.

1) Getting on the balcony:

Leaders can be so deeply tied up with firefighting problems and providing solutions that they cannot view and assess situations objectively. Thus, leaders should take a step back from the action. In this theory, this step back is represented by the metaphor *getting on the balcony.* Getting on the balcony allows the leader to "obtain a greater perspective of what really is happening and more accurately diagnose the problem" (Dugan, 2017, p. 270) and reengage again. The leader moves "back and forth between the field of action and the balcony, to reflect day to day, moment to moment, on the many ways in which an organization's habits can sabotage adaptive work" (Heifetz & Laurie, 2001, p. 5).

2) Identifying the adaptive challenge:

While on the balcony, leaders assess the situation to differentiate if the issues are of a technical or adaptive nature or a mix of both.

a. Technical challenges: Challenges, even when they are important and complex, can be handled by using the traditional authorities and the technical expertise that the leaders hold.
b. Adaptive challenges: Challenges where the challenge and the solution are not clear, cannot be easily identified, and cannot be handled using the traditional authority that leaders hold. Nor can the leaders use their technical expertise to solve the issues. Instead, "adaptive challenges require that leaders encourage others to define challenging situations and implement solutions. Not easy to tackle and often resisted, adaptive challenges are difficult because they usually require changes in people's priorities, beliefs, roles, and values" (Northouse, 2022, p. 290).

Leaders can use the following four archetypes to differentiate whether a challenge is technical or adaptive or not and decide when an adaptive change is required (Heifetz et al., 2009):

- The gap between espoused values and behavior: the organization's actions do not match with what it states the organization does.
- Competing commitments: two or more organizational commitments are in conflict with each other.
- Speaking the unspeakable: the organization has "radical ideas, unpopular issues, or conflicting perspectives that people don't dare address because of their sensitive or controversial nature. Speaking out about these is seen as 'risky'" (Northouse, 2022, p. 292).
- Work avoidance: organization avoids dealing with a difficult situation(s), and the status quo is maintained, even though the organization might be incurring a loss.

3) Regulating distress:

Heifetz and Laurie (2001) note, "adaptive work generates distress" (p. 6). When people face too much stress, they will not be able to work, but "eliminating stress altogether removes the impetus for doing adaptive work" (p. 5). They note that leaders can therefore engage in three tasks to "maintain a productive level of tension" (p. 6):

- Create a holding environment. Leaders create and nurture "a space formed by a network of relationships within which people can tackle tough, sometimes divisive questions without flying apart" (Heifetz & Linsky, 2002, p. 102). The holding environment regulates the tension and allows people who are disoriented from the adaptive work to not feel completely washed out by the stress and still be productively engaged with the adaptive challenge.

- Provide direction, protection, orientation, managing conflict, and shaping norms. Heifetz and Laurie (2001) note that the leader
    - identifies and frames the key questions and issues relating to the adaptive challenge
    - protects people by managing the rate of change
    - orients people to new roles and responsibilities by clarifying business realities and key values
    - expose conflict, viewing it as the engine of creativity and learning; and
    - finally, a leader helps the organization maintain those norms that must endure and challenge those that need to change.
- A leader must have presence and poise. A leader engages in a balancing act while engaging with adaptive challenges. If the leader cannot regulate the stress, people will wither due to the tension. If the leader removes all the stress, there will be no incentive to change. Thus "a leader has to have the emotional capacity to tolerate uncertainty, frustration, and pain [and] ... be able to raise tough questions without getting too anxious ..." (Heifetz & Laurie, 2001, p. 6).

4) Maintaining disciplined attention:
Most people prefer not to deal with change; but change is integral in adaptive work. So far, we have understood that engaging in adaptive work is disorienting and stressful. Given a choice, people can choose to avoid the change, become defensive, and engage in avoidance behavior in organizations (Heifetz & Laurie, 2001). Some examples of avoidance behavior are to "ignore the problem, blame the problem on the authority, blame coworkers for the problem, attack those who want to address the problem, pretend the problem does not exist or work hard in areas unrelated to the problem" (Northouse, 2022, p. 296). Leaders should be able to recognize avoidance behaviors and take action that maintains disciplined attention to the adaptative challenges.

5) Giving the work back to the people:
Organizations traditionally expect leaders to make various decisions and solve problems when they appear. Adaptive leadership argues otherwise. Engaging in adaptive work is challenging to the leader and the followers. Leaders find it challenging to not be in control by making decisions and/or find it difficult to support their followers while they are making decisions. Followers might believe it is not their place to make decisions that hitherto leaders were making and/or do not feel confident in tackling the adaptive challenge and making decisions. Leaders need to be mindful of two considerations when giving the work back to the people (Dugan, 2017):

- When leaders are asked for a solution to a problem, the leader must ask themselves, is this a technical or adaptive issue? If the issue is adaptive, it should be sent back to the group for them to address the challenge. The leaders should desist from making decisions on adaptive issues because if they make the decisions, the followers will fall back to their traditional passive roles.
- When the work is given back to the people, the leader must be acutely aware of the potential effects of such an action on the people who will be working on the adaptative challenges (e.g., how will it impact the relationships between various people, what will the stress level be like, how will the stress impact the work, etc.).

6) Protecting voices of leadership from below:
In the brief case study at the start of this section on Adaptive Leadership, we read how Sher (the manager) approached the Board of Directors directly. Let us assume the organization allowed such direct petitions to the Board of Directors if staff felt that senior management was potentially making decisions not conducive to specific groups. How do you think the organization's management will deal with Sher? Will Sher face retributions, as he fears? The answer depends on how invested the organization is in protecting the voices of leadership from below. The answer will also impact if this organization can engage in adaptive work.

Will the organization acknowledge that concerns about maternity leave were not a one-off issue but rather an emblematic representation of the flawed decision-making process on employee matters? By highlighting this issue, Sher might have provided the organization with an opportunity to engage in adaptive work. Heifetz and Laurie (2001) note,

Leaders must rely on others within the business to raise questions that may indicate an impending adaptive challenge. They have to provide cover to people who point to the internal contradictions of the enterprise. Those individuals often have the perspective to provoke rethinking that people in authority do not. Thus, as a rule of thumb, when authority figures feel the reflexive urge to glare at or otherwise silence someone, they should resist. The urge to restore social equilibrium is quite powerful, and it comes on fast. One has to get accustomed to getting on the balcony, delaying the impulse, and asking, What is this guy really talking about? Is there something we're missing? (p. 9)

TABLE 1.14 **Benefits and Challenges—Adaptive Leadership**

Benefits of Adaptive Leadership	Challenges of Adaptive Leadership
• Adaptive leadership is seen as a process, albeit a complex one, where the leaders and the followers interact and influence each other. • The theory is follower-centric and provides a safe environment for them to grow. • Provides opportunities for followers to develop their decision-making, reasoning, negotiating, etc., capacities when faced with challenging work situations that are not technical.	• The theory is complex and possibly too abstract for some people. • Not everything that a leader needs to engage while doing adaptive work is clear. There is a possibility that leaders will misinterpret the theory and engage in something not articulated by the theory.

Reflection Questions:

1. Of the six principles that Heifetz and Laurie (2001) describe, which of the six principles do you think you already practice or have practiced in the past? Provide an example for each principle that you have practiced, and also discuss what the impact was.
2. Of the six principles that Heifetz and Laurie (2001) describe, which principle(s) do you think will be the most important for you to use in the future? Discuss why you will engage with these principles and what changes you expect to occur.
3. Think of a situation in your organization where adaptive work might be suited. Why do you think adaptive work is suitable? What challenges might be faced, and how can those challenges be managed?

Authentic Leadership

Among the various theories discussed in this chapter, authentic leadership is the one at the most nascent stage. While we continue learning new aspects of the other theories, what we know about authentic leadership is relatively tentative in comparison (Avolio and Gardner, 2005), and there is no consensus on what authentic leadership is or can be (Dugan, 2017). One core issue relates to the difficulty in defining *authenticity* itself, an ongoing philosophical challenge that can be traced to Greek philosophers (Dugan, 2017). Despite the ongoing challenges in defining what authentic might mean, scholars increasingly use the following definition to define authentic leadership:

> a pattern of leader behavior that draws upon and promotes both positive psychological capacities and a positive ethical climate, to foster greater self-awareness, an internalized moral perspective, balanced processing of information, and relational transparency on the part of leaders working with followers, fostering positive self-development. (Walumbwa et al., 2008, p. 94)

In their definition, Walumbwa et al. (2008) have noted four components critical to authentic leadership:

1. Self-awareness: The leader demonstrates "an understanding of how one derives and makes meaning of the world and how that meaning making process impacts the way one views himself or herself over time" (p. 95).
2. Internalized moral perspective: The leader has an "internalized and integrated form of self-regulation" (p. 95).
3. Balanced processing of information: The leader "objectively analyze[s] all relevant data before coming to a decision" (p. 95).
4. Relational transparency: The leader presents "one's authentic self (as opposed to a fake or distorted self) to others" (p. 95).

These leaders are self-aware about why they are doing what they are doing and are self-disciplined to continue doing what they believe to be ethical and moral. Further,

> authentic leadership extends beyond the authenticity of the leader as a person to encompass authentic relations with followers and associates. These relationships are characterized by: a) transparency, openness, and trust, b) guidance toward worthy objectives, and c) an emphasis on follower development. (Gardner et al., 2005, p. 345)

Authentic leadership entails leaders being genuine and transparent in honest relationships and who can be trusted by their followers. Authentic leaders demonstrate numerous traits and behaviors discussed previously:

1. passion
2. strong ethical and moral values
3. the ability to create and nurture trusting relationships; and
4. the ability to practice empathetic behaviors.

TABLE 1.15 **Benefits and Challenges—Authentic Leadership**

Benefits of Authentic Leadership	Challenges of Authentic Leadership
• Leaders become more ethical and their decisions are guided by moral values; followers are inspired and motivated. • Leaders can engage with the four components (become self-aware, internalize moral perspective, process information in a balanced way, and have relational transparency) to become authentic leaders.	• While there is agreement on many of the ideas about authentic leadership, there is no universally accepted model. • It is not clear how situational factors impact authentic leadership. • It is still not known if there is a significantly strong correlation between authentic leadership and positive organizational performance.

Reflection Questions:

1. Discuss some challenges in practicing authentic leadership.
2. Walumbwa et al. (2008) list four components that are critical to authentic leadership. As a leader, how would you engage with these four components?
3. Think of leaders that you believe are engaged in authentic leadership. Why do you believe they are engaged in authentic leadership?

Conclusion

In this chapter, we have discussed various leadership theories. We have explored how leadership is increasingly understood as a complex relational process that warrants the leader to work with an ethical perspective that shows respect to followers as human beings. While effective leaders do need to exhibit certain traits and have the ability to engage in certain specific leading behaviors, potential leaders can also be developed.

References

Avolio, B. J., & Gardner, W. L. (2005). Authentic leadership development: Getting to the root of positive forms of leadership. *The Leadership Quarterly, 16*(3), 315–338. https://doi.org/10.1016/j.leaqua.2005.03.001

Bass, B. M. (1985). *Leadership and performance beyond expectations.* Free Press.

Bass, B. M. (1990). From transactional to transformational leadership: Learning to share the vision. *Organizational Dynamics, 18*(3), 19–31.

Bellou, V., & Gkorezis, P. (2016). Unveiling the link between facets of positive nonverbal communication and perceived leader effectiveness: A moderated mediation model. *Human Performance, 29*(4), 310–330. https://doi.org/10.1080/08959285.2016.1157597

Blake, R. R., & Mouton, J. S. (1964). *The managerial grid.* Gulf.

Blake, R. R., & Mouton, J. S. (1985). *The managerial grid III.* Gulf.

Blanchard, K., Zigarmi, D., & Nelson, R. B. (1993). Situational leadership after 25 years: A retrospective. *The Journal of Leadership Studies, 1*(1).

Blanchard, K., Zigarmi, P., & Zigarmi, D. (2013). *Leadership and the one minute manager: Increasing effectiveness through situational leadership II.* HarperCollins.

Dugan, J. P. (2017). *Leadership theory: Cultivating critical perspectives.* Jossey-Bass.

Fiedler, F. E. (1964). A contingency model of leadership effectiveness. In L. Berkowitz (Ed.), *Advances in experimental social psychology, Vol 1* (pp. 149–190). Academic Press.

Fiedler, F. E. (1978). The contingency model and the dynamics of the leadership process. In L. Berkowitz (Ed.), *Advances in experimental psychology Vol 11* (pp. 59–112). Academic Press.

Fleishman, E. A. (1957). A leader behavior description for industry. In R. M. Stogdill, & A. E. Coons (Eds.), *Leader behavior: Its description and measurement* (pp. 103–119). Bureau of Business Research, The Ohio State University.

Gardner, W. L., Avolio, B. J., Luthans, F., May, D. R., & Walumbwa, F. O. (2005). "Can you see the real me?" A self-based model of authentic leader and follower development. *The Leadership Quarterly,* 16, 343–372.

Grace, W. J. (1990). *A comparison of male and female ethical leaders' opinions on ethical leadership and ethical leadership development.* https://dr.lib.iastate.edu/handle/20.500.12876/64414

Grace, W. J. (1998). *Ethical leadership: In pursuit of the common good.* CEL.

Graen, G. B., & Uhl-Bien, M. (1995). Relationship-based approach to leadership: Development of leader-member exchange (LMX) theory of leadership over 25 years: Applying a multi-level, multi-domain perspective. *The Leadership Quarterly, 6*(2), 219–247.

Greenleaf, R. K. (1970). The servant as a leader. The Greenleaf Center for Servant Leadership.

Halpin, A. W., & Winer, B. J. (1957). A factorial study of the leader behavior descriptions. In R. M. Stogdill, & A. E. Coons (Eds.), *Leader behavior: Its description and measurement* (pp. 39–51). Bureau of Business Research, The Ohio State University.

Heifetz, R. A. (1994). *Leadership without easy answers.* Belknap Press.

Heifetz, R. A., Grashow, A., & Linsky, M. (2009). *The practice of adaptive leadership: Tools and tactics for changing your organization and the world.* Harvard Business School.

Heifetz, R. A., & Laurie, D. D. L. (2001). The work of leadership. *Harvard Business Review, 79*(11), 1–14. (Original work published 1997).

Heifetz, R. A., & Linsky, M. (2002). *Leadership on the line: Staying alive through the dangers of leading.* Harvard Business School.

Hersey, P., & Blanchard, K. H. (1969). Life-cycle theory of leadership. *Training and Development Journal, 23*(5), 26–34.

Hersey, P., & Blanchard, K. H. (1996). Revisiting the life-cycle theory of leadership. *Training and Development, 50* (January), 42–47.

House, R. J. (1996). Path-goal theory of leadership: Lessons, legacy, and a reformulated theory. *Leadership Quarterly, 7*(3), 323–352.

Kahn, R. L. (1956). The prediction of productivity. *Journal of Social Issues, 12*, 41–49.

Mayer, D. M. (2010). Servant leadership and follower need satisfaction: Where do we go from here? In L. C. Spears, & M. Lawrence (Eds.), *Focus on leadership: Servant-leadership for the twenty-first century* (pp. 147–154). John Wiley & Sons.

McGee-Cooper, A., & Trammell, D. (2001). The essentials of servant leadership: Principles in practice. Ann McGee-Cooper & Associates. (Revised by M. Kosec in 2013).

Mitchell, T. R., Biglan, A., Oncken, G. R., & Fiedler, F. E. (1970). The contingency model: Criticisms and Suggestions. *The Academy of Management Journal, 13*(3), 253–267.

Northouse, P. G. (2022). *Leadership: Theory and practice* (9th ed.). SAGE Publications, Inc.

Remler, D. K., & Ryzin, G. G. V. (2015). Research methods in practice: Strategies for description and causation (2nd ed.). SAGE Publications, Inc.

Robbins, S. P., & Judge, T. A. (2021). *Essentials of organizational behavior* (15th ed.). Pearson.

Spalding Minor, C. (1998). Bill Grace—Ethical Leadership | fscj.digital.flvc.org. (1998). [Florida State College at Jacksonville Collections]. Bill Grace—Ethical Leadership. https://fscj.digital.flvc.org/islandora/object/fscj%3A13379

Spears, L. C. (2010). Tracing the past, present, and future of servant-leadership. In L. C. Spears, & M. Lawrence (Eds.), *Focus on leadership: Servant-leadership for the twenty-first century* (pp. 1–16). John Wiley & Sons.

Stogdill, R. M. (1948). Personal factors associated with leadership: A survey of the literature. *The Journal of Psychology, 25*(1), 35–71.

Torraco, R. J. (1997). Theory-building research methods. In R. A. Swanson & E. F. Holton (Eds.), Human resource development research handbook (pp. 114–137). Berrett-Koehler.

van Zyl, J., & Hofmeyr, K. (2021). Leadership behaviour that facilitates shared leadership emergence in internationally dispersed non-formal teams. *South African Journal of Business Management, 52*(1), 1–13. https://doi.org/10.4102/sajbm.v52i1.2695

Walumbwa, F. O., Avolio, B. J., Gardner, W. L., Wernsing, T. S., & Peterson, S. J. (2008). Authentic leadership: Development and validation of a theory-based measure. *Journal of Management, 34*(1), 89–126.

Wendt, H., Euwema, M. C., & van Emmerik, I. J. H. (2009). Leadership and team cohesiveness across cultures. *The Leadership Quarterly, 20*(3), 358–370. https://doi.org/10.1016/j.leaqua.2009.03.005

CHAPTER 2

Ethical Leadership

By Terri A. Deems

> *It is true that integrity alone won't make you a leader, but without integrity, you will never be one.*
>
> —Zig Ziglar

Learning Objectives

After reading this chapter, students will be able to:

1. Identify the principles and characteristics of ethics and ethical leadership
2. Examine major ethical theories that people use to arrive at and justify their moral choices
3. Assess the impact that ethical leadership and ethical violations have on followers and other stakeholders
4. Identify strategies to confront ethical dilemmas and to foster a culture of ethical behavior in organizations
5. Engage in self-reflection and consider their own values, strengths, and areas for growth as ethical leaders

Introduction to Ethical Leadership

Almost daily the news is rife with reports of leaders' ethical missteps and moral failures. From leaders of "Main Street" businesses to leaders of major corporate enterprises or entire countries, we see instances of financial manipulation, negligence, and dishonesty. We see toxic leaders abusing their power, eager to take advantage of people's vulnerabilities and undermining the welfare of their followers and stakeholders. Unethical leadership is at the heart of many corporate scandals characterized by fraud, mismanagement of resources, and a lack of transparency, leading to an erosion of trust (van den Akker et al., 2009). Far too often. unethical leaders use fear, intimidation, and other manipulative strategies to exploit others and achieve short-term gains at the expense of public welfare (Hassan et al., 2023).

It is open to debate as to whether ethical leadership has declined in the 21st century or whether ethical lapses are simply more visible in our digital age than in the past. Reports suggest, however, that the COVID-19 pandemic led to additional ethical challenges and that, for example, "the incidence of significant fraud shows no downward trend over the last 14 years, spiking in 2020 at the height of the COVID-19 pandemic" (Gordon, 2022).

Increasingly, people are demanding greater moral accountability from our leaders and organizations, and interest in the field of ethical leadership has grown significantly in recent years (den Hartog & de Hoogh, 2020; Guo, 2022). A survey by the Institute of Business Ethics found that more than half of employees surveyed believe that ethical leadership has become increasingly important this past decade (2018). With reports showing that senior leaders are involved in a majority of observed ethical misconduct cases in the workplace (Ethics and Compliance Initiative, 2019), it is not a surprise that executives themselves are beginning to view ethical leadership as a top priority (Ethics Resource Center, 2020).

Leaders are confronted with a multitude of ethical choices on a daily basis—choices that will not only affect their personal careers but will also impact their employees, customers, the organization, and the larger society. In the face of competing pressures and priorities, leaders must be equipped with the self-awareness, knowledge, and skills to make ethical decisions and behave in a way that aligns with accepted ethical standards and values.

What Are "Ethics?"

When I ask my students, "Who knows the difference between right and wrong?" they overwhelmingly raise their hands. Yet their certainty often wavers upon further examination: What is the difference between right and wrong? How do we determine what is morally good or bad? Can an action be morally wrong even if the outcome is good? What if a decision we make is good for some but harmful to others—can we still say it is ethical? What can we do when faced with a situation in which all of our choices seem morally wrong? This is the realm of ethics.

Ethics is a complex, multifaceted field of study. Derived from the word *ethos*, meaning custom or character, ethics is a branch of philosophy concerned with what is morally good or bad, right or wrong, just or unjust in our treatment of others (Thiroux & Krasemann, 2016; Velasquez et al., 2010).

As described by the Markkula Center for Applied Ethics, "ethics refers to well-founded standards of right and wrong that prescribe what humans ought to do, usually in terms of rights, obligations, benefits to society, fairness, or specific virtues" (Markkula, 2010, para. 10). While specific principles and standards of ethics may vary from person to person and group to group, four principles serve as fundamental pillars of ethical behavior. While these pillars are perhaps most often associated professionally with medical ethics (Varkey, 2021), they have served as guiding principles across different ethical systems:

> *Beneficence:* Simply put, this relates to basic human kindness and doing good for others. It is commonly described in terms of mercy, charity, generosity, caring, and contributing to the welfare of others.
>
> *Nonmaleficence:* This holds that we are obligated to do no harm to others, which may include not causing pain or suffering, not causing offense, and not creating undue burdens. It calls on us to both cause no harm and to act in ways which prevent harm from occurring.
>
> *Autonomy:* Because people have an intrinsic worth, they also have the power to choose for themselves—to be self-determining. Respect for autonomy includes truth-telling, respect for privacy, confidentiality, and informed consent.
>
> *Justice:* The pillar of justice obligates us to treat others in a way that is fair and equitable, such as in how we share in the good and the bad, the benefits and the burdens of a society. This includes avoiding undue bias and ensuring we do not create unfair advantages and disadvantages for others.

Our sense of morality and what is or is not considered ethical behavior stems from multiple sources. Many people, for example, equate their ethical choices with their feelings, intuition, or what their "gut instincts" may tell them in any given situation. While our emotions can certainly influence our moral judgments, ethics extends beyond individual preferences or sentiments and calls for critical thinking, objective analysis, and the intentional application of moral principles. People also often associate ethics with religion, and many do find that their religious or spiritual practices provide a helpful moral framework and serve to motivate ethical behavior. Ethical principles, however, transcend religious doctrine and stem from various sources, which may or may not include religious belief.

In a similar vein, we cannot simply equate ethics with legal compliance. While it is true that many ethical principles are reflected in our laws, not all morally right actions are necessarily legal and not all legal actions may be morally right. Ethical considerations often go beyond legal requirements, urging people to aspire to higher moral standards (Thiroux & Krasemann, 2016). Neither can we presume that what is ethical is whatever a society determines to be so. In the United States, for example, slavery was once socially accepted in many parts of the country, yet it was never something we could ever consider "ethical."

How Do People Make (and Justify) Ethical Choices?

When it comes to choosing an ethical action, it is easy to simply say to ourselves, "I'll just do the right thing." But ethical decision-making—knowing what is right—is complex and varies significantly from one person to another. Factors such as our personal biases, emotions, and situational constraints will influence both how we make our choices and how we defend them. Our ethical decision-making processes are also heavily influenced by our values, beliefs, cultural norms and practices, reasoning abilities, and our personal experiences (Thiroux & Krasemann, 2016). Together these form a sort of moral compass that guides us in determining what is right or wrong in any given situation.

Several key ethical theories describe common approaches to decision-making and how people navigate ethical dilemmas. We can think of these as falling within two broad camps: consequentialist theories, which emphasize the consideration of outcomes or consequences of one's actions, and non-consequentialist theories, which emphasize something other than simply the outcomes of an action such as particular rules, duties, or virtues ("A Framework for Making Ethical Decisions," n.d.; Thiroux & Krasemann, 2016).

Consequentialism

Many people approach ethical choices by thinking of the potential outcomes or consequences of their actions. They weigh the potential impact and try to choose the option that brings the greatest good or that will do the least amount of harm. The focus is on the result rather than on the nature of the action. Two key theories stand out here:

> *Ethical egoism:* This theory asserts that people ought to act in their own self-interest and to maximize their own well-being. An action is ethical, then, if it promotes our self-interest even if it comes at the expense of others.
>
> *Utilitarianism:* This theory urges us to think of the well-being of others rather than just of ourselves—to do the greatest good for the greatest number. What is ethical, then, is whatever action or rule will have the biggest positive impact on the most people.

As with all ethical theories, consequentialism has its critics. For instance consequentialism, as a guide to action, requires that we anticipate what will happen, and of course we can never reliably do so. This group of theories also opens the door to thinking that "the end justifies the means" and can lead people to take reprehensible action in order to gain a desirable outcome. Finally, it requires that we somehow calculate the benefits for the greatest number and overlook potentially negative consequences for the minority.

Non-Consequentialism

This body of ethical theory suggests that an action may be immoral even if it leads to positive consequences. Rather than focusing on the outcomes only, the non-consequentialist instead will adhere to moral rules, duties, or virtues that guide their ethical choices. They believe that certain actions are inherently right or wrong, and that people should be guided by ethical principles, virtues, or obligations.

> *Deontological ethics:* This approach to ethical decision-making focuses on following rules and fulfilling certain obligations or duties; it's like having a moral rulebook that we follow. The motive behind an action also matters, so it's not just about what you do but also why you do it. The rightness of an action is determined by how it aligns with guiding moral principles or duties, regardless of the outcome. Kant's duty ethics, for example, promote a "categorical imperative," which emphasizes the universal application of a moral principle and the need to treat people not as a means to an end but as ends in themselves.
>
> *Virtue ethics:* Rather than simply following a set of moral rules or achieving specific outcomes, virtue ethics looks at the overall character of a person. It asks the question, "What kind of person should I be?" or "What would a person of good moral character do in this situation?" Virtue ethics involves cultivating virtuous qualities such as honesty, compassion, kindness, and courage.
>
> *Ethics of Care:* This theory of Carol Gilligan challenges the traditional ethical frameworks mentioned so far but fits most closely with the non-consequentialist theories. The Ethics of Care highlights the importance of caring relationships, empathy, and responsiveness to the needs of others in moral decision-making. It promotes interconnectedness, nurturing, and valuing the voices and experiences particularly of marginalized groups.

Non-consequentialist theories have also faced criticism. For example, these theories often lack specific guidance when faced with complex moral dilemmas. Critics also argue that focusing solely on duties or virtues may neglect the more practical concern for action and outcomes. Their reliance on subjective judgment may also lead to potentially biased decision-making.

Such criticisms of either consequentialist or non-consequentialist theories in no way invalidate these as approaches to ethical decision-making. They do, however, call on us to carefully consider the value of different moral perspectives and to evaluate how consistently we apply our own moral codes. As ethical decision-makers, these ethical theories or frameworks can guide our decision-making and help us to weigh competing interests and values.

BOX 2.1 **Your Ethical Framework**

Review the ethical theories presented here, and even take time to explore them further online. Then, consider ethical choices you have made recently (most of us face ethical choices on a daily basis).

1. Which of these theories best represents how you make moral choices?
2. If you find that you rely on one theory at one time but apply another in a different circumstance, what makes the difference? How do you know, for instance, when to consider the greater good and when to rely on your sense of caring, duties, or virtues?
3. What other frameworks or principles might be guiding you?

Leadership Ethics in the Workplace

With these key ethical theories in mind, let's shift our focus now to the professional landscape: ethical leadership within our organizations. In the remainder of this chapter, we will examine the purposes of ethical leadership, as well as the essential characteristics, principles, and behaviors that set ethical leaders apart as catalysts for positive change. In this way we can better equip ourselves to become effective, responsible leaders who make ethical choices and inspire others to do the same.

What Is Ethical Leadership?

Ethical leadership refers to the practice of leading in a way that is aligned with the four ethical pillars described previously—beneficence, nonmaleficence, autonomy, and justice—and the moral principles of the individual leader, the organization, and the larger society. This goes beyond gut instinct, legalities and compliance, or any particular religious doctrine people may have.

Ethical leaders are guided by a set of moral principles such as respect for others, service to others, honesty, and building community (DuBrin, 2010; Northouse, 2021). Leadership, at its essence, is about influencing people toward a common goal (Northouse, 2021). Ethical leadership is concerned with influencing human behavior and reaching those goals with integrity—in a way that is good, fair, consistent, and just (Daft, 2011).

Ethical leaders model ethical behavior themselves and foster ethical behavior among their followers. This is a central tenant of ethical leadership—that not only does the leader behave in ways consistent with recognized moral principles, but they also set a positive ethical tone for others to follow (Treviño et al., 2014). "Ethical leadership involves not only the personal character of the leader but also the norms, values, and culture of the organization that are necessary to support ethical decision-making and behavior" (Brown & Mitchell, 2010, p. 220). Overall, ethical leaders prioritize the well-being of their stakeholders (people who can, directly or indirectly, be affected by a leader's choices). They promote fairness and adhere to moral principles even in the face of challenges or temptations.

BOX 2.2 **Characteristics of Ethical Leaders**

While not an exhaustive list, the following represent some of the commonly identified characteristics of ethical leaders (den Hartog & de Hoogh, 2020; DuBrin, 2010; Northouse, 2021):

- Integrity: Ethical leaders consistently demonstrate strong moral principles, honesty in all their dealings, transparency, and consistency between their words and actions. They stick to their ethical standards even in the most challenging situations.
- Accountability: Ethical leaders take responsibility for their decisions and actions. They admit their mistakes and, more importantly, they learn from them.
- Transparency: Ethical leaders cultivate an environment of openness and transparency. They communicate openly, share information widely, and encourage feedback and dialogue.
- Empathy and Respect: Ethical leaders demonstrate empathy and respect towards others. They consider and value different perspectives and treat others with dignity.
- Fairness and Justice: Ethical leaders uphold fairness and justice in their decision-making processes. They treat people equitably and base decisions on sound reasoning and objective criteria.
- Authenticity: Ethical leaders are authentic ... genuine. They are true to themselves and their values and through this, they inspire trust and loyalty among their followers and stakeholders.
- Courage: Ethical leaders display moral courage by standing up for what is right, even in the face of adversity.

Consider ethical leaders you have known. Which of these characteristics did they demonstrate? What, if anything, would you add to this list?

Why Do We Need Ethical Leadership?

While unethical behaviors among leaders are seen almost daily in our news headlines, it is precisely because of this that ethical leaders become crucial in today's workplaces. True, there have been numerous cases where organizations have recorded significant financial success despite their leaders' unethical business practices. More often than not, however, their unethical practices eventually catch up with them, leading to sometimes severe consequences such as legal actions, reputational damage, and the loss of both employee and customer trust.

Within the organization itself, when faced with a leader's misconduct, employees may compromise their own ethical standards and are less likely to raise concerns (Ethics Resource Center, 2013). Other studies find that leaders who lack ethical behavior can negatively impact their employees' job satisfaction, commitment, and performance (Treviño, Weaver, & Reynolds, 2006; Trevor & Inkpen, 2013), as well as employee attitude and psychological well-being (Brown & Mitchell, 2010). All of this can damage an organization's reputation and credibility, foster a toxic work culture and climate, and lower employee morale and productivity (Treviño, Weaver, & Reynolds, 2006).

Such outcomes have perhaps contributed to the growing emphasis on ethics within our workplaces and on ethical leadership in particular. In many ways, this has led to rethinking just how it is we define success and ethical business practices within our business communities.

Redefining Organizational Success

The cases we see in the news of leader misconduct underscore the importance of ethical behavior for sustainable business success. Increasingly, companies are investing in such actions as integrity training (Gordon, 2022) or make public their statements of values or conduct codes. In response to societal expectations, companies are incorporating new standards for social responsibility (Gordon, 2022).

This recognized importance is reflected, for example, in the growth of B-Corporations, or B-Corps. A B-Corp company is a type of for-profit business that voluntarily meets specific social and environmental performance standards (which include justice, equity, diversity, and inclusion, among others), for which the company receives a B-Corp certification ("Measuring a Company's Entire Social and Environmental Impact," n.d.). These companies use their business as a force for good, considering both the financial bottom line and the impact of their actions on people and the planet. They commit to higher standards of accountability, transparency, and social responsibility compared to traditional corporations, and dedicate themselves to a "triple bottom line" approach.

This idea of a triple bottom line, or TBL, has gained prominence in the 21st century as more organizations embrace corporate social responsibility as a dimension of leadership ethics. Rather than looking exclusively at an organization's financial performance as the key metric for defining success, the TBL focuses on three dimensions: people, profit, and planet (Elkington, 1997; Miller, 2020). With the TBL, we consider not only the financial stability of an organization (such as by making money and ensuring efficiencies), but also how the organization affects people (like employees, customers, and communities) and the planet (such as the environment and natural resources). The TBL calls on ethical leaders to think about the impact of their actions on people's well-being and the health of the planet, in addition to achieving financial stability in a sustainable and responsible way. It is like looking at three bottom lines together to measure success, and it lies at the heart of corporate social responsibility (Byars & Stanberry, 2018).

BOX 2.3 **The Triple Bottom Line**

The Triple Bottom Line, or TBL, expands on the traditional focus on financial performance in our workplaces to also consider social and environmental factors in our ethical decision-making:

People: This emphasizes the social dimension of business ethics. Considerations include fair treatment of employees, respecting human rights, promoting diversity and inclusion, and ensuring product safety.

Profit: Economic sustainability is vital for any business to remain viable. This includes financial integrity, fair competition, transparent accounting, and responsible financial management.

Planet: This addresses the environmental dimensions of business ethics and demands consideration of how business activities impact the environment, natural resources, and ecosystems such as by minimizing pollution and waste, conserving natural resources, and addressing climate change and other environmental challenges.

1. What organizations have you known that define their success in terms of the Triple Bottom Line?
2. Think of a non-Triple Bottom Line organization; how might they look different if they adopted a Triple Bottom Line approach?

Organizational Impact of Ethical Leadership

Beyond the tangible impacts on people, profit, and planet, ethical leadership has a ripple effect throughout the entire organization, shaping the organizational climate, employee well-being, and both short- and long-term business outcomes. Ethical leaders serve as role models who influence employee job satisfaction, performance, and motivation (Bedi, Alpaslan, & Green, 2016). Because of this, "the developing notion [of ethical leadership] has brought immense advantages for worldwide businesses, compelling them to adopt moral and ethical considerations as an essential tool for [sic] organization's welfare" (Guo, 2022, para. 1).

Ethical leaders reduce legal problems and increase employee ethical conduct, organizational commitment, and job satisfaction (Treviño et al., 2000), all of which have a direct impact on performance. As leaders foster an ethical culture and climate characterized by high levels of trust and transparency, they contribute to long-term organizational success (Guo, 2022; Treviño et al., 2006).

We must acknowledge here that ethical leadership alone cannot eliminate all risk of unethical behavior. However, the presence of ethical leaders can significantly impact the culture and climate within organizations, setting a high standard and inspiring others to behave ethically. Simply put, ethical leaders encourage others to make principled choices and enhance individual, group, and organizational performance. "The importance of ethical leadership cannot be overstated in today's world. Businesses that strive to operate in a socially responsible and sustainable manner create not only long-term success but also promote positive change within their industry and community" (Terzieva, 2023, para. 10).

What Are Common Ethical Challenges in the Workplace?

The workplace is fraught with ethical challenges that require both vigilance and a commitment to ethical conduct on the part of the leader. Some of these challenges involve relatively straightforward ethical choices. We know, for example, that stealing company funds would be unethical since it involves taking something that does not belong to us. While stealing funds may be in a person's personal best interest financially, such an action would violate both virtue and duty ethics and would not be seen as being in the best interest of most other people (a utilitarian concern).

Ethical choices such as theft often pale in comparison to the larger ethical dilemmas facing leaders today, including the consideration of different stakeholder interests.

Ethical Dilemmas

On a daily basis, leaders must also grapple with complex ethical dilemmas—situations that involve making a tough choice between two or more conflicting moral principles or values. These arise when there are competing interests or conflicting values that cannot all be fully satisfied in a single decision; no clear solution exists, and each available option presents potential negative ethical consequences. As leaders, negotiating ethical dilemmas is a central part of their work, and how they resolve such dilemmas contributes to the moral tone within an organization.

The following are examples of common dilemmas faced by today's leaders:

Equality vs. Equity: Leaders must choose between treating people equally or treating them equitably in the workplace. Equality is seen when everyone is treated the same; equity emphasizes providing people with what they need to succeed, accounting for different starting points or circumstances. Striking a fair balance between these two ideals can be a challenge when designing policies, allocating resources, or addressing disparities.

Privacy vs. Transparency: The ethical leader must find the right balance between protecting employee privacy and fostering a transparent work environment. Respecting privacy involves such things as protecting sensitive information and ensuring confidentiality, while transparency promotes openness, accountability, and sharing relevant information. It can be a particular challenge for a leader when it comes to monitoring performance, data sharing, or decision-making processes.

Individual Autonomy vs. Organizational Control: Respecting individual autonomy involves truly empowering employees by allowing for freedom of expression, contributing to their own job redesign, encouraging critical thinking and independent decision-making, or even taking an action such as whistleblowing. Our organizations, however, also need structure and clear policies and standards to ensure consistency, efficiency, and legal compliance.

Profitability vs. Social Responsibility: While maximizing profits and efficiencies are necessary goals for organizations, leaders must also consider broader social implications such as environmental impact, fair labor practices, and community welfare (such as with product safety). Leaders must strike a balance between ensuring profitability and promoting shareholder interests versus fulfilling social responsibilities.

Short-term Results vs. Long-term Sustainability: Leaders may struggle daily with the ethical dilemma of pursuing short-term results or prioritizing long-term sustainability. Short-term thinking may involve making decisions based solely on immediate gains, while long-term sustainability requires thinking about the broader impacts on employees, other stakeholders, and the environment. As with other dilemmas, it is critical for leaders to find the right balance for sustainable and responsible leadership.

Loyalty to the Individual vs. Loyalty to the Organization: A final dilemma leaders face is the challenge of balancing loyalty to individual employes versus loyalty to the organization as a whole. Loyalty to employees involves serving as an advocate for their well-being, professional growth, and even work-life balance. In contrast, loyalty to the organization may require tough choices that prioritize long-term viability of the organization. Leaders must find ways to support employees while making choices that align with the organization's success.

BOX 2.4 **Ethical Dilemmas**

Scenario 1

Jasmine, the Human Resources department leader, must decide how best to allocate her very limited professional development budget. The company values fairness and also acknowledges that employees have diverse needs when it comes to professional growth. Jasmine must decide whether to distribute the training budget uniformly among all employees or consider individual circumstances and allocate resources accordingly, so that some departments may receive more development opportunities than others. This decision could impact employees' opportunities for growth, skill enhancement, and even promotion.

1. What type of ethical dilemma is Jasmine facing?
2. What potential impacts could Jasmine's decision have on employee satisfaction, professional development, and the overall workplace environment? Consider both short-term and long-term consequences. How might this decision influence the perception of fairness among employees and their trust in the company's commitment to employee growth?

Scenario 2

Recently, Jarrod, the head of EcoTech's marketing department, became aware of two employees who have been talking negatively about the company on their personal social media accounts. Other employees in the company are also aware of these negative posts. Negative rants about the company are in violation of EcoTech's Code of Conduct, which describes everyone's role in creating and supporting a positive work culture, both within and outside the company. Jarrod knows he has a duty to protect the company's reputation as well as to keep the internal work climate positive. He wonders, though, if he crosses a line by disciplining the two employees for simply expressing their views on their personal social media platforms—would that be perceived as retaliation by other employees? On the other hand, if he does nothing, will other employees see this as a lack of commitment to the company's Code of Conduct?

1. What type of ethical dilemma is Jarrod facing?
2. How might Jarrod's response to the employees' negative social media posts impact the overall workplace culture and employee morale? Consider the balance between upholding the company's reputation and fostering an environment where employees feel they have the freedom to express concerns. What steps could Jarrod take to address the situation in a way that maintains a positive work culture while addressing the Code of Conduct violation?

Scenario 3

TurbineZ, Inc. has signed a 2-year contract with GlobalMakers, a supplier located in a developing country outside the United States. GlobalMakers will be creating a unique and crucial component that TurbineZ needs for a new product line, which they hope to bring to market in six months. Recently, however, TurbineZ leaders have learned of troubling practices within GlobalMakers' operations: the use of child labor and exploitative wages, inadequate safety measures, and the discharge of untreated wastewater into nearby rivers, contributing to water pollution that affects the health of villages that rely on those water sources. Each of these practices violate the TurbineZ commitment to employee and environmental well-being. Leaders recognize that it is not TurbineZ itself that is in violation of their own Triple Bottom Line—GlobalMakers is simply part of their supply chain. What message might this send to their own employees and customers, however? Breaking their contract with this supplier, though, means their new product line will not go to market on time, and TurbineZ may face hefty penalties for breaking the contract.

1. What type of ethical dilemma are the leaders of TurbineZ facing?
2. Consider the potential messages that TurbineZ's decision could send regarding their commitment to ethical business practices, social responsibility, and environmental sustainability. Furthermore, think about the long-term consequences for brand loyalty and stakeholder trust. In light of these considerations, what strategies might TurbineZ adopt to address the ethical concerns while still meeting their contractual obligations and minimizing harm to their reputation?

Navigating such ethical dilemmas demands that a leader exercise both thoughtful analysis and moral courage. The ethical leader must be both willing and able to weigh competing values and conflicts of interest and consider implications for any trade-offs among different stakeholders. Issues such as pay disparities, hiring biases, inclusivity and respect, security, safety, new challenges presented by emerging technologies such as AR/AI, and more must all be confronted.

Weighing Stakeholder Interests

A significant concern for leaders involves how they do—or should—weigh the interests and needs of diverse stakeholders. These are the people impacted by a leader's decisions: employees, suppliers, shareholders, customers, communities, government bodies, and the environment.

Stakeholder theory gained prominence in the late 20th century and since then has evolved and influenced such areas as strategic management, organizational behavior, and corporate social responsibility. Initially introduced by Edward Freeman in 1984, stakeholder theory advanced the idea that leaders must consider the interests and impacts on a broader set of stakeholders rather than focus solely on shareholders. Today it has become a foundational concept in discussions of corporate social responsibility, ethics, and sustainable business practices and is shaping the way leaders approach their relationships and ethical responsibilities.

Whose interests should take priority—the customers? Employees? The organization as a whole? The environment? How do we arrive at a decision when, for example, an action is good for the business but harmful to the environment? What about when a product will return high profits but pose a hazard to customers? These are the kinds of questions the ethical leader must grapple with. As leaders consider various stakeholders and their often-competing interests, they must also consider how their decisions may affect stakeholders. Leaders have a moral responsibility to act in the best interest of their stakeholders and understand that their decisions can have a far-reaching impact on the lives of others. Considering all stakeholders is a way to help ensure fairness, justice, and the minimization of harm.

Leaders also understand that they are accountable to all of their stakeholders—this is vital in order to foster trust and credibility (Byars & Stanberry, 2018). Leaders who consider their stakeholders are more likely to make decisions that promote long-term success. By considering both the concerns and expectations of stakeholders, leaders can make more informed choices, identify potential risks and opportunities, balance short-term gains with long-term benefits, and assess the potential ethical implications of their choices (2018). Demonstrating their commitment to stakeholder consideration is key for enhancing a positive reputation and social responsibility.

BOX 2.5 **Who Are Your Stakeholders?**

Think about a particular organization in which you are involved. This could be your workplace, school, or some other organization in which you regularly engage. With that organization in mind:

1. Who are the stakeholders (such as employees, customers, vendors, stockholders, the environment, and so on)?
2. As you think about these stakeholders, in what ways might their needs, interests, and priorities be different?
3. What might be the needs, interests, and priorities of the leader?
4. How might these differences influence a leader's ethical decision-making?
5. Whose needs and interests should be given priority, and why?

How Do We Become Ethical Leaders?

Before examining how we can become ethical leaders, let's look first at how good people can make unethical choices. After all, few leaders set out to become unethical people; unethical behavior is generally not the result of bad people gaining power (though sometimes that occurs). Rather, unethical behavior is more often the result of an unfolding process that starts with an ethical dilemma. Despite our good intentions, it can be difficult to hold firmly to the values that are important to us when we are confronted with pressures to do otherwise. Given the right circumstances, it can be all too easy to fall victim to psychological traps that can weaken our moral resolve and strip us of our moral courage (Hoyk & Hersey, 2008).

Research suggests that ethical violations can stem from a variety of factors such as our organizational culture, social norms, and incentives, as well as our personality characteristics and biases (Treviño & Weaver, 2003). Other factors include exposure to people within our social circles who behave unethically, greed, egocentrism, and more also play a role (Belle & Cantarelli, 2017).

In general, our motivation to take any sort of action stems from a number of impulses brought about by internal or external stimuli. When it comes to choosing between an ethical and unethical course of action:

> Sometimes a stimulus is so powerful or triggers such automatic behavior that we act on it without being aware that other options exist. At other times, we are aware of other choices but the stimulus's effect overrides these potential actions. (Hoyk & Hersey, 2008, p. 6)

There are many external stimuli that can provoke us to take unethical action. Many of us, for example, have been socialized into automatically obeying someone in a position of authority. This obedience to authority is difficult to ignore; after all, if the person in authority tells us to do something, it must be the right thing to do. A sense of self-preservation can also lead us to take action in a way that violates our values or principles, as will external pressures: time pressure, the pressure to conform to a group, pressures from obligations ("You owe me this ..."), or pressure to "not stir things up" (Hoyk & Hersey, 2008, p. 6). How distant we are from the impact of an action also makes it easier to behave unethically, such as when we will never see the people affected or if we objectify or dehumanize them. "Within decision-making research, the concept of moral distance is used to explain why individuals behave unethically towards those who are not seen. Moral distance abstracts those who are impacted by the decision and leads to less ethical decisions" (Villegas-Galaviz & Martin, 2023).

Internal stimuli may also impact our ethical choices and typically take the form of personality characteristics such as psychopathy, low self-esteem, or an authoritarian or social dominance orientation (Hoyk & Hersey, 2008). Even empathy toward someone can lead us to create an unfair advantage that others will not benefit from (2008). It is also easier to take an unethical action when we can justify or minimize its impact or take other steps to absolve us of guilt or shame, which can lead us to further unethical behavior.

Given the importance of ethical leadership and its potential for positively impacting human performance and social well-being, how can we stay true to our principles and the values of our organization and help others to do so as well? After all, when it comes to promoting ethical behavior, "Unless we actually develop the leaders that can implement an embedded ethical way of operating within organisational cultures, the whole subject becomes a purely academic and unrealizable exercise" (Knights, n.d., p. 4).

The key may lie in a combination of professional growth opportunities, practical experience, and self-reflection. When faced with an ethical dilemma, leaders must approach it with integrity, transparency, and a commitment to ethical decision-making. This typically includes a heightened self-awareness as well as thoughtful considerations of key steps for resolving an ethical dilemma.

Cultivating Self-Awareness

Self-awareness refers to the conscious knowledge and understanding of ourselves and our internal experience. This may include our emotions, thoughts, personality, motivations, strengths, biases, values, and beliefs and the ways in which these influence our actions and interactions with others. Self-aware leaders have an accurate and realistic understanding of their abilities, limitations, and areas for growth. This develops through an ongoing process of self-reflection and self-examination, which allow us to gain insights into our own preferences and patterns of behavior. As we cultivate self-awareness, we can enhance our decision-making, emotional intelligence, and interpersonal relationships, leading to further growth and more effective leadership (Gallo, 2019).

Increasing self-awareness is an ongoing process that takes time and patience—it's a lifelong journey that requires effort and practice. Here are just a few of the steps we can take to foster our own self-awareness:

A. *Take time for self-reflection.* Understanding our personal values and biases can lead us to see how those personal perspectives may influence our judgment and decision-making and their potential impact on our ethical choices (Chugh, 2018). Dedicating time for self-reflection may include journaling, meditation, or simply examining the reasons behind our actions.
B. *Recognize emotional responses.* Ethical decision-making can be complex and evoke strong emotions. Working to both identify and manage our emotions can reduce the likelihood that they will interfere with our ability to make ethical choices and allow us to make our choices with greater clarity and rationality (see, for example, Marques, Dhiman, & Biberman, 2011). Self-reflection and practicing mindfulness are good ways to observe our emotions and physical sensations, particularly when we face uncomfortable situations.
C. *Identify blind spots.* Being aware of our blind spots can help us to seek diverse perspectives and make more informed ethical decisions. Blind spots are those areas where we may lack knowledge, experience, or awareness, including, for instance, our own limitations and biases. Actively seeking feedback from others can help us gain insight into our blind spots or biases, and many leaders make use of various self-assessment tools such as the MBTI to better understand themselves and potential blind spots.
D. *Build empathy and perspective taking.* These allow us to gain a deeper understanding of how our decisions may impact others. As leaders we must consider the well-being and interests of all stakeholders involved. To build empathy and understand different perspectives, we can learn more about diverse groups and individuals, practice active listening, and simply take time to put ourselves in someone else's shoes to understand what they may be feeling or the factors that impact their perspective.
E. *Commit to authentic and transparent leadership.* We foster trust and openness by being trusting, trustworthy, authentic, and open (Frei & Morriss, 2020). Leaders who are self-aware and can acknowledge their own fallibility are more likely to engage in open dialogue, seek feedback, and admit mistakes. Through this, they promote an ethical culture of accountability and continuous improvement.
F. *Align actions with values.* Self-aware leaders make sure their actions fit their stated values. They find quiet moments to think about their actions and examine how closely those actions fit with their ethical principles. This alignment promotes credibility, trust, and respect among their teams.

By cultivating self-awareness, leaders can better make ethical choices, positively influence their organizational culture, and inspire ethical behavior in their teams (Eurich, 2018).

Resolving an Ethical Dilemma

When faced with an ethical dilemma, such as when our stakeholders have competing interests, leaders must approach it with self-awareness, thoughtfulness, transparency, and a commitment to ethical decision-making.

Addressing and resolving an ethical dilemma starts by recognizing that a dilemma exists. Ethical leaders work first to understand the conflicting values, interests, and principles among stakeholders, and recognize the potential ethical implications for their decisions. To gain clarity around the situation, ethical leaders gather relevant information by researching the issue, consulting experts, or simply talking with stakeholders to gain their perspectives and insights.

Once the leader has a firm grasp of the situation, they can take the following steps:

1. *Analyze the situation.* Ethical leaders need to think through the potential consequences of each available option and evaluate the impact on all stakeholders. A key question to consider is simply this: Among the stakeholders, whose interests or needs will take priority if not all needs or interests can be met? How a leader weighs competing needs and interests often rests with how they align with the leader's own ethical principles and the organization's values and sense of public duty.
2. *Apply ethical frameworks.* Turning to the basic ethical frameworks (such as utilitarianism, virtues, duty ethics, or care) or applying decision-making models can help guide a leader's analysis of the dilemma. These frameworks or models can provide a systematic approach and help to ensure that the leader is making principled decisions.
3. *Use ethical reasoning and reflection.* Ethical leaders take time to engage in thoughtful ethical reasoning and reflect on their personal values, organizational values, and the ethical implications of their decisions for all stakeholders. This introspection helps leaders align their choices with their own ethical compass and the espoused values of the organization.
4. *Consult with and engage stakeholders.* Involve relevant stakeholders in the decision-making process whenever possible. This may include seeking input from people directly affected by the dilemma or who possess expertise in the issue. Open dialogue and considering diverse perspectives can foster trust and promote fairness and inclusivity in our decision-making.
5. *Identify and evaluate alternatives.* The ethical leader will generate and evaluate different courses of action in order to resolve the dilemma. What will create the most good or do the least harm to stakeholders? What options align best with the stated organizational values? What are the priorities in terms of stakeholder interests and well-being?
6. *Take responsibility for the decision.* Ultimately, a decision must be made, taking into account the analysis, ethical considerations, and available information. Among the options, which one best aligns with ethical principles, respects the rights and well-being of stakeholders, and promotes the long-term interests of the organizations and the broader impact on society? Ethical leaders own their actions, accept responsibility for their choices, and are prepared to stand behind their decisions. If mistakes are made, ethical leaders accept responsibility and work to fix them (Terzieva, 2023).
7. *Communicate effectively to implement the decision.* Ethical leaders communicate their decision transparently and clearly to the relevant people. While doing so, they also provide a rationale for their decision, emphasizing the ethical considerations and the values that guide their choice. As with any other decisions a leader must make, effective implementation must include clear instructions or expectations, necessary resources, and ongoing monitoring to assess the results.

Navigating ethical dilemmas transparently and thoughtfully, while considering all stakeholder perspectives, can demonstrate a leader's commitment to ethical conduct and help promote a culture of integrity within the organization. Transparency in particular helps to foster ethical behavior in their teams as well.

How Can Leaders Foster a Culture of Ethical Behavior and Accountability?

We can view ethical leadership as a shared responsibility that involves, impacts, and is affected by people in all levels of an organization. As leaders—either designated or emergent—we have an opportunity to create an environment that supports this shared responsibility and thus minimize the risk of people making unethical choices when confronted with tough decisions. Central to this environment is the work culture, commonly understood as the shared values, beliefs, norms, behaviors, artifacts, and practices that exist within a workplace. This includes the attitudes, expectations, and social dynamics that shape the work environment and influence employee behavior and interactions (Hofstede, 2010; Schein, 2004).

Research in organizational behavior and ethics supports the idea that an ethical culture, characterized by ethical leadership, ethical practices, and strong ethical norms, is associated with reduced counterproductive behavior (see, for example, Treviño, Weaver, & Reynolds, 2006). When people perceive a strong ethical culture, they are more likely to embrace high ethical standards, report misconduct, and act in ways that promote the organization's best interests. Conversely, the work culture may become the strongest predictor of counterproductive behavior (Peng & Kim, 2020).

It is important to note here that other variables such as individual characteristics, personal values, and situational factors can also influence counterproductive behavior. A significant body of research, however, suggests that we acquire much of our knowledge, skills, attitudes, and behaviors by observing and imitating others in our social circles (Bandura, 1976; Rotter, 1972). In other words, we often take our cues as to what is acceptable by observing the role models around us. Within the workplace, the leader serves as a central model.

The Leader's Role

A leader plays a critical role in fostering a positive and ethical work culture. They do so by promoting ethical values, fostering open communication, and setting clear expectations. A leader sets the tone through their own actions, making decisions based on integrity and holding themselves accountable. They create an environment of trust where employees feel safe to voice concerns, report unethical behavior, and take part in ethical discussions. A leader also cultivates a climate supporting learning and growth, encouraging people to develop their ethical decision-making skills and providing opportunities for learning and development. By actively promoting ethical conduct, emphasizing transparency, and both recognizing and rewarding ethical behavior, a leader shapes the organizational climate as well as culture.

Just how an organization creates and sustains an ethical work culture varies from one organization to another. In many workplaces, an organizational code of conduct or code of ethics is used to articulate ethical expectations. That is a good start, but ethical leadership must go beyond simply creating a set of rules to guide our actions. Rather, we must foster an entire work culture that not only supports, but insists upon, ethical decision-making and accountability.

Creating an ethical work culture can reduce the likelihood of ethical violations and promote ethical behavior throughout the organization (Brown & Treviño, 2006). It's not a simple thing to do, though. A recent survey conducted by the Ethics Resource Center found that 68% of senior leaders believe the creation of an ethical work culture is a significant challenge facing their organizations (Ethics Resource Center, 2020). In spite of the challenges, cultivating and reinforcing an ethical work culture remains a critical responsibility for leaders and requires an ongoing effort, consistent attention, and commitment.

We commonly see ethical leaders take these types of actions:

> *Lead by example.* Leaders serve as role models for their teams and must embody ethical behavior, consistently demonstrating integrity, transparency, and ethical decision-making in their actions. This sets the standard for ethical conduct within the organization. When seen as being ethical themselves, leaders become a strong predictor of employee ethical behavior (Bedi, Alpaslam, & Green, 2016; Guo, 2022).
>
> *Clearly communicate expectations.* Ethical leaders communicate their expectations on ethical behavior and the organization's values. This includes establishing a code of conduct, ethics policies, and clear guidelines that outline the standards of behavior that are expected. This calls for more than simply placing posters on the wall or talking about expectations during an orientation. Employees must see these standards being clearly applied as a part of any decision-making, problem solving, or other daily interactions.

Foster open communication. Encourage a culture of open and transparent communication where people feel comfortable discussing ethical concerns or dilemmas. Create channels and mechanisms for open communication such as anonymous reporting systems or regular team discussions to facilitate such conversations, and ensure that ethical concerns are addressed promptly. It's not enough to simply tell people you want them to speak freely; they must have genuine, firsthand encounters so that open and transparent communication becomes a lived rather than an appropriated, superficial experience (Aktouf, 1992).

Provide ethics training and education. Offer ethics as a part of employee learning and development efforts to enhance people's understanding of ethical principles, values, and decision-making frameworks. Studies indicate that ethics training is positively associated with ethical conduct, helps people develop their ethical awareness, leads to higher intentions to behave ethically, and better equips them to navigate ethical challenges (Kaptein & Schwartz, 2008; Treviño, Weaver, & Reynolds, 2006).

Establish systems for accountability and consequences. Hold people accountable for their actions and decisions by establishing not only clear standards but also clear consequences for ethical misconduct. The fair and consistent enforcement of ethical standards sends a strong message about an organization's commitment to principled action and maintaining an ethical work culture.

Provide guidance, resources, and supporting processes. Create an environment where people are encouraged to make ethical decisions. Support them by providing guidance, resources, and processes such as through active listening and empathy, helping people to weigh the consequences of an action, brainstorming alternatives, and ensuring confidentiality so people feel safe to speak freely or can report misconduct without fear of retaliation. Ensure policies are consistent with the organization's stated values, and provide guidelines to help people address such things as conflicts of interest or gifts from suppliers.

Recognize ethical behavior. Shine the spotlight on ethical behavior wherever possible (except when to do so would violate confidentiality). Acknowledge people who consistently demonstrate ethical behavior and who contribute to an ethical work culture. Recognize people's actions and encourage others to follow suit.

Regularly assess and improve. Examine and evaluate the organization's ethical climate and culture through feedback mechanisms such as surveys or ethical audits. Use the insights gained to identify areas for improvement and implement changes transparently to reinforce the ethical work culture.

Is it worth all this effort? Numerous leaders, experts, and researchers suggest it is! We know, for instance, that a strong work culture in general is essential for maintaining trust, fostering employee engagement, and ensuring long-term organizational success (Schein, 2004). The ethical work culture not only creates a firm foundation for employee morale, commitment, and retention, but also enhances productivity and attracts top talent (see, for example, Kerns, 2005; Paine, 2003).

A culture of ethics and integrity will serve to strengthen relationships with customers and other stakeholders and minimize both legal and reputational risks by inspiring ethical conduct at all levels of the organization (Paine, 1994). The ethical work culture fosters a collaborative and inclusive environment (Raimi & Kah, 2022) where diversity of thought is both expected and respected, and ethical dilemmas are openly discussed and addressed.

BOX 2.6 **Organizational Code of Conduct**

An organization's code of conduct (also known by other names such as a Code of Ethics) is a formal document that outlines the expected behavior, values, and ethical standards for all members of the organization. It serves as a guide or reference point for people's actions and decisions, promoting a culture of integrity, professionalism, and ethical conduct.

Though unique to each organization, industry, or professional association, typical codes of conduct include:

- Ethical principles
- Conflicts of interest
- Compliance with laws and regulations
- Workplace behavior
- Confidentiality, privacy, and data protection
- Gifts and gratuities
- Use of company resources
- Reporting and whistleblowing

Consider an organization, industry, or profession you are familiar with, then:

1. Conduct an information search to find its code of ethics or code of conduct.
2. Which of the above do you see represented within the code?
3. What other areas are defined in the code you found?

Conclusion

Ethical leadership plays a pivotal role in shaping today's workplace and fostering a culture of integrity, trust, and accountability. This chapter has explored the essence of ethical leadership, highlighting its significance when facing complex ethical challenges. We've also considered ways to become ethical leaders ourselves and seen how fostering a culture of ethical behavior and accountability is vital for organizational success.

Ethical leadership isn't just about following a set of rules or sticking to our moral principles; it's about inspiring others to do the right thing and engaging in conversation to examine what that means within the organizational context. It's about making tough choices with integrity and being a role model for ethical conduct. When leaders act ethically, it sets the tone for the entire organization and contributes to an environment of trust and respect.

Ethical leaders understand the importance of considering the interests of multiple stakeholders, promoting fairness, transparency, and respect. They demonstrate moral courage in confronting ethical dilemmas, and their actions create a ripple effect throughout the organization. Ethical leaders foster a supportive environment by setting clear expectations for ethical behavior, providing guidance and resources, and recognizing and reinforcing ethical behavior. Becoming an ethical leader begins with self-awareness and includes seeking feedback and insights from others and reflecting on our own values, strengths, and areas for growth. Through self-reflection, education, and expanding on our experiences, we can develop our moral reasoning skills and continuously strive to improve ourselves.

In essence, ethical leadership serves as a compass, guiding organizations toward responsible and sustainable practices, ensuring that they not only achieve financial goals but also meet broader societal obligations. By embracing ethical leadership, organizations reap numerous benefits, including an enhanced reputation among diverse stakeholders, increased employee engagement and performance, and sustained organizational success in an ever-evolving and ethically complex world. Through our collective efforts as ethical leaders, we can make a real and positive difference in the workplace and beyond.

References

A framework for making ethical decisions. (n.d.). Brown University: Science and Technology Studies. https://www.brown.edu/academics/science-and-technology-studies/framework-making-ethical-decisions#:~:text=Ethical%20theories%20are%20often%20broadly,making%20ethical%20decisions%20about%20particular

Aktouf, O. (1992). Management and theories of organizations in the 1990s: Toward a critical radical humanism? *Academy of Management Review, 17*(3), 407–431.

Arnold, B. G., Beauchamp, T. L., & Bowie, N. E. (2020). *Ethical theory and business* (10th ed.). Cambridge University Press.

Bandura, A. (1976). *Social learning theory.* Pearson.

Beauchamp, T. L., & Bowie, N. E.

Bedi, A., Alpaslan, C. M., & Green, S. A. (2016). Meta-analytic review of ethical leadership outcomes and moderators. *Journal of Business Ethics* 139, 517–536.

Belle, N., & Cantarelli, P. (February 2017). *What causes unethical behavior? A meta-analysis to set an agenda for public administration research.* American Society for Public Administration. https://doi.org/10.1111/puar.12714

Brown, M. E., & Mitchell, M. S. (2010). Ethical and unethical leadership: Exploring new avenues for future research. *Business Ethics Quarterly, 20*(4), 583–616. https://doi.org/10.5840/beq201020439

Brown, M. E., & Treviño, L. K. (2006). Ethical leadership: A review and future directions. *The Leadership Quarterly, 17*(6), 595–616. doi: 10.1016/j.leaqua.2006.10.004

Byars, S. M., & Stanberry, K. (2018). *Business ethics.* Openstax.

Chugh, D. (2018). *The person you mean to be: How good people fight bias.* Harper Business.

Daft, R. L. (2011). *The leadership experience* (5th ed.). Thomson, South-Western.

den Hartog, D. N., & de Hoogh, A. H. (2020). Ethical leadership: A review and future directions. *Journal of Business Ethics, 165*(3), 385–406.

DuBrin, A. J. (2010). *Principles of leadership* (6th ed.). South-Western Cengage Learning.

Elkington, J. (1997). *Cannibals with forks: The Triple Bottom Line of 21st century business.* Capstone; Oxford Centre for Innovation.

Ethics and Compliance Initiative. (2019). *The state of ethics and compliance in the workplace: A look at global trends.* Global Business Ethics Survey. https://www.ethics.org/research/gbes

Ethics Resource Center. (2020). *2020 global business ethics survey.* https://www.ethics.org/global-business-ethics-survey-gbes

Ethics Resource Center. (2013). National Business Ethics Survey of the U.S. Workforce. https://lowellmilkeninstitute.law.ucla.edu/wp-content/uploads/2015/10/Thomas-Jordan_Ethics-Resource-Center-National-Business-Ethics-of-the-U.S.-Workplace.pdf

Eurich, T. (January 2018). What self-awareness really is (and how to cultivate it): It's not just about introspection. Harvard Business Review. https://hbr.org/2018/01/what-self-awareness-really-is-and-how-to-cultivate-it

Freeman, R. E. (2010). *Strategic management: A stakeholder approach.* Cambridge University Press.

Frei, F. X., & Morriss, A. (May-June 2020). *Begin with trust.* Harvard Business Review. https://hbr.org/2020/05/begin-with-trust

Gallo, S. (2019). *The importance of self-awareness in leadership.* Training Industry. https://trainingindustry.com/articles/leadership/the-importance-of-self-awareness-in-leadership

Gordon, A. (February 2022). *Tunnel vision or the bigger picture? The EY Global Integrity Report 2022 reveals how a focus on governance can help reimagine corporate integrity.* EY. https://www.ey.com/en_us/forensic-integrity-services/how-a-focus-on-governance-can-help-reimagine-corporate-integrity

Guo, K. (May 2022). The relationship between ethical leadership and employee job satisfaction: The mediating role of media richness and perceived organizational transparency. *Frontiers in Psychology.* doi: 10.3389/fpsyg.2022.885515

Hassan, S., Kaur, P., Muchiri, M., et al. (2023). Unethical leadership: Review, synthesis and directions for future research. *Journal of Business Ethics* 183, 511–550. https://doi.org/10.1007/s10551-022-05081-6

Hofstede, G. (2010). *Cultures and organizations: Software of the mind* (3rd ed.). McGraw-Hill.

Hoyk, R., & Hersey, P. (2008). *The ethical executive: Become aware of the root causes of unethical behavior: 45 psychological traps that every one of us falls prey to.* Stanford Business.

Institute of Business Ethics. (2018). *Ethics at work: 2018 survey of employees.* United Kingdom. https://www.ibe.org.uk/uploads/assets/ba9cd14a-a195-4c79-b12c68f7b06fd203/IBESurveyReportEthicsatWork2018surveyofemployeesEuropeINT.pdf

Johnson, C. E. (2017). *Meeting the ethical challenges of leadership: Casting light or shadow* (6th ed.). Sage.

Kaptein, M., & Schwartz, M. S. (2008). The effectiveness of business codes: A critical examination of existing studies and the development of an integrated research model. *Journal of Business Ethics 77*, 111–127. https://doi.org/10.1007/s10551-006-9305-0

Kerns, C. D. (2005). *Value-centered ethics: A proactive system to shape ethical behavior.* HRD Press.

Knights, J. (n.d.). *How to develop ethical leaders* [white paper]. Routledge: Transpersonal Leadership Series. https://www.routledge.com/rsc/downloads/Transpersonal_Leadership_WP1.pdf

Lewis, A. (October 2022). *Good leadership? It all starts with trust.* Harvard Business Publishing Corporate Learning. https://www.harvardbusiness.org/good-leadership-it-all-starts-with-trust/#:~:text=Be%20transparent&-text=Don't%20withhold%20resources%20from,performance%E2%80%94both%20positively%20and%20constructively

Marques, J., Dhiman, S., & Biberman, J. (2011). Ethical leadership and emotional intelligence. In Marques, J., Dhiman, S., & Biberman, J. (Eds.). *Managing in the twenty-first century.* Palgrave Macmillan. https://doi.org/10.1057/9780230116719_4

Measuring a company's entire social and environmental impact. (n.d.). Bcorporation. https://www.bcorporation.net/en-us/certification

Miller, K. (December 2020). *The triple bottom line: What it is and why it's important.* Harvard Business School Online. https://online.hbs.edu/blog/post/what-is-the-triple-bottom-line

Northouse, P. G. (2021). *Leadership: Theory and practice* (9th ed.). Sage.

Paine, L. S. (2003). *Value shift: Why companies must merge social and financial imperatives to achieve superior performance.* McGraw-Hill.

Paine, L. S. (March-April 1994). Managing for organizational integrity. *Harvard Business Review, 72*(2), 106–117.

Peng, A. C., & Kim, D. (2020). A meta-analytic test of the differential pathways linking ethical leadership to normative conduct. *Journal of Organizational Behavior, 41*(4), 348–368.

Raimi, L., & Kah, J. M. L. (Eds.). (2022). *Mainstreaming diversity, equity, and inclusion as future workplace ethics.* IGI Global.

Rotter, J. B. (1972). *Applications of a social learning theory of personality.* Holt, Rinehart and Winston.

Schein, E. H. (2004). *Organizational culture and leadership* (3rd ed.). John Wiley & Sons.

Terzieva, K. (February 2023). *The rise of ethical leadership in modern business enterprises.* Forbes Coaches Council. https://www.forbes.com/sites/forbescoachescouncil/2023/02/28/the-rise-of-ethical-leadership-in-modern-business-enterprises/?sh=69f3bae237dd

Thiroux, J. P., & Krasemann, K. W. (2016). *Ethics: Theory and practice* (12th edition). Pearson.

Treviño, L. K., den Nieuwenboer, N. A., & Kish-Gephart, J. J. (2014). (Un)ethical leadership and identity: What did you do? Who, me? Why? In D. M. Rousseau (Ed.), *The Oxford handbook of evidence-based management* (pp. 123–148). Oxford University Press.

Treviño, L. K., Hartman, L. P., & Brown, M. (Summer 2000). Moral person and moral manager: How executives develop a reputation for ethical leadership. *California Management Review, 42*(4), 128–142.

Treviño, L. K., Weaver, G. R., & Reynolds, S. J. (2006). Behavioral ethics in organizations: A review. *Journal of Management, 32*(6), 951–990.

Treviño, L. K., & Weaver, G. R. (2003). Managing ethics in business organizations: An integrative model and fields of practice. In M. Ehnert, & M. Harry (Eds.), *Diversity and ethics in the workplace* (pp. 177–194). Palgrave Macmillan.

Trevor, C. O., & Inkpen, A. C. (2013). A social network perspective on leader ethical decision making. *Journal of Business Ethics, 113*(1), 1–12.

van den Akker, L., Heres, L, Lasthuizen, K., & Six, F. (2009). Ethical leadership and trust: It's all about meeting expectations. *International Journal of Leadership Studies 5*(2), 102–122.

Varkey, B. (February 2021). Principles of clinical ethics and their application to practice. *Medical Principles and Practice* 30(1), 17–28. https://doi.org/10.1159/000509119

Velasquez, M., Andre, C., Shanks, S. J., T., & Meyer, M. J. (rev. 2010). *What is ethics?* Markkula Center for Applied Ethics, Santa Clara University. https://www.scu.edu/ethics/ethics-resources/ethical-decision-making/what-is-ethics/

Villegas-Galaviz, C., & Martin, K. (March 2023). *Moral distance, AI, and the ethics of care.* National Library of Medicine, AI and Society, 1–12. doi: 10.1007/s00146-023-01642-z

UNIT II

LEADING SELF

CHAPTER 3

Leadership Courage

By Amy Cox

Courage is what it takes to stand up and speak; courage is also what it takes to sit down and listen.

—Winston Churchill

Learning Objectives

After reading this chapter, students will be able to:

1. Describe the attributes essential to leadership courage
2. Analyze scenarios using the essential attributes of leadership courage
3. Discuss one thing you learned from the chapter and describe how you will use this knowledge going forward

Introduction to Leadership Courage

The concept of courage is universal, and numerous examples of courage can easily be identified. However, defining courage is a complicated task. There are many different definitions of courage throughout the literature. Christopher Rate and colleagues (2007) conducted a comprehensive review of these descriptions using numerous sources, which included philosophy, psychology, ancient and modern literature, and more. After analyzing their findings for similarities and differences, Rate et al. (2007) consolidated their results into scenarios in which study participants rated the scenarios as more or less courageous. The stories that were rated as more courageous had common features, which led the investigators to describe courage as (a) a willful, intentional act; (b) performed after mindful deliberation; (c) involving risk to the actor; (d) to achieve a noble or worthwhile outcome; (e) at times, despite the presence of fear. This description is based on the external circumstances in which leaders find themselves, and their cognitive knowledge and understanding, discretional (rational), emotional, and motivational, and therefore internal, environment.

So, what internal environment, or attributes, does the actor need to demonstrate courage, and how does this apply to leadership in the workplace? Below, we explore the interplay between the leader's external surroundings and inherent characteristics necessary to navigate leadership, and leadership courage, successfully.

Will and Intent

In a portion of the literature, research results indicate that participants believe that for an act to be courageous, the actor must voluntarily enter into the action (Rate et al., 2007), but action undertaken as a result of pressure or coercion is not considered courageous (Detert and Bruno, 2017). However, courage described in this manner can be subjective. For instance, imagine a scenario in which an employee is threatened by her manager to be reassigned (demoted) if she does not execute a specific request by the manager, a request that is against the employee's wishes and that of her colleagues. Despite the employee's reservations, she decides to carry out the manager's request. This would appear to be an act based on fear, but the employee will need to call upon some level of personal fortitude to take an action that she knows is against the wishes of her colleagues, regardless of the driving factor (threat or free choice). Perhaps the employee's position and associated salary make the difference between her family being able to pay rent or not, and the employee must therefore make the choice between maintaining her position and the well-being of her family or maintaining a harmonious relationship with her peers. This scenario leads us to appreciate the significance and complexity of intent and the realization that, while free will may seem like a necessary component of courage, the practical conclusion may be that the degree of free choice moderates the degree of courageousness, rather than whether an act is courageous at all (Detert and Bruno, 2017).

Furthermore, in the example above, while it may appear that neither the manager nor the employee was acting in an ethical manner, we don't know whether the manager's request was truly unethical or a request that might be unpopular with the employees but serve the good of the organization overall. A leader's intent should derive from the leader's moral compass. Ethical leaders are regarded to be honest, trustworthy, fair, and principled decision-makers who care about others and behave ethically in their personal and professional lives (Brown & Treviño, 2006). As demonstrated, there can be many complicating factors. We explore how to navigate these challenging situations in the following discussions.

Mindful Deliberation

Much like the degree of free choice moderates the degree of courageousness, it is useful to think about the degree of deliberation or contemplation prior to an action moderating the degree of courageousness. For instance, heroic acts can be spontaneous with little to no deliberation but are nevertheless determined to be courageous. However, an employee who stands up to her manager regarding a request that the employee does not agree with can be considered foolhardy if the employee takes no time to consider the manager's request and the repercussions of denying that request. In this example, if the employee takes the time to consider the manager's request and consider her own circumstances (as in the situation presented above with potential repercussions of decreased pay) and, after learning as much as she can about the request and why it was made, the employee then refuses to carry out the manager's request based on the employee's personal moral compass, this then could be considered a courageous act. But again, this is a subjective description of courage. One way that a person can anticipate making difficult decisions is for the person to clarify what is important ahead of time (Gebelein, 2004). Thinking about personal values and having a strong understanding of personal morals and beliefs will help you make reasonable decisions when placed in challenging circumstances. While this strong moral and ethical foundation is important, so too is awareness of the situational context in which a decision must be made and utilizing judgment within that situational context appropriately.

Situational Awareness (Context) and Judgment

We've acknowledged that there are several unknowns in the hypothetical scenario presented earlier but hypothesized some extenuating circumstances (unknown pressures on the manager, family circumstances of the employee, etc.). Leaders with the ability to understand the context in which they are making decisions increase their chances of making better informed decisions and of being more effective leaders (Kerns, 2015). A leader needs to be aware of multiple common situational influences on their environment at the same time, recognizing that the significance of the different influences will ebb and flow for them over time. The four spheres of influence affecting leaders can be categorized into core organizational identity, (organizational) internal environment, transactional environment, and extended external environment (Kerns, 2015). The core organizational identity defines the organization, separates it from others, and includes the purpose and values of the organization. The (organizational) internal environment is the organization's culture, people, structure, and processes, and this is where we proposed we needed more information in the earlier example regarding the pressures the manager might be facing, such as from her own boss. The transactional environment includes customers, suppliers, and competitors, and also influence from the local community, including the extended family of the organization's workforce. Finally, the extended external environment, such as government legislation, demographic changes, technology, and the economy, can have a significant impact on a leader's decision-making.

Once a leader is aware of the situational context in which they must take action, the leader must also practice judgment of the circumstances that influence their decision. How do we know which sphere of influence is more important in the given situation? Most likely, there will be multiple spheres of influence at play. Are they opposed to each other? What will be the outcome if one is considered more heavily than the other? Are there inconspicuous influences at play?

Judgment has a significant impact on a leader's decision-making. Human beings are naturally judgmental. Being able to assess a situation or the current environment has helped us survive and evolve as a species. From basic survival such as noting the effects of eating a particular food, to observing the interactions among one's social group and negotiating the dynamics of the social hierarchy, judgment allows us to navigate the environment around us. What distinguishes us from our ancestors and our fellow primates, however, is the ability to moderate judgment and use it to our advantage. To use judgment to our advantage requires recognizing that any circumstance which moves us out of our comfort zone will activate the judging mechanisms in our brain. We can use judgment to make decisions objectively and wisely, but we must be conscious of using judgment rather than bias in our decision-making. One way to do this is to adopt a curious mindset or a questioning attitude toward ourselves, others, and situations (Textbox 3.1).

BOX 3.1 **Adopting a Curious Mindset**

1. Recognize when you are starting to judge
2. Ask yourself why you are judging something as "good" or "bad"
3. Gather all the facts you can. If you do not understand something, learn about it
4. Replace "why" with "why not?"
5. Be kind to yourself as you are learning and transforming your thoughts
6. Keep practicing a questioning attitude at work and at home

Risk to the Actor

In addition to known and unknown influences that a leader must consider, there will be known and unknown risks that a leader will face while making decisions. The complexity of risk includes differing risk types, such as physical, social, career, and psychological (Detert, 2021) and varying degrees of these different risks. Judgment must be used not only to assess the situational context in which decisions must be made, but also when weighing risk to the actor. In an evolutionary context, human instinct guides us to be willing to take risks for those to whom we are more closely genetically related and not toward those with whom we may be in the same social group but are not related. Although our example above in which the employee is worried about taking care of her family relates to this concept of risk, many times the risk we encounter in the workplace will not have the potential to impact us in a way that directly impacts our family. Sometimes we will be called upon to assume risk on behalf of our colleagues. Our instincts will try to guide us against assuming this risk, but we must make a conscious choice to act against these instincts in the appropriate situations (Detert, 2021). When a leader voluntarily takes on risk, he or she is choosing to act from a state of vulnerability.

Vulnerability

Within the context of leadership and leadership courage, vulnerability can best be defined as "a willingness to be transparent and emotionally exposed in a relationship with another individual" (Lopez, 2018). This brings us back to the concepts of will and intent as components of courage. Vulnerability is considered a choice that leaders make, willingly entering into a communion with another person that may involve risk due to personal exposure in some form—emotional, psychological, or moral. Vulnerability is not oversharing, but rather a state of openness. It must be genuine, or the intent will appear to be manipulation. Ideally, both parties are trustworthy, which can decrease the degree of vulnerability one or the other feels. Realistically, the person exposing themselves must trust that they are able to navigate the circumstances despite the degree of exposure in the specific scenario.

In other words, vulnerability must be learned and practiced. When an individual becomes proficient with vulnerability, they are able to behave in an ethical manner, acting from commitment to their personal values and morals, and demonstrating genuine intent. Textbox 3.2 has a method to practice your vulnerability.

BOX 3.2 **Deliberate Practice of Exposure**

Purposely expose yourself to things that are different to take away the power of discomfort. Avoiding discomfort gives strength to whatever is causing the discomfort and anxiety. If you choose to avoid situations that trigger an undesired response (anxiety, self-doubt, etc.), you are choosing to give power to the discomfort.

Instead, use an additive approach to desensitize yourself to uncomfortable things or situations. For example, if you have trouble giving constructive feedback to your fellow employees, practice having a "mock" conversation about constructive feedback with a trusted friend or family member. Concurrently, you could solicit assistance with difficult conversations with your employer's organizational development group. Once you practice these conversations with people whom you feel comfortable with and trust, seek situations in which you can at least be witness to some crucial conversations, so that you are again exposed to an uncomfortable situation and can learn additional tools to use during these uncomfortable situations.

What other situations can you think of that may be uncomfortable for you and from which you would benefit experiencing?

Achieve a Noble or Worthwhile Outcome

People generally believe their own courageous actions are taken in pursuit of worthwhile goals, and they tend to be able to clearly articulate those goals at a later time (Lester & Pury, 2011). If we are acting from a place of integrity, holding ourselves accountable to our own principles and morals, acknowledging our mistakes, making amends, and extending generosity when warranted (Brown, 2018), then it makes sense that we perceive our courageous actions to be taken in pursuit of a worthwhile goal. But if we act out of alignment with our morals and principles, or we act in an arrogant or self-serving manner, even if we are able to achieve the same outcome, it will not feel as and may not be perceived as a noble or worthwhile outcome.

Taking Action in Face of Fear

An actor who is being courageous may be experiencing fear, but it is not an essential component to demonstrating courage (Rate et al., 2007; Lester & Pury, 2011). Awareness of personal risk may lead to fear, but this is not necessarily true in all cases. Examples of courageous individuals who do not experience the subjective (psychological distress, anxiety, impulsiveness, etc.) or physiological elements (increased blood pressure, heart rate, respiratory rate, etc.) of fear include military personnel (Lester & Pury, 2011), extreme athletes (Monasterio et al., 2016), public servants (Próchniak, 2012), and others in the general population. However, for many of us, awareness of personal risk, whether it be physical risk or moral risk, elicits some type of uncomfortable (fear) response. Below is a useful exercise to have a better understanding of your feelings and physiological responses to them. The exercise can be performed alone or paired with the deliberate practice of vulnerability and exposure exercise (Textbox 3.3). Once you become proficient at recognizing and experiencing your feelings, you can then begin to manage your personal emotional microcosm and make reasonable decisions after a rational assessment (judgment) of the current situational context and risks and based on genuine and ethical intent. You will become self-monitoring and self-regulating, selectively processing information and basing decisions and actions on reality, rather than on the thoughts or feelings you are telling yourself that come from fear and discomfort.

BOX 3.3 How to Experience Your Feelings and Move Through Them

We have all been there—an unpleasant feeling arises and our mind launches into whatever inner story accompanies this feeling (Everyone is quiet so I must have said something wrong, If I do not meet my boss's expectations, I will lose my job, etc.). When you are doing this, your thoughts are directing your feelings (by initiating physiological responses).

1. Stop.
2. Redirect your mind away from these thoughts and into the sensations in your body. Mentally describe the sensations (my chest is tight, my heart rate is elevated, and so forth).
3. Take deep breaths and breathe into the feeling/sensation.
4. Your mind will want to go back into storytelling mode. When this happens, redirect your awareness back into your body, take more deep breaths, keep feeling into your body, let the feeling exist and trust that it will leave, observe it changing, watch it go, notice that the unpleasant feelings have diminished, and you have endured.
5. Repeat this practice of recognizing, acknowledging, and naming your feelings as often as needed as circumstances arise.

Final Point on Attributes of Leadership Courage

As with other leadership competencies, it is important to consistently exemplify the attributes of leadership courage rather than just espouse them. While it is possible to learn the attributes associated with the competencies and imitate them, an inauthentic leader will ultimately fail as those who the leader guides begin to suspect a lack of sincerity and come to recognize the impostor. Rather than inspire others to follow in the footsteps of the leader and work as a team, an inauthentic leader will generate distrust in his or her employees and corrode the culture of an organization. Authentic leaders who demonstrate the attributes they advocate will inspire their employees, colleagues, managers, and leaders; these genuine, positive values will permeate the organization.

How to Use Leadership Courage in the Workplace

As a leader, you will face challenges or risky situations in which you will need to choose courage to take the appropriate action. You can prepare yourself for leadership courage situations in the future by considering these questions now:

1. Clarify what is important to you. Ask yourself the following questions:
   - What do I value?
   - What am I passionate about?
   - Which situations might I encounter that I would need to stand up for an issue or an employee's well-being?
2. Think about the distinction between sound decision-making based on situational context and based on biased judgments. Give examples of when you have used both and when you could have made a different choice.
3. Ask yourself how you would like people to describe you to someone else. What would you like them to say about your leadership and your values? Are there people in your organization whom you'd like to emulate? Ask to have a conversation with this person about their approach to leadership and leadership courage.
4. What is your response when you feel uncomfortable or in a situation in which there is personal risk? How might you respond differently?
5. Do you champion new ideas and initiatives, or do you want things to stay the way they are? Think about how to inspire others, especially when it comes to out-of-the-box thinking.
6. What are your goals? What are the goals of your community, your school, or your workplace? Are you able to describe these goals clearly when asked?

Application

Use these scenarios to apply what you have learned in this chapter about leadership courage. As you read each scenario, consider the opportunity to display leadership courage, what you need to consider, what you will do and why, and the impact your actions will have on yourself and others.

Scenario A

Top-Notch Accounting is a large accounting firm with many Fortune 100 companies as clients. You are a leader of a team of senior accountants. In addition to your client work, you and your team are under pressure from upper management to develop and implement multiple initiatives to improve processes and promote collaboration across the organization. Despite the increased tasks placed on you or your team, additional resources will not be provided for this work.

As a leader, you feel very frustrated by this.

1. Describe the possible "leadership courage" situation.
2. Keeping in mind the information from this chapter, what do you need to consider?
3. What are your next steps?
4. What impact will each of these steps have on you, your team, the environment, your results?

Scenario B

You are a leader at Healthy You Insurance where you lead a national sales team. Prior to your promotion into leadership 6 months ago, you were a member of the national sales team and were consistently the top salesperson. Because of your firsthand knowledge and experience with the work of this team, you redesigned the sales approval process so it is streamlined and easier for you to understand the process and results of each of your salespeople. Unfortunately, many of the salespeople do not like it and feel it is "extra work" for them.

1. Describe the possible "leadership courage" situation.
2. Keeping in mind the information from this chapter, what do you need to consider?
3. What are your next steps?
4. What impact will each of these steps have on you, your team, the environment, your results?

Scenario C

You are a manager at Power Up Marketing and lead a team of 6 marketing analysts. You and your team recently developed a marketing campaign for a regional restaurant chain. You and your director present the campaign to the customer. During the presentation, your director presents the idea as if he created the idea. The customer loves the idea and gives the green light to move forward with it.

1. Describe the possible "leadership courage" situation.
2. Keeping in mind the information from this chapter, what do you need to consider?
3. What are your next steps?
4. What impact will each of these steps have on you, your team, the environment, your results?

Scenario D

You are the student coordinator of the inclusion club, a university-recognized student-run organization. During a club outing at the campus bowling alley, you notice that Pat, a highly functional student with autism spectrum disorder, is making inappropriate comments about Chris each time Chris approaches the lane using forearm crutches. It seems everyone is laughing, except Chris.

1. Describe the possible "leadership courage" situation.
2. Keeping in mind the information from this chapter, what do you need to consider?
3. What are your next steps?
4. What impact will each of these steps have on you, your team, the environment, your results?

References

Brown, B. B. (2018). Dare to lead. *Vermillion.*

Brown, M. E., & Treviño, L. K. (2006). Ethical leadership: A review and future directions. *The Leadership Quarterly,* 17(6), 595–616.

Detert, J. R. (2021). Choosing courage: The everyday guide to being brave at work. *Harvard Business Review Press.*

Detert, J. R., & Bruno, E. A. (2017). Workplace courage: Review, synthesis, and future agenda for a complex construct. *Academy of Management Annals,* 11(2), 593–639.

Gebelein, S. H., & Personnel Decisions International. (2004). Successful manager's handbook: Development suggestions for today's managers (7th ed.). *Personnel Decisions International.*

Kerns, C. D. (2015). Situational context: A core leadership dimension. *Journal of Leadership, Accountability and Ethics,* 12(1), 11.

Lester, P. B., & Pury, C. (2011). What leaders should know about courage. Digitalcommons.unl.edu

Lopez, S. O. (2018). Vulnerability in Leadership: The Power of the Courage to Descend. Doctoral dissertation, Seattle Pacific University.

Monasterio, E., Mei-Dan, O., Hackney, A. C., Lane, A. R., Zwir, I., Rozsa, S., & Cloninger, C. R. (2016). Stress reactivity and personality in extreme sport athletes: The psychobiology of BASE jumpers. *Physiology & behavior,* 167, 289–297.

Próchniak, P. (2012). Traits of personality and preferred values among fearless and courageous policemen. *International Journal of Psychological Studies,* 4(4), 113.

Rate, C. R., Clarke, J. A., Lindsay, D. R., & Sternberg, R. J. (2007). Implicit theories of courage. *Journal of Positive Psychology,* 2, 80–98.

Rijamampianina, R. (2018). Leaders and decision making: A study of the drivers of courage. *Problems and Perspectives in Management,* 16(1), 320.

CHAPTER 4

Emotional Intelligence

By Christie Cremer

Anyone can become angry—that is easy. But to be angry with the right person, to the right degree, at the right time, for the right purpose, and in the right way—that is not easy.

—Aristotle, The Nicomachean Ethics

Learning Objectives

After reading this chapter, students will be able to:

1. Know the difference between Intelligence Quotient (IQ) and Emotional Quotient/Intelligence
2. Understand the competencies as areas of possible growth
3. See the need for high EQ/EI in the workplace and other areas of life

Introduction to Emotional Intelligence

Emotional Intelligence Defined

Emotional intelligence is an important competency for leaders. Researchers and business leaders alike have recognized its importance in enhancing our performance at work and in our personal relationships as well. Emotional intelligence is defined as "an ability to recognize the meanings of emotion and their relationships, and to reason and problem-solve on the basis of them. Emotional intelligence is involved in the capacity to perceive emotions, assimilate emotion-related feelings, understand the information of those emotions, and manage them" (Mayer, Caruso, & Salovey, 1999, p. 267).

Building on the work of Mayer, Caruso, and Salovey, Daniel Goleman's book *Emotional Intelligence* brought the concept to mass audiences. His premise is that people could be taught to recognize the meanings of their emotions (feelings) and then think about and manage the behaviors that often come from those feelings. Goleman advocates for a merging of our emotions with reasoning and using both as an integrated whole to understand others and manage our behaviors. "Emotional Intelligence reconciled what had been seen as two opposites: our feelings and our reasoning (Goleman, 2005, p. xi)." Goleman and others see a person's EI (Emotional Intelligence) as pliable and able to be grown and developed, whereas IQ (Intelligence Quotient) is somewhat fixed.

IQ Defined

Intelligence Quotient (IQ), or intelligence, can be defined as "the capacity to reason validly about information" (Mayer, 2004). The word *capacity* usually means that once the limit is reached, that's it. A person can learn more things but usually not increase their IQ. A more detailed definition,

> Simply put, IQ is a measure of an individual's intellectual, analytical, logical, and rational abilities. As such, it's concerned with verbal, spatial, visual, and mathematical skills. It gauges how readily we learn new things; focus on tasks and exercises; retain and recall objective information; engage in a reasoning process; manipulate numbers; think abstractly as well as analytically; and solve problems by the application of prior knowledge. If you have a high IQ—the average is 100—you're well equipped to pass all sorts of examinations with flying colors, and (not incidentally) to score well on IQ tests. (Stein & Book, 2011)

IQ matters. It is important for success in school and to acquire certain jobs. A person's IQ will influence how quickly they learn new skills, how they can critically think about those skills, and how they can cross-apply knowledge to enhance those skills. For example, certain positions such as physicists, doctors, and high-level executives, may only be attainable by those with higher IQs. However, once in those jobs, is IQ enough to propel them to outstanding performance and gathering followers (in essence becoming a leader)?

The Importance of Emotional Intelligence

BOX 4.1 **The Future of Leadership**

In the future, business leaders will need significantly greater skills in emotional intelligence. Self-awareness and self-management will be essential for mastering critical thinking in complex environments. Empathy and collaborative skills will be essential for retaining and leveraging top talent in increasingly cross-functional, disbursed teams. The leaders who master these components of emotional intelligence will capture the loyalty of those who will play the greatest roles in long term success. (Price, 2022, personal interview)

—Ron Price, coauthor, *The Complete Leader: Everything You Need to Know to Become a High Performing Leader*

When we reduce the idea of leadership to its purest root form, we can see that, as Peter Drucker said, "The only definition of a leader is someone who has followers" (Kruse, 2013). When we strip away the constructs where people are forced to "follow" their "leader," we are left with the responsibility squarely on the shoulders of those who lead to learn what it means to lead well. The competencies of emotional intelligence will help us lead well, in whatever context we have followers.

> IQ is not sufficient to predict, once you're in that position, that you will emerge as an outstanding performer, as a leader. Unknown if you'll emerge as a leader at all. So, when it comes to leadership, you're dealing with a different skill set. You need to have self-mastery, you need to lead yourself as they say, and you need to persuade, empathize, listen, communicate, elaborate, do all those things that require people skills. That's the emotional intelligence domain. In other words, once you're in a high-level situation, IQ matters less in distinguishing stars from average performers. It is the interpersonal skills that make the difference. (Haynes, 2022)

Daniel Goleman suggests that a person's Intelligence Quotient (IQ) accounts for about 20% of their success on the job, in relationships, and in the world. That leaves about 80% of the possibilities for success unanswered (Goleman, 2005, p xii). Simply put, there is a wide variety of factors that could help or hinder a person's success. Other factors, including external factors such as available opportunities, country of origin, childhood experiences, and poverty all may play a role in a person's success.

In their book *Emotional Intelligence 2.0*, Bradberry and Greaves show that those with the highest levels of cognitive intelligence (IQ) outperform their peers with average IQs only 20% of the time, while people with average IQs can outperform those with the highest IQs a whopping 70% of the time (Bradberry & Greaves, 2009, p. 7). These findings left researchers puzzled. As the theories and research in emotional intelligence began to emerge, one of the missing links was found in the joining of reason and feelings.

Johnson & Johnson conducted a study of 358 managers to see if there were identifiable leadership competencies that could distinguish high-performing managers from average performers. The participants were rated by their managers, their peers, and their direct reports. Results showed that the highest-performing managers had significantly more emotional competence than other managers. There was strong agreement among Supervisors, Peers, and Subordinates that the competencies of Self-Confidence, Achievement Orientation, Initiative, Leadership, Influence, and Change Catalyst differentiate superior performers (Cavallo & Brienza, 2006).

What Are Emotions?

As humans, we can have hundreds and possibly thousands of emotions throughout the course of one day. Most of our emotions are born out of a blend of naturally occurring feelings and life experiences. The intensity of our emotions is also strongly tied to our experiences. These include primary emotions, and then often an undetectable blending of one or more primary emotions.

The James Madison University Counseling Center (2015) provided a list of eight primary emotions and sub-emotions.

- Anger: fury, outrage, wrath, irritability, hostility, resentment, and violence
- Sadness: grief, sorrow, gloom, melancholy, despair, loneliness, and depression
- Fear: anxiety, apprehension, nervousness, dread, fright, and panic
- Joy: enjoyment, happiness, relief, bliss, delight, pride, thrill, and ecstasy
- Interest: acceptance, friendliness, trust, kindness, affection, love, and devotion
- Surprise: shock, astonishment, amazement, astound, and wonder
- Disgust: contempt, disdain, scorn, aversion, distaste, and revulsion
- Shame: guilt, embarrassment, chagrin, remorse, regret, and contrition.

Often our emotional patterns and the behaviors that follow are rooted in childhood. This can make growing beyond these emotional patterns and behaviors even harder. However, unlike IQ, which is pretty much set, our EQ can be significantly raised, thus raising our success as individuals and as leaders. "Emotional Intelligence can be learnt and acquired; brain elasticity is bringing breakthrough strategies and processes" (Verma, 2016). It is often easier to learn a new skill that involves our IQ than it is to sharpen and grow our EI/EQ. Remember to face each growth opportunity with a growth mindset. This foundation will set you up for success as you lead all who follow you in every area of your life.

Competency Models of Emotional Intelligence

Models of EI/EQ

There are many Emotional Intelligence models, and all could be utilized for growth and applicable to different areas of life and work. We will use and define the model formulated by Daniel Goleman (Goleman, 2005, p. xiv).

This model (Riopel, 2019), which Goleman calls the competencies of Emotional Intelligence, is organized with two rows: personal or self (having to do with you) and social (having to do with others) and two columns: recognition (being aware of the emotion and need) and regulation (managing your emotion and behavior). The result is a 2x2 matrix that includes the domains of Emotional Intelligence: Self-Awareness, Self-Management, Social Awareness, Relationship Management.

1. Self-Awareness
    a. Emotional Self-Awareness

Self-Awareness means that when our brains produce emotions, we become very aware of how those emotions make us feel and how we typically act or react to them. For example, if I am a very neat and tidy person and my friends are not, I will often have an emotion rise. See the list above—would this be disgust? Self-awareness would help me to know that it is the feeling of disgust, but to also reason *why* I feel it. I might feel disgust because my friend is not living up to my set of values and morals.

	Recognition	**Regulation**
Personal Competence	**Self-Awareness** • Self-confidence • Awareness of your emotional state • Recognizing how your behavior impacts others • Paying attention to how others influence your emotional state	**Self-Management** • Keeping disruptive emotions and impulses in check • Acting in congruence with your values • Handling change flexibly • Pursuing goals and opportunities despite obstacles and setbacks
Social Competence	**Social Awareness** • Picking up on the mood in the room • Caring what others are going through • Hearing what the other person is "really" saying	**Relationship Management** • Getting along well with others • Handling conflict effectively • Clearly expressing ideas/information • Using sensitivity to another person's feeling (empathy) to manage interactions successfully

FIGURE 4.1 Daniel Goleman's Four Domains of Emotional Intelligence

2. Self-Management
    a. Emotional Balance
    b. Adaptability
    c. Achievement
    d. Positivity

Self-Management is the next domain. Once we have become aware of our emotions, can label them, know why we feel them, and most importantly examine them from a rational mindset, we then can manage our behaviors through self-management. Using the scenario above, I might *feel* disgusted at the messy ways my friend lives, but Self-Management helps me to *feel the feeling* and then make a conscious decision whether to *act on that feeling.* The four key points within this competency are useful tools in this process: Emotional Balance, Adaptability, Achievement, and Positivity.

3. Social Awareness
    a. Empathy
    b. Organizational Awareness

As we become Self-Aware and practice Self-Management, the next domain, Social Awareness, requires that we become others-aware. With Social Awareness, we look outside ourselves and cultivate a desire to gain a strong awareness and understanding of others. Social Awareness must be rooted in Empathy, where we seek to understand and remain curious about the words and actions of others.

4. Relationship Management
    a. Influence
    b. Coach
    c. Conflict Management
    d. Teamwork
    e. Inspire

Once we become Socially Aware, we learn to practice Relationship Management. Just as we learn to manage ourselves based on our self-awareness, we then learn to manage ourselves within our relationships and manage our role in the relationships. This domain includes five important traits: Influencing, Coaching, Conflict Management, Teamwork, and Inspiration.

How to Use Emotional Intelligence in the Workplace

Actively Increase Your Knowledge of Self and Others

Actively expanding insight and knowledge of myself and others is one important way to use emotional intelligence in the workplace. Self-Awareness is the ability to gain knowledge about ourselves and our behaviors. Social Awareness is the ability to grow our knowledge and understanding of others. In the workplace, this can be achieved by reflecting at the beginning or end of each day. Ask yourself these questions:

1. What went well yesterday? What didn't go well?
2. What did I do to contribute to positive outcomes? How do I contribute to poor outcomes?
3. How can I learn more about others on my team and partner with them to create better outcomes today?

Management of Yourself and Your Relationships

Self-Management helps us to apply reason and knowledge to our own actions. It helps us control otherwise unrestrained emotional behaviors. Relationship Management helps us to navigate misunderstandings and miscommunications. It helps us to be better listeners.

Active Listening is a foundational principle of good communication and of Relationship Management. In the workplace, we often stop listening to others and start planning our next comment. We can't do both at the same time. An Emotionally Intelligent person almost always listens to learn instead of listening to speak. As you learn to become a more active listener, you can use these techniques as you manage yourself and your relationships with others:

1. When someone is speaking, intentionally listen to learn
2. Practice asking at least one question so you can learn more about the other person's ideas.
3. Connect your comments to the conversation by using what you learned from them and adding your ideas.

Staying Aware and Managing the Impact of Unbridled Emotions

Self-Management helps us to stay thoughtful and aware of our emotions and to learn competencies that will help us grow. This includes adaptability, positivity, achievement, and emotional balance. The key is to recognize when your unbridled inner world is negatively affecting your dreams and goals.

In the workplace, it's a healthy practice to review your future dreams and goals to align your career goals. Our unmanaged emotions—and the behaviors that follow—can become impediments to our own career dreams and goals. Learn to recognize your emotions as you go through your workday. As those emotions come and you feel rushed to speak or respond, practice these techniques:

1. Pause to allow your rational brain to engage before you react
2. Don't act out of emotion, but try to align your actions with achieving your goals
3. Stay adaptable and positive about your dreams and goals.

Become Others Aware

Being Socially Aware helps us to unpack bias, change any preconceived ideas of other individuals, groups, and cultures and to recognize the humanity in everyone. Examples of this include growing and developing empathy and compassion for others, becoming aware of your ability to manage conflict to bring desired growth in yourself and others, inspiring others toward growth, and becoming a team player.

In the stress of the workplace, it is easy to draw unfounded judgments of others based on how their behaviors make us feel. When disagreements occur, we can feel hurt, and if we don't pause, we can lash out and behave in ways that keep us from achieving our goals. Emotional Intelligence helps us to build our awareness of others from a foundation of empathy and compassion. When we have that foundation, the next step is to assume positive intent and focus on our goals and the work. Consider the following:

- 40% of emotionally intellgent companies reported strong customer loyalty.
- 90% of top workplace performers were highly emotionally intelligent.
- A Fortune 500 company added EQ criteria, increasing annual provit by $32 million and retaining 67% of staff.

FIGURE 4.2 The Importance of Emotional Intelligence in the Workplace

1. How can I learn more about others on my team and partner with them to create better outcomes today?
2. When someone is speaking, intentionally listen to learn from a foundation of empathy and compassion
3. Pause to allow your rational brain to engage turning your emotions into passion for your work.

Develop a Growth Mindset

One of the traits that may be useful to those with high Emotional Intelligence is possessing and using a Growth Mindset as opposed to a Fixed Mindset. To be able to recognize the importance of growth can be helpful in the workplace. "The passion for stretching yourself and sticking to it, even (or especially) when it's not going well, is the hallmark of the growth mindset. This is the mindset that allows people to thrive during some of the most challenging times in their lives" (Dweck, 2020).

Jason was a newly hired employee in the Agent Licensing Department at a large insurance company. He was fresh out of college with a business degree and was excited about using all that he had learned in college to help the company create better processes for state-by-state licensing of insurance agents. On his first day, he met Jack. Jack had worked in the same role and department for over 30 years and thus had many years of experience and knowledge.

In this situation, it would be beneficial to Jason to learn from Jack's long history of success in this department. However, it would also benefit Jack to collaborate with Jason and learn some of the latest business theories for process improvement. If both employees took the opportunity to have a ready and open mind to learn from the other, the benefits to the department would be exponential.

Application of Emotional Intelligence in the Workplace

> *Before you have any hope to lead someone else, you must first lead yourself. And of everyone you lead, you are the person who will need the most attention and care if you intend to serve your people in a way that brings them to new levels of engagement, fulfillment and performance while also delivering outstanding results.*
>
> —Jeff Harmon, Brilliance Within Coaching & Consulting

William's Story

William was a manager of a diverse team at a call center. It is typical practice for call centers to collect data regarding how many calls, the length of calls, and the issue resolution rate for each staff member. William had experiences, education, and knowledge regarding collecting this type of data and often impressed the company's executives with his charts and reports regarding trends, calls, known issues, and staffing.

Every Friday, William had one-on-one meetings with each staff member. He created reports with each staff member's numbers for the previous week and would report the "winners" and the "losers." He put the winners' names in a winners' circle on his whiteboard, and the losers in probation prison on the same board. His expectations were that the "losers" would improve their rates the next week. William's leadership style was direct. He would often say, "The data tells the truth about your performance, and I expect you to fix your problems." He would often tell the "losers" on the team to find out how the "winners" did it and to copy them.

William was certainly successful at data analysis. However his approach left his direct reports unhappy and fearful. We might call this a *toxic environment*. We can clearly see that William was indeed smart, but it was his behavior due to low EI/EQ that was causing harm to his work and others. The data, the charts, the black-and-white facts are all necessary, but William did not emerge as a high-performing leader due to his lack of emotional intelligence.

FIGURE 4.3 Call Center Staff

A trained Emotional Intelligence coach was hired by William's company. William took an Emotional Intelligence assessment, which measured his abilities in Self-Awareness, Self-Management, Social Awareness, and Relationship Management. One of William's lowest scores came from the Social Awareness Quadrant of the assessment.

Now that you have read William's story, take the information above and identify: what did William do wrong? And what did William do right? Here is a list of questions for you to ponder:

Exercise 1:

1. As you consider the four quadrants of Goleman's Competencies of Emotional Intelligence Model, which quadrant do you think is William's weakest quadrant? Why?
2. What impact is low Emotional Intelligence in this quadrant having on William? His team members? His results? Why?
3. What specific actions would you recommend to William to improve his Emotional Intelligence in this quadrant? How will these actions improve his Emotional Intelligence?
4. When William implements these actions, what impact might it have on William? His team members? His results? Why?
5. Is there an Emotional Intelligence quadrant in which William is strong? How do you know? What is the impact?

Exercise 2:

1. Think of a situation where you saw a manager or leader act Emotionally Intelligent
   a. What was the situation?
   b. What did they do or say?
   c. What was the impact on you? On your performance?

2. Think of a situation where you saw a manager or leader act Emotionally Unintelligent
   a. What was the situation?
   b. What did they do or say?
   c. What was the impact on you? On your performance?
3. Consider Goleman's Competencies of Emotional Intelligence model and *you*
   a. In which quadrant are you strong? Why? What is the impact of being strong in this quadrant?
   b. In which quadrant are you less strong? Why? What is the impact of being less strong in this quadrant?
   c. Identify three specific actions you can take to improve your Emotional Intelligence in the quadrant you identified in (b). Why and how will these actions help improve your Emotional Intelligence in the quadrant? When you implement these actions, what might be the impact?

References

Bradberry, T., Greaves, J., & Lencioni, P. M. (2009). *Emotional Intelligence 2.0*. TalentSmart.

Cavallo, K., & Brienza, D. (2006). Emotional competence and leadership excellence at Johnson & Johnson. *Europe's Journal of Psychology*, 2(1). https://doi.org/10.5964/ejop.v2i1.313

Dweck, Carol S. (2020). Goodreads.com. *Mindset: The new psychology of success*. https://www.goodreads.com/author/quotes/217172.Carol_S_Dweck

Goleman, D. (2005). *Emotional intelligence: Why it can matter more than IQ* (10th anniversary ed.). Random House.

Harmon, J. (2015) https://brilliancewithincoaching.com/leader-lead-thyself/

Harris, R. (2008). *The happiness trap: How to stop struggling and start living: A guide to ACT* (1st ed.). Trumpeter.

Haynes, M. (July 22, 2022). *What makes a leader? Daniel Goleman*. BUSINESS & LEADERSHIP. Retrieved July 23, 2022, from https://www.businessandleadership.com/leadership/item/33518-what-makes-a-leader/

James Madison University Counseling Center (January 20, 2015). Retrieved December 22, 2023, from: https://www.jmu.edu/counselingctr/files/About%20Emotions.pdf

Kruse, K. (2013). https://www.forbes.com/sites/kevinkruse/2013/04/09/what-is-leadership/?sh=4fd652c75b90

Mayer, John D. (2004). "What is Emotional Intelligence?" UNH Personality Lab. 8.

Mayer, J. D., Caruso, D., & Salovey, P. (1999). Emotional intelligence meets traditional standards for an intelligence. Intelligence, 27, 267–298.

Price, R. (2022). Personal interview.

Riopel, L. (2019). Emotional intelligence frameworks, charts, diagrams & graphs. https://positivepsychology.com/emotional-intelligence-frameworks/

Stein, S. J., & Book, H. E. (2011). *The EQ edge: Emotional Intelligence and your success* (3rd ed.). Jossey-Bass.

van der Kolk, B. A. (2014). *The body keeps the score: Brain, mind, and body in the healing of trauma*. Viking.

Verma, Y. V. (2016). *Emotional intelligence: 10 things you must know*. Entrepreneur India. https://www.entrepreneur.com/article/270060

Wiest, B. (February 5, 2018). *7 things emotionally intelligent people don't do at work*. Forbes. https://www.forbes.com/sites/briannawiest/2018/02/02/7-things-emotionally-intelligent-people-dont-do-at-work/?sh=17dc36f5ff0c

Credits

Fig. 4.1: Leslie Riopel and Daniel Goleman, "Daniel Goleman's Four Domains of Emotional Intelligence," https://positivepsychology.com/emotional-intelligence-frameworks/. Copyright © 2019 by PositivePsychology.com B.V.

Fig. 4.2: Adapted from Al Hartman, "The Importance of Emotional Intelligence in the Workplace." Copyright © 2022 by Al Hartman.

Fig. 4.3: Copyright © 2014 Depositphotos/Wavebreakmedia.

UNIT III

LEADING OTHERS

CHAPTER 5

Motivation

By Robert W. Lion

A hallmark of wisdom is knowing when it's time to abandon some of your most treasured tools—and some of the most cherished parts of your identity.

—Adam Grant

Learning Objectives

After reading this chapter, students will be able to:

1. Understand and distinguish between different motivation frameworks
2. Recognize that different workplace situations and circumstances call for different approaches to the utilization of motivational frameworks
3. Correctly utilize motivation frameworks to cultivate higher levels of motivation

Introduction to Motivation

The study of motivation focuses on why we do what we do. Concurrently, it also examines the mitigating constructs that influence our behaviors. Consistent among all motivation frameworks, they stem from human need fulfillment, whether that be safety and security, relationships and connections, or growth and identity development. Needs drive people to seek out solutions to safety and survival risks at the most fundamental level (deficiency needs) or self-actualization at the highest level (growth needs). All of the theories and frameworks presented in this chapter are based on the premise of need-fulfillment. However, not all motivation frameworks have the same salience in the workplace or among scholars. In recognition of the range of motivational theories and frameworks available, this chapter features a mix of classic and emerging theories to help you see the complements and conflicts among the different perspectives.

Over the years, there has been a lot of debate over the *truths* of motivation. Certain groups cite the redeeming value and importance of such things as financial incentives and rewards, whereas others denounce such strategies, as the behavioral change is often based on the reward/incentive, and once the reward/incentive is removed, the new behavior is not sustainable. This chapter contains a mix of perspectives, and it is up to you to determine what makes the most sense for you and your team. However, prior to getting into this, there is an important factor that is at the heart of the motivation discussion as it relates to the workplace, and that is if we pay people a fair/reasonable wage, we control for compensation as a mitigating factor in the motivation equation (Olafsen & Deci, 2020). This is important for two specific reasons. First, it is important to understand that there is a difference between compensation (the rate of which you are paid for your work) and financial incentives. Incentives are add-ons, typically above and beyond base compensation. Second, while the rate of pay may be fair or reasonable when one begins a job, we are not suggesting that will not change. People's needs change over time, and while a level of pay was acceptable when they started the position, conditions may eventually present themselves where they need to look for new employment with higher levels of pay. Or what we see too frequently in the workplace is that while the rate of pay is generally still acceptable, the quality of the work experience is not. This was a major contributor to the mass resignations and shuffling of positions during COVID-19. It is important to recognize this as what you will read moving forward will hopefully help you improve your leadership skills and prevent poor working experiences for your people.

Motivation in the Workplace

Motivation is not about what you *do to others*, it is more reasonable to think about this in terms of what I can do *with others* to cultivate higher-quality (intrinsic) motivation. A common misunderstanding is that a manager can fix or *motivate* others. Motivation is an internally managed phenomenon but can be influenced by external factors, such as people, status, material items, etc. However, it is important to be aware of what we can do, as well as avoid, to nurture higher-quality motivation in others. Also, by better understanding the factors that influence motivation, we are empowered to manage our own motivation and experiences better.

The mainstream/pop culture understanding of motivation is often based on a binary model of motivation that flows from one of two places, either internally or externally. Internal motivation, more commonly known as intrinsic motivation, focuses on factors that are meaningful or important to the person, such as feeling like they are accomplishing something, helping others, alignment with their own purpose and passion, and so forth. Joy, fulfillment, and job satisfaction are often an outcome of a person being intrinsically motivated. Of the two forms of motivation, intrinsic motivation is the most desired as it is the highest quality of motivation. High levels of intrinsic motivation have been found to be better aligned with health outcomes (Ng et al., 2012), persistence (Grant, 2008), and engagement (Cho & Perry, 2012).

External, also known as extrinsic motivation, is concerned with items of importance such as a reward (monetary or not), incentive, etc. The difference between the two is based on where the impetus to accomplish a task originates. Simply put, if I receive satisfaction from this work, I do the work for the joy it brings (think about artists and the joy their craft brings them). This is an example of intrinsic motivation. Whereas if you want to sell more widgets to receive the bonus or win a prize, this is an example of extrinsic motivation.

In both intrinsic and extrinsic situations, the individual wants or desires something. What occurs with extrinsic motivation is that something is based outside of the individual. For example, a high school student really wants a specific brand of sneaker. While the desire may seem to be internal, it is influenced by external factors. They may very well want it; however, in this instance it is against the backdrop of how others may regard them (social influences) because they have a particular brand of sneaker, as brands are often associated with status. The same can be said about receiving a sales commission. While the person may or may not want to do the work, the sales commission is an external reward to the person. Just for comparison purposes, an intrinsically motivated person would prioritize the value and satisfaction they receive doing the work above the value of the commission.

Popular Motivational Theories

Over the past 100 years, numerous motivation theories and frameworks have emerged in the academic arena and the practitioner/world of work arena. They all aim to demystify how humans behave as well as

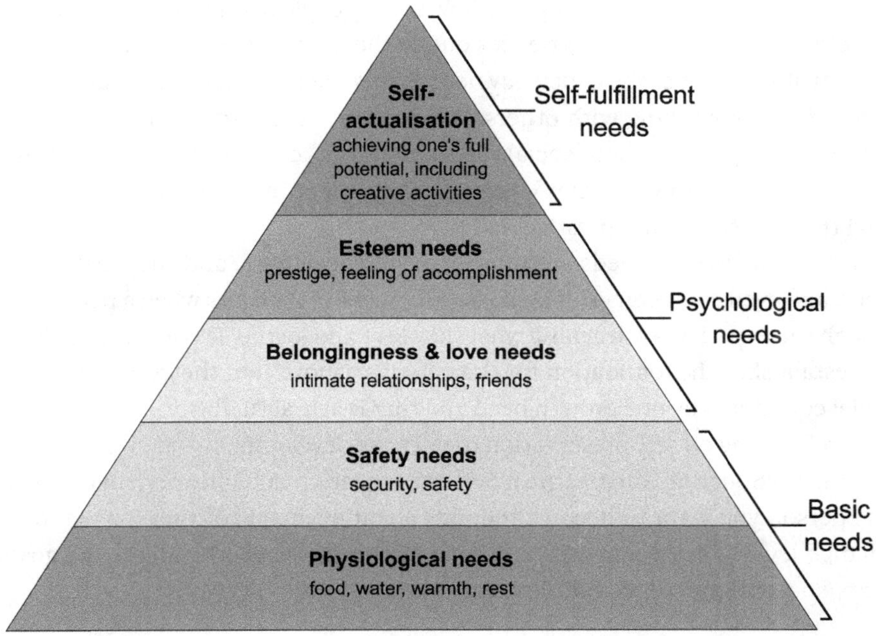

FIGURE 5.1 Maslow's Hierarchy of Needs

what is needed to improve the internal drive and focus of humans. The following four theories are among the most popular motivational theories. While no one theory is all-encompassing of the human experience, together these theories provide the practitioner with a strong framework.

Maslow's Hierarchy of Needs (1943)

In 1943, Abraham Maslow introduced his hierarchical model of needs for mentally healthy humans. The five needs are physiological needs, safety needs, love and belonging needs, esteem needs, and self-actualization. His model is built upon four lower-order foundational needs, also known as deficiency needs, and one higher-order need known as growth needs. The design of the model is stepwise, meaning that you move from one level to the next without skipping levels.

Physiological needs (first of the deficiency needs) are needs stemming from one's body such as food, water, and sleep and other physiological processes such as breathing, reproduction, etc. Maslow argued that needs must be met prior to progressing to the next needs. However, he did not claim that they must be 100% fulfilled prior to moving on (Compton, 2018), so while the concept is a stepwise progressive model, it allows for some deviation.

The next need is the need for safety. Once the physiological needs are met, a person works to fulfill their safety needs, whether that be safe shelter, economic stability, and/or emotional and physical safety. These needs can fluctuate quickly due to a variety of factors such as encountering a violent situation or relationship or economic recession. Turmoil due to such factors can move a person that is at the love and belonging level or the esteem level back down to this level, pausing the pursuit of higher-order needs fulfillment until the need for safety is addressed.

The love and belonging needs are sometimes also called social needs. This is based on the belief that humans need connection or, as one of our later theories calls it, relatedness. Prior to the experience of COVID-19, loneliness was identified as one of the highest public health concerns and even found to be greatest among men (Mansour et al., 2021). This need can be a lifelong struggle for many and by better understanding this model, we begin to recognize how some people in our communities may not be able to focus on self-development or growth experiences due to the current need deficiencies.

The esteem needs are the last of the deficiency needs. This refers to increasing our understanding of self through the experiences of working with others. We develop our sense of self through experiences that are external to us such as learning about social rules and norms, community behaviors and decorum, and broader topical interests. For some, higher levels of engagement in external factors may result in being highly influential through status and prestige.

The second part of the esteem needs are more internally oriented, and they lead to concepts of self-worth, confidence, and even competence. It is the development that occurs when a person begins to develop themselves through the experiences, learning what they love and loathe. It is an extremely important phase of discovery and establishes the foundation for the person to move into the growth needs phase.

Maslow's model contains only one growth need and that is self-actualization. Self-actualization, simply put, is moving from focusing on self-preservation to purpose development and even the shift toward altruism and selflessness (D'Souza & Gurin, 2016). Self-actualization is highly dependent on self-awareness, as becoming the person you want to become requires a commitment to consciousness. At this level, the individual has a high level of self-awareness and draws upon their beliefs, values, and goals to synthesize these into more purposeful pursuit of fulfilling experiences.

Herzberg's Two-Factor Theory of Motivation (1959)

Hertzberg's two-factor theory is also known as Herzberg's motivation-hygiene theory. In 1959, Frederick Herzberg introduced his work-specific motivation framework. Factor one, things that bring satisfaction to the person, examines work aspects that bring energy to the person. Items that will bring satisfaction to the individual include a variety of items that Maslow's self-actualization points toward, but since Herzberg's work is focused on the work domain, it is much more explicit around the job and work experience. Satisfiers include the work itself, recognition, advancement opportunities, increased responsibility, and the nature of the work. All these items are in line with current concerns in the workplace and have been part of the point of contention in the workplace during the COVID-19 pandemic.

The second factor in Herzberg's theory are hygiene issues, which lead toward diminished levels of motivation. These tend to be items that are not central to the person; however, they are an aspect of the work experience that can often become obstacles and barriers to fostering high levels of intrinsic motivation. The challenge with most of these items is that they are central to the operation of organizations. This is where the leader has opportunity to recognize these potentially demotivating factors and help the organization and team navigate the path forward with appropriate inclusion of them. Dissatisfiers include, but are not limited to, policies, negative relationships with peers and leaders, work conditions, salary, and issues concerning status and bureaucracy.

McClelland's Theory of Needs (1961)

In the prior frameworks, the two predominant needs were growth and deficiency needs. McClelland's (1961, 1975, 1985) theories needs are more closely aligned with the growth needs stated earlier. He posits that there are three specific needs that fall within this category. They include achievement needs, first coined by Murray (1938), which refer to the drive for accomplishment; power needs, which state that the individual has a need to be influential; and affiliation needs, which include reciprocal and close relationships with colleagues (Robbins, 2003). Unlike Maslow's stepwise needs fulfillment, these needs are concurrent and independent of each other, resulting in individuals having some level of motivation from each and, in many cases, having stronger preference of one over the other. McClelland's 1977 article reported that he found high-level managers tend to have a high need for power, but only a low need for affiliation.

McClelland's research found that fulfillment of the needs yielded different outcomes and the needs fueled different motives. For example, those with high levels of the power need aim to find positions that fulfill this need such as leadership positions where they can "compel the actions of others" (Royle & Hall, 2012, p. 26). They are likely more commanding in nature due in part to the need orientation of influencing others in the direction that the leader desires. Those with high affiliation needs, with a focus on interactions with others (McClelland & Koestner, 1992), are likely to be more collaborative. For those with a high level of achievement needs, success is about personally meeting or exceeding a standard of excellence and is intentional. These people seek out opportunities to problem solve (McClelland, 1985), and when they fall short on their goal, they experience higher levels of sadness and disappointment (McClelland & Koestner, 1992). However, something noteworthy about those with high achievement needs is that they value appropriate feedback to assist them with the goal pursuit, improving more desirable outcomes (McAdams, 1994; Emmons, 1997).

Self-Determination Theory

While Maslow (1943), Herzberg (1959), and McClelland's (1961) work laid the foundation for future research in motivation, these theories have received less exploratory research attention in recent decades. However, those theories have served as springboards for the development of the most robust body of motivation literature in the present day called self-determination theory (also known as SDT).

In 1985, Edward Deci and Richard Ryan introduced self-determination theory as an explanation of how motivation occurs within humans. Self-determination theory is actually known as a meta-theory because it is built upon six mini-theories. They are Cognitive Evaluation Theory (Deci & Ryan, 1980), which is concerned with intrinsic motivation; Organismic Integration Theory (Deci & Ryan, 1985), which studies extrinsic motivation; Causality Orientations Theory (Deci & Ryan, 1985), which examines motivation through the lens of it being autonomous (internal/intrinsic), controlled (external/extrinsic), and amotivation (absence of motivation); Basic Psychological Needs Theory (Deci & Ryan, 2002), which is based on three nutriments essential for cultivating high levels of intrinsic motivation. The three basic psychological needs are autonomy, competence, and relatedness. The last two mini-theories are Goal Contents Theory (Kasser & Ryan, 1993), which examines goal orientation, specifically, the link between intrinsic and extrinsic goals' impact on motivation; and Relationships Motivation Theory (Deci & Ryan, 2014), which homes in on the relational aspect of the basic psychological need of relatedness.

The body of research that supports SDT is substantial and continues to grow. For the practitioner, self-determination theory can be most effectively understood when organized by 1) the basic psychological needs; and 2) motivation regulation, which draws upon several of the mini-theories.

Basic Psychological Needs

As introduced above, the basic psychological needs are autonomy, competence, and relatedness. These are the foundational aspects that lead to human (arguably all organismic) flourishing. Prior to further exploring the concepts of intrinsic and extrinsic motivation, it is important to understand that the three basic psychological needs are essential for optimal human functioning and are directly related to intrinsic motivation. Autonomy is having agency, discretion, and/or independence over one's work (Lion & Burch, 2018). People need to feel like they have volitional choice over their personal and professional activities (Fowler, 2014). Too often, leaders can be overbearing or too demanding, and this could drive down one's autonomy. The same can be said of significant others in relationships that are controlling. That controlling behavior exerted over another person can lead the person to experience diminished levels of motivation.

Competence is being able to complete a specific task consistently and accurately (Lion & Burch, 2018). Because people often begin new jobs as not being fully competent, just as a new first-time parent is not fully competent as a parent, the goal of any leader should be to develop an onboarding and training experience that leads to competence as soon as possible to fuel high levels of motivation.

The literature on relatedness is significant and spans many different academic disciplines, ranging from psychology and sociology to family studies and gerontology. Relatedness refers to the belonging and connection people experience with others through meaningful relationships (Baumeister & Leary, 1995). The relatedness component poses some interesting challenges in the workplace, and people tend to have different expectations concerning how they want to connect with others at work (frequency, activity type, etc.). However, in order for a person to have optimal levels of intrinsic motivation, relatedness is an important need to fulfill whether that is through personal relationships, professional relationships, or a blend of the two.

According to research, a deficiency in any one or more of the basic psychological needs has a detrimental effect on levels of intrinsic motivation. As we consider this with employees in the work environment, a lack of autonomy in their position will erode intrinsic levels of motivation, possibly to the point that more extrinsic motivation factors become important. Consider the saying "I don't get paid enough for this." This sentiment demonstrates that the work is not enjoyable, which does not align with a person's intrinsic ambitions, and now, even the extrinsic rewards are not enough to satisfy the employee.

Just as low levels of autonomy can reduce levels of intrinsic motivation, the same can be said for competence and relatedness. However, relatedness does not carry the same need as the other two. Relatedness is an important part of the motivation equation; however, everyone has different needs and expectations as it relates to relatedness. For one employee, they may have a high level of relatedness in their personal life, so they do not necessarily need the same amount or intensity of relatedness in the workplace. For another employee, staff get-togethers, lunch meetings, and happy hours play an important role in bringing joy to their life through work-specific relatedness.

The 4-Item Motivation Regulation Framework

A much more accurate and refined way to think about motivation is understanding how the self-determination theory work has identified several forms of regulation, which refers to how people respond to different motivational factors. The regulation research pushes back on the traditional binary motivation model of intrinsic versus extrinsic motivation (see Figure 5.2 below). Simply put, research has demonstrated that there is a range of four different regulations that relate to motivation. They are: external, introjected, identified, and intrinsic. The significance of this research for the workplace is that better understanding of how to manage these four items, as opposed to the 2-item approach (intrinsic versus extrinsic), will empower leaders and employees to be able to better cultivate an environment that leads to higher levels of intrinsic motivation.

The value of using this 4-item approach to motivation is that it is a more nuanced approach to working through issues of motivation and it provides a much more detailed view of how factors influence a person. Few of us have ever received formal education on the 2-item approach. It seems that most people have learned the terms intrinsic and extrinsic motivation with not much depth or detail; it is a poorly articulated concept that we have latched onto to help us have an answer to the motivation puzzle. Because of that, it is tricky to operationalize in the workplace because most people do not have discretion over incentives, pay raises, and bonuses—all of which are extrinsic rewards.

Intrinsic Regulation

This is the ideal and optimal state for motivation; it is the highest quality motivation a person can possess. Intrinsic regulation leads to higher levels of job satisfaction, flow, and higher states of commitment. Simply put, a person is intrinsically motivated when they find joy and satisfaction in the activity or experience.

Arguably, at that point, the fulfillment experienced from the activity is of greater importance and internally valuable than the compensation for the task.

External Regulation

External regulation is doing the work simply for the rewards or to avoid the consequences or punishments which may come with not completing the work (Gagné et al., 2015). This is what the motivation adage of "carrots and sticks" refers to. It is the belief that incentives, rewards, and punishment will lead employees to desired performance levels. The self-determination theory body of research has consistently refuted this and cannot find evidence that supports a relationship between incentives or punishments and sustained intrinsic motivation. Studies consistently demonstrate that once incentives are removed because they are an external factor, not an internal factor, performance and drive consistently wane.

To further assist with the understanding of what constitutes external regulation, this category can be broken down into two different subgroups, *social* and *material*. Social refers to factors such as peer pressure or other social factors that influence a person to do something (i.e., buy a particular brand of purse because of the implied status affiliated with the brand). In the workplace, a person may put in long hours, not because they love the work, but because their officemates put in lengthy days, and they do not want to be perceived as less than their colleagues.

Material refers to factors of pay or job security. An employee may choose to work the weekends because of a financial incentive. Or a salary-earning employee may put in extra hours, not because of the importance of being respected (external-social), but because they believe this will increase job security. In both situations, these are factors external to the employee; these situations are not aligned with internal (intrinsic) factors such as self-worth, passion, purpose, or any of the other items that fuel high-quality motivation.

Introjected Regulation

Introjected regulation stems from impositions in the workplace. For example, your leader tells you that you should fix something or do something that you did not consider. While feedback is an important and valuable part of the leader-employee relationship, if not handled well it can leave a bad taste in one's mouth, not to mention serve as a demotivator. Introjection is akin to advice, and in many instances the leader has the best interests of the employee in mind. However, what research has demonstrated with advice is that if advice is not requested by the recipient, it can have a significant negative impact on motivation. This is a very important consideration for workplace and homelife. While offering advice is often heartfelt, it can create problems with the recipient. A classic example is the overbearing parent and rebellious teenager. The parent introjects their opinion, based on many of their hard-learned life lessons and the teenager does just the opposite.

Imposing tasks or commands on coworkers should be avoided. It makes sense why we often resort to introjection because we are too busy to take more time to help inform the person, or we learned our lessons and we feel like our imposition is a gift. Unfortunately, not everyone has the same regard for that type of gift. If we are trying to avoid external or extrinsic motivators, then we should avoid introjection as it is an external concept to the recipient. Instead, if they are not intrinsically motivated to the work, then operating from the identified regulation phase is a much better approach.

Identified Regulation

Identified regulation is much closer to internalized motivation, but it still begins outside of the person. If you consider the previous two categories, according to the research, external regulation is the least desirable, followed by introjected, as they are both originating from outside the individual. With identified regulation it still originates outside the person, but there is an alignment that occurs between the external source

Organization of SDT Motivational Framework

Historical practitioner's binary view of motivation	Extrinsic		Intrinsic	
4 Item Motivation Regulation Framework (Gagné et al., 2015; Ryan & Deci, 2017)	External *Material & Social*	Introjected	Identified	Intrinsic
Source of motivation stimulus	External	Somewhat External	Somewhat Internal	Internal
Lion's Proposed New 4 Factor Practitioner Motivational Framework (based on existing theory)	Extrinsic *Material & Social*	Imposed	Aligned	Intrinsic

FIGURE 5.2 Organization of SDT Motivational Framework

and the internal operations of a person. To help improve relations among employees, it would be valuable to help people better understand how to spend more time in this category.

Time is often limited in a busy workplace (at least that is what we continue to claim; however, we have a tendency to overestimate just how busy we are), assisting employees through an identified lens is often more time consuming. It may be helpful to differentiate introjection regulation from identified regulation. Introjection regulation is telling/imposing on the subject, whereas identified regulation is much more about alignment and a coaching-centric approach. For example, a new opportunity just came up for your division; it will require a group of people to work over the weekend due to the tight deadline. Your leader thinks you would be a great fit for this, and it may lead to a future promotion. However, because it is the weekend, it may not be all that desirable to you. The leader has several different approaches to sharing this information. They can impose it on you—"I would really like you to represent our office in this initiative," or they can work to find alignment between your interests and the opportunity. "I would like to share this opportunity I just learned about. It is, however, on a Saturday and Sunday, but I believe you might be interested in this; I thought of you immediately. Would you like to hear more about this?" At this point, the leader is working to align you with the opportunity. They are not insisting that you do it. Instead, the leader takes time (aligning and coaching require time) to have a healthy, two-way conversation to explore the benefits and opportunities of the experience. This opens the floor for dialogue so that you feel like you can make an informed decision based on your wants, interests, and availability. With identified regulation, a person finds value in the proposed experience and sees how it aligns with their own internal values, goals, etc.

Figure 5.2 takes the traditional binary view of motivation and presents it with the 4-item regulation framework that has emerged in the self-determination theory literature followed by a proposed *new* four-factor framework for practitioners.

How Motivation Can Be Used in the Workplace

As established at the beginning of this chapter, motivation is not something we do to people; it is something that people must work through internally, subject to the stepwise nature of needs and external influences (this is where the leader plays a major role). However, the leader's role as it relates to their team members' motivation is significant because the decisions leaders make can enhance or diminish motivation. What further complicates this is that for each person their motivation needs may differ and how they differ may shift over the course of a day due to external factors.

The following are three common motivation scenarios leaders encounter in the workplace.

Be Mindful of Gimmicks or Quick Fixes

One of the biggest challenges leaders encounter relates to the wants and wishes for incentives or extrinsic rewards. There is often top-down pressure to improve work performance, and the use of incentives is frequently viewed as the preferred means to accomplish this. There is no question that people like free things; however, when the incentive circumvents the addressing of needs (for instance, hygiene needs such as unfair policy, poor pay, toxic supervision), the incentive is merely a gimmick, and any performance or behavioral change tied to the incentive will likely dissipate shortly after the incentive is received. Perhaps in a perfect world, where we had no hygiene concerns, research would show that incentives work and result in sustainable change. However, at this time and for the foreseeable future, there are too many factors that will continue to erode the efficacy of incentives.

How about bonuses or commissions? Will they work? The answer to this will vary by the person receiving the reward. However, if the organization cannot commit to sustaining bonuses or commissions, there is an extremely high risk of the desired performance not sticking. People learn quickly how to game systems as well as how to exist among others, and if they are in a system that does not prioritize cultivating intrinsic motivation and honoring the esteem, self-actualizing, and satisfying needs identified by our researchers, bonuses and commissions may only be as effective as a gimmick.

Question What You are Observing When Diagnosing Motivational Needs

Often when working with clients, organization development consultants experience a gap or discrepancy between what the client expresses is the issue and what truly *is* the issue. Leaders also get caught in this trap. What tends to happen is that the people working within the system are too close to the problem and do not accurately diagnose the issue. Instead of seeking to identify the root cause, which often becomes the consultant's first step, leaders tend to want to address what they are observing, which is often a symptom of a deeper issue. For example, when an organization puts their staff through computer system training for the second, third, or fourth time to address an accuracy deficiency in processing auto loan paperwork (goal is less than 5% rejection on loan application paperwork), instead of investigating the situation to determine what is truly contributing to the problem, the organization is at risk of squandering valuable resources. Taking people out of their position to receive training is an extremely expensive process and should only occur if an analysis determines that all or most of the staff need this type of intervention. Unfortunately, many leaders do not think about that as the people are already at work. This can be avoided if the leader spends time learning a) who are the people responsible for errors; and then b) determining the reason(s) these people (or individual) are making errors. It is very possible that upon investigation the incidents of error are isolated to only a few people, which often results in a different solution or intervention approach.

If it is a situation where only a few people are struggling and they share that they need further assistance, then the best intervention should be applied to address the deficiency, which may not be more training. In this instance, it may not have anything to do with a motivation issue, but instead a competency or confidence issue. However, in some situations, a motivational issue may be at the root leading to the deficiency. For example, a person's loan preparation accuracy may be compromised during a time where they are working through a challenging situation, such as working with debt collectors to avoid a home foreclosure (a stressful situation that can be quite demanding of the person's resources). This is an example of why it is important to be cognizant of motivational needs, as work performance may be tied to need fulfillment.

While the scenario may be different in your organization, it is possible that leaders are rendering judgments on people and misattributing the issues or problems. One of the most commonly cited areas of concern among leaders is that people/individuals are *unmotivated*. When a person labels another person or group as unmotivated, they are often overlooking variables that contribute to the poor performance and instead chalk it up to being unmotivated. Have you ever heard an employee being called lazy or entitled or some other derogatory term? In many instances, this labelling occurs in small groups, even leader groups, without the person knowing it. Labeling often occurs because people are misdiagnosing the sources of the issue, which can often be tracked back to a lack of motivation need-fulfillment for the person. Take, for example, Henry, who works in a call center. He has been coming into work late 3 days a week, every week. He has established quite a reputation for himself among colleagues and leaders because of his tardiness. However, instead of the leadership discussing this directly with him, they begin to pull together a disciplinary process—or worse, they do not discuss this at all and choose to remove him. What the leaders and colleagues may not know is that he only gets his young children 3 days a week and he must get them to a more affordable day care on the other side of town, closer to where the children's mother lives. This is an example of one of the deficiency needs being a factor preventing him from fulfilling some of his job responsibilities.

Question What People Tell You

I want to state right away that people really do know themselves best. However, and it is a big, bold **HOWEVER**, they often do not have the communication or language skills to articulate what they truly and accurately want, aspire for, or even need. Research continues to demonstrate that people's actions are not strongly tied to what they *believe* they will do. For example, let's say you are starting a new two-year master's program in Leadership Studies. However, prior to receiving approval on the program, you must complete a feasibility study targeting stakeholders, specifically the people you hope to enroll. After administering your survey, your results come back very favorably. Over 85% percent of the 450 in your audience indicated that they are interested in this new program and wish to enroll. Fast-forward three years and the administration is demanding higher enrollment numbers and question your feasibility study ... "So, where are all of those students?" What happened? Year one enrollment was on target, year two was down 30%, and year three is down 60% from year one. Why aren't those stakeholders enrolling in the program? The simplest answer is "it's complicated," due to many factors such as timing, life events, economic conditions, etc. So, did they lie to you? No, they didn't. It is quite likely that they really are (still) interested in the program, but any number of other factors have assumed greater priority, likely due to several of the need-fulfillment items listed earlier. As such, it is those items that are preventing them from participating.

As we learn more about how people make decisions, it is becoming clear that people excel at telling you what they do not want as opposed to what they do want. Consider a time when you went to a new restaurant and you could not decide what to choose for dinner. If you are like most people, you clearly knew what you did not want: "I definitely don't want the clams," but you likely struggled to narrow your dinner selection down to one item. It is because of these two scenarios leaders should proceed with caution on taking what people tell them as absolute truths. People may tell you that they would love some specialized training on a topic like self-leadership or diversity, equity, and inclusion. Yet while they may show up and participate, they may not retain the information or apply the information because one or several deficiency needs are not being met.

Application

Activity 1 - Intrinsic Versus Extrinsic Motivation

This exercise has four steps, with the goal of leading toward a conversation that explores beliefs and assumptions surrounding the topic of motivation.

1. Begin with the question "What motivates you?" and interview people to examine their beliefs about what motivates them. There is a chance that they may have never considered this. Record their

answers (paper, computer, etc.) and listen closely for key intrinsic (joy, meaningful work, passion, make a difference, etc.) and extrinsic words (paycheck, vacation time, benefits, bonus, etc.).

2. Next, ask them "What motivates others?" They may ask you for more information or clarification, such as "Others, like everyone?" You may need to revisit your initial question to recalibrate it to focus on a person or certain people of their choice; "everyone" is too broad of a category. Record these answers.
3. Next, ask them for their opinions on the difference between intrinsic motivation and extrinsic motivation. At this point, the question-and-answer time should shift to a dialogue, producing a meaningful conversation about beliefs, experiences, and so forth.
4. Finally, after the discussion, capture your thoughts and impressions about the experience.

Activity 2 - Build Your Own Motivation Model

Take all the theories presented in the chapter and build one universal model for motivation. Feel free to add other theories to enhance your model. The goal is to develop the best, most comprehensive motivation framework you can use to assist you in your personal and professional life.

Other motivation theories that might be of interest to you may include Vroom's Theory of Expectancy, Social Cognitive Theory, McGregor's Theory X and Theory Y, Alderfer's ERG Theory, Reinforcement Theory, Locke's Goal-Setting Theory, Adam's Equity Theory of Motivation, Theory Z, and Hull-Spence Drive Theory.

Activity 3 - Check Your C-A-R

Utilizing the self-determination framework, complete an audit (we will call it a "check-in" or just "check") on yourself and others as it relates to the three basic psychological needs of autonomy, competence, and relatedness. However, reorganize those needs to spell C-A-R (competency - autonomy - relatedness). Just like your own vehicle, there are things you need for it to function well, such as air in your tires, fuel in the tank, and brakes that work. Using the C-A-R approach, complete a C-A-R check on your own motivation for both your personal (home domain) and professional life (work domain). Explore the differing levels of intensity of each item. Consider how deficiencies in one category may be spilling over and affect other categories. Also, explore how the intensities in one domain are potentially affecting the other domain in terms of satisfaction, success, and aspirations. As you explore these, revisit the various needs presented in the chapter and aim to articulate your findings as they relate to needs fulfillment.

References

Baumeister, R., & Leary, M. (1995). The need to belong: Desire for interpersonal attachments as a fundamental human motivation. *Psychological Bulletin, 117*, 497–529. https://doi.org/10.1037/0033-2909.117.3.497

Cho, J. Y, & Perry, J.L. (2012). Intrinsic motivation and employee attitudes: Role of managerial trustworthiness, goal directedness, and extrinsic reward expectancy. *Review of Public Personnel Administration, 32*(4), 382–406.

Compton, W. C. (2018). Self-actualization myths: What did Maslow really say? *Journal of Humanistic Psychology.* https://doi.org/10.1177/0022167818761929

Deci, E. L., & Ryan, R. M. (1980). The empirical exploration of intrinsic motivational processes. In L. Berkowitz (Ed.), *Advances in Experimental Social Psychology, 13*, 39–80. Academic Press. https://doi.org/10.1016/s0065-2601(08)60130-6

Deci, E. L., & Ryan, R. M. (1985). *Intrinsic motivation and self-determination in human behavior.* Plenum.

Deci, E. L., & Ryan, R. M. (2002). Self-determination research: Reflections and future directions. In E. L. Deci, & R. M. Ryan (Eds.), *Handbook of self-determination research* (pp. 431–441). University of Rochester Press.

Deci, E. L., & Ryan, R. M. (2014). Autonomy and need satisfaction in close relationships: Relationships motivation theory. In N. Weinstein (Ed.), *Human motivation and interpersonal relationships* (pp. 53–77). Springer. https://doi.org/10.1007/978-94-017-8542-6_3

D'Souza, J., & Gurin, M. (2016). The universal significance of Maslow's concept of self-actualization. *The Humanistic Psychologist, 44*(2), 210–214. https://doi.org/10.1037/hum0000027

Emmons, R. A. (1997). Motives and life goals. In S. Briggs, R. Hogan, & J.A. Johnson (Eds.), *Handbook of personality psychology* (pp. 485–512). Academic Press.

Fowler, S. (2014). What Maslow's hierarchy won't tell you about motivation. *Harvard Business Review, 92*(11).

Gagné, M., Forest, J., Vansteenkiste, M., Crevier-Braud, L., van den Broeck, A., Aspeli, A. K., ... Westbye, C. (2015). The Multidimensional Work Motivation Scale: Validation evidence in seven languages and nine countries. *European Journal of Work and Organizational Psychology, 24*, 178–196. doi:10.1080/1359432x.2013.877892

Grant, A. M. (2008). Does intrinsic motivation fuel the prosocial fire? Motivational synergy in predicting persistence, performance, and productivity. *Journal of Applied Psychology, 93*(1), 48–58. https://doi.org/10.1037/0021-9010.93.1.48

Herzberg, F., Mausner, B., & Snyderman, B. B. (1959). *The motivation to work* (2nd ed.). John Wiley.

Kasser, T., & Ryan, R. M. (1993). A dark side of the American dream: Correlates of financial success as a central life aspiration. *Journal of Personality and Social Psychology, 65*, 410–422. https://doi.org/10.1037/0022-3514.65.2.410

Mansour, K. A., Greenwood, C. J., Biden, E. J., Francis, L. M., Olsson, C. A., & Macdonald, J. A. (2021). Pre-pandemic predictors of loneliness in adult men during COVID-19. *Frontiers in Psychiatry, 12*. https://doi.org/10.3389/fpsyt.2021.775588

McAdams, D. P. (1994). *The person: An introduction to personality psychology* (2nd ed.). Harcourt Brace.

McClelland, D. C. (1961). *The achieving society*. Free Press.

McClelland, D. C. (1975). *Power: The inner experience*. Irvington.

McClelland, D. C. (1985). *Human motivation*. Cambridge University Press.

McClelland, D., & Burnham, D. (1977). Power is the great motivator. *Harvard Business Review, 81*(1), 117–126.

McClelland, D. C., & Koestner, R. (1992). The achievement motive. In C. Smith (Ed.), *Motivation and personality: Handbook of thematic content analysis* (pp. 143–152). Cambridge University Press.

Murray, H. A. (1938). *Explorations in personality*. Oxford University Press.

Ng, J. Y., Ntoumanis, N., Thøgersen-Ntoumani, C., Deci, E. L., Ryan, R. M., Duda, J. L., & Williams, G. C. (2012). Self-determination theory applied to health contexts: A meta-analysis. *Perspectives on Psychological Science, 7*(4), 325–340. https://doi.org/10.1177/1745691612447309

Olafsen A. H., & Deci, E. L. (2020). Self-determination theory and its relation to organizations. *Oxford Encyclopedia of Psychology*. https://doi.org/10.1093/acrefore/9780190236557.013.112

Robbins, S. P. (2003). *Organizational behavior* (10th ed.). Prentice-Hall.

Royle, M. T., & Hall, A. T. (2012). The relationship between McClelland's theory of needs, feeling individually accountable, and informal accountability for others. *International Journal of Management and Marketing Research, 5*(1), 21–42.

Ryan, R. M., & Deci, E. L. (2017). *Self-determination theory: Basic psychological needs in motivation development and wellness*. Guilford.

Credit

Fig. 5.1: Copyright © by Androidmarsexpress (CC BY-SA 4.0) at https://commons.wikimedia.org/wiki/File:Maslow%27s_Hierarchy_of_Needs2.svg.

CHAPTER 6

Setting Expectations

By Sheila Grebert

Disappointment is unmet expectations. The more significant the expectations, the more significant the disappointment.

—Brene Brown

Learning Objectives

After reading this chapter, students will be able to:

- Explain why expectations are vital to your success as a leader
- Set clear expectations for your direct reports and others

Introduction to Setting Expectations

Setting clear expectations is vital to the success of all leaders, but it is an often-overlooked skill that many leaders do not understand or do well. This chapter will focus on what expectations are, how they differ from goals, common mistakes leaders make around expectations, why they are so important, and how leaders can successfully establish and communicate expectations.

What Are Expectations?

The *Oxford Advanced Learner's Dictionary* defines expectation as "a strong belief about the way something should happen or how somebody should behave." Brown (2021) says, "When we develop expectations, we paint a picture in our head of how things are going to be and how they're going to look" (p. 43). We create these pictures in our heads for ourselves and others and may or may not articulate them. Whether we share our expectations out or not, they drive how we respond to both our actions and the actions of others.

Expectations vs. Goals

Before we learn more about expectations, it is important to understand the difference between expectations and goals. Research is clear that goals are important to employee success. "Specific, difficult goals lead to higher performance than no goals as well as vague, abstract goals such as 'do our best'" (Locke & Latham, 2013, p. 5). If goals are *what* an employee is working toward, expectations are the guidelines you establish for *how* employees will behave to get there. These expectations may be for how employees will achieve the goal, expectations for their role, or for how employees will work together.

Categories of Expectations

While goals are typically well documented and explained to employees as a desired result to work toward, expectations may be unspoken or ill defined. If leaders do not define and explain their expectations, it will be impossible for employees to meet the expectations and difficult for employees to successfully achieve the desired goals.

Brown (2021) talks about two categories of expectations: unexpressed and unexamined expectations, and expressed and examined expectations.

Unexpressed and Unexamined Expectations

When expectations are either unexpressed or unexamined, we are setting others up to fail. Both of these components are required in order to successfully set expectations, yet often one or both are overlooked.

Unexpressed Expectations

As a leader, if you are holding people accountable to expectations that are unexpressed, it is unlikely they will ever meet your expectations since they don't know what your expectation is. According to Rigoni and Nelson (2016), only about half of workers strongly agree they know what is expected of them.

Here are two examples of how these unexpressed expectations can lead to unmet expectations.

A small community center with a leader and one employee is open nightly until 6:00 p.m. A few nights a week, the center holds events that go until 6:00 or later, with customers leaving after 6:00. The employee is scheduled to work from 2:00–6:00. The employee's role includes helping customers and helping with these events.

The leader observed that the minute the clock turns 6:00, the employee was out the door, even if there were still customers in the building or an event was not over. This left the leader alone to finish the day and clean up after the event. The leader became more and more frustrated, as it happened week after week. The employee picked up on the leader's frustration and was confused by this since she was working until her scheduled end time of 6:00 p.m. The confusion and frustration were due to unexpressed expectations. The leader felt the employee should stay until the events were over and all customers had left, to help clean up and shut down for the evening. To do this, the employee would sometimes need to work beyond 6:00. The employee was not aware of this expectation and often made other plans and so needed to leave right at 6:00 to ensure she could meet her other commitments. A simple conversation about the expectation to stay later than 6:00 p.m. and the why behind it could have avoided this confusion and frustration.

Another example comes from an organization where a leader expected to see an agenda for all meetings a day prior to the meeting or she would not attend. A new employee was not aware of this expectation and was very confused when her leader did not attend any of the meetings she scheduled. Once the employee was made aware of the expectation, she began sending agendas and her leader began attending the meetings she scheduled.

Unexamined Expectations

When our expectations have been expressed, we can still become disconnected with our direct reports if we have not examined and created clarity for what these expectations mean to all involved. As we think about expectations and behaviors, each of us may look at things differently based on our individual experiences. Our experiences influence how we see the world, interpret expectations, and show up each day. Without examining these assumptions and biases, and making sure we are clear on the expectations, we can talk about the same set of expectations but interpret them differently.

For example, if we have a meeting at 10:00 a.m. and I say I am going to *move our meeting up an hour.* Is our meeting at 9:00 or 11:00? The answer could differ based upon your experience. We think we are being clear since we stated our expectation, but it can be interpreted differently based on the employee's experience and perspective.

Let's look at another example. If one of my expectations is to be on time, that seems like an easy expectation everyone would understand. However, if "on time" to me is in the office ready to work 5 minutes before your start time, and your definition of "on time" is in the parking lot by your start time, we are going to have some unmet expectations and confusion.

Let's say coaching each other is an expectation you have for your employees. What does that expectation mean? You might feel that coaching others is teaching them how to do specific tasks. You might feel coaching others is providing constructive feedback, providing answers, and solving problems. You might feel that coaching is asking great questions, listening more than talking, and being a thought partner who draws answers and ideas from others versus telling or solving. If employees are not sure how you define coaching others, they will likely miss the mark on this expectation because you do not have shared clarity on what this means.

Examined and Expressed

What we strive for when setting expectations is to both examine and express our expectations. When we do this, we are setting the framework for a successful partnership where unexpressed or unclear expectations do not sabotage the relationship or the desired performance. Even with care in setting expectations, there may still be instances when expectations are not met. When this happens, it is important to provide feedback and hold your direct reports accountable to the agreed-upon expectations. Without accountability, expectations are worthless. This could include conversations to provide feedback about how the expectation was not met, reexamine the expectation, and/or even reset the expectation.

As a new leader, I had a number of instances where I fell short on holding my team accountable and found it hard to then enforce the set expectation. For example, I had the weekly expectation that my team completed a form outlining where they spent their time that past week. Individually and as a team we had agreed to do this so we could use the data to demonstrate to the business leaders where we spent our time in order to make adjustments to our responsibilities or staffing as needed. I initially reminded employees when they did not get their forms completed each week. However, as I got busier, I did not check these each week. Weeks would go by and there would be no data captured. By the time I followed up, the data submitted was less accurate. This went on until employees were many months behind in tracking their time. It would have improved performance, reduced my frustration and employee frustration if I had provided feedback much earlier and provided consequences for not meeting the expectation. This was a valuable lesson for me on the importance of not only expressing and examining the expectations but also holding employees accountable to those expectations. "Improper guidance and feedback are the single largest contributors to incompetence in the world of work, and a principal culprit at school" (Gilbert, 2007, p. 91).

Gilbert (p. 87) goes on to say if you want to set employees up to *fail*, do the following:

1. Don't let people know how well they are performing.
2. Give people misleading information about how well they are performing.
3. Hide from people what is expected of them.
4. Give people little or no guidance about how to perform.

How to Use Setting Expectations in the Workplace

Setting Expectations

The key to setting expectations is to be clear, deliberate, and up front with all your expectations. Take the time to ensure everyone has clarity and is on the same page with *what* the expectations are, *why* you have those expectations, and what *success* looks like. It is also vital to continually revisit these expectations through ongoing feedback and conversations to ensure you stay on the same page and your direct reports know how they are doing. See Box 6.1 for the steps to use when setting expectations.

Let's look at a few examples.

Example 1: Expectation—Be On Time

What this looks like: at your desk, ready to work by 5 minutes before your start time.

Conversation:

- How does this differ with your definition of "on time?" What is missing? What do you disagree with?
- Is this a realistic expectation you can meet? If not, talk about what is.
- Discussion around how this will be tracked (i.e., I will be able to see if you are online or I will see if you are at your desk each morning) and the consequences if it is not met (i.e., two warnings, then moving to disciplinary action).
- Discussion around feedback (i.e., if I see or am made aware of instances when you are not on time, per this definition, I will provide feedback within 48 hours).

Example 2: Expectation—Good Communicator

What this looks like:

- Communicates timely (within 24 hours for request)
- Concise (using bullets, graphs, tables versus paragraphs)

BOX 6.1 **Setting Expectations**

Step	Action
1	**Ensure you don't have unexpressed expectations.** Make a list of all your expectations and confirm they have all been communicated.

2	**Ensure your expectations have been examined / discussed with your direct reports.**
	Examine all your expectations to make sure you have
	• clearly defined your expectations and the why behind them.
	• provided specific examples of what this behavior looks like when it is done well.
	• a conversation with your direct report about the expectation to ensure
	  ◦ you are both seeing what success around this expectation looks like.
	  ◦ the expectation is realistic.
	  ◦ you both know how success will be tracked/monitored and the consequences if not met.
	  ◦ each party knows how/when feedback will be provided.

3	**Provide feedback about how the individual is doing.** Discuss if they are meeting the agreed-upon expectations, if the expectation needs to change, what they are doing well, and what they need to improve.

- Uses appropriate method of communication (text, email, IM, phone call, etc.) (you may need to provide guidelines on when to use each method if you have expectations around this)
- Good customer service skills
- If verbal: uses appropriate tone, empathetic, etc.
- If written: written well, including grammatically correct, proofread, in logical order, to the point, took into consideration audience's needs

Conversation:

- How does this differ with your definition of a good communicator? What is missing? What do you disagree with?
- Is this a realistic expectation you can meet? If not, what is?
- Discussion around how this will be tracked (i.e., by feedback from customers, peers, and quality review that is randomly done monthly) and the consequences (i.e., if multiple complaints are received and/or quality is under 98% for three consecutive months, disciplinary actions will begin)
- Discussion around feedback (i.e., if I see or I am made aware of examples where these expectations are not met, I will reach out to share feedback within 48 hours from notification)

Application

Reflection: Your Expectations for Others

Identify an employee (or others such as family members or friends if you are not in a leadership role).

1. List the expectations you have for this person.
2. Which of the expectations on your list are unexpressed expectations?
3. Which of the expectations are not examined? Are they clear, realistic, and agreed upon with your employee (others)?
    - If not, for each expectation, create your description of what the expectation is, why this expectation is important, and what success looks like for the employee.
4. Have a conversation with the employee (others).
    - Share your expectations, the descriptions of the expectations, why this expectation is important, and what success looks like for the employee.
    - Discuss the expectations to assure the employee and you have agreement on the expectation.
5. Be prepared to discuss these conversations, including what went well, what did not go well (and what you would do differently), the impact this conversation had on you, the employee, the performance.

References

Brown, B. (2021). *Atlas of the heart*. Random House.

Gilbert, T. (2007). *Human competence: Engineering worthy performance*. Pfeiffer.

Locke, E. A., & Latham, G. P. (2013). *New developments in goal setting and task performance*. Routledge.

Oxford Advanced Learner's Dictionary. Oxford Advanced Learner's Dictionary at Oxford Learner's Dictionaries | Find meanings and definitions of words. (n.d.). Retrieved June 19, 2022, from https://www.oxfordlearnersdictionaries.com/definition/english

Rigoni, B., & Nelson, B. (2016). Do employees really know what is expected of them? *Business Journal*. Retrieved October 9, 2022, from Do Employees Really Know What's Expected of Them? (gallup.com)

CHAPTER 7

Giving and Receiving Feedback

By Robin Lindbeck

We all need people who will give us feedback. That's how we improve.

—Bill Gates

Learning Objectives

After reading this chapter, students will be able to:

1. Define feedback and describe why it is important
2. Identify the components of an effective feedback message
3. Describe the behaviors for receiving feedback
4. Create and deliver effective positive and negative feedback messages

Introduction to Feedback

Our job as leaders is to help our employees be engaged and successful in the workplace so we can meet organizational goals and expectations. Organization productivity is determined by employees' efforts and engagement (Anitha, 2014; Musgrove, Ellinger, & Ellinger, 2014). Feedback is a powerful tool for leaders to give employees information on how they are performing and so they know what they need to do to continue or improve their performance. In addition to providing clarity, "good feedback is associated with a heightened sense of personal accountability, a wide range of worker satisfaction factors, and enhanced performance" (LaFasto & Larson, 2001, p. 46).

What Is Feedback?

Feedback is "actions taken by an employee's supervisor to provide information regarding performance" (Kluger & DeNisi, 1996, p. 255) and it's "how we learn about ourselves from our experience and from other people" (Stone & Heen, 2014, p. 4). According to recent studies by Gallup, "80% of employees who say they have received meaningful feedback in the past week are fully engaged" (McLain & Nelson, 2020, para. 1). However "only 26% of employees strongly agree that feedback they receive helps them do work" (Wigert & Dvorak, 2019, para. 1). The key here is to give—and receive—*meaningful* feedback. When done well, feedback allows individuals to have an honest perspective of their performance and know what they need to do to sustain or improve their performance (LaFasto & Larson, 2001). What are the elements of meaningful feedback? Meaningful feedback is:

Well intentioned. The purpose of providing feedback is to *help* the individual improve or sustain their performance. It is not to "catch them" doing something wrong, or even to evaluate them. The purpose of feedback is to share information to help the individual be as successful as possible.

Focused on behavior. Separate the story you have in your mind from the individual's behavior. Meaningful feedback does not include the motives or reasons you think someone behaved in a particular way; you do not know why the individual behaved the way they did. Meaningful feedback focuses on specifically *what* the individual did or said and the impact that had on the situation.

Describes the impact. Describing the impact of the behavior lets the individual know *why* the behavior mattered. This connects the feedback to the outcome of the behavior.

Clear. Sometimes we are reluctant to give feedback. Know what you want to say in your feedback message and say it. Do not try to surround your negative feedback with excess words to try to make it more appealing to the individual. Your feedback is well intentioned; say it as clearly as possible. The more you give feedback, the easier it is to do.

Timely. Whenever possible, feedback should be as close to the behavior as possible. This does not necessarily mean immediately, but within a reasonable timeframe so the individual, and you, have the time to consider and discuss the feedback while the behavior is still fresh in your minds.

Frequent. Feedback that is given on a frequent or regular basis is more impactful on performance than feedback that is given once a month, once a quarter, or once a year. This is what Gallup refers to as *fast feedback*. Fast feedback is frequent, focused, and future oriented (McLain & Nelson, 2022). Getting frequent, regular feedback lets individuals confirm and correct their behavior so they can be as successful as possible.

Part of a conversation. For feedback to work, "it has to come from a good place and land well. It should be a 2-way communication" (Huston, 2021, p. 14). There may be times when you give a feedback message and the individual agrees with the feedback and only a brief conversation is needed. More often, the feedback message will be the start of a conversation where you and the individual gain clarity on the behavior and the impact, discuss next steps, and identify a time to check in on progress.

Why Do We Need Feedback?

But why do we need feedback? Can't we assess our own performance and improve? Apparently not. A meta-analysis of 22 studies found a low correlation between individuals' self-evaluations and the assessment of their work skills (Zell & Krizan, 2014). Asking for feedback ranked last of 30 leadership behaviors of 2.5 million individuals who completed the Leadership Practices Inventory (Kouzes & Pozner, 2016, p. 160). In addition to inaccurate self-evaluation of our performance, we may be unaware of areas of our performance and the impact it has on others. The Johari Window (Luft & Ingham, 1955) illustrates potential gaps in our awareness about our performance.

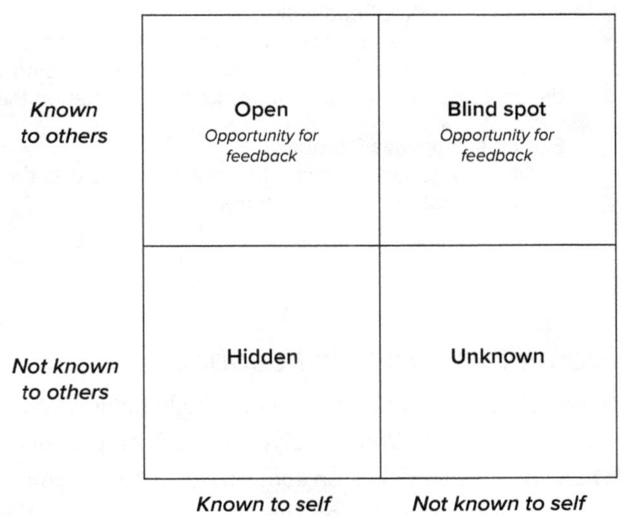

FIGURE 7.1 Johari Window

The Johari Window is divided into four areas, two of which have the potential for feedback (Welch, 2023):

Open: Represents what is known to the person and to others. This is an opportunity to get feedback from others to supplement your own self-assessment of your performance.

Blind Spot: Represents what is unknown to the person but known to others. This is an important opportunity to get feedback from others to provide information that you do not know.

Hidden: Represents what is known to the person but not to others.

Unknown: Represents what is unknown to both the person and others.

Types of Feedback

Positive vs. Negative Feedback

We often think of feedback as information on the *effectiveness* of someone's behavior. We give positive feedback when we want to provide information to someone on what they are doing well that we want them to continue doing. We give negative, or corrective, feedback when we want to provide information on what is not going well that we would like changed. The positive or negative feedback is a statement that, when used effectively, often starts a conversation about how to continue (positive feedback) or modify (negative feedback) behavior in the future.

Sometimes, in an attempt to make everyone more comfortable with negative feedback, it might be called "constructive" feedback. *All* feedback should be constructive feedback whether it is positive or negative feedback. But feel free to call it negative feedback, constructive feedback, corrective feedback, or anything else. What's important is that you provide it!

BOX 7.1 **Positive and Negative Feedback Examples**

Example: Positive Feedback

Maria, you did a great job with your presentation today. You were poised and friendly, you talked at a good pace, checked in with the group on their understanding, and answered their questions completely. This helped the group to be engaged and to get the information they needed to move forward with our new process.

Example: Negative Feedback

Maria, when you are late to work, it means that there is no one available to answer customer calls, and that is frustrating for our customers.

Product vs. Process Feedback

In addition to the effectiveness of the behavior, you also want to consider the *type* of behavior for which you give feedback. You can give feedback on product behaviors or process behaviors. Product feedback is when you give feedback on something that happened. You provide feedback on the outcome, on the thing that was accomplished, on the *what* that happened. Much of the feedback you have given or received in the workplace is likely product feedback. You can also provide process feedback, which is feedback on how someone went about doing something regardless of the ultimate outcome or product.

BOX 7.2 Product and Process Feedback Examples

Example: Product Feedback (positive)

Gabe, in the meeting today you reminded the customer service reps that we have two primary measures for phone calls: average speed of answer and the quality or customer's satisfaction of the call. You shared your expectation that although we care about average speed of answer, we care more about the quality of the call to be sure customers get their questions answered and feel supported, even if that means the call takes a little longer. Several of the reps shared that hearing your expectation was very helpful for them and provided the clarity they needed to be confident in spending the time they needed with the customers to fully solve their issues.

Example: Process Feedback (positive)

Gabe, we were getting bogged down in the meeting today and when you said, "so it sounds to me like there are basically three issues" and summarized those issues, it got us all on the same page and helped us move forward and figure out what we needed to do.

Formal vs. Informal Feedback

Finally, you want to consider *when* you give feedback. Formal feedback occurs in planned settings such as monthly one-on-one meetings, annual performance evaluation meetings, and project debrief meetings where there is an expectation that performance will be discussed. Of even more importance is informal feedback. Informal feedback is the feedback you share as part of your day-to-day interactions with others. When you see someone doing something well, you give them positive feedback. When you see someone doing something not-so-well, you give them negative, corrective feedback. This day-to-day feedback provides others with an ongoing understanding of how they are performing and allows for behavior corrections on a regular basis.

How to Use Feedback in the Workplace

Giving Feedback

When we think about giving effective feedback, there are two things we need to consider: first is the *quantity* of the feedback that we're giving, and the second is the *quality* of the feedback that we're giving. Let's begin with the quantity of feedback.

Quantity of Feedback

When do we typically give feedback?

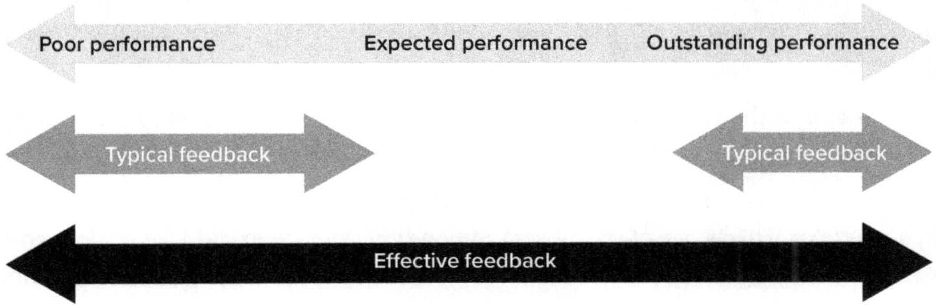

FIGURE 7.2 Performance and Feedback Continuum

In Figure 7.2, you see the performance continuum that goes from poor performance on the left to outstanding performance on the right. We typically give feedback when the individual is performing below expectations (negative feedback) or when the individual is doing such an outstanding job that we feel compelled to give them positive feedback.

What is missing in this typical feedback? We miss providing feedback, positive feedback, when the individual is performing as expected or slightly better than expected. People need feedback all along the performance continuum, including when they are doing what we expect them to do. Of course, you want to keep the feedback proportionate—you need not be excessive in your enthusiasm for expected performance. But if you want expected performance to continue, or improve, you need to provide feedback. For optimal performance, you will provide feedback all along the performance continuum.

Why don't we give enough positive feedback?

TABLE 7.1 **Common Reasons for Not Giving Positive Feedback**

Reason	Response
They know they are doing things right if I don't say anything.	This is not feedback! To reinforce, sustain, and adjust behavior, people need feedback.
If I give them positive feedback for doing what they are supposed to do, they will expect a raise or an outstanding rating on their performance review.	Keep the feedback proportionate for the behavior and connect it to expectations. For example: Erica, when you are here, ready to answer the phones at 8:00, that means that our customers will get the service they need even if they call first thing in the morning. This is exactly what I expect and I appreciate it.
If I give them positive feedback for "doing their job," it will not sound genuine.	Be sure to give a positive feedback message using one of the feedback models. By including all the relevant information, including the impact of their behavior—why it mattered—it will be genuine.
I don't have time to give feedback.	It's true that leaders are very busy. But is it about time? Or is it about priority and skill? The first step is prioritizing feedback as something important to do. When you see someone doing something right, don't just observe it, say it! And once you are practiced at giving feedback, a positive feedback message will likely take less than a minute. And that minute will make a difference for a behavior you want to reinforce and sustain.

Quality of Feedback

We also need to consider the *quality* of the feedback we are giving. Many of us think that we're giving feedback, but we are giving incomplete feedback messages. For example, I might say,

> Susan, I appreciate what you did today. Thanks.

Is that feedback? Does Susan know what behavior she did well or not so well? Does she know why I am bringing it up? This is a nice sentiment, and Susan might appreciate hearing it, but it is not feedback. Let's try again. I might say,

> Susan, I was late to the meeting today and you got it started without me. I really appreciate it. Thanks.

Is this feedback? Does Susan know the behavior she did? Yes. Does she know why I think it matters that she did this behavior? No. This is one of the most common types of "feedback" that leaders give in the workplace. They describe the what, but not the why-it-matters. This is not feedback. Let's try again. I might say,

> Susan, I was late to the meeting today and you got it started without me, which meant we could get everything done and still finish on time. I really appreciate it. Thanks.

Is this feedback? Does Susan know the behavior she did? Yes. Does she know why I think it matters? Yes. This is feedback.

Feedback Models

A feedback model is a framework for providing feedback that allows you to include the information you need to share to provide a high-quality, complete feedback message. The advantages of using a feedback model is that you are more likely to include all the information necessary for effective feedback, and this may increase the effectiveness of your feedback as well as your confidence in providing feedback. A scan of the internet or conversations with professional colleagues will uncover many possible feedback models. It does not matter which feedback model you use; what matters is that you have a framework to help you provide high-quality, effective feedback. Use the model that makes the most sense to you! Here are three common feedback models.

SBI Feedback Model (Situation-Behavior-Impact)

The SBI Feedback model was created by Sloan Weitzel at the Center for Creative Leadership (Weitzel, 2003; CCL, n.d.). The steps and definitions are described on the Center for Creative Leadership web page.

TABLE 7.2 **SBI Feedback Model**

Step	Definition	Example Feedback Message
Situation	Describe the specific situation in which the behavior occurs.	At the department meeting when I was describing the new hybrid work option.
Behavior	Describe the actual, observable behavior.	You asked the first question about how much choice employees had with this new work option.
Impact	Describe the results of the behavior.	This broke the ice in the meeting for asking questions, and your specific question raised a concern that was likely on the minds of everyone in the room.

STAR Feedback Model (Situation/Task-Action-Result)

The STAR model was created by Developmental Decisions International (DDI, n.d.). The steps and definitions are described on their web page.

TABLE 7.3 **STAR Feedback Model**

Step	Definition	Example Feedback Message
ST: Situation/Task	Explain the situation or task so others understand the context.	In the sales call yesterday, you were describing the new, increased pricing to the manufacturing manager.
A: Action	Give details about what you or another person did to handle the situation.	He was very angry about the price change. You did a great job of listening to him, asking questions about his concerns, and responding to those concerns while remaining calm.
R: Result	Describe what was achieved by the action and why it was effective.	Because you were calm and focused on him and his concerns, he was able to continue in the conversation, calm down, better understand the situation, and ultimately stay with our product.

DESC Feedback Model (Describe-Express-Specify-Consequence)

The DESC model and script was developed by Sharon and Gordon Bower (1976) and includes the following steps and definitions (pp. 89–94):

TABLE 7.4 **DESC Feedback Model**

Step	Definition	Example Feedback Message
Describe	Describe the behavior.	We just had a fairly difficult conversation about your performance on your quarterly goals. You were calm during the discussion, you were honest about your performance and offered explanations, not excuses, and took accountability for your performance.
Express	Express what you feel and think about the behavior. Use "I" statements for your feelings rather than "you" statements.	I am happy that we can have open conversations, even when the topic is difficult.
Specify	Specify the specific behavior you want to continue (positive feedback) or the specific behavior you would prefer happen instead (negative feedback).	I want you to continue to be honest with me in our conversations.
Consequence	State the consequence (payoff or penalty) of continuing or adjusting behavior. Whenever possible, state the consequence as a positive.	This will allow us to identify steps to improve your performance so you can be successful in achieving your goals.

There is another common feedback model that we do not recommend: the Feedback Sandwich. With the Feedback Sandwich, you start with a piece of positive feedback to start the conversation, deliver a piece of negative feedback, and finish with another piece of positive feedback. The idea is to "soften" the negative feedback by sandwiching it between two pieces of positive feedback. This is not effective for several reasons: (1) if the negative feedback is delivered with the intention to help the individual improve their performance and effectiveness, and the feedback is specific in the behavior and the impact of the behavior, it does not need to be "softened"; (2) the individual will likely see the pattern of the sandwich and discount the positive feedback and focus only on the negative feedback; and (3) combining positive and negative feedback in the same feedback message can be confusing to the individual and leave them unsure how to interpret the feedback. Your feedback message will be more effective if you use the SBI, STAR, or DESC feedback models.

Receiving Feedback

Just as feedback is important for us to give to others so they can sustain or improve their performance, the same is true for us. Without regular, meaningful feedback, we will not have the information *we* need to perform as well as possible. Hopefully you have individuals who are willing to give you regular, meaningful feedback. If not, you can ask for feedback. Here are some things to keep in mind when you receive feedback:

Listen. Listen to the feedback. Don't try to disprove it, don't rebut it. Focus on what the other person is saying and take it in. It was important enough for them to say it, so listen to it.

Don't get defensive. We sometimes hear that feedback is a gift ... but we do not always like the gifts we are given! If someone is willing to give you feedback, it *is* a gift. Stay open to what they have to say. Getting defensive may shut down the feedback giver now and may stop them from giving you feedback in the future. You do not need to agree or disagree with the feedback now; just stay open and see what you can learn from the feedback. Why do we feel defensive when receiving feedback? We might feel defensive because they are not sharing the feedback in the most effective way. We might feel defensive because the feedback is feeling accurate. Stay open so you can understand the feedback they are giving you.

Ask for clarification. Despite our best efforts to stay open to feedback, we sometimes jump to conclusions about what the feedback giver is saying to us. Ask for clarification or examples to help you better understand the feedback they are giving you. This is not asking them to *prove* what they are saying because you think they are not correct; this is asking questions to help you more fully *understand* the feedback.

Thank them for the feedback. It takes time, energy, thoughtfulness, and sometimes courage to give someone feedback. This person was willing to give you feedback, so thank them for it and let them know that you appreciate that they shared it with you or whatever you can genuinely say to them.

Take time to consider the feedback. Take the time to consider the feedback and how you can continue the behavior (positive feedback) or what you might do differently in the future (negative feedback). Even if you think you disagree with the feedback, take time to consider it and the ways the feedback might be accurate. This person thought it was worth sharing with you, and there may be at least a kernel of information that you can act on to be more effective. Depending on the feedback, you may not be obligated to act on it, but you are obligated to consider it.

Close the loop. Again, it takes time, energy, thoughtfulness, and courage to give someone feedback. Close the loop with them on the feedback. This could be as simple as letting them know you have been thinking about what they said and here is what you did (or plan to do) differently and that you appreciate their feedback or whatever you can genuinely say to them.

Application

It's time to try out your new skills in providing feedback.

1. Identify someone at work (or in your nonwork life) and provide them with positive (or constructive) feedback.
    a. Plan your feedback message to include specifically what they did or said and the impact.
    b. Decide when you will deliver this feedback message.
    c. Deliver the positive feedback.
    d. Consider the following questions:
        i. What happened when you delivered the positive feedback message?
        ii. What was the reaction of the person who received the positive feedback?
        iii. What was your reaction?
        iv. What was the impact of providing this person the positive feedback? (Or what do you think the impact will be of providing this positive feedback?)
        v. Anything else that you learned from this activity?
2. Now that you have had some practice delivering feedback, do it again. Repeat the activity in step 1.
3. Think about your direct reports or coworkers (or other people in your life). Make a list of who needs feedback, create the feedback messages, and plan when you will provide them with feedback.

References

Anitha, J. (2014). Determinants of employee engagement and their impact on employee performance. *International Journal of Productivity and Performance Management, 63*, 308–323. doi:10.1108/ijppm-01-2013-0008

Bower, S. A., & Bower, G. H. (1976). *Asserting yourself: A practical guide for positive change.* Addison-Wesley.

Center for Creative Leadership (CCL). (n.d.). *Use situation-behavior-impact (SBI)TM to understand intent.* https://www.ccl.org/articles/leading-effectively-articles/closing-the-gap-between-intent-vs-impact-sbii/

Developmental Decisions International (DDI). (n.d.). *Star method.* https://www.ddiworld.com/solutions/behavioral-interviewing/star-method

Huston, T. (2021). *Let's talk: Make effective feedback your superpower.* Penguin Group.

McLain, D., & Nelson, B. (January 1, 2022). *How effective feedback fuels performance.* https://www.gallup.com/workplace/357764/fast-feedback-fuels-performance.aspx

Kluger, A. N., & DeNisi, A. (1996). Effects of feedback intervention on performance: A historical review, a meta-analysis, and a preliminary feedback intervention theory. *Psychological Bulletin, 119*(2), 254–284.

Kouzes, J. M., & Posner, B. Z. (2016). *Learning leadership.* Wiley.

LaFasto, F. M. J., & Larson, C. E. (2001). *When teams work best: 6,000 team members and leaders tell what it takes to succeed.* Sage.

Luft, J., & Ingham, H. (1955). The Johari window, a graphic model of interpersonal awareness. *Proceedings of the Western Training Laboratory in Group Development.* University of California, Los Angeles.

Musgrove, C., Ellinger, A. E., & Ellinger, A. D. (2014). Examining the influence of strategic profit emphases on employee engagement and service climate. *Journal of Workplace Learning, 26,* 152–171. doi: 10.1108/JWL-08-2013-0057

Stone, D., & Heen, S. (2014). *Thanks for the feedback: The science and art of receiving feedback well.* Penguin Group.

Weitzel, S. R. (2003). *Feedback that works: How to build and deliver your message.* Center for Creative Leadership.

Welch, J. (2023). Visioning strategy through the "Johari window": Discovering critical "unknowns" in a rapidly evolving context. *Strategy & Leadership, 51*(5), 30–35.

Wigert, B., & Dvorak, N. (2019). *Feedback is not enough.* https://www.gallup.com/workplace/257582/feedback-not-enough.aspx

Zell, E., & Krizan, Z. (2014). Do people have insight into their abilities? A metasynthesis. *Perspectives on Psychological Science, 9*(2), 111–125.

Credit

Fig. 7.1: Joseph Luft and Harrington Ingham, "Johari Window," https://commons.wikimedia.org/wiki/File:Johari_Window.PNG, 1955.

CHAPTER 8

Coaching

By Terri A. Deems

I never cease to be amazed at the power of the coaching process to draw out the skills or talent that was previously hidden within an individual, and which invariably finds a way to solve a problem previously thought unsolvable.

—John Russell

Learning Objectives

After reading this chapter, students will be able to:

1. Define coaching and differentiate between coaching and more traditional ways of leading others
2. Defend the use of a coaching mindset and strategies within the workplace
3. Identify the essential elements, skills, and strategies for effectively coaching followers, including the GROW model and structuring a coaching conversation.

Introduction to Coaching

Whether an organization has a marketing team or a football team, sells groceries or builds cars, provides insurance or serves meals to the homeless, one fact holds true for them all: an organization that is stagnant will not survive. To be a sustainable, thriving business—either for-profit or nonprofit—leaders must continually seek ways to develop people and promote a culture of continuous learning and improvement.

A leader's primary role can be boiled down to this: to help people be successful. To bring their "best self" to work, every day. Traditionally, this was often attempted by using authoritative, command-and-control approaches to leading others (Bass, 1996; Wheatley, 1997). Work was seen as little more than a transaction—you do this work, and we'll pay you these benefits. In today's workplace, however, such an approach (though still widely used) is not enough (see, for example, Grint, 2020; Nerland & Goh, 2021).

Increasingly, leaders are adopting revolutionary business models and a more transformational leadership style that emphasizes the development of individuals and teams. Instead of command-and-control, leaders apply a coaching mindset as a vehicle to drive meaningful, sustainable change and growth. Particularly over the past 20 years, a variety of coaching models and competency frameworks have been developed, some of which we will touch on in this chapter. A common element across these models and frameworks is simply this: employee performance is accelerated by having a coach, not simply a boss.

BOX 8.1 Critical Thinking Activity: Coaches You Have Known

Consider effective coaches you have known—people who perhaps coached you on a sports team or elsewhere at some point in your life and made a difference for you. Call up this person's image in your mind: really remember what it was like to engage with this person, to talk with them, and what difference they may have made in your life or performance.

- What personal qualities or characteristics did this person have that seemed to positively impact your relationship?
- What did this person DO as they coached you (e.g., they taught, listened, advised, and so on)?
- What did this person help YOU do?

Coaching Myths and Realities

A quick online search will provide many variations as to what coaching is and how it is best accomplished. It's no wonder, then, that many leaders are confused about coaching and may even resist it as one more task to fit into their already full schedule.

Let's start by clearing up some common misconceptions.

Myth #1: Coaching is a form of corrective action—a tool we use when we need to "fix" people or to close a gap between current and desired performance. It's a last-ditch effort for people whose jobs may be on the line.

Reality: While coaching is used to strengthen a person's performance, it should never be used only as corrective or punitive action. Most organizations have other procedures for those situations. Rather, coaching is about creating a future—enhancing work habits, gaining an advantage, or removing obstacles by encouraging reflective, critical thinking and problem solving. A common aim is to help others identify and take self-corrective action.

Myth #2: Coaching is like therapy and a way of being "soft" with employees.

Reality: Therapy is used to address mental health challenges and typically focuses on the past and/or the present. In contrast, coaching is performance oriented and focuses on the future. It's a collaboration between the coach and the one being coached, where both parties bear responsibility for advancement and goal attainment. There's nothing "soft" about it!

Myth #3: Coaching is time consuming—and leaders just don't have time for it.

Reality: While coaching may demand a commitment of time, it does not need to be an added burden. Leaders take advantage of coaching moments throughout their day as well as scheduled conversations. Many find that coaching helps to save time in the long run as those being coached increase their own problem-solving abilities, accept greater responsibility for their performance, and develop their skills more quickly than through more traditional methods such as training.

Myth #4: Employee coaching is the same as mentoring.

Reality: Though there may be some similarities, coaching and mentoring are two distinct processes. A mentor is more of an adviser, someone who has achieved what a mentee wants and is willing to share their experience, knowledge, and insights in order to help further the mentee's career. In contrast, a coaching leader focuses on short-term goals, issues, and areas for development. The focus is on performance gains rather than long-term career planning and strategies.

Myth #5: Coaching is a planned event that occurs in a scheduled meeting between a leader and follower, usually in someone's office.

Reality: Coaching is not an isolated event, though it certainly may include planned coaching conversations to help accelerate growth. But just as often, coaching occurs on the shop floor or over lunch or while counting inventory in the storeroom. Any instance is an opportunity for a coaching conversation when you adopt a coaching mindset.

Defining Coaching

The practice of coaching in general draws on a number of disciplines and theories, including behaviorism, humanistic psychology, lifespan and adult development, positive psychology, even transpersonal psychology and neuroscience, among others (see, for example, Williams, n.d.). This may account for some of the variation found when we seek a clear definition or set of standards or strategies for coaching. In spite of this, there are many consistencies we can find, whether we think of an external professional coach or when a leader coaches their followers.

While we often talk about coaching skills and strategies (and we will examine these later in this chapter), coaching starts with a **mindset** we bring to our work as leaders. It is about a way of being in a relationship with others rather than simply what we are doing. As Canadian coach Michael Stanier describes, coaching is about causing people's success and helping them move from good work to great work (2016).

The International Coaching Federation, perhaps the leading global organization for advancing the coaching profession, defines coaching as partnering with others "in a thought-provoking and creative process that inspires them to maximize their personal and professional potential. The process of coaching often unlocks previously untapped sources of imagination, productivity and leadership" (About ICF, n.d.).

Let's break down that definition. First, coaching is a **partnership** between a leader and a follower who have a shared commitment to the follower's growth and development. It's also a **process** rather than an event. The process used in coaching is both **intellectual and creative**. It requires both reflection and imagination to consider what has not been considered—what entrepreneur and coaching expert Robert Hargrove describes as "the Impossible Future" (2008), where we dream and imagine even if the path itself remains unclear. The **purpose** of coaching is to help people realize their potential and tap into sources they may not have previously recognized.

Coaching can take many forms. For example, a leader may hire an outside professional coach as a way to accelerate their own growth and development; together, they work on specific goals the leader has and track his or her progress toward those goals. We can also think of coaching as a style used by a leader when working with followers, such as described in Hersey and Blanchard's situational leadership model (see, for example, Blanchard, Zigarmi, & Zigarmi, 1985; Hersey, 1984), where coaching is one of four styles a leader chooses from in order to enhance the performance and confidence of their followers.

For the purposes of this text, we are focusing first on coaching as a mindset a leader adopts, where the leader relates to their followers as a coach rather than simply as a boss. A 2019 study from the International Coaching Federation and the Human Capital Institute (HCI) found that organizations' use of coaching as a key development tool has increased substantially in recent years, and that 83% of the study's respondents indicated they plan to increase the use of managers and leaders using coaching skills within the next five years (ICF, Building a coaching culture).

The coaching mindset begins with a leader's commitment to the coaching process, the coaching vision, and to the development of the person being coached. With these commitments, "An effective manager-as-coach asks questions instead of providing answers, supports employees instead of judging them, and facilitates their development instead of dictating what has to be done" (Ibarra & Scoular, 2019, para. 6). Central to this is the focus on development rather than fixing some perceived deficiency—we consistently watch for coachable moments in a continuous press for growth.

Leaders who embrace a coaching culture view coaching as a central component of their leadership responsibilities. They recognize the benefits of coaching for motivating and developing others and fostering a supportive and high-performance environment (Dennis, 2022).

Coaching Benefits

In the United States, the external coaching industry overall has seen substantial growth over the past 10 years, even with the slight decline seen during the COVID-19 pandemic. Recent industry reports show the coaching industry has grown an average of 2.8% annually since 2017, and it is anticipated that the industry will see a revenue of $14.2 billion for 2022 (Business Coaching Industry in the US, 2022).

Why are businesses willing to invest so much in coaching? The answer is simple: because coaching is an effective and cost-efficient way to foster high performance and development among individuals, teams, and organizations (see, for example, Bozer & Jones, 2018; Theeboom et al., 2013). This is why so many organizations around the world are working to turn their leaders into coaches.

There are many compelling reasons for a leader to coach rather than to simply manage in the workplace and lots of opportunity to do so. Managing is, of course, a vital part of what many leaders do. Too often, though, managing takes a deficit approach focusing on what's wrong and how to control or fix it. Coaching takes a more appreciative, positive approach to developing others, focusing on what's right, what's wanted, and what's needed to get there. We know from the research going back decades that people tend to live up to (or down to) our expectations—one person's positive expectation of another's abilities often becomes a self-fulfilling prophecy (Rosenthal & Jacobson, 1968). Coaching is a proactive way of leading, taking advantage of both opportunities and challenges.

When a leader coaches employees—rather than simply directing them—the leader not only can accelerate growth and productivity, but the inquiry-based approach a coach uses is also integral to promoting problem-solving and critical thinking skills. Coaching can help employees improve their work habits, strengthen knowledge transfer, and develop new competencies often more quickly than traditional training might. Coaching can even serve as a vehicle for greater support of organizational change. Through coaching a leader can optimize performance, inspire people to tackle new challenges, and quickly close gaps that may limit performance.

The coaching process can add clarity to expectations and choices, increase individual or team self-awareness, enhance collaboration, and serve to leverage core strengths in ways that other leadership techniques may not. Not only can coaching have a positive impact on productivity, but it has also been shown to have a positive impact on other organizational metrics such as retention and morale (Theeboom et al., 2013).

BOX 8.2 **Critical Thinking Activity: Coaching vs. Managing**

Take time to conduct an online information search to identify the kinds of tasks and responsibilities that a manager has and that a performance coach has (or talk to a manager and to a coach, if you know people who fill those roles). Use this table to record your findings (add more rows to your table as needed).

A manager ...	**A coach ...**

As you study these tasks and responsibilities, consider the following questions:

1. What, if any, similarities do you find between a manager and a coach?
2. What key differences do you see?
3. Why might a manager choose to coach rather than "manage" people's performance?

How to Use Coaching in the Workplace

Coaching techniques can be used in a variety of situations. The following are just a few of the opportunities for coaching employees:

- Daily communication with team members
- Engaging or inspiring people
- Sharing honest feedback
- Solving problems
- Recognizing someone's contributions
- Redirecting someone's path
- Removing barriers
- Sharing knowledge and expertise
- Preparing for or assisting with transitions

Remember, coaching is both a mindset and a process rather than a particular event. A leader needs some way, however, to structure their coaching. There is a variety of approaches that can be used.

The Coaching Structure

The coaching structure is highly individualized based on the strengths of the leader and the personal and situational needs of the employee. A leader will have to decide how formal or structured their coaching must be, as well as whether the situation calls for being more directive or more nondirective.

Formal vs. Informal Coaching

The most structured form of coaching is the formal coaching meeting, where the leader and employee agree on a set time and place for the session. This might take the form of a regularly scheduled meeting such as a monthly session, or it could be part of an annual or biannual performance review. Both people understand the purpose of the session is to address performance needs or challenges or in some way enhance the capabilities of the employee. The leader typically has a planned format for the session, including specific questions and feedback they want to provide, and specific action plans are often one of the meeting outcomes. Formal coaching sessions may be used for such needs as performance appraisals, setting performance goals, training, creating or reviewing development plans, or to clarify the goals, needs, or direction of a particular project.

In contrast, informal coaching is less structured, though many of the same coaching tactics are used. With informal coaching, a leader takes advantage of "coachable moments," as they observe the employee in action. Informal coaching is more spontaneous than formal coaching and can take place as the leader and employee walk down the hallway together or when they are out on the shop floor or construction site. The conversation could take 5 minutes or 15, and it's typically more conversational than a formal coaching session. Does that mean that every conversation a leader has with an employee is a coaching conversation? No, though the opportunity for coaching is always there. A leader will have many performance-focused conversations in the course of a day, the purpose of which is to fix a problem or address some kind of challenge. A coaching conversation, though, differs in that it is always focused on the employee's development—it's about the person dealing with an issue rather than about a particular issue itself (Stanier, 2016).

Directive vs. Nondirective

In addition to thinking about how formal or informal coaching is, we can also view coaching as being more directive or nondirective.

A leader uses directive coaching when they need to give advice or to demonstrate a particular way of doing something. The focus here relies on the leader's expertise and sharing that with the employee. This directive approach is appropriate when time is short, when an employee is completely stuck, or when there is a specific skill or process that must be used in a certain way—the employee simply needs to be told what to do or how to do it. For instance, if Natalie is unable to access an equipment part to be replaced, her leader might tell her what has worked most easily for him or show her how to do it.

Nondirective coaching, though, focuses more on getting the employee to think through the problem or to think differently about it. Instead of offering his advice, Jamal, as Natalie's leader, might instead help Natalie create her own solution. He does so first by actively listening to Natalie's description of the problem, then posing questions to help her think through possible solutions: What have you tried so far? What seems to be getting in the way? How might doing x be different than y? Let's see what happens when you do z? In this way, Natalie ultimately creates her own solution (and has strengthened her problem-solving skills in the process). A nondirective coaching approach may take more time than a directive approach, but the outcome will be the same; through the coaching conversation, we help foster greater confidence, efficacy, and critical thinking with the employee than we would otherwise. The goal here is to support the employee in their development while solving the problem rather than simply providing answers.

In any coaching conversation, a leader may find they need to shift between being directive and nondirective at different points in the conversation.

BOX 8.3 **Coaching Roles**

A coach fills multiple roles based on the needs of the person being coached at any given time. Robert Hargrove, thought leader and founder of Masterful Coaching, Inc., describes these roles as "coaching caps" a coach puts on and takes off (2008).

7 Coaching Caps:

1. Declaring Possibilities: Use this cap to brainstorm alternative possibilities when a person struggles to see their options, break habits, or perceive any path forward.
2. Thinking Partner: Use this cap to offer new ideas or perspectives when a person faces problems or puzzles with no obvious answer.
3. Drawing Others Out: Use this cap when a person struggles to express their ideas or are feeling misunderstood.
4. Reframing Thinking & Attitudes: Put on this cap when a person needs to see themselves differently or is using limiting beliefs, attitudes, or assumptions.
5. Teaching & Advising: This cap can be used to make a distinct point, offer practical advice, or when you see a teachable moment to add clarity.
6. Forwarding the Action: Use this cap when people have had enough thinking or strategizing and are ready to take action.
7. Giving Honest Feedback: Put on this cap to help increase people's awareness of strengths and gaps or when actions have led to unintended consequences.

Types of Coaching

The different structure and roles tell us that coaching is more than just a single technique, style, or opportunity. It is highly individualized, can take many different forms, and can be used with all levels of employees. Within the workplace, we also see different types of coaching, which are used to meet different purposes.

Executive coaching: Though executive coaching is often done by hiring a professional coach from outside the organization, it can also occur with any more senior leader within the organization. As with all coaching, this involves a strengths-based approach designed to help a leader achieve a personal performance goal through self-awareness and reflection, revealing barriers in a leader's thinking, creating practice fields, and developing an effective action plan.

Peer coaching: A leader is not the only person who can coach employees, and leaders often find that the more they use coaching practices, the more their employees make use of these practices with each other. That is the crux of peer coaching—a formal or informal arrangement where two or more coworkers interact with each other using the coaching mindset and a nondirective approach to problem solving. Together, peer coaches work with each other to learn together, exchange ideas, and address problems, while at the same time creating stronger relationships and helping each other enhance their critical thinking and problem-solving skills (Verlinden, n.d.).

Team coaching: As the name suggests, team coaching involves coaching an entire team rather than an individual. And just as with other types of coaching, team coaching can use different structures and methods. It can be quite structured, such as when a leader may take a team out on a work retreat and sets the agenda, or an unstructured meeting with the team to foster team thinking and decision-making (Center for Creative Leadership, 2020). Team coaching may focus on a particular team project or be designed to help foster more effective team processes or interactions over time.

Virtual coaching: The Center for Creative Leadership (2020) has identified virtual coaching as the most common form of workplace coaching in recent years since so many employees are dispersed or work remotely. Virtual coaching can be used with executives, individual contributors, or entire teams and is an effective way for a leader to fit coaching into everyone's hectic schedules. With virtual coaching, a leader engages in much the same way as they do in face-to-face situations.

The GROW Framework

Whether we are doing individual coaching or team coaching, virtual or face-to-face, formal or informal, a common framework leaders use is the GROW model. If you look online you will find several similar versions of this framework, such as the WOOP method (Oettingen, 2015), and any may be useful not just for coaching conversations but also for other meetings and projects. Because GROW is a common method used by leaders and professional coaches today, we will focus on this method.

With its origins in sports and influenced by Tim Gallwey's work with "the inner game" (Parsloe & Wray, 2000), the GROW model (Figure 8.1) was developed in the 1980s and 1990s by business coaches Sir John Whitmore, Graham Alexander, and Alan Fine (Kamarudin, Kamarudin, Darmi, & Saazai, 2020). It is a

G	R	O	W
Goal	**Reality**	**Obstacles/ Options**	**Will/ Way forward**
What do you want to achieve?	What is going on? What are you at now?	What is getting in your way? What choices do you see? What could you do?	What will you commit to doing? What are your next steps?

FIGURE 8.1 GROW Model

simple but powerful coaching method used to set goals, identify barriers, brainstorm ideas, and to create a path for taking action.

Much of the attraction to the GROW model is its simplicity and flexibility. This technique can be used on all kinds of problems—technical, adaptive, interpersonal, and more. It can also be used for individual or team coaching or by peers working together to meet a challenge. Let's look at the four components.

Goal: This is the target—where the person being coached wants to be or what they want to achieve. It may start in the form of a wish or a dream. We find that a goal is most effective when it is defined in a clear way that includes how you will know when the goal has been achieved. Many coaches and the employees find it most helpful to frame this goal as a S.M.A.R.T. goal—one that is specific, measurable, achievable, realistic, and timely. Set "stretch" goals that will challenge people but that are also realistic and achievable. We have also found that the more personal and meaningful the goal is to the employee, the more likely they are to achieve it.

Reality: Once the goal has been set, it is important to also get a clear picture of where the employee is now in relation to the goal. This is typically done by the leader asking questions to help raise awareness and deepen the understanding of the present situation.

Obstacles or Options: Different versions of the GROW model may emphasize one or the other, but it is helpful to include both once the goal has been clarified and the present reality is known. The questions posed while clarifying the reality often lead naturally to identifying obstacles getting in the way. What's making goal achievement difficult? Once the obstacles are known, the conversation shifts to thinking about the options to remove, reduce, or work around the obstacles. What is a different way to think about the challenges? What new choices could be made or actions taken? This is the time to brainstorm ideas with the employee and to help them see that there ARE options.

Will or Way Forward: As the leader and employee work through the obstacles and options, what does and does not work becomes more clear. Now the employee makes a commitment ("Here's what I will do ...") based on one or more of the options identified and lays out a path to get there ("Here's my plan of action ...").

The use of the GROW technique might look something like this:

Imagine that Ric has become increasingly frustrated with his sales calls—he seems able to close easily most of the time, but in some situations he gets nowhere with a potential client. His district leader, Justin, sits down with him to coach him through to an actionable plan. They start with Justin asking some goal-oriented questions: What leads you to think you need to increase your sales? What do you want to most change? What's your ideal outcome? What will happen if you do not achieve your goal? From this conversation they create a S.M.A.R.T. goal: Ric will increase his closings by 12% by the end of the year. Now Justin poses new questions and listens carefully to help them both get a clear picture of what the present reality is. What is your closing rate now? How does this compare with others on your team? How have you tried to improve your sales? What products do you close most easily? What type of customer is most challenging? What do you notice you do differently with customers who buy and those who don't?

Once they have a clear picture of what is currently happening, they focus on what's making it difficult for Ric to close. Again, Justin asks more questions in order to help Ric think this through in terms of his obstacles and his options. What makes it most difficult for you to close? What resources do you need but do not have? How do you correct yourself if you get off track? What has worked in the past? What if you did x rather than y? Who could provide more support? What is another way to approach your prospects? Finally, they consider what Ric can and will commit to and his plan for moving forward. What can your team do to support you? What will you do next? What motivates you to hit this goal? If x happens, what will you do? What actions do you most (or least) want to take? What might stop you from moving forward, and how will you overcome this? When should we talk again?

It will be important for both Ric and Justin to set a date when they can meet again to talk about Ric's progress and review his action plan to see what is working, what isn't, and what adjustments need to be made.

As you think about this scenario (and others that come to mind), note that Justin spends much of his time asking questions rather than simply telling Ric what to do. Perhaps the most important skills for a leader are the ability to ask good questions and to actively listen to what the employee is saying.

The Coaching Conversation

We spoke earlier of the coaching mindset and our commitment to the development of employees so they can be their best selves at work. When we enter into a coaching conversation, that mindset must be front and center; we must be clear as to our purpose and just who we need to be in this conversation. Am I a teacher or an adviser? A challenger? A thinking partner? A sounding board?

There is no single right way to coach, but within the GROW model or other coaching models, there is one constant: the most effective coaching occurs in conversation by asking powerful questions and actively listening. This is what an inquiry-based approach is all about. Gallup management consultants Kar and Watkinson (2021) describe it this way:

> Coaching starts with *asking more and telling less* [original emphasis]—becoming more inquisitive about employees as human beings. What do employees need? What are their strengths? What are their goals? The best coaches display a genuine interest in the individual by asking coach-like questions on a regular basis. For example, in a 10-minute conversation, a manager might ask an employee, "What's going well for you today (and what isn't)? How can I best support you?" Then, the best coaches listen to understand. They listen to truly comprehend employees' circumstances, goals, challenges and needs.

Active Listening

Listening actively—on purpose and with intention—is a core skill for every effective leader. As first described by Rogers and Farson (1987), active listening is key to fostering change in others. People who have been actively listened to are generally less defensive and more open to new ideas and ways of thinking. They also tend to listen to themselves and work to be very clear concerning what they are thinking and feeling (1987).

When we listen actively rather than passively, we intentionally remove distractions so we can focus on listening. That means setting aside a report we might be reading, an email we were writing, or some problem we were mentally working through. Instead, we intentionally turn our attention to the speaker in ways the speaker will recognize, such as through our eye contact and body language. We pay attention to not just the words someone is speaking but also to the nonverbals like the speaker's tone, pace, emotion, and body language. As an active listener, our goal is to understand what the other person is saying, feeling, and thinking rather than planning what we want to say next (as so often happens in conversation).

Active listening also involves responding to the speaker to show our understanding. Typically, this means raising questions to draw the speaker out and paraphrasing what the speaker has said to check that we have understood correctly. This gives the other person the chance to either correct our understanding or to confirm it. Our purpose with active listening is to fully grasp what the person is communicating to us—to see things from his or her point of view. Doing so opens the door to further inquiry and honest, two-way dialogue. In this way, quality listening becomes an interaction between the listener and speaker rather than passively hearing a person's words.

BOX 8.4 **Critical Thinking: What Great Listeners Do**

Below are just a few of the actions that great listeners take. Which of these describe how you listen, and which would you like to strengthen?

1. Prepare to listen (physically, cognitively, and emotionally).
2. Clear away distractions.
3. Create a safe (nonintimidating) environment/put the speaker at ease.
4. Ask questions that promote discovery, insight, and understanding.
5. Show that they are listening.
6. Ensure feedback flows in both directions.
7. Listen for emotion; empathize.
8. Recognize and set aside personal assumptions, preconceptions, and biases.
9. Defer judgment.
10. Signal encouragement.
11. Summarize/paraphrase/check for understanding.
12. Show interest.
13. Exercise patience and avoid interruption.
14. Listen to get the whole picture.
15. Evaluate information prior to responding.

Think about specific times you have felt really listened to. How did this affect you as the speaker?
Think of a time when you felt you were not being listened to or heard. How did this affect you as the speaker?
Based on your experiences, how does the quality of listening impact our conversations?
How might your conversations change by increasing your active listening?

Asking Powerful Questions

In addition to active listening, effective coaching also calls for powerful questions. A great many leaders will tell you this: when it comes to developing others through coaching, it's more about the questions than the answers. When joined with active listening, a powerful question asked at just the right time can lead an employee to new insights, new possibilities, and a new way forward. A leader's questions, though, should not take the form of an interrogation. Rather, a leader poses questions that encourage reflection, insight, and discovery, and gives the employee time to really think before responding.

Coaching questions most often are open-ended rather than closed-ended. A closed-ended question is one that can be answered with a simple "yes" or "no" or which requires a brief, factual response. For example, "Did you complete the project?" "What time will you get here?" or "Which form did you use?" are all closed-ended questions. Sometimes those are necessary and useful. Closed-ended questions by themselves, though, do not encourage thoughtful reflection, and that is where open-ended questions come in.

Open-ended questions require a longer, more subjective response based on a person's opinions, ideas, explanations, and perspectives. These questions generate discussion and discovery and call for a more elaborate response than closed questions do. For instance, "What will success look like?" "How will you mark your progress?" and "Why is this goal important to you?" are all open-ended questions. Be cautious about using "Why?" questions, however, especially if the question starts with "Why did you ...?" Questions that begin with "why" can easily lead someone to think they must defend a choice that they made. Rather than ask, for example, why someone did x rather than y, it can be more helpful to say, "Tell me about your thinking when ..."

When having a more structured coaching conversation, we might plan our questions in a sequential way. This is often useful when applying the GROW model. Using GROW, a leader will start by asking goal-oriented questions, then shift to questions designed to gain clarity on the present reality. Once the reality has been fully understood and examined, the leader will begin asking questions to identify both the obstacles and/or the options, then end with questions to draw out the way forward.

With a more spontaneous coaching conversation, the questions may be less sequential but typically still follow a format that moves from "where do we want to go" regarding an issue to "how do we get there." Coaching conversations in general focus on some aspect of change, and many leaders find it helpful to frame their questions around the change—what is driving the desire for change, why that's important, what choices are made or actions taken, and/or how we will sustain the change.

Remember that a leader's focus is on furthering the development of the person or team being coached, and that we take an appreciative rather than deficit approach to doing so. It's less about what is wrong and more about how we together create the desired future. Use questions that stimulate reflection and personal insight and that encourage critical thinking and problem solving.

BOX 8.5 Sample Questions for the Coaching Conversation

A coaching leader makes minimal use of directives and instead engages in conversation to foster change and development. Here are some suggested questions. Many more can be found online:

What drives you? What is important to you? Leaders uncover what is important to their staff in order to improve performance and align their efforts with the organization's vision and direction.

- What do you want in this project/your career/this position that you don't currently have?
- What do you want to be doing that you aren't currently doing?
- What are you doing now that you don't want to be doing?
- What areas do you want to strengthen, improve, or develop?
- What are the three most important things you would like to accomplish right now?

What is the problem? Why is change important? It's often difficult for us to identify a meaningful need for change, since we often ignore information that threatens the status quo or challenges our current perceptions. Coaches can help reveal the blind spots by encouraging self-reflection.

- As you think about your goal, what's not working well?
- What are the consequences of this issue for you and for the other people involved?
- Looking ahead, what will happen if you don't change?
- What is making it difficult for you to accomplish what you want to accomplish?
- What do you want to do differently next time?

What's your decision? What action(s) do you choose to take? This is a crucial moment because it marks the point when you begin to see different possibilities ahead. Commitment and focused effort are required to do something new and make it stick.

- What have you decided to do differently, and why?
- What exactly will you do, and when will you do it?
- How will you measure progress—what will be happening to tell you that you are making progress?
- What stands in the way or may make change difficult, and how will you overcome these barriers?
- What if this is harder than you think?

How do we sustain change? Encouragement builds momentum, and coaches should provide frequent reinforcement and celebrate successes to bolster confidence and help avoid slipping back into old patterns.

- What impact has your new behavior had on you and others?
- What accomplishments are you proud of achieving?
- What might be a step to help you build momentum?
- As your coach, how can I reinforce your commitment to action?
- What additional support would help you strengthen your resolve?

Summary

The coaching approach to leadership has the potential to transform learning and workplace relationships (Whitmore, 2017). Coaching is a mindset, a process, and a partnership involving straight talk with employees and a committed desire to help others see something they didn't before. A leader makes sure that each person leaves the coaching conversation with greater clarity and a path forward for taking action. Masterful coach Robert Hargrove describes a coach's fundamental question in this way: what's missing that, if provided, will make a difference (2008)?

While there is no set formula for how to do it "right," we do know that employee coaching occurs over time. It may occur in scheduled meetings or by taking advantage of coachable moments as leaders observe others in action. The leader fills multiple roles, depending on the situation and employee or team. Sometimes they may teach or advise, while other times they may be a needed thinking partner or reality checker. Regardless of the situation, open communication and a give-and-take between leader and employee are required. The leader's commitment to meaningful growth and development is always at the forefront. As a coach, the leader encourages employees to develop a plan of action to which they can commit, and not telling the employee how the leader thinks things should be done.

Coaching is highly individualized, and how a leader coaches one employee may look different from how he or she coaches another simply because each employee is different. Regardless of method or style, active listening is a core skill, and the most effective coaches recognize its value. A coach guides the employee by asking powerful, open-ended questions, becoming more directive only when employees are stuck.

In this way, the leader not only fosters high performance but also promotes high morale and satisfaction by building relationships characterized by trust and respect. Through focused reflection, employees also enhance their own critical thinking and problem-solving skills.

BOX 8.6 **Seven Common Coaching Mistakes**

The leader fosters collaboration, open communication, trust, and respect for others as they work toward meaningful growth and development of their followers. We can reduce unnecessary frustration by staying aware of these common coaching mistakes:

#1 – Don't Rock the Boat: Too many people assume that the best way to build strong relationships is to keep quiet, keep your head down and eyes closed. The worst thing you can do when you have a concern is to let it fester. Instead, ask, talk, and engage people in the spirit of inquiry and understanding.

#2 – Delay: Some leaders put off a coaching conversation by saying to themselves, "I will make a move at the right moment when I am not so busy," as if there will be an ideal time to talk. As a result, we do more damage as we wait for this magical moment to appear. Budget time to talk with people, to explore situations, and to find solutions.

#3 - Dump: Many leaders "save up" coaching topics until the list of topics is long and the leader dumps it all at once. When you dump, people react defensively or shut down completely. It's better to be selective and focused with conversation topics rather than comprehensive. People appreciate talking about one or two issues at a time. Don't swamp them with too many suggestions and changes.

#4 - Dominate: Too many managers inadvertently dominate coaching discussions by simply talking too much. We mistakenly believe that we have more to say, more expertise, and more wisdom. Plan ahead. Rehearse your thoughts. If you spend more than 55% of the time talking, you are overstepping the boundaries.

#5 - Prescribe: Many of us take pride in our expertise and feel that we have a lot to offer, that we know what is best. But management coaching is about guiding rather than dictating. Ask questions before you start advocating. Find out what the other person knows and what solutions they have in mind.

#6 - Attack: When an employee feels attacked, he or she will simply cover up, deflect responsibility, or withdraw. People cease acting like the creative, empowered contributors we want to have. When you attack, you make the issue personal rather than objective. Step back to look at all the factors—usually serious problems have many roots. Look, too, for your own contribution to the situation. This will help defuse the fireworks.

#7 - Denial: It is easier to see the faults and needs of others than to identify them in ourselves; we create a "self-serving bias." Encourage and seek out feedback from others. If leaders model a willingness to develop and improve, others around will also. Be open, up-front, and candid. Don't get defensive if others see your own shortcomings. Thank them for their openness and willingness to speak up.

(Source: Adapted from Stowell, n.d.)

Application

1. Pair up with a peer (or a work colleague) to have a coaching conversation. Decide who will be the coach and who is the one being coached. That person will tell the coach of a change they a) want to make; b) are in the process of making; or c) have recently made. The coach, then, will select questions appropriate to the situation the coached has described (you may use some of the GROW questions or see Textbox 8.5). Remember that, as a coach, your purpose is to help the other person clarify their direction and create a path forward.

   When coaching, challenge yourself to ONLY ask questions—do not offer advice or tell stories from your own experiences.

   After 10 minutes of coaching, reverse roles so each partner has a chance to be the coach.

   Reflection questions:

   a. When you were the coach, how easy or difficult was it for you to only ask questions rather than to give advice or share your own stories?
   b. In what ways, if any, would your coaching conversation be different if the coach had immediately started to give advice rather than ask questions?
   c. What other takeaways do you have from this exercise?

2. Conduct an information search to discover more coaching questions. Which questions do you find most powerful, and why?
3. Imagine that your colleague Derrick, a middle manager like you, has come to you for help. He is struggling with how to boost the performance of one of his team members, Sarah. Since joining his team last year she has been one of his top performers but so far this year her performance has dropped and her morale seems to be deteriorating. Derrick describes, "I've talked with Sarah several times now about the importance of stepping up her game, and even warned her that her job could be at stake, but so far nothing has worked."
   a. What recommendations would you give to Derrick to help him move from telling Sarah what to do to more of a coaching approach?
   b. How would you approach this conversation with Derrick, and why?

Here are just a few additional resources you may find helpful online:

International Coach Federation (ICF): http://www.coachfederation.org

- This is a nonprofit organization formed by professionals who practice coaching, including executive coaches, leadership coaches, life coaches, and many more from around the world. The ICF is the leading global organization, with over 18,000 members, dedicated to advancing the coaching profession.

Peer Resources: http://www.peer.ca/bestcoachsites.html

- Peer Resources provides a great list and description of online resources for coaches. Includes general information, virtual assistants, assessments, and more.

Top Coaching Blogs: http://www.ekgclasses.org/100-best-life-and-career-coach-blogs

- Links to many of the top coaching blogs on the internet.

Box of Crayons: http://www.boxofcrayons.biz

- Master coach Michael Bungay Stanier's website is full of good resources, all with a focus on helping others do more "Great Work."

References

Bass, B. (1996). *A new paradigm of leadership: An inquiry into transformational leadership.* U.S. Army Research Institute for the Behavioral and Social Sciences.

Blanchard, K. H., Zigarmi, D., & Zigarmi, P. (1985). *Leadership and the one-minute manager: Increasing effectiveness through situational leadership II.* William Morrow.

Bozer, G., & Jones, R. J. (2018). Understanding the factors that determine workplace coaching effectiveness: A systematic literature review. *European Journal of Work and Organizational Psychology, 27*(3), 342–361. doi: 10.1080/1359432X.2018.1446946

Business Coaching Industry in the US: Market research report (June 2022). IBISWorld. https://www.ibisworld.com/united-states/market-research-reports/business-coaching-industry/

Center for Creative Leadership (November 2020). *Your organization should consider these 4 types of coaching.* https://www.ccl.org/articles/leading-effectively-articles/4-types-of-coaching/

Dennis, H. (March 1, 2022). A 4-step framework for creating a coaching culture. *Training Industry.* https://trainingindustry.com/articles/strategy-alignment-and-planning/a-4-step-framework-for-creating-a-coaching-culture/#:~:text=A%20coaching%20culture%20exists%20when,a%20supportive%20high%2Dperformance%20environment

Grint, K. (2020). Leadership, management and command in the time of the Coronavirus. *Leadership, 16*(3), 314–319. doi: 10.1177/1742715020922445

GROW model questions: 60 questions to enable employee growth (n.d.). Personio. https://www.personio.com/hr-lexicon/grow-model-questions/

Hargrove, R. (2008). *Masterful coaching* (3rd ed.). John Wiley & Sons/Pfeiffer.

Hersey, P. (1984). *The situational leader.* Center for Leadership Studies.

Ibarra, H., & Scoular, A. (November-December 2019). *The leader as coach: How to unleash innovation, energy, and commitment.* Harvard Business Review. https://hbr.org/2019/11/the-leader-as-coach

International Coaching Federation (2020). *ICF team coaching competencies: Moving beyond one-to-one coaching.* https://coachingfederation.org/app/uploads/2021/10/Team-Coaching-Competencies_10.4.21.pdf

International Coaching Federation (n.d.). *About ICF: Leading the global advancement of coaching.* Retrieved November 13, 2022, from https://coachingfederation.org/about

Kamarudin, M., Kamarudin, A. Y., Darmi, R., & Saazai, N. (June 2020). A review of coaching and mentoring theories and models. *International Journal of Academic Research in Progressive Education and Development 9*(2): 289–298. doi:10.6007/IJARPED/v9-i2/7302

Kar, R., & Watkinson, A. (September 24, 2021). *Don't overcomplicate the best management practice: Coaching.* Gallup Workplace. https://www.gallup.com/workplace/354758/don-overcomplicate-best-management-practice-coaching.

aspx?gclid=Cj0KCQiA37KbBhDgARIsAIzce16lUGMQwL6PMpFhi-tM_d53qx5TwFc3DeLHNqh6lVjgljvBHS__B6EaApVeEALw_wcB

Nerland, D., & Goh, A. (February 2021). Why command and control managers are obsolete. Medium. https://nerland.medium.com/why-command-and-control-managers-are-obsolete-62b9a6de2311

Oettingen, G. (2015). *Rethinking positive thinking: Inside the new science of motivation*. Current.

Parsloe, E., & Wray, M. J. (2000). *Coaching and mentoring: Practical methods to improve learning.* Kogan Page.

Rosenthal, R., & Jacobson, L. (1968). *Pygmalion in the classroom: Teacher expectation and pupils' intellectual development*. Crown House.

Rogers, C. R., & Farson, R. E. (1987). *Communicating in business today.* D. C. Heath.

Stanier, M. B. (2116). *The coaching habit: Say less, ask more & change the way you lead forever.* Page Two Books.

Stowell, S. J. (n.d.). How to avoid 7 common management coaching mistakes. Center for Management & Organization Effectiveness. https://cmoe.com/how-to-avoid-coaching-mistakes/

Theeboom, T., Beersma, B., & van Vianen, A. (September 2013). Does coaching work? A meta-analysis on the effects of coaching on individual level outcomes in an organizational context. *The Journal of Positive Psychology, 9*(1), 1–18. doi: 10.1080/17439760.2013.837499

Verlinden, N. (n.d.). *Peer coaching: Benefits and best practices.* Academy to Innovate HR. https://www.aihr.com/blog/peer-coaching/#:~:text=is%20peer%20coaching%3F-,A%20definition,workplace%20(Robbins%2C1991

Wheatley, M. (July 1997). Goodbye, command and control. *Leader to Leader, 5*(3), 21–28.

Whitmore, J. (2017). *Coaching for performance: GROWing human potential and purpose: The principles and practice of coaching and leadership* (5th ed.). Nicholas Brealey.

Williams, P. (n.d.). The theoretical foundations of coaching. *Choice* 4(2).

CHAPTER 9

Influence

By Robin Lindbeck

The key to successful leadership today is influence, not authority.

—Ken Blanchard

Learning Objectives

After reading this chapter, students will be able to:

1. Describe the importance of a leader's effective influence in the workplace
2. Describe the influence process
3. Create a clarity message
4. Plan and conduct an influence conversation

Introduction to Influence

In his book *To Sell Is Human* (2012), Daniel Pink states that 40% of your day is spent influencing others; and if you are in sales, it is even higher. It is likely that leaders also spend more than 40% of their day influencing others. Why? Because "leadership is intentional influence" (Grenny et al., 2023, p. 5). The role of a leader is to support and develop employees to increase their engagement and success and to meet the goals for the organization.

> Leadership is about mobilizing *others* to achieve the vision, challenge the status quo, build breakthrough products, and execute flawlessly on lofty plans ... True leaders possess the repeatable capacity to influence rapid, profound, and sustainable behavior change to produce valued results. (Grenny et al., p. 6)

In this chapter, we will learn how to influence others, to help them and the organization be as effective and successful as possible.

What Is Influence?

At its most basic, influence is the ability "to affect or change how someone or something develops, behaves, or thinks" (Cambridge Dictionary). Others say that influence answers two questions: "1. Why are they doing *that*? 2. How can I help them do *this* instead?" (Grenny et al., 2023, p. 5). That influence is "a negotiating and learning process through which a persuader leads colleagues to a problem's shared solution ... moving people to a position they don't currently hold, but not by begging or cajoling ... by careful preparation, the proper framing of arguments, the presentation of vivid supporting evidence, and the effort to find the correct emotional match with your audience" (Conger, 1998, p. 86). And that the three outcomes of influence attempts are: resistance, in which the individual is opposed to the influence attempt; compliance, in which the individual accepts the influence behavior with minimal effort; and commitment, in which the individual agrees with the influence and is enthusiastic in the influence behavior (Yukl, 2006). Using these definitions and adding context for the workplace, a working definition of influence in the workplace is:

> Influence in the workplace is the ability to create a strategy and conversation to persuade, minimize resistance, and gain commitment from others to develop and change, in order to accomplish organizational goals and objectives.

BOX 9.1 **What Is Persuasive to You?**

Think about a time someone influenced you to do something different or to adopt a different point of view.

1. Briefly describe the situation, the roles of the influencer and you, and on what they wanted to persuade you.
2. What did they do or say that was persuasive to you? Why?
3. What did they do or say that was *not* persuasive to you? Why?
4. What was the outcome of the influence attempt? How did you feel?

BOX 9.2 **Influence vs. Manipulation**

Some people influence with no plan. They try something to influence and if it works, they are happy but may not be sure exactly why it worked. Effective influence involves deliberate planning, including considering, what you are influencing on, what you know about the individuals you are influencing, and determining the most effective influence approach for them. This amount of planning for influencing may seem manipulative to people who do not plan their influence. Let's look at the difference between manipulation and influence.

> Manipulation is persuading people (often in an unscrupulous way) to do something they would not ordinarily do and from which they get no benefit.
>
> Influence is persuading people to do something they would not ordinarily do and from which they get benefit.

The difference between manipulation and influence is the intention of the influencer and the impact on the individual being influenced. With manipulation, the influencer often has as a goal to benefit themselves with no benefit for the individual. With influence, the influencer is trying to make the individual more successful and capable in order to benefit the individual.

Considerations for Influence

How can a leader effectively influence? Often, people influence from a position of power. French and Raven (1959) describe five types of power in organizations: legitimate or positional power, rewarding power, coercive or punishing power, expert or expertise power, and referent or status power (Lunenburg, 2012; Yukl, 2006). Leaders can take a coercive or command-and-control approach to changing the behavior of people in the workplace to get compliant behavior; but to engage individuals and influence them to be committed to a new direction, a more robust approach to influence is required (Kaiser et al., 2012). Researchers and practitioners have developed recommendations to consider when influencing. Below is a selection of these recommendations.

Researchers Laker & Patel (2020) conducted a meta-analysis of literature on influence and leaders and identified two approaches to influence: transactional influence and transformational influence:

> The first approach—transaction—emphasizes actual, actionable transactions between a leader and their subordinates. It focuses on improving an immediate situation by determining the steps that need to be taken in the short term. In the second approach—transformation—leaders act as role models and motivators who offer vision, excitement, encouragement, morale boost, and satisfaction to the followers. (para 6)

This meta-analysis, and follow-up interviews with 1,000 leaders, led them to four recommendations for influencing: build rapport with the people you want to influence, become an active listener rather than a transmitter, commit to your team (sharing your vision for success and why it is important), be focused, and set an excellent example (Laker & Patel, 2020, para. 16–19).

Conger (1998) interviewed managers known for their outstanding influence and identified four steps for persuasion: establish credibility, frame goals for common ground, provide evidence, connect emotionally (pp. 87–88).

In their book *Critical Influence* (2023), Grenny et al. recommend a three-step approach to influencing: begin with a "focus on results" (p. 19) and be able to clearly articulate those results; identify the new "vital behaviors" (p. 20) individuals need to embrace to accomplish the results; and use six sources of influence to persuade the individual to embrace the vital behaviors. The six sources of influence consider the motivation and ability of the individual, the people around them, and the non-people influences that might help or hinder the adoption of the new behaviors (pp. 36–39).

In his book *Influence* (2021), Robert Cialdini highlights the importance of including the reason *why* during the influence attempt and describes six principles of persuasion: liking, reciprocity, social proof, commitment and consistency, authority, and scarcity.

Glass (2018), a member of the Forbes Coaches Council, recommends five principles for influencing others: influence is a persuasive process and does not happen all at once; influence is a product of trust; when people feel heard, they're more open to being influenced; influence requires persuasively communicating; and influence isn't about winning, it's about solving problems.

Looking across these five approaches to influence, we can identify common themes for influencing:

- Influence is a process with multiple elements, conversations, and ideas to consider while influencing.
- Influence is about relationships and the people, not just the outcome. It is important to develop trust and rapport, a focus on the individual, and empathy for their concerns and questions.
- Influence is a balance of providing leadership, commitment, and consistency with the influence attempt while being open to the individual's concerns, ideas, and suggestions.
- Influence is a conversation (multiple conversations). This requires effective communication skills and emotional intelligence, including active listening, questioning, and clear communications. These conversations are the chance to describe the behavior change, why it is important, the benefits for the individual and the organization, and to share evidence and examples. It is a time to raise and address questions and concerns, identify ideas, and whenever possible, cocreate a shared solution for how to get to the desired behavior.

How to Use Influence in the Workplace

Influence Process

Using the information from the previous section, we can create a process for influencing that identifies the stages of influence and the three outcomes of resistance, compliance, and commitment.

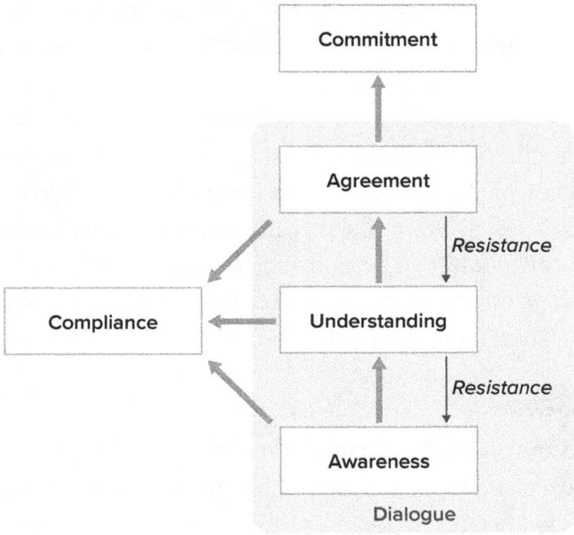

FIGURE 9.1 The Influence Process Model

Possible Outcomes of Influence

Resistance. Resistance describes an outcome in which the individual is actively opposed to the influence attempt (Yukl, 2006, p. 147). Leaders may be tempted to give up on the influence attempt at this point because the individual is actively disagreeing with you. Active resistance is the second-best thing that can happen during an influence attempt. The best thing that can happen is if the individual is easily influenced and committed. But if they actively resist you, they are *active*. This is, in effect, the individual saying to you, "I don't yet understand. Please help me understand." It is an invitation to engage in a conversation to probe to understand why they are resistant, provide more information, and continue the dialogue until they, and you, can move forward in the influencing conversation. As you see in the Influence Process Model (Figure 9.1), resistance will prevent you from moving forward and may move you backward in the process.

Compliance. Compliance describes an outcome in which the individual is willing to do what is asked (Yukl, 2006, p. 147). Compliance is generally a transactional process (Laker & Patel, 2020) that includes a consequence for the behavior: either a positive consequence (reward) for doing the behavior or a negative consequence (punishment) for not doing the behavior (a carrot or a stick). When compliance is the outcome, it is the consequence that is persuasive more than the influence conversation. Compliance-based performance is less robust than commitment-based performance because the individual is doing the behavior because of the positive or negative consequence and because they may lack sufficient information to fully engage in the performance. For example, a leader may attempt to influence by saying, "I know you are busy, but corporate needs you to write a new marketing plan before end of day Friday or you will have to work all weekend to get it done." The individual may be compliant because they do not want to work all weekend (negative consequence), but they may work grudgingly and may not have sufficient information to successfully complete the marketing plan.

Because compliant performance relies on positive or negative consequence and the individual may lack sufficient information to address variations in the performance, the performance may need to be monitored more closely for effectiveness. Repeated feedback may be needed to sustain the performance. Consequences for compliant behavior may lose potency over time and require "bigger carrots and bigger sticks" to maintain the persuasion. For example, if sales teams are influenced to exceed sales targets by 20% so they can qualify for a trip to Las Vegas, after several years a Las Vegas trip may not be a sufficient reward for the behavior. The reward of the trip may need to be increased to a cruise, then a trip to Europe, then a trip to Africa to continue to motivate the compliant behavior.

Commitment. Commitment describes an outcome in which the individual internally agrees with an influence request (Yukl, 2006, p. 147). Because the individual internally agrees with the influence request, they engage in the behavior because they know what it is, they understand why it is necessary or important, and they agree with the new behavior. They engage in the behavior whether or not there is a positive or negative consequence. Committed behavior is transformational (Laker & Patel, 2020) and individuals engage in the behavior because it makes sense to them and they believe and have bought in to the fact that this is what is needed.

Committed behavior tends to be more robust behavior because the individual has sufficient information, understanding, and engagement to effectively perform and to navigate unanticipated events when they come up. Committed behavior also requires less monitoring and reinforcement from the leader because the individual has sufficient information, understanding, and engagement to effectively perform. Of course, all individuals *need* monitoring, feedback, and coaching to be as successful as possible, but committed behavior does not need the same constant monitoring and feedback to sustain the performance that is needed to sustain compliant behavior.

Stages of the Influence Process

Awareness. This is the *what* of the influence attempt. During this stage, you describe the situation and what needs to happen. It is possible for an individual to go from awareness to compliance; you tell the individual what needs to happen and then provide a positive or negative consequence to persuade them. For example, "You need to complete the annual security awareness training by the end of the week or your name goes on a list with HR." The individual knows what they need to do, but not necessarily why they need to do it. They will likely do it because of the potential negative consequence of having their name on a list with HR. It is not possible to go from awareness to commitment because the individual does not have enough information to understand and agree with the influence. This stage may or may not include a dialogue and will be the lowest level of performance because the individual only knows *what* needs to happen. The behavior is sustained because of the positive or negative consequence.

Understanding. This adds the *why* to the influence attempt. During this stage, you describe why the influence behavior needs to happen. As Conger says, "work today gets done in an environment where people don't just ask what should I do? But why should I do it?" (1998, pp. 85–86). This stage requires dialogue for the individual to understand the why of the influence. This might include why this behavior or event needs to happen, why the behavior is required, why you need to change your behavior, why the timeline is what it is, why we do or do not have input on this, or any other why that is relevant to the influence attempt. During this stage of the influence process, you will ask questions to check for understanding, probe for questions and concerns, address the concerns, and then continue checking for understanding, and probing for questions and concerns until the individual understands the why of the influence. This stage results in compliance. This compliant behavior has the potential to be more robust than behavior that goes from awareness to compliance because the individual understands the what *and* the why of the influence. It is not possible to go from understanding to commitment. The behavior is sustained because of the positive/negative consequences.

Agreement. This adds agreement and acceptance of the behavior or influence by the individual. During this stage, you continue the dialogue. During that dialogue, you continue questioning, raising and addressing concerns, compromising and recreating actions, timeline, resources, etc. The result of this stage is that the individual agrees with and accepts the influence and adopts and embraces the behavior. The outcome of this stage can be compliance or commitment. If compliance, it potentially represents the highest level of compliant performance because the individual knows what, why, and is in agreement. But if the influence is ultimately because of a positive or negative consequence, it is compliant behavior. If the outcome is commitment, the individual is motivated to continue the robust, high-quality behavior because they agree with the influence and will continue the behavior whether or not a consequence is in place. For example, Paulo has several influence conversations with Laura about a new monthly report that needs to be created for the sales teams to provide information that will help them follow up with existing customers and has the potential to increase sales by 25% each quarter. This report will add a significant amount of work to Laura each month. After several rich conversations to align Laura on the what and why of this project, Paulo and Laura together create changes in her workload and schedule that make creating the report doable for Laura. Is Laura compliant or committed? Her level of performance may be the same in both instances. If she is compliant, she will stop generating the report as soon as the sales team stops asking for it. If she is committed, she may continue generating the report and attempt to influence the sales team because she is committed to the value of this information for the sales team and the impact it can have on the organization.

BOX 9.3 **Influencing to Compliance vs. Commitment**

If committed behavior gives us the most robust performance, should we always have commitment as the desired outcome for our influence attempts? Not necessarily. It's a question of time spent versus desired performance.

Influencing someone to commitment has the potential for more robust performance that requires less monitoring and reinforcement to sustain the behavior but takes more time. Influencing someone to compliance will likely have less robust and informed performance and will take more monitoring and reinforcement to sustain the performance but can be faster to influence the individual to compliance. As a leader, time is a finite resource that you need to manage strategically. It is up to you as a leader to decide which influence attempts require commitment and need the time spent influencing individuals to commitment; which influence attempts are sufficient with compliant behavior will take less time.

For example, if you need everyone to complete their annual appraisals by a particular date, you may decide compliant behavior is sufficient. They need to know what to do, why they need to do it; and then just do it with the negative consequence that if they don't do it, they will not be eligible for a raise. Although it would be optimal if they were committed to completing the annual performance appraisal, by influencing them to compliance you get sufficient behavior and save some time that you can use to influence them to commitment on other behaviors.

BOX 9.4 **Enthusiastic Compliance vs. Commitment**

The only way to gain commitment and sustained, high-quality performance over time, is to go through the awareness, understanding, and agreement stages. But it is possible to jump to what might seem like "instant commitment" without going through the three stages of the influence process. Because compliance is often less robust behavior, we may associate effective behavior and enthusiasm only with commitment. However, it is possible to have enthusiastic compliance with robust behavior if there is a positive or negative consequence that is particularly meaningful for us.

Example 1: Being influenced by a strong, value-related appeal

Imagine you have a personal value related to hunger and sufficient food for everyone. You are at a meeting and see a presentation on the impact of hunger on adults and children in your area, with a request for volunteers to work at a local food bank. Because you have a value of sufficient food for everyone, you are influenced to volunteer. You feel "committed" to volunteering. It is likely your behavior will be sustained because your values are serving as a strong positive/negative consequence for your enthusiastically compliant behavior for volunteering for the food bank. In this case, the influence is because of your values rather than the influence attempt made during the presentation. If your values (the consequence) change, it is likely you will not continue the volunteering behavior without going through awareness, understanding, and agreement.

Example 2: Being influenced by a personal relationship

Imagine Erica is your mentor at work. She has played an important role for you as an advice giver and sounding board over the last four years, and your conversations have had a positive impact on your development, your success, and your career. Erica calls you into her office and asks you to take on a new project. You immediately say yes. You are excited to do the project and anxious to get started. It is likely that you are enthusiastically compliant. In this case, the influence is because your relationship with Erica represents the positive or negative consequence that may sustain your performance. However, if the consequence is removed (Erica gets a job at a different company), it is likely your performance will no longer continue at the same level without going through awareness, understand, and agreement.

Example 3: Influencing yourself by doing

Imagine your manager assigned you to a project. She told you what to do (awareness) and the consequence of not doing it. You are compliant. However, as you continue to work on this project over time, you begin to understand why this project is important and the benefit to the customers of your company. Over time you see that this project needs to be done and agree it is important for your company. By participating in the project, you learned the *why* and the impact to the company along the way. You have moved from compliant (or enthusiastically compliant) to committed. You influenced yourself through your participation!

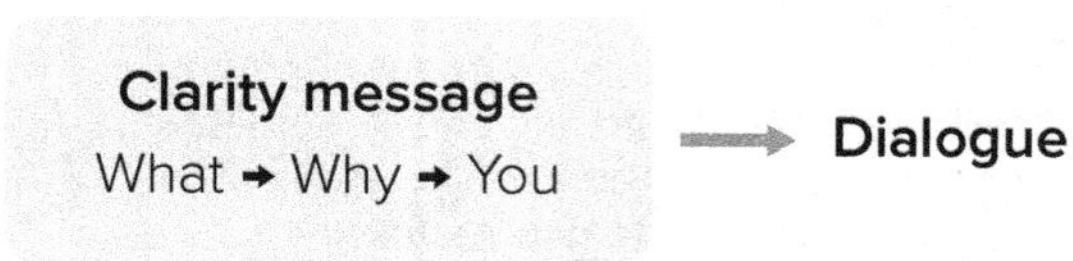

FIGURE 9.2 The Clarity Model

Creating a Clarity Message

Creating clarity is an essential skill for leaders. You need to create clarity in formal meetings. You need to create clarity in informal and "hallway" conversations. And you need to create clarity when influencing. Starting your influence attempt with a clarity message will provide a strong (and clear) foundation to your influence conversation.

The clarity model (Figure 9.2) has two parts: the clarity message and dialogue. The clarity message includes three components. The first component is to describe the *what*. The second component is to describe the *why*. And the third component is to describe the *you*. The *you* is the WIIFM, or the "what's-in-it-for-me" for the individual. Including the *you* adds relevance and makes the clarity message personal to the individual. The problem is that often when we are trying to give a WIIFM, we instead give a WIIFO: a what's-in-it-for-the-organization. And although people care about the organization, a WIIFM will be more impactful for them. After you deliver your clarity message (what-why-you), you can start a dialogue to check for understanding, uncover questions and concerns, etc. Creating a strong clarity message will get you started on the awareness and understand stages of the influence process.

BOX 9.5 **WIIFM vs. WIIFO**

It is often more natural to think of a WIIFO (what's in it for the organization) instead of a WIIFM (what's in it for me/the individual) because we are creating clarity on something that came from the organization. But a WIIFM is more impactful for the individual than a WIIFO.

Example with a WIIFO:

Everyone in the department needs to attend the annual sexual harassment prevention training. (What)

This will give all of us the information we need to understand what sexual harassment is, to avoid sexual harassment, and to know what we need to do if we see or experience sexual harassment. (Why)

The more we can avoid sexual harassment, the less chance that we will have lawsuits which can put the company's assets as risk. (WIIFO)

Example with a WIIFM:

Everyone in the department needs to attend the annual sexual harassment prevention training. (What)

This will give all of us the information we need to understand what sexual harassment is, to avoid sexual harassment, and to know what we need to do if we see or experience sexual harassment. (Why)

The more we can avoid sexual harassment, the less chance that we will have lawsuits which can hold you liable and put *your* assets at risk as well as the company's assets. (WIIFM)

With this small change of letting the individuals know that they can be held financially liable for sexual harassment, this changes from a WIIFO to a WIIFM (actually a combinate WIIFO and WIIFM). You can see that the WIIFM is a *why* that is more relevant to the individual than the WIIFO alone.

What if you can't think of what's in it for the individual? Keep thinking! Or ask yourself why you are planning to influence the individual on something that has no benefit for them and reconsider the influence attempt.

Influence Tactics

You have an influence process. You can create a clarity message. But what do you *say* to try to influence someone else? Most of us influence in a way that would be persuasive to *us*. It makes sense: if it's persuasive to us, we assume it will be persuasive to everyone else. The problem is that everyone else is not us, and for optimal influence effectiveness, we need to include influence strategies that work with us and influence strategies that do not work with us but that work with others. We need influence strategies that focus on the facts, and we need influence strategies that focus on the person and relationships. We need influence strategies that focus on us and the individual, and we need influence strategies that utilize others.

Yukl (2006, p. 166) identifies 11 influence tactics you can use during your influence attempts (Table 9.1). All of the influence tactics are effective depending on the situation and the individual; however, the four influence tactics identified as most effective most often for targeting commitment are rational persuasion, consultation, collaboration, and inspiration. Combining two or more influence tactics can be more effective than a single tactic, depending on the combination of tactics (pp. 173–174). Some of these influence tactics may be familiar and comfortable to you, and some of these may be tactics you never use. But *all* of these tactics are effective sometimes and can be part of your influencing tactics repertoire.

TABLE 9.1 **Yukl's 11 Influence Tactics**

Rational Persuasion	Using logical arguments and factual evidence to show a proposal or request is feasible and relevant to attaining important task objectives.
Apprising	Explaining how carrying out the request or supporting a proposal will benefit the individual.
Inspirational Appeals	Making an appeal to the values and ideas or arousing emotions to gain commitment for a request or proposal.
Consultation	Encouraging the individual to suggest improvements in a proposal or to help plan an activity for which the individual's support is desired.
Collaboration	Offer to provide relevant resources and assistance if the individual will carry out a request or approve a proposed change.
Ingratiation	Using praise and flattery before or during the influence or expressing confidence in the individual's ability to carry out the request.

(Continued)

TABLE 9.1 *(Continued)*

Personal Appeals	Asking the individual to carry out a request or support a proposal out of friendship or as a personal favor.
Exchange	Offering an incentive, exchange of favors, or willingness to reciprocate at a later time if the individual will carry out the request or support the proposal.
Coalition Tactics	Seeking the aid of others to persuade the individual to do something or using the support of others to get the individual to agree.
Legitimating Tactics	Seeking to establish the legitimacy of the request or verifying the authority to make it by referring to rules, policies, contracts, or precedent.
Pressure	Using demands, threats, frequent checking, or persistence reminders to influence the target to carry out a request.

BOX 9.6 **Influence Tactics and You**

Many of us do not use the full range of influence tactics. We have our "favorite" influence tactics that we use all the time (whether they are effective all the time or not) and the influence tactics we do not use. Consider the following:

1. Which one to three influence tactics do you use most often? For each of these influence tactics:
   a. What is the advantage of using this influence tactic? (On you, on the individual, on the influence attempt outcome?)
   b. What is the disadvantage of overusing this influence tactic? (On you, on the individual, on the influence attempt outcome?)
2. Which influence tactics do you seldom or never use?
   a. What is the disadvantage of not using this influence tactic? (On you, on the individual, on the influence attempt outcome?)

BOX 9.7 **Which Influence Tactics?**

Review the scenarios below and determine which influence tactic(s) you would use and why.

1. Due to the increasing emphasis on customer satisfaction, the hours of operation in your department are being expanded by 2 hours: 1 hour earlier in the morning and 1 hour later in the afternoon. You are about to meet with your team to discuss this change and would like half of your staff to start their day an hour earlier and the other half to end their day an hour later. Which influence tactic(s) will you use? Why?
2. One of your neighbors has invited you to a neighborhood meeting to discuss the annual 4th of July picnic. Last year's picnic was almost ruined when a child from the neighborhood was slightly injured by fireworks. You would like to see an emphasis on safety this year. At the upcoming meeting, which influence tactic(s) will you use to influence your neighbors? Why?
3. Your supervisor has sent a note to you and your teammates seeking a volunteer for an assignment. You are very interested in the assignment because it matches your skills and abilities perfectly, and it is in Hawaii. You are aware that several of your teammates would also like the assignment. You are

about to meet with your supervisor to express your interest. Which influence strategies will you use to influence your supervisor to select you for the assignment? Why?

4. Your supervisor has asked you to make a presentation to her peers about a highly successful quality control system you implemented in your department. The system is easily transferable to other functions, and an improvement in quality would help your division meet its customer satisfaction goals. Which influence tactic(s) will you use when you meet with your supervisor's peer group? Why?
5. A peer has asked for your input on a report she has written summarizing the completion of a project. The report concludes with a recommendation with which you disagree. You are about to meet with this peer and want to convince them that if this recommendation is approved, it would be detrimental to the department. Which influence tactic(s) will you most likely use? Why?
6. You are very excited to learn about a new deli featuring your favorite type of sandwich. You have a coworker who shares your fondness for these sandwiches, but she is usually so busy she skips lunch. You are about to pick up the phone to invite her to lunch. Which influence tactic(s) will you use to influence her to accept your invitation? Why?

[1] *Thanks to Dr. Caryn Staebler for her help creating these scenarios.*

Application

Now that you have learned about influencing, it is time to put it into practice.

1. Clarity: Identify someone with whom you need to have a clarity conversation.
   A. Create your clarity conversation. Be sure to include the What, Why, You.
   B. Have your clarity conversation.
   C. Write your reflections on the influence conversation.
      1. What went well?
      2. What went not so well? How will you improve on this for your next clarity conversation?
      3. What was the outcome of this clarity conversation?
      4. What will you continue to do in the future when creating clarity?
      5. Other reflections.
2. Influence and clarity: Identify a situation in which you want to influence someone.
   A. Plan your influence conversation. Consider:
      1. What is the outcome you want: compliance or commitment?
      2. What is the path you will take to get there? Awareness? Understanding? Agreement?
      3. Given the person you are trying to influence and your influence outcome, what do you need to consider in your approach influencing this person?

   B. Create your clarity message.
   C. Have your influence conversation (or your *first* influence conversation; it may take several conversations!).
   D. Write your reflections on the influence conversation.
      1. What went well?
      2. What went not so well? How will you improve on this for your next influence conversation?
      3. What was the outcome of the influence conversation?
      4. What will you continue to do when influencing?
      5. Other reflections.

3. Influence, clarity, influence tactics: Identify a situation in which you want to influence someone.
    A. Plan your influence conversation. Consider:
        1. What is the outcome you want: compliance or commitment?
        2. What is the path you will take to get there? Awareness? Understanding? Agreement?
        3. Given the person you are trying to influence and your influence outcome, what do you need to consider your approach influencing this person?
    B. Create your clarity message.
    C. Which influence tactic(s) will you use to begin this influence attempt?
    D. Have your influence conversation (or your *first* influence conversation; it may take several conversations!).
    E. Write your reflections on the influence conversation.
        1. What went well?
        2. What went not so well? How will you improve on this for your next influence conversation?
        3. What was the outcome of the influence conversation?
        4. What will you continue to do when influencing?

References

Cambridge Dictionary (n.d.). Influence. https://dictionary.cambridge.org/us/dictionary/english/influence

Cialdini, R. B. (2021). *Influence: The psychology of persuasion*. Harper Business.

Conger, J. A. (1998). The necessary art of persuasion. *Harvard Business Review, 76*(3), 84–95.

French, J., & Raven, B. H. (1959). The bases of social power. In D. Cartwright (Ed.), *Studies of social power* (pp. 150–167). Ann Arbor, MI: Institute for Social Research.

Glass, A. (October 5, 2018). Five principles to follow if you want to influence others. *Forbes Coaches Council*. https://www.forbes.com/sites/forbescoachescouncil/2018/10/05/five-principles-to-follow-if-you-want-to-influence-others/?sh=1b6d42cd6e29

Grenny, J., Patterson, K., Maxfield, D., McMillian, R., & Switzler, A. (2023). *Crucial influence: Leadership skills to create lasting behavior change* (3rd ed.). McGraw-Hill.

Kaiser, R. B., McGinnis, J. L., & Overfield, D. V. (2012). The how and the what of leadership. *Consulting Psychology Journal: Practice and Research, 64*(2), 119–135.

Laker, B., & Patel, C. (August 28, 2020). Strengthen your ability to influence people. Harvard Business Review. https://hbr.org/2020/08/strengthen-your-ability-to-influence-people

Lunenburg, F. C. (2012). Power and leadership: An influence process. *International Journal of Management, Business, and Administration, 15*(1), 1–9.

Pink, D. (2012). *To sell is human: The surprising truth about moving others*. Riverhead Books.

Smith, F. (February 5, 2021). 7 ways to influence other people. *Entrepreneur*. https://www.entrepreneur.com/leadership/7-ways-to-influence-other-people/361700

Yukl, G. (2006). *Leadership in organizations* (6th ed.). Pearson Prentice-Hall.

CHAPTER 10

Conflict Resolution

By Tracy Gibson

Every conflict we face in life is rich with positive and negative potential. It can be a source of inspiration, enlightenment, learning, transformation, and growth—or, rage, fear, shame, entrapment, and resistance. The choice is not up to our opponents but to us and our willingness to face and work through them.

—Cloke & Goldsmith, 2001

Learning Objectives

After reading this chapter, students will be able to:

1. Describe the importance of conflict resolution
2. Recognize what triggers a "threat" (or conflict) response in people and what are the physical and psychological responses
3. Describe assertive and cooperative behaviors to conflict and when to use
4. Identify skill sets for de-escalating and navigating conflict
5. Summarize the steps involved in a productive problem-solving conversation

Introduction to Conflict Resolution

Conflict is a social experience. Anytime you find yourself in disagreement with someone, you experience conflict. Conflict is "a critical mechanism by which we navigate the variety of personalities, goals, interests, and values in social interaction" (Oore et al., 2015, p. 306). Conflicting views, change, and disagreements are natural parts of our lives and the lives of every team and organization. Workplace conflicts can range from minor disagreements to more significant altercations. Conflict is inevitable due to intense social and relational interaction in organizations. You may be frustrated by a colleague failing to meet a deadline. You may need to facilitate a meeting between two department members or two departments. Alternatively, you may feel exhilarated by a brainstorming session with multiple opposing ideas being shared. Your ability to navigate conflict influences whether the result will be positive or negative, so good conflict resolution skills are essential.

Your Brain on Conflict: The Psychological and Neurological Response to Conflict

People tend to associate conflict primarily with negative emotions. Conflict often evokes an emotional response of threat or fear, and people say things like, "Oh, I avoid conflict at all costs," or "I hate the drama of conflict." An effective conflict resolution process is necessary to navigate conflict for organizational effectiveness. In the workplace, you experience both **functional and dysfunctional conflicts** (Menon et al., 1996). Functional conflict propels a workplace forward. It encourages people to be creative problem solvers and to develop a strategy and structure that supports innovation. Functional conflict leverages the benefits of diverse employees and groups. Diverse functional workgroups contribute to organizational effectiveness because they foster more diversity of thought, leading to more and better ideas in the workplace. Functional conflict encourages healthy competition, strengthens team participation, and bridges the communication gap. When conflict goes sideways, however, psychological and emotional effects often lead to low productivity and active disengagement. These are dysfunctional conflicts. It is important to note that how the conflicts are handled will determine the outcome as functional or dysfunctional.

Several common cognitive and emotional traps, many of them unconscious, can exacerbate conflict and contribute to the need for conflict resolution. We will examine three frameworks for understanding conflict: the first identifies the brain's response to conflict, the second is a framework for examining potential emotional traps of conflict, and the third is a framework for understanding "conflict styles"—how individuals tend to navigate conflict.

The first framework we will examine is the SCARF model. This comes from David Rock, from the Neuroscience Leadership Institute (2008). The SCARF model provides a framework for understanding **the five domains of human social experiences**. Using brain scan technology, David Rock (2008) and his team found that during our social experiences, five social domains activate. These five domains are **Status, Certainty, Autonomy, Relatedness, and Fairness (SCARF)** (Rock, 2008). These five areas can trigger a threat or reward response based on how we experience and interpret the situation. When we experience dysfunctional conflict, we often experience the threat response side of the SCARF model.

The drama triangle, developed by Stephen Karpman (1968), is the framework for identifying potential emotional traps. The drama triangle is a model of social interactions and illustrates a dysfunctional power game involving three roles: **Victim, Rescuer, and Persecutor**. Each role represents a point in the drama triangle and describes a common and ineffective response to conflict. Most people are neurologically programmed to play these three roles and often gravitate toward one of them when conflict begins. You enter the drama triangle when you take on one of these three roles. Once in the triangle, a person might switch roles as the conflict progresses, leading to other people changing roles (Lac & Donaldson, 2002). The journey around the triangle can be made with just yourself or another person, such as a spouse, child, coworker, etc.

A framework for resolving conflict is the Thomas-Kilmann Conflict Mode Instrument (TKI), created by researchers Kenneth Thomas and Ralph Kilmann (1974). Conflict occurs whenever people disagree. This model provides a way of keeping conflict functional instead of dysfunctional by helping people identify and use the best approach in response to conflict. This conflict management approach includes two dimensions: how assertive we are in meeting our needs and how cooperative we are in meeting the needs of others. The five conflict resolution strategies are **Competing, Avoiding, Accommodating, Collaborating, and Compromising** (Kilmann & Thomas, 1974). These five strategies represent different approaches to managing conflict with different strengths and weaknesses. The best approach depends on the specific circumstances at hand.

Successful leaders in the workplace need the skills to navigate conflict successfully and create environments that promote healthy, functional conflict while eliminating dysfunctional conflict. These three models—SCARF, the Drama Triangle, and the TKI—provide you with the knowledge and skills to do so. In the next section, we will examine each model in depth.

What Is the SCARF Model?

In 2008, David Rock developed the SCARF model based on research by neuroscientists. SCARF is an acronym for five critical areas called domains that influence our behavior in social situations. According to Rock (2008), these five are:

1. **Status**—our relative importance to others and our self-worth.
2. **Certainty**—our ability to predict the near future.
3. **Autonomy**—our perception of control and capacity for self-governing.
4. **Relatedness**—involves deciding whether someone is a friend or foe; this is also the degree to which we feel we belong in the workplace.
5. **Fairness**—our perception of how just exchanges play out. (Mind Tools, 2023)

The model is based on neuroscience research identifying the brain's response to varying situations. The research shows that the brain's overarching organizing principle categorizes incoming data as either a **threat** or a **reward** (Rock, 2008). The brain processes information in this way at all times, often subconsciously. The body's threat response is activated when the brain categorizes something as a threat. Conversely, the body's reward response is activated when the brain categorizes something as a reward. The five domains of SCARF provide a helpful way to understand what is likely to trigger a threat or reward response in the workplace.

The human brain wants to minimize threats and maximize rewards that trigger behavior. This primitive reaction helps explain the sometimes strong emotional responses we can have to social situations and why it is often hard to control them (Mind Tools, 2023). It is instinct; we cannot just turn it off.

For example, when left out of an activity, we might perceive it as threatening our status and relatedness. Research has shown that this response can stimulate the same brain region as physical pain (Tabac, 2021). In this situation, our brain is sending out the signal that we are in danger.

Furthermore, releasing cortisol (the "stress hormone") affects our creativity and productivity when we feel physically or socially threatened. We literally cannot think straight, increasing the feeling of being threatened. Glucose and oxygen move from the prefrontal cortex to our extremities, readying our body for flight and further limiting our ability to engage in problem solving and emotional regulation (Rock, 2008).

On the flip side, when we feel rewarded (for instance, when we receive praise for our work), our brains release dopamine, the "happy hormone" (Tabac, 2021). And, of course, we want more! So, we seek out ways to be rewarded again.

BOX 10.1 **SCARF in the Workplace**

Marcia served as legal counsel for a government agency. She led a team of about 40 people and reported to the chief administrative officer (CAO). During a one-on-one meeting, the CAO offered what he thought was a small, nonthreatening suggestion for improving Marcia's performance. This suggestion triggered Marcia's threat response for autonomy and status. Marcia got increasingly animated as her threat response took hold. What was a small issue to the CAO became very significant in Marcia's mind. The CAO did not recognize what was happening. Rather than seeking to alleviate Marcia's threat response by affirming the five domains of SCARF, he repeated the small performance change he sought. Marcia's emotions took over, and she quit her job immediately. Within 20 minutes, she packed her office and emailed her team that she was quitting. This is an extreme example of a threat response. In this case, the CAO spoke to his counterpart in Human Resources (HR). That person understood SCARF and could explain what was likely happening to Marcia. They gave her time to unhook from the physical response to her perceived threat, then offered to meet and discuss further. Marcia did return to work and performed successfully, thanks to the HR leader's effective use of SCARF.

How Does the SCARF Model Apply to Conflict Resolution?

Conflict, remember, is the experience of a disagreement between you and another person (or several people). In functional conflict, the five domains of SCARF are experiencing the situation positively. For example, you and a coworker have differing views on how to handle a customer complaint. As you talk together, you create a new solution that is better than either of the options you individually identified. You feel creative and supported by your coworker in the conversation, triggering the reward response for the status and relatedness domains. On the other hand, when the conflict is dysfunctional, that situation could trigger a threat response for autonomy if you think your coworker is telling you what to do and not appreciating your perspective (Nichols, 2020).

You can use the SCARF model to create an environment that promotes functional conflict by triggering the reward response in the five domains and avoiding the threat response. If you are leading a team and initiating a change, you might seek to emphasize how the change will increase your team's autonomy in the workplace or how team members can support each other through the change (relatedness).

How to Use the SCARF Model

Status

Status is in the eye of the beholder, meaning individuals decide what determines status (Rock, 2008). For one person, this could be having an office with a window. For another, it could be high pay; for another, it could be attending meetings with senior executives. As a leader, you will want to understand how your team members define status and then use that to minimize threats and maximize rewards.

Certainty

Certainty is the degree to which we can predict the future (Rock, 2008). Certainty means that what people expect to happen actually happens in the workplace. Certainty is one reason why change is so difficult for many people—they want predictability, and change creates uncertainty. As a leader, you will seek opportunities to create stability and certainty. When introducing change, emphasize what stays the same and what people can predict. Even if it is just the timeline of the change, that can be helpful. For example, one leader had to inform his employees about layoffs. That type of announcement generates significant threat responses in several SCARF domains. In this case, the leader shared exactly what employees could expect, the decision-making process, and the specific timeline for them. This provided a small amount of certainty for employees.

Autonomy

Autonomy is the amount of control we have over our environment (Rock, 2008). In the workplace, positions have different levels of autonomy. For example, in one position, it may be expected to have to request a bathroom break, while in other positions, an employee could expect to set their own hours. During the COVID pandemic, many employees experienced higher levels of autonomy while working from home. When some employers then asked employees to return to the workplace, this lowered the autonomy they had come to expect in their work environment. Many employers described backlash to this request as employees refused to return to the workplace (Tsipursky, 2023). To minimize a threat response, leaders should avoid decreasing an employee's level of autonomy from what they have been in the past.

Relatedness

The reward response is triggered when we feel part of the group and belong. Relatedness speaks of feeling welcomed, appreciated, and in positive relationships with others (Rock, 2008). This is why many employee surveys will ask whether employees feel they have a friend at work. To minimize a threat response and maximize the reward response, employers should do what they can to create a sense of belonging in the workplace (Rock & Cox, 2012).

Fairness

Fairness speaks to our sense of whether exchanges in the workplace are just (Rock, 2008). Employees want to know that they are being treated fairly. They also want to know that others are treated fairly. Consistent application of policies and rules can help maximize this fairness domain.

EXAMPLES OF SCARF IN THE WORKPLACE

	Threat	**Reward**
Status	Performance review, changes to the title, location, pay, critical feedback	Present to higher levels, joining a leadership team, positive feedback
Certainty	Not knowing expectations, someone acting incongruently	Clear objectives at the start of a discussion, breaking major initiatives/projects into smaller steps
Autonomy	Frequent directions, directions of each step, requests for progress reports, limiting self-expression in a workspace	Organizing own workflow, determining working hours
Relatedness	New team, new individual, missing the "inside joke," not being invited to an event	Mentoring/coaching, having a friend at work, team development
Fairness	Lack of ground rules, no way to surface concerns, talking negatively about someone else (especially boss with favorites)	Mentoring/coaching, having a friend at work, team development

When the SCARF model is used, you can work alongside others more effectively. You can often prevent or mitigate conflict by understanding what will likely trigger a threat response. It is beneficial when collaborating with or coaching others by minimizing perceived threats and maximizing the positive feelings generated by rewards. If someone reacts strongly to something you view as minor, do not ignore it. Use the SCARF model to determine first what they feel threatened or fearful about and why. Ask them how they would like you to approach similar situations in the future.

Using the SCARF model effectively will help you to understand the people around you. Before you act, consider the individual needs of the other person. Put yourself in their position: What would they see as a threat? What reward would they most desire?

Escaping the Drama of Conflict and the Karpman Drama Triangle

The drama triangle was conceived by Stephen Karpman (1968). While the SCARF model helps us understand what can cause a conflict between people, the Karpman Drama Triangle is a framework for understanding the emotional traps of dysfunctional conflict.

The drama triangle puts the conflict in perspective with "actor roles" named as the Persecutor, the Victim, and the Rescuer (Karpman, 1968).

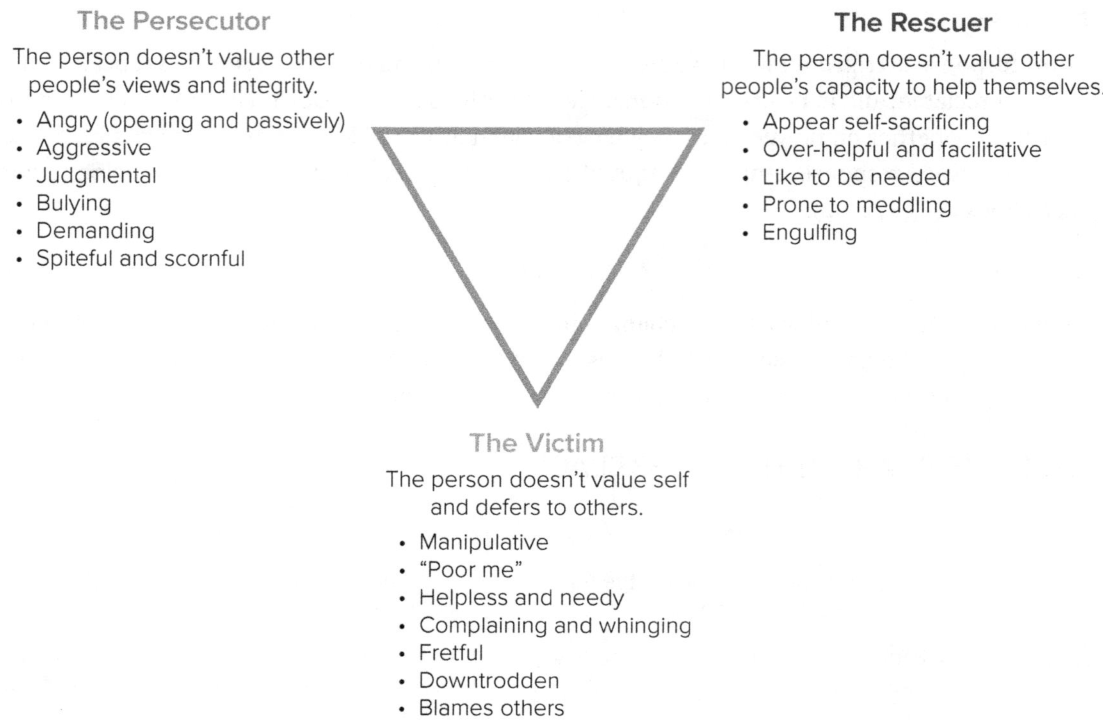

FIGURE 10.1 The Karpman Drama Triangle

The Victim Role: In Karpman's (1968) triangle role, this usually means someone acts like a victim—and is not necessarily an actual victim. Nevertheless, the *victim* genuinely feels wronged, overloaded, helpless, hopeless, incapable, humiliated, and unable to move forward with making decisions, solving problems, or achieving insight. The *victim*'s stance is, "Woe is me!" "Ugh, why does this always happen to me?"

The Persecutor: The *persecutor* is controlling, blaming and shaming, critical, domineering, angry, imposing, inflexible, and self-righteous—superior (Karpman, 1968). The *persecutor* insists, "It is all your fault." Or "I would rather be mad than vulnerable."

The Rescuer: The rescuer is the classic enabler (Karpman, 1968). The rescuer feels good about rescuing and confuses their actions as helping others. Who doesn't want to jump in and be the hero? However, their rescuing is often unsolicited and has adverse effects by keeping the *victim* reliant on the rescuer and giving the *victim* role permission to fail. It also feeds the *rescuer*'s role in focusing energy on someone else's problems, not recognizing their behavior. The *rescuer*'s language is, "Let me help. I'll do this for you." "I can help you do it better." "Let me help you do it right."

Karpman's triangle is a valuable tool for understanding the dysfunctional dynamics of the different roles we can fall into in conflict, mapping how the role changes as the conflict grows, and learning the actions that will move us out of the dysfunction to functional conflict with resolution (Lac & Donaldson, 2002).

How the Drama Triangles Form

Being in the drama triangle is ineffective and not something happening *to* you; it is what you do *with* someone else. The drama triangles involve at least two people and can affect even more when linked triangles form.

The drama triangle forms because we are predisposed to adopt the roles of self-interest (Karpman, 1968). There are motivations (often subconscious) for each person, and without pausing to assess the situation, we can find ourselves in the drama triangle. The drama triangle ensues because each person gets some needs met and feels justified in their role. Often we do not realize the dysfunction and harm that are being created. So, in the drama triangle, each participant acts upon self-satisfying but unhealthy roles rather than pausing and assessing the conflict by considering the others' needs, fears, and concerns.

The victim role often starts or generates the development of the drama triangle. The victim will seek a persecutor to prove that it is not their fault, but someone is doing it to them, or a rescuer will "save" the day and perpetuate the victim's negative emotional state. According to Karpman (1968), we are now setting the stage for forming a drama triangle. If we are not honest about our feelings, fears, and concerns and do not take responsibility for them, we make ourselves out to be the victim.

Imagine you are driving in heavy traffic and someone cuts you off. What is the first reaction you have? Have you been wronged? Did the other person do this to you? Fear is what we feel because we could have been in a wreck. After all, we feel they did not follow the rules of the road, so we experience fear and jump into the victim role. "Why does this always happen to me? Wow, that car cut me off!" Next, what often happens is that we quickly jump roles from victim to persecutor by yelling at the other person in the car, who cannot even hear us. Or worse, we use visual cues to let the other person know they are to blame. "It's all your fault!" Unconsciously, we are in the state of "I would rather be mad than a victim (persecutor role)."

The persecutor is a learned behavior as a protection to avoid being vulnerable (Karpman, 1968). The above example of being cut off in traffic and how we process that initial fear demonstrates how easy it is to move from the victim to the persecutor role. We move from being perceived as weak or scared (victim role) to blaming (persecutor role) to take the onus off ourselves.

The rescuer has a simple motive of resolving the problem but takes action without being asked and appears to make great efforts to solve it. "I am here to save the day!" Even unconsciously, we can think we are doing the right thing by helping, but often there is a hidden motive. We may feel we can do it better or don't want to look bad because of other people's decisions. This role perpetuates having someone dependent on you and reinforces the victim role in others.

The drama triangle conceals the real issues and possible solutions. The actions of the participants in dysfunctional conflict start to divide and become increasingly polarized with counteractions. This behavior perpetuates the roles of the *victim*, *persecutor*, and *rescuer* role to shift, and this can polarize and create more conflict. For example, the *victim* can strike back at the *persecutor* or the *victim* can seek out their *rescuer*, creating overlapping drama triangles by introducing another person into the mix.

According to Karpman (1960), we tend to have a primary role (victim, rescuer, persecutor) when we land in a dysfunctional conflict. We assume a habitual role in finding relief when there is dysfunctional conflict. While roles can become chronic and start to feel natural and often familiar, they prevent conflict resolution from success (Lac & Donaldson, 2002).

Based on Acey Choy's (1990) work *The Winner's Triangle*, David Emerald (2015) describes the transformation process from dysfunctional to functional conflict through the power of *The Empowerment Dynamic (TED)*. Assume the **creator role** when you find yourself in the victim role instead. The creator's role is learning to pause and be aware of the space between the incoming stimulus and your reaction. This awareness builds your capacity to make an active choice rather than simply reacting to the situation (Womeldorff, 2021). Instead of thinking, "Poor me," think, "I can do it." The persecutor role shifts to the **challenger role**, a learning role (Emerald, 2015). Ask, "What can I learn or understand from this situation?" In the persecutor mindset, we use blame and judgment. Switching to the challenger role, we focus on continuous learning for ourselves and others and listen with genuine curiosity. Instead of "It's your fault," approach with "I am willing to listen; what happened?" The rescuer takes on the **coach role** (Emerald, 2015). The coach's role is to encourage others to work toward action rather than becoming embroiled or controlling. In the coaching role, we provide support using questions to help a creator develop an action plan instead of doing it for them or taking other rescuing actions. Switch from "You need my help" to "Do you need help with this?"

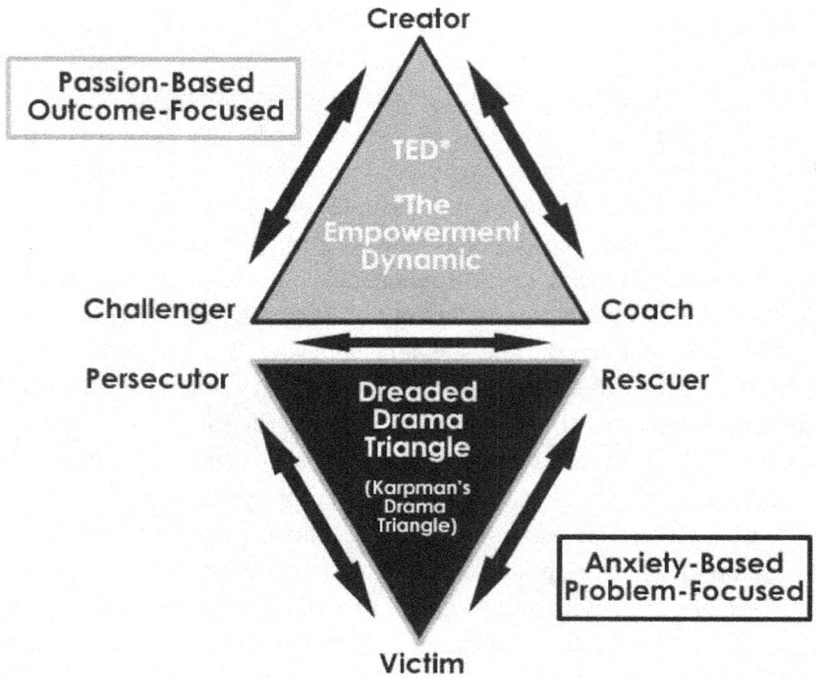

FIGURE 10.2 The Empowerment Dynamic Triangle (TED)

We can accept and recognize our actions by taking responsibility for our involvement in perpetuating drama. Steps to break out of a drama triangle:

1. Recognize that you are in a drama triangle.
2. Consider how important it is to you to stop the drama. Are you willing to work to step out of contributing to the drama? What is the payoff for doing so?
3. Step back mentally and analyze what is happening. Who is playing what role? When and how do the roles change? What benefits do they gain by behaving in this way? How can we become emotionally detached from the drama triangle and move to productive problem solving?
4. Invite others to join you in analyzing the situation. Where do we agree and disagree? How do we want this relationship to function or the problem to be solved?
5. Work with them in committing to move into The Empowerment Dynamic (TED) using the creator, challenger, and coach roles when conflict arises (Emerald, 2015).

BOX 10.2 **The Empowerment Dynamic (TED) Triangle in the Workplace**

Lawrence was a senior-level executive. His peer, Rajeesh, had a direct report named Althea. Lawrence was leading a meeting that Althea was supposed to attend and missed. When Lawrence followed up with Althea, she jumped right into the victim role: "Why didn't you wait until I could attend? You always hold these meetings and make decisions without me. No one bothers to include me." This was a common response for Althea, so Lawrence contacted Rajeesh to discuss what to do next. Rajeesh met with Lawrence and Althea, and both Lawrence and Althea felt Rajeesh had taken the other person's side. No one felt satisfied with the outcome of this conflict. Lawrence checked in with his executive coach, who helped Lawrence explore the elements of the drama triangle at play and introduced The Empowerment Dynamic. Using TED, Lawrence was able to assume that Althea was fully capable, and he was prepared to help coach Althea into some new options the next time Althea jumped into victim mode.

Conflict Management TKI Model

We have explored the SCARF model, which can help identify ways people respond to conflict. The drama triangle shows how certain emotional traps lead to dysfunctional conflict. Now let's explore the Thomas-Kilmann Conflict Mode Instrument (TKI), which describes five conflict styles. These conflict styles are situational, so knowing which style to use can help you manage conflict effectively.

Kenneth Thomas and Ralph Kilmann (1970) developed this classic conflict management model. It is well used in the workplace today, along with the TKI assessment tool used to measure what behavior we are each most likely to use in conflict. It is a great assessment to understand our habitual pattern and learn how and when to rely on other behaviors in a conflict situation.

The Thomas and Kilmann model assesses people's behavior in conflict situations. The authors described people's behavior as having two dimensions in a graph pattern. The vertical axis in the model is assertiveness. Assertiveness is the extent one satisfies their needs and personal concerns during conflict resolution. The horizontal axis is cooperativeness. Cooperativeness is the extent one is willing to address others' needs and concerns. These two basic dimensions of behaviors define five different modes of responding to conflict-handling dispositions: avoiding, accommodating, collaborating, competing, and compromising.

Five Conflict Management Styles

Here are the five conflict management styles according to Thomas and Kilmann (1974):

1. **Avoiding** is using low assertive behavior and low cooperation (Thomas & Kilmann, 2001). This style avoids the issue altogether, or you don't care or engage with the other person or persons about the problem or issue. The avoiding approach works when the emotions are high and you must take a break. It can also be a good approach when the issue is small or you have time to wait for a different solution to emerge. Avoiding a conflict is not usually an effective long-term strategy. Conflict is not like a fine wine; it does not improve with age, and you must return to it.
2. **Accommodating** is using highly cooperative behavior and low assertive behavior (Thomas & Kilmann, 2001). This approach is effective when you have little to lose, "no dog in the fight," the

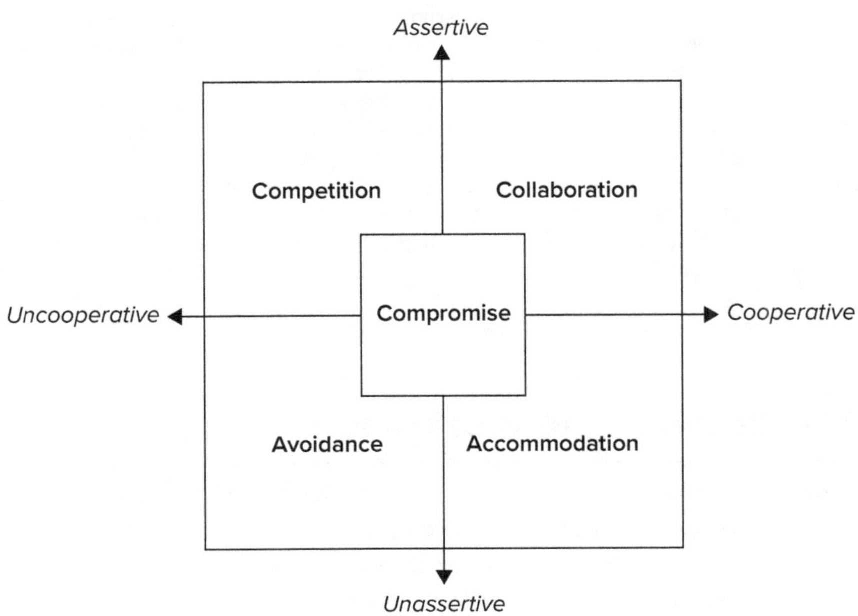

FIGURE 10.3 Thomas-Kilmann Conflict Styles

outcome has little impact on you, or the other party is more knowledgeable about the problem. Accommodating is a great way to show empathy and willingness to work with the other person. It works great for maintaining relationships, especially when the relationship is more important than the issue. This approach can be overused or misused, and you should recognize that it works against your own needs, ideas, and desired outcomes.

3. **Collaborating** is partnering with the other party to achieve your goals. Collaborating is high assertiveness and high cooperativeness (Thomas & Kilmann, 2001). Collaborating is how you break free of the "win-lose" paradigm and seek the "win-win." This style can be effective for complex scenarios where you must find an innovative solution. Collaborating can redefine the challenge or problem to create a bigger space for more possibilities. The downside to collaboration is that it requires a high degree of time and effort to involve everybody on board, synthesize all the ideas, and create consensus for the solution.
4. **Competing** is a "win-lose" approach (Thomas & Kilmann, 2001). It may be at the other party's expense if I act assertively to satisfy my needs and achieve my goals without seeking cooperation from the other party. This approach is best used for emergencies when time is of the essence, quick, decisive action is required, or where winning is the goal, like sports and competitions.
5. **Compromising** is a "win some-lose some" scenario, where neither party achieves what they want. This style uses both assertiveness and cooperation behavior and can leave both parties unhappy with the outcome but moving forward (Thomas & Kilmann, 2001). It is best used as a temporary solution, or each party has important issues, and time is of the essence to create forward action. It is also effective when resources are constrained and everyone must "give a little" to keep going. Often, compromising becomes a habit we can fall into as an easy way out when collaborating will produce better solutions for all involved.

By knowing our default patterns, we improve our self-awareness and adjust to best adapt to the situation. We can better recognize the patterns, behaviors, threats, and rewards at play.

BOX 10.3 **Conflict Styles in the Workplace**

Josie was a successful policy leader for a large government agency. Her job was to develop the best possible policy with the best chance of getting approved by the legislature. Josie leaned heavily on collaboration conflict management style as her primary approach for getting policies passed. She was known for leading groundbreaking policy changes that positively impacted citizens through highly charged political situations. Some of these policy changes took 2–3 years to complete. As Josie was promoted up through the workplace, she eventually had a team of people working for her. Like many leaders, Josie continued to use the conflict style she knew best: in her case, the collaboration style to conflict management. Over time, her team became frustrated and grumbled that meetings were time consuming and unproductive and that Josie did not seem to decide independently. To her surprise, she was losing credibility due to the very source of her previous success. Josie learned to utilize other conflict styles like competing, avoiding, and accommodating to match the situation.

Conflict Resolution in the Workplace

When you are faced with a conflict or an issue that needs to be resolved, the worksheet can help. The five steps to the worksheet are used to identify the problem, explore your perspective and the other person's, and use the conflict resolution tools discussed in this chapter to clarify how we contributed to the situation and strategies to find common interests and possible solutions.

The first step to resolving conflict is **identifying the problem or behavior** being addressed. This step may involve stepping back and reflecting on the situation to understand what is happening clearly. This section requires looking at your perspective on this situation and the other person's viewpoint. **Explore your perspectives**. Write down your thoughts, feelings, and needs about the issue. This step may involve asking yourself questions such as "What are my goals in this situation?" "What assumptions am I making about the other person's perspective?" and "What emotions am I experiencing as a result of the conflict?" **Consider the other person's point of view**. Put yourself in the other person's shoes and write what you believe their thoughts, feelings, and needs are about the issue.

The next step in the worksheet is to examine the conflict management tools and consider what you did or did not do that might have contributed to the conflict. Using the SCARF (status, certainty, autonomy, relatedness, and fairness) model, explore the potential threat you might be triggering or which are triggers for you. Examining the drama triangle explores the high emotions and seeks to understand the actor roles (victim, persecutor, or victim) we took on in the conflict. The third step is to **seek understanding to find common/mutual interests**. The action is first to **neutralize** the conflict by asking yourself some questions. For example, "Am I taking a stance on the issue, or am I focusing on the interest of both parties? In what ways is the other person right?" Next is to think of ways to use empathy to show that you listen to and understand their concerns, needs, or wants in the situation. The third part of this section is **inquiry** to create questions you can ask for clarification; for example, "Will you clarify what you mean by ...?" or "What I think you said is ... Is that correct?" Lastly, in this section, you seek **the facts and observations** instead of judgments and assumptions that show up when emotions are high. Step four is brainstorming possible solutions. In this column, list the possible solutions you can think of to resolve the conflict or issue. Which conflict management style from the TKI model is best for each potential solution? Finally, consider all possible solutions and select the one that works for the current situation, recognizing each part's commitment to creating the best possible outcome.

Conflict is rarely resolved the first time. Revisit the worksheet's early steps and ensure the problem is clearly defined because the apparent conflict is often not about the real issue. Be sure to find a common interest to generate options with mutual respect. Stick to the facts and observations in the discussion to keep judgment and assumptions to a minimum. Lastly, implement options and solutions with integrity versus superiority or inferiority (drama triangle).

Conflict Resolution Worksheet

Step 1	**Issue:** Write a brief description of the problem or behavior you want to resolve.	**My Perspective:** Write your thoughts, feeling, and needs about the issue.	**Other Person's Perspective:** Write what you think their thoughts, feelings, and needs are about the issue.
Define the problem or the behavior.			
Step 2	**Strategies**	**What did I do or not do to contribute to the conflict?**	
Examine the conflict tools and accept responsibility.	**SCARF:** What are the potential threats being activated for each party? What are the possible rewards? **Drama Triangle:** What is the fear or vulnerability at risk for each party? **The Empowerment Dynamic (TED):** How can I assume the creator, challenger, or coach role in this situation?		

(Continued)

Step 3	**Strategies**	**How will you revisit the situation?**
Seek understanding to find the common/ mutual interests.	**Neutralize** (in what small way are they right?) **Empathy** for their feelings and concerns **Inquiry** (what questions can you ask or need to be answered?) **Seek the facts and observations** (versus judgment and assumptions)	
Step 4	**Find 3 Solutions**	**Which conflict management approach is best to use for each solution and why? (avoid, accommodate, compete, compromise, collaborate)**
Identify options.	1. 2. 3.	
Step 5	**Who commits to what?**	**What does the best possible outcome look like?**
Choose the best solution.		

Application

Now it is time for you to think about conflict management and you.

1. Describe a time you were in a conflict situation. Use the worksheet to assess the situation.
2. What was the outcome of this conflict situation?
3. What would you do differently in this situation? Why would this be a better approach?
4. As you think of future conflicts, which conflict management tools in this chapter will you use the next time you encounter conflict? Why?

References

Choy, A. (1990, January). *The Winner's Triangle. Transactional Analysis*, 40–46.

Cloke, K., & Goldsmith, J. (2001). *Resolving conflicts at work: A complete guide for everyone on the job.* Bass.

Emerald, D. (2015). *The power of TED (The Empowerment Dynamic)* (3rd ed.). Polaris.

Karpman, S. (1968). Fairy tales and script drama analysis. *Transactional Analysis Bulletin, 7(26)*, 39–43.

Kilmann, R. H., & Thomas, K. W. (1974). *Thomas-Kilmann Conflict Mode Instrument (TKI)*. APA PsycTests. Retrieved from https://doi.org/10.1037/t02326-000

Lac, A., & Donaldson, C. D. (2002). Development and validation of the Drama Triangle Scale: Are you a victim, rescuer, or persecutor? *Journal of Interpersonal Violence, 37*, 7–8. Retrieved from https//doi-org.libpublic3.library.isu.edu/10.1177/0886260520957696

Listening Partnership (2023). *Listening Parntership, LTD.* Retrieved from About the Drama Triangle—and how to escape it. https://www.listeningpartnership.com/insight/about-the-drama-triangle-and-how-to-escape-it/

Menon, A., Bharadwaj, S. G., & Howell, R. (1996). The quality and effectiveness of marketing strategy: Effects of functional and dysfunctional conflict in intraorganizational relationships. *Journal of the Academy of Marketing Science*, 299–313.

Mind Tools. (2023). *Mindtools.* Retrieved from David Rock's SCARF Model: Using neuroscience to work effectively with others. https://www.mindtools.com/akswgco/david-rocks-scarf-model

Nichols, A. O. (2020, August 17). *Making conflict suck less: The basics.* Boise State eCampus. Retrieved from Boise State Pressbooks. https://boisestate.pressbooks.pub/makingconflictsuckless/

Oore, D. G., Leblanc, D., & Leiter, M. (2015). Individual and organizational factors promoting successful responses to workplace conflict. *Canadian Psychology, 56(3)*, 301–310.

Rock, D. (2008). SCARF: A brain-based model for collaborating with and influencing others. *NeuroLeadership Journal* (1).

Rock, D., & Cox, C. (2012). *NeuroLeadership Journal*, 4, 1–14. Retrieved from https://www.academia.edu/25000956/SCARF_in_2012_updating_the_social_neuroscience_of_collaborating_with_others

Tabac, M. (2021, February 10). *SCARF Model in the times of Covid-19*. Retrieved from Magdatabac Mind Training Applied Psychology. https://magdatabac.com/the-scarf-model-in-the-times-of-covid-19/

Thomas, K. W., & Kilmann, R. H. (2001). *Thomas-Kilmann Conflict Mode Instrument Sample Report.* CPP. Kilmann Diagnostics. Retrieved 2023 from chrome-extension://efaidnbmnnnibpcajpcglclefindmkaj/https://kilmann-diagnostics.com/wp-content/uploads/2018/03/TKI_Sample_Report.pdf

Tsipursky, G. (2023, February 23). *Why employers forcing a return to office is leading to more worker power and unionization.* Retrieved from Entrepreneur: https://www.entrepreneur.com/leadership/why-employers-forcing-a-return-to-office-is-leading-to-more/446004

Womeldorff, D. E. (2021, Februaty 12). *Shifting from victim to creator.* Retrieved from 3 Vital Questions: https://3vitalquestions.com/shifting-from-victim-to-creator/

Credits

Fig. 10.1: Adapted from Listening Partnership, "The Karpman Drama Triangle," https://www.listeningpartnership.com/insight/about-the-drama-triangle-and-how-to-escape-it/. Copyright © 2023 by Listening Partnership.

Fig. 10.2: Copyright © by Davidemerald (CC BY-SA 3.0) at https://commons.wikimedia.org/wiki/File:Drama-Triangle-The-Empowerment-Dynamic.jpg.

Fig. 10.3: Adapted from Kenneth W. Thomas and Ralph H. Kilmann, "Thomas-Kilman Conflict Styles," https://

www.psychometrics.com/assessments/thomas-kilmann-conflict-mode/. Copyright © 2015 by Psychometrics.

CHAPTER 11

Building Collective Efficacy

By Wendy Ruchti

If you want to go fast, go alone; if you want to go far, go together.

—African proverb

Learning Objectives

After reading this chapter, students will be able to:

1. Define collective efficacy and describe its relationship to self-efficacy
2. Describe the impact of strong collective efficacy
3. Describe conditions and actions for enhancing collective efficacy
4. Analyze workplace situations to enhance collective efficacy

Introduction to Collective Efficacy

Have you ever wondered what makes some groups work effectively while other groups seem to lack cohesion and flounder as they try to work together toward a common goal? When working with teams of people, it isn't just talent or ability to do a job that makes a group effective. We can have a group of talented people who still perform poorly or don't achieve the outcomes that we would like to see. A group's collective efficacy, defined as a group's shared belief that they are capable to organize and execute required courses of action, can affect the choices a group makes, their resilience to adversity, vulnerability to stress, and also performance accomplishments (Bandura, 1998). As modern workplaces are shifting toward a greater degree of teamwork due to enhanced technology, competition and downsizing, and increasing globalization (Salas & Fiore, 2004), collective efficacy becomes increasingly important. A basic requirement of effective group leadership is the ability to enable and foster collective action. As humans become more and more interdependent, collective agency becomes influential in workplace settings. Increasing collective efficacy can increase group members' willingness to try new approaches, put in greater effort, or feel an increased commitment to the work. Research has shown us that this is true in in the workplace, the neighborhood, politics, the gym, the classroom, or anywhere groups exist.

This chapter explores the transformative power of collective efficacy first through the examination of self-efficacy and how the recognized contributions of mastery experiences, social modeling, social persuasions, and psychological responses function also to support collective efficacy in groups.

Self-Efficacy

To better understand collective efficacy, we must first understand self-efficacy. In his book *Self-Efficacy in Changing Societies*, Bandura (1995) defines self-efficacy as "the belief in one's capabilities to organize and execute the courses of action required to manage prospective situations" (p. 2). Self-efficacy continues to be an important topic because self-efficacy can influence people's behaviors and their motivation to pursue goals, how we go about accomplishing goals, and what we think about our performance.

Self-efficacy is a major determinant of people's choice of activities. Self-efficacy has a strong record of application in the workplace, including a major impact on learning, effort, goals, and persistence when tasks get difficult (Bandura, 1982). In addition, Stajkovic and Luthans (1998) found that self-efficacy influences four specific areas for employees in the workplace: choice of tasks, goals, level of effort, and persistence when learning new tasks. People with strong self-efficacy develop deeper interest in activities in which they participate. They are more committed to their success and do not focus on personal failings and negative outcomes.

Self-efficacy starts developing in early childhood and continues to evolve throughout a person's life. Each of us experiences a range of situations that contributes to our self-efficacy that shape and mold our sense of efficacy. Bandura named four major sources of self-efficacy:

Mastery Experiences

When tasks are performed successfully, it strengthens our sense of self-efficacy. When we are unsuccessful at a task or challenge or perceive we are unsuccessful, self-efficacy is typically weakened. An employee's past performance has been documented to impact their self-efficacy (Stajkovic & Luthans, 1998).

Social Modeling

Seeing others perform a task successfully, or vicarious experiences, can also strengthen our sense of self-efficacy, especially if we see people similar to ourselves succeed.

Social Persuasions

Verbal encouragement or persuasions from others can support a strong sense of self-efficacy, helping people overcome self-doubt and focus on giving best effort.

Psychological Responses

A person's response and emotional reactions such as our mood, anxiety, or stress level, can also mold our sense of self-efficacy. In addition, emotional cues have been shown to support an employee's self-efficacy. Bandura noted, however, that "it is not the sheer intensity of emotional and physical reactions that is important, but rather how they are perceived and interpreted" (Bandura & Watts, 1996).

Collective Efficacy

In the workplace, understanding and fostering self-efficacy is important because of the influence on the individual's behavior, but we often need to work together to achieve what cannot be accomplished by individuals alone. Much of what needs to be accomplished in the workplace, the outcomes, are achievable only through work that relies on others' strengths and abilities. It's not uncommon for groups with members who are talented individually to perform poorly collectively because the members cannot work well together as a unit. Collective efficacy can be a powerful tool if the work relies on collective interdependent effort. Fostering, enabling, and shaping collective efficacy in the workplace has the potential to impact the workplace in many ways, and these will be addressed in this chapter (see Figure 11.1).

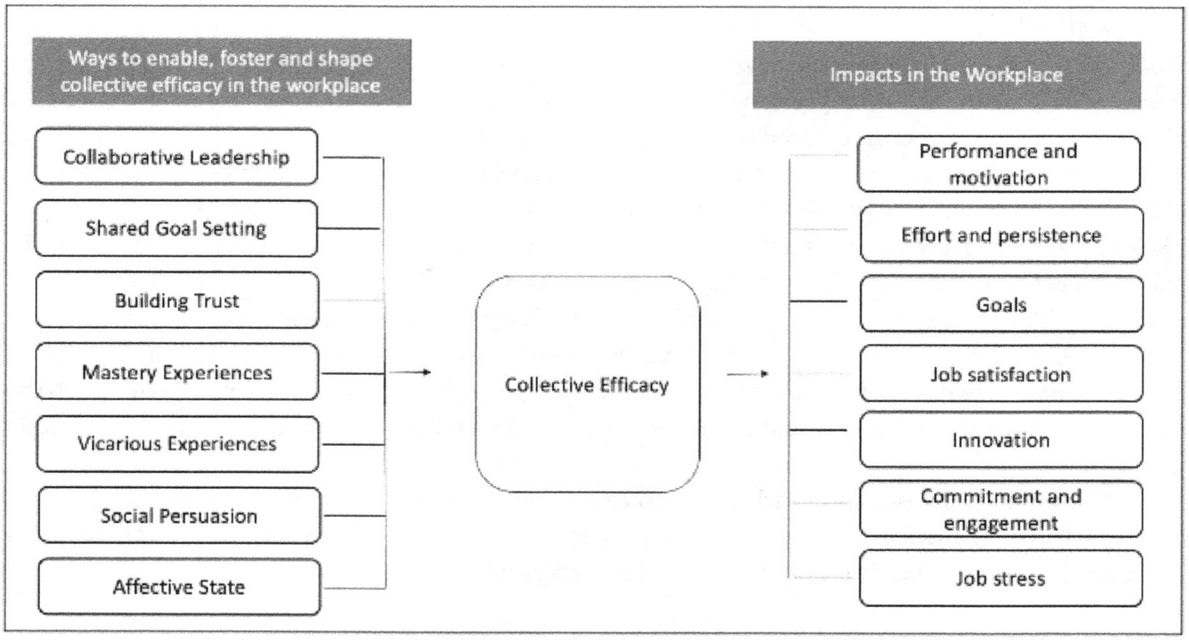

FIGURE 11.1 Collective Efficacy Overview

Collective efficacy is the shared perception that together a group can shape outcomes. Bandura (1998) explained that "personal and collective efficacy differ in the unit of agency, individual or collective, but in both forms efficacy beliefs have similar sources, serve similar functions, and operate through similar processes" (p. 478). Bandura (2000) differentiates between different units of agency, which could be personal (make choices ourselves), proxy (have someone make choices for them), or collective (participate in making choices in a group). Studies have shown that greater collective efficacy can impact many types of workplace settings, organizations, educational, and sports systems. Collective efficacy has been shown to affect political interests (Richert et al., 2017), business organizations (Earley, 1994; Hodges & Carron, 1992; Little & Madigan, 1994), athletic teams (Carron et al., 2002; Feltz & Lirgg, 1998; Mullen & Copper, 1994; Spink, 1990), combat teams (Jex & Bliese, 1999; Lindsley et al., 1994), neighborhood problems (Sampson et al., 1997), and environment behaviors (Bonniface & Henley, 2008). Teacher collective efficacy is one of the strongest predictors of student performance in a school (Fisher et al., 2016).

Collective efficacy can be defined and measured in a variety of ways, depending on the operational definition and context. Bandura (1998) explained collective efficacy as a property of the group, stemming from the interactions of its members. Riggs and Knight (1994), who also saw collective efficacy as a group construct, developed a seven-item measure to assess collective efficacy by asking respondents to think about their department and rate the group's abilities to perform their jobs (see Textbox 11.1).

BOX 11.1 **Collective Efficacy Beliefs Scale**

Think about the department in which you work. This department may be an office group, a maintenance crew, an academic department, etc. When responding to the following items, answer in reference to this group's work-related ability. Respond with SA for strongly agree, A for agree, AS for agree somewhat, DS for disagree somewhat, D for disagree, and SD for strongly disagree.

1. The department I work with has average ability.
2. This department is poor compared to other departments doing similar work.
3. This department is not able to perform as well as it should.
4. The members of this department have excellent job skills.
5. Some members of this department should be fired due to lack of ability.
6. This department is not very effective.
7. Some members in this department cannot do their jobs well.

As you review your answers, you will get an idea of your beliefs of the collective efficacy of your department.

Matt L. Riggs and Patrick A. Knight, Selection from "The Impact of Perceived Group Success-Failure on Motivational Beliefs and Attitudes: A Causal Model," *Journal of Applied Psychology*, vol. 79, no. 5.

What Is the Impact of Strong Collective Efficacy in the Workplace?

People's shared beliefs in their collective efficacy have similar consequences to those of personal beliefs, including how well they use their resources, how much effort they put into their group endeavor, their staying power and resilience, their vulnerability to discouragement (Bandura, 2000). Like self-efficacy, but at the group level, collective efficacy is based in the idea that unless people believe that they can produce desired effects and forestall undesired ones by their actions, they have little incentive to act. Improving collective efficacy in an organization would be valuable based on the number of consequences or effects of greater collective efficacy in the workplace, including the following:

Performance and Motivation

People and groups of people want to learn and perform those tasks that they believe they will be able to perform successfully. If the group believes they can be successful, they are more motivated to complete tasks and complete them well (Bandura, 2000; Rapp et al., 2021).

Effort and Persistence

A key factor in a group's collective efficacy is the amount of effort a group puts into achieving its shared goal. The amount of effort generally corresponds to the degree to which it expects success (Bandura, 2000; Goddard et al., 2000; Rapp et al., 2021). If groups have high collective efficacy, they tend to work harder to learn how to do novel tasks, likely because they feel their efforts will be successful. They are more likely to persist in their efforts, even when problems arise. Conversely, groups who have low collective efficacy, will provide less effort and are inclined to stop trying because they do not believe their effort will be successful, resulting in lower levels of performance (Tschannen-Moran & Barr, 2004).

Goals

Those groups with strong collective efficacy tend to set higher or more difficult goals and are more committed to those goals than those with lower collective efficacy. Challenging group goals can be important to improve group performance, and groups with specific goals perform better than groups with vague goals (Weldon & Weingart, 1993). Group performance is reflected in those goals, and people perform at levels consistent with their collective beliefs and goals. Those groups with high efficacy have likely had higher past performance and more success in achieving their goals, so will likely set goals that are equal to or higher than past performance. (Zander & Medow, 1963). Groups with higher efficacy will also be more persistent and more committed to the group's goals.

Job Satisfaction

Job satisfaction results from an evaluation of the tasks, activity, job, or other related experience. Job dissatisfaction is associated with more job-related stress. Individuals' communication skills and collective efficacy both had positive direct effects on both individual and group task satisfaction in a gaming context (Luu & Narayan, 2017). Tucker et.al (2013) found that "a group's shared perceptions of competence and agency provide individuals with the contextual cues that give them confidence to exercise personal control to manage stressors in the workplace" (p. 16). Increasing collective efficacy seems to help individuals to cope with job stress by helping them think about their role in a positive light, therefore increasing job satisfaction. Role conflicts is a stressor that arises when a person has conflicting expectations or roles that are overlapping with other work or work groups. Since role conflict happens in virtually all occupations and work settings, it's important to note that the negative effects of role conflict can be partially lessened when individuals perceive their groups to be highly efficacious (Tucker et al., 2013; Zellars et al., 2001).

Innovation and Willingness to Try New Approaches

High collective efficacy has been linked to more innovative performances (Salanova et al., 2012) as well as actual innovations (Choi & Chang, 2009). When collective efficacy is high, "teachers are more accepting of change and more likely to try new approaches" (Ross & Bruce, 2007).

Commitment and Engagement

Commitment to and engagement in the work is a key factor influencing the success of groups. Highly efficacious staffs show increased commitment and a willingness to exert effort on behalf of the organization (Lee et al., 2011). Multiple studies have linked high levels of efficacy beliefs with intrinsic motivation (i.e., work engagement) both at individual and organizational levels. Optimistic views raise aspirations and maintain motivation, so people take greater advantage of their talent and contribute to personal achievements.

Job Stress

High levels of collective efficacy were negatively related to psychological strain and positively related to job satisfaction and organizational commitment. Collective efficacy (CE) moderated the relationship between work overload and job satisfaction. Collective efficacy beliefs foster a positive interpersonal climate of cooperation. When CE is low, individuals will lack a positive and supportive work context. High levels of collective efficacy were negatively related to psychological strain and positively related to job satisfaction and organizational commitment. Also, high CE moderated the relationship between work overload and job satisfaction, regardless of the level of individual-level job demands. When collective efficacy was low, job satisfaction suffered under conditions of high workload (Jex & Bliese, 1999).

How to Use Collective Efficacy in the Workplace

There are many benefits to developing collective efficacy in many organizations, especially in the workplace. The rewards of strong collective efficacy are well documented and include increased performance and motivation, greater effort and persistence, setting higher goals, and increased job satisfaction. Additionally, higher CE resulted in reduced stress for employees, increased commitment, engagement, and willingness to try new approaches and innovation. In order to develop strong collective efficacy in the workplace, several supports are key and can be developed through effective leadership.

Enabling, Fostering, and Shaping Collective Efficacy

Given the significant positive impacts from increased collective efficacy, it is important to then understand and implement ways of enabling, fostering, and shaping collective efficacy. Fortunately, beliefs about our own capabilities and our beliefs about our group's capabilities can change and can be impacted by workplace leaders. Our beliefs can be influenced by several sources, many of which are interrelated to each other (see Figure 11.1):

- Collaborative Leadership
- Shared Goal Setting
- Building Trust
- Mastery Experiences
- Vicarious Experiences
- Social Persuasion
- Affective State

Collaborative Leadership

When group members are given opportunities to make decisions as a group, collective efficacy can be increased. Bandura (1998) argued that "collective enablement programs take many different forms, but the shared assumption is that they work in part by enhancing people's sense of efficacy to bring about change in their lives" (p. 503). By increasing opportunities to participate in decision-making or lead groups of people who make decisions, teams can build more mastery experiences and can also experience social persuasion through their colleagues' feedback (Lewis, 2009). In addition, leadership roles can positively affect collective efficacy. When group members are entrusted with the responsibility to make important decisions, they feel more empowered and more ownership of the efficacy of the group.

Shared Goal Setting

Closely related to collaborative leadership, group goal setting can affect people's motivation, self-evaluation, and beliefs about the level at which they are capable of performing (Bandura et al., 1999). Kurz and Knight (2004) explored the relationship between collective efficacy in teachers and their goal consensus or vision and found them to be highly correlated. Finding shared beliefs with all involved, administration and coworkers, seems to impact not only job satisfaction but also overall effectiveness in the workplace. Shared goal setting can also be motivating and increase collective efficacy, as it supports a better understanding of the problems, perceived strengths and challenges, areas of tension, as well as increased feelings of empowerment. Groups are more likely to be successful when goals are well defined and measurable and when the group is in agreement on the goals. As leaders connect followers' personal beliefs to the mission of the group, they can raise followers' identification with the group and increase their willingness to contribute to group objectives (Kark & Shamir, 2002).

Building Trust

When trust exists, organizations are more likely to see broader employee buy-in and collective decision-making, which in turn supports stronger collective efficacy. Trust in an organization can be elusive, but also essential to building collective efficacy. Stephen Covey (2006) defines trust as the feeling of confidence we have in another's character and competence. Trust is built through integrity or how honest we are and how aligned our actions are with what we say. In the workplace, individuals interact with one another and are continually consciously or unconsciously examining the intentions embedded in the actions and words of others. In addition, trust is built through confidence in each other's competence in their core role responsibilities; i.e., whether we feel they have the skills, abilities, attitudes, and knowledge that are needed for the organization. Trust can be undermined when negligence or incompetence exists and is allowed to persist.

Mastery Experiences

When teams experience success and attribute that success to causes within their control, collective efficacy is increased as teams come to expect that effective performances can be repeated (Goddard et al., 2004). In short, past success helps influence belief in future success. However, all of us perceive and attribute various causes when considering factors that contribute to success and/or failure, and these could be external or internal. Attribution is important to leveraging the power of mastery experiences to influence collective efficacy. If success is attributed to internal or controllable causes such as ability or effort, efficacy beliefs are strengthened. If success is attributed to luck or the intervention of others, efficacy may not be strengthened (Pintrich & Schunk, 2002).

Vicarious Experiences

When teams see others who are faced with similar opportunities and challenges perform well, expectations are generated that they too can overcome obstacles. Vicarious experiences can be in-person visits, watching videos, or reading about others' work. Leaders can also influence team members' collective efficacy by highlighting their team members' individual work as well. It makes sense that a better understanding and knowledge of others' work would be an influence on their perception of the group's ability to complete tasks. Members of the group need to feel empowered to take the actions needed to make a difference. For example, telling employees that they can be successful in increasing sales is not sufficient for collective efficacy to increase; the employees need support and to be allowed to reach customers in new and innovative ways.

Social Persuasion

To a certain extent, social persuasion by credible and trustworthy persuaders can influence others to overcome challenges and support innovation, thereby increasing collective efficacy. The more believable the source of the information, the more likely efficacy expectations will change (Bandura, 1977). Social persuasion "depends on establishing norms of openness, collaboration, and cooperation" (Adams & Forsyth, 2006, p. 631) to persuade others that they constitute an effective team. A leader's inspiration and motivation can give self-worth for their employee's contribution and support them when challenges arise (Bass & Avolio, 1994).

Affective States

Bandura (1977) explained that "people rely partly on their state of physiological arousal in judging their anxiety and vulnerability to stress" (p. 198). The mood, emotions, and physiological state of the individuals and the group can contribute to their perception of the group's capability or incompetence collective efficacy. Affective states such as feelings of excitement or anxiety can influence how groups interpret and react the myriad challenges they face. Note that Bandura (1977) stated, "it is not the sheer intensity of emotional and physical reactions that is important but rather how they are perceived and interpreted" (p. 212). For example, sometimes high emotional arousal like anxiety before giving a speech could be interpreted as a facilitator of performance, or could increase self-doubt and become debilitating. Leaders must learn to interpret moods and emotions and acknowledge prior history of a group, especially in challenging situations, and support using high emotional arousal for positive outcomes.

Application

Apply what you have learned in this chapter to the following scenarios.

1. Your community has seen an increase in illegal drug activity. One group in the community wants to put a stop to it but does not think anything can be done. Many community members feel that someone else, such as the police or the mayor, should deal with the problem. This group wants to write letters and complain to officials. A second group in the community are confident that they can solve the problem and reclaim their neighborhood. Their group members suggest a crime watch, cleanup of several vacant lots, and neighborhood education on how to observe and report suspected criminal activity.
   a. What might be some of the barriers to strong collective efficacy these groups could have?
   b. How might you find out if those barriers exist?
   c. What might you do to overcome those barriers? Why is this a good approach?
   d. How does this fit with the Collective Efficacy Overview (see Figure 11.1)?
2. You are working with several departments in your company supporting the implementation of a new sales initiative. You have presented the initiative, the reasons for the initiative, and the ways that management is going to support each employee to implement their part. Everyone seems to be on board in the meetings, but later you receive emails from several employees expressing concerns about how this new initiative will affect them and stating that the goals will be impossible for their particular group to accomplish.
   a. What might be some of the barriers to strong collective efficacy these groups could have?
   b. How might you find out if those barriers exist?
   c. What would you do next to support the collective efficacy of the group? Why is this a good approach?
   d. How does this fit with the Collective Efficacy Overview (see Figure 11.1)?
3. Your hospital department has recently had several instances of missed nursing care, where nursing care for patients has been delayed, partially completed, or not completed at all. This is a problem because the nurses coordinate, provide, and evaluate many interventions prescribed by others to treat illness in hospitalized patients. You notice that many of the nurses don't follow set protocols and also don't interact much with each other. When asked, many of the nurses do not know their colleagues, as many are substitutes from other parts of the hospital, are temporary nurses, or those who work different shifts. Leadership changes often due to changing roles at the hospital, temporary positions, and/or high turnover.
   a. What might be some of the barriers to strong collective efficacy these groups could have?
   b. How might you find out if those barriers exist?
   c. How could you apply the principles of collective efficacy to decrease instances of missed nursing care and increased desired patient outcomes? Why is this a good approach?
   d. How does this fit with the Collective Efficacy Overview (see Figure 11.1)?
4. Your community service agency had merged with other agencies to respond to a natural disaster in your community. After creation of a Unified Command, you are leading the various agencies, each with their own expertise necessary to support an effective response to the incident. Individuals who play leadership roles in their individual agencies now must merge into the new leadership organization and may not have the same roles they have in their home agency. It has been difficult to plan strategically and accomplish the mission of the larger group since each agency is vying for their own agenda.
   a. What might be some of the barriers to strong collective efficacy these groups could have?
   b. How might you find out if those barriers exist?
   c. What would you do next to support the collective efficacy of the group and respond effectively to the natural disaster? Why?
   d. How does this fit with the Collective Efficacy Overview (see Figure 11.1)?

References

Adams, C. M., & Forsyth, P. B. (2006). Proximate sources of collective teacher efficacy. *Journal of Educational Administration*, *44*(6), 625–642.

Bandura, A. (1977). Self-efficacy: Toward a unifying theory of behavioral change. *Psychological Review*, *84*(2).

Bandura, A. (1998). Personal and collective efficacy in human adaptation and change. *Advances in Psychological Science*, *1*(1), 51–71.

Bandura, A. (2000). Exercise of human agency through collective efficacy. *Current Directions in Psychological Science*, *9*(3), 75–78.

Bandura, A., Freeman, W. H., & Lightsey, R. (1999). Self-efficacy: The exercise of control. Springer.

Bandura, A. (1995). Exercise of personal and collective efficacy in changing societies. In A. Bandura (Ed.), *Self-efficacy in changing societies* (pp. 1–45). Cambridge University Press. https://doi.org/10.1017/CBO9780511527692.003Bandura, A., & Watts, R. E. (1996). Self-efficacy in changing societies. Springer.

Bandura, A. (1982). Self-efficacy mechanism in human agency. *American Psychologist*, *37*(2), 122–147. https://doi.org/10.1037/0003-066X.37.2.122

Bass, B.M. and B.J. Avolio (1994). Transformational leadership and organizational culture. *The International Journal of Public Administration, 17 (3-4): 541-554. https://doi.org/10.1080/01900699408524907*

Bonniface, L., & Henley, N. (2008). "A drop in the bucket": Collective efficacy perceptions and environmental behaviour. *Australian Journal of Social Issues*, *43*(3), 345–358.

Carron, A. V., Colman, M. M., Wheeler, J., & Stevens, D. (2002). Cohesion and performance in sport: A meta analysis. *Journal of Sport and Exercise Psychology*, *24*(2), 168–188.

Choi, J. N., & Chang, J. Y. (2009). Innovation implementation in the public sector: An integration of institutional and collective dynamics. *Journal of Applied Psychology*, *94*(1), 245.

Covey, S. R., & Merrill, R. R. (2006). *The speed of trust: The one thing that changes everything.* Simon & Schuster.

Earley, P. C. (1994). Self or group? Cultural effects of training on self-efficacy and performance. *Administrative Science Quarterly*, 89–117.

Feltz, D. L., & Lirgg, C. D. (1998). Perceived team and player efficacy in hockey. *Journal of Applied Psychology*, *83*(4), 557.

Fisher, D., Frey, N., & Hattie, J. (2016). *Visible learning for literacy, grades K–12: Implementing the practices that work best to accelerate student learning.* Corwin Press.

Goddard, R. D., Hoy, W. K., & Hoy, A. W. (2000). Collective teacher efficacy: Its meaning, measure, and impact on student achievement. *American Educational Research Journal*, *37*(2), 479–507.

Goddard, R. D., Hoy, W. K., & Hoy, A. W. (2004). Collective efficacy beliefs: Theoretical developments, empirical evidence, and future directions. *Educational Researcher*, *33*(3), 3–13.

Hodges, L., & Carron, A. V. (1992). Collective efficacy and group performance. *International Journal of Sport Psychology.*

Jex, S. M., & Bliese, P. D. (1999). Efficacy beliefs as a moderator of the impact of work-related stressors: A multilevel study. *Journal of Applied Psychology*, *84*(3), 349.

Kark, R., & Shamir, B. (2002). The influence of transformational leadership on followers relational versus collective self-concept. *Proceedings of the Academy of Management, USA, 2002*(1). https://doi.org/10.5465/apbpp.2002.7517557

Kurz, T. B., & Knight, S. L. (2004). An exploration of the relationship among teacher efficacy, collective teacher efficacy, and goal consensus. *Learning Environments Research*, *7*(2), 111–128.

Lee, J. C.-k., Zhang, Z., & Yin, H. (2011). A multilevel analysis of the impact of a professional learning community, faculty trust in colleagues and collective efficacy on teacher commitment to students. *Teaching and Teacher Education*, *27*(5), 820–830.

Lewis, S. G. (2009). *The contribution of elements of teacher collaboration to individual and collective teacher efficacy.* ProQuest.

Lindsley, D., Mathieu, J., Heffner, T., & Brass, D. (1994). Team efficacy, potency, and performance: A longitudinal examination of reciprocal processes. Annual Meeting of the Society for Industrial and Organizational Psychology. Nashville, Tennessee,

Little, B., & Madigan, R. (1994). Motivation in work teams: A test of the construct of collective efficacy. Annual meeting of the Academy of Management, Houston, Texas,

Luu, S., & Narayan, A. (2017). Games at work: Examining a model of team effectiveness in an interdependent gaming task. *Computers in Human Behavior, 77*, 110–120.

Mullen, B., & Copper, C. (1994). The relation between group cohesiveness and performance: An integration. *Psychological Bulletin, 115*(2), 210.

Pintrich, P. R., & Schunk, D. H. (2002). *Motivation in education: Theory, research, and applications*. Prentice-Hall.

Rapp, T., Maynard, T., Domingo, M., & Klock, E. (2021). Team emergent states: What has emerged in the literature over 20 years. *Small Group Research, 52*(1), 68–102.

Richert, C., Erdlenbruch, K., & Figuières, C. (2017). The determinants of households flood mitigation decisions in France on the possibility of feedback effects from past investments. *Ecological Economics, 131*, 342–352.

Riggs, M. L., & Knight, P. A. (1994). The impact of perceived group success-failure on motivational beliefs and attitudes: A causal model. *Journal of Applied Psychology, 79*(5), 755.

Ross, J., & Bruce, C. (2007). Professional development effects on teacher efficacy: Results of randomized field trial. *The Journal of Educational Research, 101*(1), 50–60.

Salanova, M., Lorente, L., & Martínez, I. M. (2012). The dark and bright sides of self-efficacy in predicting learning, innovative and risky performances. *The Spanish Journal of Psychology, 15*(3), 1123–1132.

Salas, E. E., & Fiore, S. M. (2004). *Team cognition: Understanding the factors that drive process and performance*. American Psychological Association.

Sampson, R. J., Raudenbush, S. W., & Earls, F. (1997). Neighborhoods and violent crime: A multilevel study of collective efficacy. *Science, 277*(5328), 918–924.

Spink, K. S. (1990). Collective efficacy in the sport setting. *International Journal of Sport Psychology*.

Stajkovic, A. D., & Luthans, F. (1998). Self-efficacy and work-related performance: A meta-analysis. *Psychological Bulletin, 124*(2), 240.

Tschannen-Moran, M., & Barr, M. (2004). Fostering student learning: The relationship of collective teacher efficacy and student achievement. *Leadership and Policy in Schools, 3*(3), 189–209.

Tucker, M. K., Jimmieson, N. L., & Oei, T. P. (2013). The relevance of shared experiences: A multi-level study of collective efficacy as a moderator of job control in the stressor-strain relationship. *Work & Stress, 27*(1), 1–21.

Weldon, E., & Weingart, L. R. (1993). Group goals and group performance. *British Journal of Social Psychology, 32*(4), 307–334.

Zander, A., & Medow, H. (1963). Individual and Group Levels of Aspiration. Human Relations, 16(1), 89-105. https://doi.org/10.1177/001872676301600105

Zellars, K. L., Hochwarter, W. A., Perrewe, P. L., Miles, A. K., & Kiewitz, C. (2001). Beyond self-efficacy: Interactive effects of role conflict and perceived collective efficacy. *Journal of Managerial Issues*, 483–499.

CHAPTER 12

Respect for Others and Integrating Diversity

By Ashley Farmer-Hanson

Differences are not intended to separate, to alienate. We are different precisely in order to realize our need of one another.

—Desmond Tutu

Learning Objectives

After reading this chapter, students will be able to:

1. Recognize the benefits and challenges of a diverse workplace
2. Understand the scaffolding and process of diversity training
3. Describe implicit bias

Introduction to Respect for Others and Integrating Diversity

It is increasingly important to create a work environment that allows for and integrates diversity, one which provides respectful space for everyone and honors people's differences. As described in *What Companies Need to Know About Gen Z's Diversity, Equity, and Inclusion Expectations* (2021), a cultural shift is underway, where employees now frequently assume diversity, equity, and inclusion (DEI) will be a part of the workplace. They expect differences to be discussed and celebrated, rather than treated as inappropriate topics for on-the-job conversation. Making space for these discussions does not distract from the task at hand; rather, research shows that teams with a culture of respect are likely to foster successful, high-performing environments (McClendon, 2022; Minot, 2021). Williams and Mihaylo (2019) found that diverse teams "outperform homogeneous ones" (n.p.); as Westover (2021) states, "diversity enhances collaboration, creativity, innovation, decision making, and individual and team productivity" (p. 25).

The benefits of DEI and training add up financially for organizations in many ways. Long gone are the days where people stay with one employer for their whole career. People are more mobile, and if they don't feel like they are being treated with respect as individuals, they will not hesitate to leave (Liu et al., 2023). It is well understood that employee satisfaction is a moderating influence in productivity and employee dissatisfaction may be a destructive force on employee retention (Sageer et al., 2012, and Suffian et al., 2018; as cited in Ntimba et al., 2021); when employees want to work in an inclusive environment, they may well be willing to move elsewhere in search of it (Stanley et al., 2019). Anytime someone leaves, it creates real costs; paying current employees overtime or hiring temps to pick up the extra work created by vacant positions is expensive, and recruitment and new-hire training are also significant expenditures.

The challenge facing employers is how to implement a culture of respect within the workplace as frictionlessly as possible. Most companies do not currently have a chief diversity officer, and as more progressive organizations are seeking to hire them (while "red" states' legislative bodies are restricting their work), the market for qualified personnel is becoming incredibly competitive (Mallick, 2020). This process is complicated by the fact that corporate officers often have not been trained to implement DEI; when I speak with business leaders, many say they value this work, but do not know how to begin. Their uncertainty is exacerbated by a fear that if they do it wrong, it will have the opposite effect and make the workplace feel less inclusive, hurting the organization's image and driving people away.

To ease the process, I use the outline below to help leaders get to a place where diversity and differences are celebrated. One of the critical things that people trying to start DEI initiatives need to recognize is that this work isn't done in a vacuum, and it can take years of incremental change to reshape organizational culture (Hecht, 2020; McClendon, 2022). Being patient and persistent in the pursuit of an equitable workplace is key.

Integrating Diversity and Respect for Others into the Workplace

Step 1: Fostering Trust

The first step to creating an inclusive environment is creating a culture of trust (Sakpal, 2019). Employees must genuinely believe that the space is safe from retribution and that they are free to share stories about their personal background and the things that make them unique (Dewar, 2021). The best formalized way to ensure safety is to have a non-retaliation policy that employees can see in action. For example, having an anonymous whistleblower hotline for reporting harassment is a good practice, but it is only effective if there be a way to report back to the caller with a summary of the inquiry and its findings. Without feedback, the process is opaque to the reporter, which does not engender trust. Fortunately, the technology exists to allow a caller to remain anonymous while still engaging with the investigator; providing a clear summary of the investigation and its findings demonstrates that concerns are taken seriously and shows the organization's resolve in enforcing its policies. Shielding employees from having to identify themselves to report violations helps everyone; it makes reporters feel safe and thus more willing to call attention to issues that might otherwise go unnoticed until they grow large enough to cause significant organizational disruption.

In order to foster inclusion, leaders and managers must demonstrate a commitment to it; by being vulnerable and willing to share about themselves, while listening attentively and nonjudgmentally to the stories of others, they can help create an environment where everyone feels comfortable following suit. Team-building activities and other exercises allowing for self-disclosure and connection should be offered to employees, helping them create and build relationships.[1] It is important to start off slow, focusing on setting the norms for group interactions. Early discussions, for example, should cover how to address instances when people have said things that intentionally or unintentionally hurt one another, which sets the tone for later discussions, as well as providing a framework for dealing with and defusing similar situations in the future. Once these norms are established, post them at every meeting and refer to them; it provides a gentle and convenient reminder of group conventions for when people are emotionally reacting to one another.

1. Adams et al. 1997 provide an excellent overview of theoretical and conceptual frameworks upon which to build activities; their work and subsequent editions of the release offer full curriculum designs for trainers to consider.

From here, a leader can introduce activities that encourage personal self-disclosure, helping people get to know one another beyond the surface level. An example of such an activity is having everyone share a PechaKucha based on a specific theme. *PechaKucha*, Japanese for "the sound of conversation" or "chit chat," usually takes the form of a 20-image slideshow, with participants verbally sharing about the designated topic for 20 seconds per slide. The leader can prompt individuals to share about themselves: their childhood and significant events, their motivations, and the things that bring them joy, as well as challenges they want to solve. The key is to gently encourage the team to be vulnerable with—and supportive of—each other.

Once the participants have grown comfortable with one another, the next step is to start providing space for sharing diversity-related experience. With teams, one exercise I like to do is Peggy McIntosh's (1989) "White Privilege: Unpacking the Invisible Knapsack" activity. This is a self-examination of the ways individuals may have benefited from privilege, without ever knowing that privilege existed. Done well, it provides an opportunity for participants to learn about the lived experience of others and reflect upon their own lives. Once a team feels safe communicating about these topics, they have established a basis of understanding and respect that opens the door to more difficult and nuanced conversations, and further efforts to promote diversity and inclusion may come more easily.

Step 2: Education and Training

As I conduct training, I always take a scaffolded approach. I often work with individuals of the majority culture, who have never had to think about cultural differences or the power and privileges they hold. My goal is to help them identify their own unique backgrounds first, which serves as a starting point for understanding other people's experiences and viewpoints. Step by step, we want to build upon that knowledge until they become comfortable not only advocating for themselves, but also for others. This can be done through activities such as the Iceberg Activity. This activity involves identifying what people see when they look at you, the area above the water with the visible part of the iceberg, and the things they cannot see lurking below the surface (see Figure 12.1 for an illustration).

Above water might be an individual's gender, race, physical disability, marital status, etc. Under the surface might be lurking an invisible disability, religion, socioeconomic status, etc. This activity gets people thinking about how others see them personally, and through discussion, helps them learn more about other people and the challenges they may be facing. As this exchange continues, expand the scope beyond the individual; invite those who are willing to answer questions about their culture and how it shapes their worldviews.[2] The goal is to help the team develop their own self-awareness and begin to build an understanding of others that extends beyond the people they know.

Whatever form trainings may take, research has shown that they should be genuinely voluntary, as compulsory sessions may discourage openness and understanding (Kulik et al., 2007; Murphy, 2018; Stahl, 2020). Leaders should spend time helping their staff to recognize their personal identities in development sessions; as participants grow comfortable sharing and discussing identity, the concept of privilege can be introduced, and they can begin to examine how it impacts their own experiences (Sakpal, 2019). The process of articulating self-identity and the place it holds within society leads to conversations about that intersection, further developing cultural competency. As participants gain a basic understanding of bias, the stage is set for further exploration of the role they could play in combating societal biases. All the following steps build on one another, so education should be ongoing throughout the year (McClendon, 2022; Minot, 2021), including a mixture of events and trainings. Set aside time for periodic evaluations

2. This exercise, known as a *cultural genogram*, has been shown to be an effective teaching tool; for an excellent overview that goes beyond the scope of this chapter, Shellenberger et al. (2007) offer insights into the practice, with reflections from participants.

for learning and employee commitment, as well as opportunities for reflection and self-assessments.

Step 3: Cultural and Ethnic Training

Earlier exercises, focused on making teams comfortable with one another and establishing norms for discussion, have laid the groundwork for more specific trainings. Beginning with broad discussions around cultural and ethnic identity is a good first step because when we think about inclusion, this is often the first topic that comes to mind. It might be because "we have always lived in an ethnically diverse society; we are all operating in an increasingly culturally diverse environment where we need to be able to interact, communicate, build relationships, and work effectively with people from diverse cultural and ethnic backgrounds" (Guzman et al., 2016, n.p). Because these differences are often immediately recognizable while interacting with people, the concept is easy to identify and relate with.

FIGURE 12.1 Below the Iceberg

The company should consider researching key stakeholders' cultures to ensure the employees know a basic understanding of those they interact with the most. This can take any form from distributing an anonymous questionnaire to employees asking demographic questions, to hiring a marketing firm to better understand their customer base, to bringing in outside experts to help devise strategy. Companies with a DEI officer often have them keep track of demographics and provide updates to senior leaders on the various cultures, faiths, and genders present in the workplace; other organizations without a dedicated officer could have a committee lead this charge.

One thing to keep in mind is that if the workplace has one dominant culture, the employer may want to reach out to members of minority cultures to see if there be any interest in celebrating them. It is imperative that these sessions do not make those in the minority feel pressured to agree to such celebrations or to take on the role of cultural ambassador if they are not interested or comfortable doing so. Too often, the role of DEI educator is informally shunted onto these individuals instead of the organization itself taking responsibility for providing information about cultural resources.

Step 4: Faith and Spiritual Training

Often, we avoid conversations about religion and politics in public spaces. The trouble with this is that a person's faith or spiritual background impacts their personal values and how they navigate their workplaces. By neglecting discussions about how faith manifests itself in employees, we are ignoring a vital piece of what makes people who they are and overlooking what that may bring to the workplace. As Harvey (n.d.)

states, "employers who embrace these conversations [about aspects of identity] openly and honestly ... can benefit from the momentum created" (n.p.). During this training, it is worthwhile to examine which holidays are celebrated, how staff interact with clients during them, and what seasonal decorations are put up throughout the year. While it may seem difficult to keep track of all the different religious holy days, it is actually quite simple for an employer to accommodate everyone. An easy solution is to provide floating holidays, which can be used at the employees' discretion, allowing each to celebrate the days that are important to them personally. These days could be used in ways similar to vacation time or paid time off but would be offered in lieu of company-wide holidays for Christmas or New Year, allowing staff to celebrate on alternative days that hold religious or cultural significance.

Step 5: Gender Identity and Expression

Gender identity is the subjective experience of one's own gender, which is expressed through clothing, pronouns, hairstyle, or behavior. Until recently, gender identity and its expression were not on the radar for most people, and organizations conducting DEI training should be aware that this could be a new concept or discussion item for some individuals (Cletus et al., 2018). As different modes of gender expression may be outside the experience of many, it may take some time to familiarize participants with the many forms that expression can take. While Generation Z is, as a rule, an incredibly diverse group of people comfortable with openness around gender identity (DiMillo et al., 2021), cultural norms and inclusive language are still developing, particularly around dress, pronouns, and bathroom use. Workplaces must help their teams understand and use best practices in these regards (Chaney & Sanchez, 2018; Coon et al., 2023; Knutson et al., 2019; Pinter et al., 2020).

Step 6: Personal Bias

After a few trainings, it is always good to stop, assess for learning, and formally introduce the concept of unconscious bias. This construct describes the ways the cultural lenses through which we judge others and their actions can rely upon negative stereotypes about minority populations. As Stahl (2020) outlines, "we make snap judgments and assumptions about others based upon learned behaviors and biases that are so entrenched in our system and insidious that we breathe them in like air without even realizing it" (n.p.). These biases are accepted as norms without conscious recognition of their impact. Because they are unrecognized, personal biases can seem like "just how things are," and we often gravitate to information that validates them and surround ourselves with people who are similar to us. Often, many people are unaware they even have a bias until they engage in activities and education. "Leaders can start addressing this by helping employees understand how individuals are impacted by unconscious bias, and what actions continue to reinforce biases" (McClendon, 2022). Quizzes and activities can help participants identify their biases and then build intentional plans to keep bias in check and push back on it. When addressing bias, it is essential to provide space for people to process new skills, reflect on their feelings, and apply what they have learned. From my experience, some staff can feel ashamed as they begin to recognize the influence unconscious bias had on their thoughts and attitudes. Support and reassurance must be evident as they work through these uncomfortable feelings; discomfort can lead to avoidance, leaving problems with bias unresolved. People should understand that these are unintentional behaviors and attitudes; most of us do not wake up and say to ourselves, "I really want to be driven by my personal biases today!" These are learned behaviors that have been instilled in us and developed over many years, and it can take a lot of time, reflection, and space for a person to change—but going through this process improves the organization as a whole, providing a path to creating an inclusive environment (Cletus et al., 2018).

Step 7: Bystander Intervention Training

Bystander intervention training, which teaches staff how to intervene when they may witness a discriminatory act, is essential to combating bias within the workplace (Gurchiek, 2021). While the immediate goal is to disrupt or stop the interaction from happening, the long-term desired effect is de-normalizing discrimination. As individuals become comfortable and confident in recognizing and discouraging biased behavior, people automatically begin to check their own actions and thinking, shifting the norms of organizational culture (Szilágyi, 2008). At the beginning, though, it can be difficult for people to actively intervene to disrupt these interactions.

Often, it feels like violating a societal norm to step in, which puts onlookers in uncomfortable situations. Reputable training offers participants a structured outline for intervening, which makes it easier to understand when and how to get involved.[3] Remember that the goal of any intervention should be to call people in instead of calling them out; this means making a good-faith effort to communicate and bring the issue to attention. Calling people in is an opportunity to understand each other's viewpoint, hopefully providing a springboard for paradigm shifts in thinking (Tufts University, n.d.). The real focus is on getting an individual to reflect on their actions or words that were harmful, rather than on the recipient's reaction to them. This is only possible, however, if all participants have mutual respect and the work environment is conducive to such discussions. Interventions should not create a hostile work environment, but part of the onus is on the people being called in; these trainings should include practice accepting feedback and applying it in real time. Scott (2002) shared that it is the manager's role to create a safe environment that allows for feedback to be given at all levels within the organization. Accountability, support, and follow-up are crucial to changing behaviors and setting expectations.

At this point, we can move from advocacy to taking action. Bystander intervention training gives one the skills to effectively apply their knowledge, providing them an opportunity to actively participate and see how they can have a direct impact on company culture.

BOX 12.1 **Examples of Intervention**

The first step in successful intervention is to just observe the environment and examine the things we take for granted. Williams and Mihaylo (2019) suggest we look for instances where some people may be allowed more leeway in their behavior than others, see if specific groups have to work harder than others to be recognized for their efforts, and watch for cases where minorities compete with one another for scarce resources.

For example, look to see if women are being asked more to do the office housework, such as preparing the space for events and cleaning up afterward. If so, suggest that these duties be shared on a rotating basis, or specifically ask others if they would lend a hand. In meetings, does everyone have an equal chance to speak, or are majority group members taking most of the airtime? Specifically ask those you have not heard from if they have anything they would like to contribute to the conversation. Does your workplace have a budget for celebrating cultural holidays? Make sure it has enough funds so that everyone has an equal opportunity to hold their events, without competition.

---

3. Gurchiek (2021) offers a framework with five simple steps: "1. Notice the event; 2. Interpret the situation as a problem; 3. Assume personal responsibility; 4. Know how to help; 5. Step up and take action" (n.p.).

Ensuring Long-Term Success

A company's backbone comes from the strength of its employees; those same employees are the foundation for an effective diversity initiative. Such programs must address the literal needs of staff if they are to gain traction, and thus a climate survey is an appropriate place to begin. Such surveys are designed to gather information about the workplace environments (Baum, 2021; Dewar, 2021; Energage, 2021), including demographic information, how individuals feel about the company's culture, respondents' unmet needs, and gaps in communication or information. To maximize the value of responses, it should be clear that the questionnaire is both voluntary and anonymous; while not everyone will respond, the data received likely reflects the actual needs and preferences of least empowered and most dissatisfied employees. With that information, leaders can gain insights into the challenges and concerns faced by employees and identify key issues with which to begin.

By being involved in the needs-assessment process, employees gain a voice in shaping the programs and services that are designed to support them. This participatory approach not only enhances the quality and relevance of the initiatives, but also fosters a sense of ownership and engagement among the workforce. Feedback on the effectiveness of programs and policies allows an organization to prioritize spending its efforts and resources on addressing identified gaps in service provision. By leveraging this information, a company can ensure that its initiatives are responsive, impactful, and tailored to meet the specific needs of its employees. Because not everyone may respond to the climate survey, leadership should continue to host focus groups and department meetings to further identify areas for development and get a sense of how employees are feeling. It may take a few rounds of data collection and observation before a leader can truly understand the culture of the community. Over time, though, more people should be willing to share their thoughts as training sessions create opportunities for building trust among employees. The more this is done, the more people will be willing to share their personal experiences.

From what I've seen, leaders risk getting caught up in negative comments or findings when analyzing gathered data. Too often, they get discouraged and overwhelmed. Don't let those emotions take the driver's seat! DEI work is hard and personal, and feelings of doubt can slow down or stall the process. This is why it is essential to celebrate progress and share the work among a reliable team that can help each other stay motivated and focused.

For DEI training to take root and bring lasting change, we must create systems of support. No single person can successfully do this work alone. Time and time again, companies hire a diversity officer and assume everything will be fine; without providing ongoing resources in support of diversity initiatives, however, the project is doomed to failure (Howard, 2021). It is unrealistic to expect a diversity officer to be effective unless leadership makes efforts to implement DEI at all levels within the organization.

BOX 12.2 **Case Study: Successfully Supporting DEI Through Communication**

ABC Co., launching a new diversity initiative, faced resistance from some employees and managers. To overcome this resistance, the head of the DEI team focused on making the process open, transparent, and implemented at all levels. She held town hall meetings to address concerns and misconceptions about DEI initiatives, taking questions and answering as best she could—and more importantly, subsequent town halls opened with follow-up discussions of topics broached earlier.

In addition to this outreach to general staff, the organization also provided training resources to inform management about the business case for diversity and inclusion, working hard to bring leadership on board. Additional development was offered to help leaders learn to model behavior and communicate its importance to their teams, ensuring that no single person was entirely responsible for the initiative's success or failure. By fostering dialogue and providing education, ABC Co. and its leadership collectively overcame resistance, creating a more inclusive workplace by modeling what they hoped to see in the future.

I cannot stress enough that higher-ups must demonstrate their commitment, both by word and deed. Not only must they fund diversity initiatives, but they must also publicly acknowledge and create space for leaders to grow and develop. By modeling behavior, communicating clearly, and diligently following company policy, leaders create a culture receptive to DEI.

Grievance and Complaint System

As a company works on creating a culture of respect, one of the first things to focus on is the process for reporting grievances and complaints. The U.S. Equal Employment Opportunity (EEO) Commission (n.d.) states,

> Participating in a complaint process is protected from retaliation under all circumstances. Other acts to oppose discrimination are protected as long as the employee was acting on a reasonable belief that something in the workplace may violate EEO laws, even if he or she did not use legal terminology to describe it. (n.p.)

In establishing a grievance process, however, I encourage organizations to go above and beyond the letter of the law. As I noted earlier in "Fostering Trust," making the process anonymous is hugely important, as people who fear retaliation will often keep silent about issues rather than risk the social and economic fallout that could follow a public complaint. Diversity officers and leadership should be aware of and knowledgeable about the law but should also consider how the workforce believes they will be protected; employees need to have faith that they can report issues freely and that policy will be fairly and reliably enforced.

When asked, people often say that they did not come forward to report policy violations because they were worried about their position at the company or because they have seen previous complaints made, but no one did anything about them (Stahl, 2020). This silence ensures that problems are not brought to the organization's attention, and thus the company does not implement measures to address or fix them. While a system for anonymous reporting can help people feel safer reporting violations or concerns, a rigid process for formal complaints can be daunting. Dobbin and Kalev (n.d.) found that too much focus on formal procedures can actually "slow workforce integration," and they encourage organizations to "adopt a menu of alternatives [to formal complaints], including ombuds programs and dispute-resolution systems" (p. 24). A healthy balance of formal and informal channels is key to success; having options and different paths for people to follow will allow them to make independent decisions and feel like they have some control over the outcome and process. It is important to provide support, though, even when proceeding informally. A neutral party such as an ombudsperson can provide policy interpretation and lay out options for how the individual can move forward. These roles are designed to help resolve conflict, and ombudspersons are also responsible for bringing systemic issues they discover to the attention of leaders for a long-term solution.

Analyzing and Fixing Systemic Barriers

Systemic barriers are the written and unwritten things in policies, procedures, and practices that create barriers to success for particular groups. Companies must spend time digging into their policies and assessing if any of them are making it difficult for underserved populations to succeed (McClendon, 2022; Energage, 2021). For example, is the company dress code written for all genders, or does it fixate on one? When the company has a picnic, are the halal and kosher offerings cooked on separate charcoal grills? Do those who conduct interviews for new hires take part in antibias training, so they can recognize and push back on their personal biases when hiring people?

Hiring practices are particularly important; people tend to prefer candidates and offer jobs to those who are similar to themselves (Stahl, 2020). While this is natural behavior, it has the effect of reducing diversity, which can affect performance. As Sakpal (2019) notes, "Having diversity of thought can be what saves a team from groupthink and allows it to achieve better outcomes" (n.p.). Fostering a diverse workforce strengthens an organization, but doing so requires a deliberate effort to include a wide range of people at all levels. The more diversity a decision-making body has, the more likely it will be to consider everyone's needs when crafting policy, which is vital to improving retention and satisfaction.

It is crucial to monitor progress and adjust policy or programs as needed to further DEI goals. Assess what people need to be successful. Is it difficult to maintain diversity because of high turnover? Create a mentorship program that supports minorities and guides them to move up within the company (Creary et al., 2021; Minot, 2021). Track the representation of different demographic groups at all levels of the organization, including data collection on the diversity of applicants, new hires, promotions, and exits. Do people feel undervalued? Start affinity groups that bring small communities of people who share interests or culture together, allowing them to support one another. These groups can be built around almost any shared construct but are particularly helpful for specific cultural or minority groups that may need space to meet and build community outside of traditional roles within the organization. Step back with an equity lens and examine policies and institutional culture with a group of diverse people. Leaders will be surprised by what they find.

Assessing Success

As training and implementation proceed, it is important to celebrate the big and small wins (Sakpal, 2019; Mackenzie & Wehner, n.d.) achieved by DEI programs. This work is hard; the problem can feel overwhelming when we start by identifying all the areas in which we can improve, and progress can come slowly and hard to identify at first. I recommend that teams build a plan that establishes small goals, with frequent reassessment as they are reached. Those evaluations quantify progress so it can be communicated to stakeholders (McClendon, 2022); a plan also holds everyone accountable to the company's expectations.

One method of doing this is through a logic model, "a graphical representation of ... the resources (inputs) and activities that will take place, [and] the deliverables (outputs) and goals (outcomes) that the program will produce" (Suber, 2019, n.p.). This method gives a leader an easy-to-grasp overview of the work ahead, helping them to map out intentional actions and assign them to individuals or groups. It is a great tool when communicating internally and externally about what the organization wants to achieve and what actions it will take to get there. Below is an example of a logic model.[4] The user would start out with the Problem/Objective box and work through from left to right. It is good to workshop the model as a team; the common thread of this chapter is including a diversity of views and thoughts, after all! When the model is complete, be sure to regularly check in on progress, and share updates with the entire organization.

4. Royse et al. 2016 cover logic models in depth as a part of their work on program evaluation. For an extensive completed example with explanations, the Centers for Disease Control and Prevention (2020) has exceptional materials, such as https://www.cdc.gov/tb/programs/evaluation/Logic_Model.html.

TABLE 12.1 **Logic Model for Gender-Inclusive Restroom Project**

Program Logic Model				
Goal: To evaluate a DEI workplace effort				
Focus Population: XYZ Organizational Employees				
Project Objectives: (1) Catalyze multigenerational support for gender-inclusive restrooms (2) Assess attitudes toward implementation of gender-inclusive restrooms				
Inputs	**Tactics and Activities**	**Outputs**	**Short-term Outcomes**	**Long-term Outcomes**
Project coordinator—appoint or hire	Campaign to focus on gender identity as a DEI initiative. Form project team. Gather information about employee attitudes.	Project-team meetings. Materials produced to market campaign. New training sessions written up, organized by type/method. Ongoing strategies to achieve objectives. Number of employees using gender-inclusive restrooms.	Expanded awareness of the issue. Acceptance of the practice as legitimate. Increased sense of belonging for gender-diverse employees.	Increased % of employees publicly supporting gender-inclusive restrooms. All gender identities included and supported.
Assumptions: (1) Leadership will support the redesign of a pilot group of restrooms. (2) Coordinators and managers of the project will continue DEI programming aimed at rationalizing gender-inclusive restrooms. (3) Employees want to work in an inclusive and welcoming workplace for all gender identities.				

As the logic model and goals are being built, be mindful that not everything will need a new policy. While a program that starts a tradition of celebrating a new cultural holiday or event shows progress, so does something as simple as a staff member catching their own bias and changing practices.

Activities

1. Think about where you have seen diversity, equity, and inclusion discussed or implemented at school or the workplace. What did leaders do well? What could they improve to make the experience more effective?
2. Find your school or employer's grievance process. Do the policies laid out provide a path for your voice to be heard? Are there also informal channels for reporting issues—and if so, where did you learn about them? What would make either one of these processes better?
3. Think of a few questions you could ask that would help define your university or workplace culture. Why are those questions important, and what would you do with the answers?

Conclusion

Drafting a DEI policy is just the first step in a long process. As shown in this chapter, organizations must devote time and resources to ensure that diversity initiatives thrive. This requires building a culture of inclusion, providing ongoing training and support, measuring the success of the initiative, and overcoming resistance and obstacles along the way. Leaders should always be learning and growing, striving to identify ways to improve organizational culture. Above all, they must keep in mind that it will take group effort to truly implement real, lasting change within an organization. I believe that by following the tactics described here, organizations can create workplaces that foster equality, innovation, and overall business success. Remember, diversity and inclusion are not just buzzwords; they are essential for creating better futures for all. Workplace leaders should set worthwhile goals and be willing to take real risks during this process. The companies will thank them later.

Application

Exercise: Case Study

Tracey has just taken a position at All Advance Together (AAT), a regional technology company that is expanding nationwide. He is feeling especially nervous, as this is not only his first day at a new company, but also his first time in a managerial role. After filling out paperwork for HR, Tracey's first day begins at 9:00 a.m. when he is scheduled to meet with his manager, Joey. He is escorted to a conference room, where he patiently waits for Joey to arrive. A few minutes later, Joey peeks in. He says, "Oh, sorry 'bout that! I've got the wrong room!" and turns to leave. Recognizing him, Tracey speaks up: "Hi Joey, it's me, Tracey." Joey immediately looks embarrassed and comes into the room, saying, "Hey, sorry. I saw your name on my sheet, and thought you were supposed to be a girl." Tracey puts on a smile and replies, "I get that quite a bit; it's okay. Should we get started?"

Joey sits down and begins to outline the major responsibilities of the job. Tracey listens intently but begins to wonder when they will start talking about diversity and inclusion within the organization. This was presented as a key part of AAT's mission and values during earlier interviews, and that focus was a large part of the reason he wanted to take the position. Tracey waits in vain, and Joey never mentions anything about DEI. After a while, Joey pauses and asks if Tracey has any questions. "Can you tell me what my role will be in creating a respectful work environment and integrating diversity? The recruiter told me that AAT recently began a big diversity-and-inclusion program, and I want to make sure I do a good job with it. This is my first time in this sort of position, so I wanted to know if there were any specific trainings for managers or anything."

Joey looks a little surprised and seems unsure how to answer the question. "Well, I think we've got an online module thing you can watch. It's not really a big deal; most people here are pretty average guys, so there's not a lot that's especially involved or anything. Mostly we just try to tone down the caveman stuff and keep the womenfolk comfortable, y'know? We're just normal people, and we get along pretty well. Anybody says the wrong thing, something not P.C. enough, just know they don't mean any harm. People are just too sensitive these days," he says, shaking his head.

Heart sinking, Tracey pushes on. "Well, what about holidays and stuff? Do we have a calendar or guide for, uh, nonmainstream celebrations, or anything like that?" Joey cocks his head and looks bemused. "Like, you mean Kwanzaa or something? I mean, it's basically Christmas, and we all get time off from the 23rd through New Year's Day, so pretty much everybody's covered. I think Hanukkah moves around, so maybe some people use vacation time for that, but I don't know if any of us are Jews. I guess you could ask HR if you needed to," he says. "Other than that, we do the usual. Long weekend for Easter, Fourth of July, Labor Day, all that."

Tracey is getting increasingly uncomfortable. Joey is obviously unconcerned with the company's DEI policies, and from what he's saying, it sounds like the organization mostly considers Christian holidays when making their schedule. As a Muslim, Tracey is getting worried about whether he can even take time out in the middle of the day for afternoon prayers—never mind asking about a flexible schedule during Ramadan. He doesn't want to be labeled the "loud person" or a troublemaker on his first day, but he wants to be an ally for underserved populations, and he feels like he needs to try one more time. "Well, what do I need to do for the diversity program? Are you trying to recruit or retain more people of color? Does that population have a high turnover here?" Again, Joey doesn't seem to have any answers. "I don't think so. I mean, we don't keep track of those things. We value people here; we don't see color," he says. Checking his watch, Joey wraps things up. "It looks like we have run out of time. Let's check in again with each other later in the week, okay? It's good to have you here!" As Joey walks out of the room, Tracey gathers his things, and wonders what he got himself into. He is beginning to think he may have made a huge mistake taking this new job.

Study Questions

1. After reviewing this case study, what steps do you think Tracey should take to integrate diversity training into his division?
2. Joey demonstrated multiple acts of unconscious bias and *–isms*. As a new hire, Tracey is understandably uncomfortable calling Joey's attention to his actions. How can he interrupt and try to prevent it from happening again?
3. What are some systemic changes this organization can implement to create a more inclusive work environment?
4. What specific actions or trainings would you provide to help Joey push back on his bias and avoid making the same mistakes in future orientations?

References

Adams, M., Bell, L. A., & Griffin, P. (1997). *Teaching for diversity and social justice.* Routledge.

Baum, B. (2021). Diversity, Equity, and Inclusion Policies: Are organizations truly committed to a workplace culture shift? *Journal of Business and Behavioral Science*, *3*(2), 11–23.

Centers for Disease Control and Prevention. (2020, November 7). *Developing a logic model.* https://www.cdc.gov/tb/programs/evaluation/Logic_Model.html

Chaney, K. E., & Sanchez, D. T. (2018). Gender-inclusive bathrooms signal fairness across identity dimensions. *Social Psychological and Personality Science, 9*(2), 245–253. https://doi.org/10.1177/1948550617737601

Cletus, H. E., Mahmood, N. A., Umar, A., & Ibrahim, A. D. (2018). Prospects and challenges of workplace diversity in modern day organizations: A critical review. *HOLISTICA—Journal of Business and Public Administration, 9*(2), 35–52. https://doi.org/10.2478/hjbpa-2018-0011

Coon, J. J., Alexander, N. B., Smith, E. M., Spellman, M., Klimasmith, I. M., Allen-Custodio, L. T., Clarkberg, T. E., Lynch, L., Knutson, D., Fountain, K., Rivera, M., Scherz, M., & Morrow, L. K. (2023). Best practices for lgbtq+ inclusion during ecological fieldwork: Considering safety, cis/heteronormativity and structural barriers. *Journal of Applied Ecology, 60*(3), 393–399. https://doi.org/10.1111/1365-2664.14339

Creary, S. J., Rothbard, N., & Scruggs, J. (2021, May). Improving workplace culture through evidence-based diversity, equity and inclusion practices. Wharton School. https://doi.org/10.31234/osf.io/8zgt9

Dewar, J. (2021). 10 ways to improve diversity, equity, and inclusion in the workplace. Sapling HR. https://www.saplinghr.com/blog/10-ways-to-improve-diversity-equity-and-inclusion-in-the-workplace

DiMillo, V., Brown, A., & Harrington, B. (2021). Addressing race in the workplace: Advancing diversity, equity, and inclusion. Boston College Center for Work & Family: Executive Briefing Series.

Dobbin, F., & Kalev, A. (n.d.). Making discrimination and harassment complaint systems better. *What works: Evidence-based ideas to increase diversity, equity, and inclusion in the workplace*. Center for Employment Equity. UMass Amherst. Making Discrimination and Harassment Complaint Systems Better | Center for Employment Equity | UMass Amherst

Energage. (2021, July 1). Diversity, equity, and inclusion in the workplace. *Top Workplaces*. Diversity, Equity, and Inclusion in the Workplace (topworkplaces.com)

Gurchiek, K. (2021, July 6). Bystander intervention can disrupt the flow of bad behavior. SHRM. Bystander Intervention Can Disrupt the Flow of Bad Behavior (shrm.org)

Guzman, M. R., Durden, T., Taylor, S., Guzman, J., & Potthoff, K. (2016, February). Cultural competency skill set for the 21st century. *Youth and Family.* Nebraska Extension

Harvey, D. (n.d.). Embracing open conversations to foster empathy and equity. Kforce Staffing & Solutions. Fostering Diversity, Equity and Inclusion in the Workforce

Hecht, B. (2020, June 16). Moving beyond diversity toward racial equity. *Harvard Business Review.* https://hbr.org/2020/06/moving-beyond-diversity-toward-racial-equity

Howard, R. (2021, December 7). So, you hired a chief diversity officer. Now what? *HR Executive.* Moving Beyond Diversity Toward Racial Equity (hbr.org)

Knutson, D., Koch, J. M., & Goldbach, C. (2019). Recommended terminology, pronouns, and documentation for work with transgender and non-binary populations. *Practice Innovations,* 4(4), 214–224. https://doi.org/10.1037/pri0000098

Kulik, C., Pepper, M., Roberson, L., & Parker, S. K. (2007). The rich get richer: Predicting participation in voluntary diversity training. *Journal of Organizational Behavior,* 28(6), 753–769. https://doi.org/10.1002/job.444

Liu, J., Zhu, Y., & Wang, H. (2023). Managing the negative impact of workforce diversity: The important roles of inclusive HRM and employee learning-oriented behaviors. *Front Psychol,* (14). https://doi.org/10.3389/fpsyg.2023.1117690

Mackenzie, L., & Wehner, J. (n.d.). Context matters: Moving beyond "best practices" to creating sustainable change. In *What works: Evidence-based ideas to increase diversity, equity, and inclusion in the workplace.* Center for Employment Equity. UMass Amherst. Context Matters: Moving beyond "Best Practices" to Creating Sustainable Change | Center for Employment Equity | UMass Amherst

Mallick, M. (2020, September 11). Do you know why your company needs a chief diversity officer? *Harvard Business Review.* Do You Know Why Your Company Needs a Chief Diversity Officer? (hbr.org)

McClendon, D. (2022, June 21). *How to promote diversity, equity, and inclusion in the Workplace.* Intelligence at work. How to promote diversity, equity, and inclusion in the workplace (ceridian.com)

McIntosh, P. (1989). "White privilege: Unpacking the invisible knapsack." National SEED Project on Inclusive Curriculum. January 28, 2009 (nationalseedproject.org)

Minot, L. (2021). *9 proven strategies to improve diversity, equity & inclusion at your workplace. Great Place to Work.* 9 Proven Strategies to Improve Diversity, Equity & Inclusion at Your Workplace | Great Place To Work®

Murphy, W. L. (2018). Distinguishing diversity from inclusion in the workplace: Legal necessity or common sense conclusion? 49, Academy of Legal Studies in Business National Procedures. http://alsb.org/alsb-resources/alsb-proceedings/2018-alsb-national-proceedings/

Ntimba, D., Lessing, K., Swarts, I. (2021). Job satisfaction and dissatisfaction as outcomes of psychological contract: Evidence from the South African workplace. *JHRSS,* 03(09), 484–502. https://doi.org/10.4236/jhrss.2021.93031

Pinter, H. H., Bloom, L., Rush, C., & Sastre, C. (2020). Best practices in teacher preparation for inclusive education. In *Handbook of Research on Innovative Pedagogies and Best Practices in Teacher Education* (pp. 52–68). https://doi.org/10.4018/978-1-5225-9232-7.ch004

Retaliation. (n.d.). US EEOC. Retaliation | U.S. Equal Employment Opportunity Commission (eeoc.gov)

Royse, D., Thyer, B. A., & Padgett, D. K. (Eds.). (2016). Chapter 5: What are formative and process evaluations? In *Program evaluation: An introduction to an evidence-based approach* (6th ed., pp. 121–151). Cengage.

Sakpal, M. (2019). CIOs must harness diversity and an inclusive mindset to build cohesive and successful teams. Gartner. CIOs should embrace DEI to build successful teams (gartner.com)

Scott, S. (2002). *Fierce conversations: Achieving success at work & in life, one conversation at a time.* Viking.

Shellenberger, S., Dent, M. M., Davis-Smith, M., Seale, J. P., Weintraut, R., & Wright, T. (2007). Cultural genogram: A tool for teaching and practice. *Families, Systems, & Health,* 25(4), 367–381. https://doi.org/10.1037/1091-7527.25.4.367

Stahl, A. (2020). 10 Steps businesses can take to improve diversity and inclusion in the workforce. Forbes. https://www.forbes.com/sites/ashleystahl/2020/07/21/10-steps-businesses-can-take-to-improve-diversity-and-inclusion-in-the-workforce/?sh=7ff512c9343e

Stanley, C., Watson, K., Reyes, J., Varela, K. (2019). Organizational change and the chief diversity officer: A case study of institutionalizing a diversity plan. *Journal of Diversity in Higher Education, 3*(12), 255–265. https://doi.org/10.1037/dhe0000099

Suber, L. (2019, April 3). *What are logic models, and when should you use them?* NC State Industry Expansion Solutions. What are logic models, and when should you use them? - NC State University Industry Expansion Solutions (ncsu.edu)

Szilágyi, B. (2008). The relationship between the organizational culture and the individual attitude, particularly the question of individualism and collectivism. *Acta Agraria Debreceniensis, 29*, Article 29. https://doi.org/10.34101/actaagrar/29/2981

Tallo. (2021, July 12). *What companies need to know about Gen Z's diversity, equity, and inclusion expectations.* https://tallo.com/blog/gen-z-workplace-diversity-equity-inclusion/

Tufts University (n.d.). Calling out vs. calling in: Diversity and inclusion. Tufts. Interrupting Bias: Calling Out vs. Calling In - Diversity and Inclusion (tufts.edu)

Westover, J. H. (2021). The importance of diversity, equity, inclusion, and belonging in the workplace: Maximizing the human capital potential of our people. *Leadership Excellence*, 38(2), 23–27. https://www.hr.com/en/resources/coronavirus/the-importance-of-diversity-equity-inclusion-and-b_kkn04sxk.html

Williams, J. C. and Mihaylo, S. (2019). How the best bosses interrupt bias on their teams. *Harvard Business Review.* November-December, 2019. How the Best Bosses Interrupt Bias on Their Teams (hbr.org)

Credit

Fig. 12.1: Copyright © 2021 Unsplash/Simon Lee.

UNIT IV

LEADING THE ORGANIZATION

CHAPTER 13

Creating and Sharing Vision, Mission, and Values

By J. Vincent Nix

It's tough to make predictions, especially about the future.

—Yogi Berra

Learning Objectives

After reading this chapter, students will be able to:

1. Articulate the meanings of vision, mission, and values
2. Understand the concept of competencies
3. Identify the competencies which are critical to creating and sharing vision, mission, and values
4. Isolate individual competencies which may need development
5. Create and share vision, mission, and values in their respective professional roles

Introduction to Vision, Mission, and Values

First, let us approach the construct of vision. What, precisely, is a vision, and how does a leader create one—particularly if their organization does not yet have one articulated? A straightforward definition of the construct is "an aspirational image that informs actions and catalyzes long-term efforts toward organizational improvement." A vision statement should be a sort of Platonic ideal, announcing what the organization strives to be and do as it interacts with the world. It should state the ideal clearly and motivate and inspire people to take action toward realizing that vision. Yet, as a forward-looking aspiration, the goal should be an ever-receding one; as the ideal approaches realization, the vision should be revisited, extended, and improved upon. After all, if an organization's goals have been reached, why does it exist; for this reason, if a vision does include a logical stopping point, it is imperative to plan for what comes next once that is reached. This focus on the future is vital, as it ensures organizational consistency across years, even as leadership changes. For example, the revered filmmaker Federico Fellini was also known for being a multigenerational visionary whose work lives on in several contemporary filmmakers; Scorsese, Lynch, Gilliam, and Burton have all stated that Fellini's vision heavily influenced their own work (Fellini, 2023). Three quotes attributed to him are an appropriate backdrop to this chapter.

These quotes are illustrative as we examine how to effectively create and share a vision.

BOX 13.1 **Federico Fellini on Vision**

Nothing is more honest than a dream.

The visionary is the only realist.

Realism is a bad word. In a sense everything is realistic. I see no line between the imaginary and the real.

The Vision

At its heart, a vision is a dream of a possible future in which the organization effects a desired outcome; simply put, it offers an alternative idea of what the world can and should be.[1] Second, we need to understand reality and be able to describe it if we wish to elaborate the changes needed to bring the vision about. This requires an honest recognition of the organizational and personal values and attributes that drive all action, which is crucial to creating organizational strategy (examined in depth in Chapter 17). Remember, though, that while it is necessary to have a realistic understanding of one's situation, capabilities, and challenges, a good vision should not be bound by those things. Reluctance to espouse a transformative vision because it is perceived as impractical, unreasonable, or unnecessary can be obstinacy masquerading as risk-averse behavior, often reinforced by groupthink. Those who are willing to depart from "the way it's done" or "the natural order of things'" are truly visionaries, and their successes are transformative.

Vision is closely connected with mission, working together to form a foundation for action. A vision statement specifies an organization's desired future state and articulates its long-term aspirations, setting the course and providing a framework for decision-making. Putting that vision into action requires a mission, which describes the overall purpose of the organization, what it hopes to achieve, and how it intends to get there.

The Mission

A mission serves as a roadmap, laying out the path for reaching the vision. It serves as a benchmark against which performance can be measured and provides justification for making the necessary adjustments to stay on track. Ideally, it also serves to rally employees around the organization's common goals and helps to instill a sense of purpose.

The mission should be specific and achievable and should be structured in a way that makes it easy to use as a guide in decision-making. As such, the mission statement should be communicated to all stakeholders in a clear, concise manner and must be regularly reviewed and updated to keep it relevant. When the mission and vision are aligned, the organization can more effectively pursue its goals and objectives. By having a clear mission and vision, organizations can stay focused and ensure that their efforts are aligned to the desired outcome.

Thus, a properly written mission statement should describe how an organization intends to manifest its values and vision in the world at large. For example, if an institution values compassion and its vision is of a world where no one has to struggle to meet their needs for safe food and water, a reasonable mission

1. Note that this applies equally to all institutions, be they driven by altruism or profit. Even the most rapacious robber baron had a vision of an alternative, ideal reality: namely, one in which they were rolling in money and had crushed their competition.

would be "to expand access to clean water and healthy food by leading projects that drill wells and provide efficient irrigation in rural villages." Each time an organization looks into expansion or taking on a new project, its leaders should ask, "Does this support our mission?"

There is no one-size-fits-all best template to follow when crafting a mission statement, but I often refer to David and David (2016), who suggest addressing the following elements: clients, services, markets, technology, growth and profits, philosophy, organizational self-concept, public image, and employees (p. 48). When I facilitate a session, I make sure that each of these components is discussed; when an organization decides to omit one, justification should be provided. Often, I find that these elements are thoughtlessly excluded by people who fail to think deeply enough about what a mission statement should be.

For example, I often have seen a mission statement which fails to address an organization's employees. If the mission be an externally facing one, it may seem unnecessary to explicitly describe internal elements; I argue though that including employees in a mission statement is an important part of any company's success. Doing so fosters an environment of trust and respect and engenders motivation and morale. It demonstrates the company's appreciation for its people and conveys the message that they are a part of the company's core values and principles. This helps to create a sense of belonging and purpose, which in turn helps keep employees engaged and committed, striving to perform their best. Collaboration and innovation improve, and as the people within it devote effort to improving their own skills and outputs, the company itself will perforce constantly strive to improve its operations and processes. Similarly, the other elements set forth by David and David (2016) are also vital to fostering excellence by forging a link between organizational excellence, goals, and success.

A well-structured mission statement provides a map to achieving the vision and also points toward the core values and beliefs of the organization, as shown by its stated goals and objectives. Thus, we turn now to values, which should be clearly defined and explicitly state how the organization intends to use them as the compass that guides its decision-making in times of disruption, opportunity, and change.

The Values

Establishing a set of guiding values is one of the top three most important organizational activities during the strategic-planning process. Organizational values should correspond with and support the vision, but they must be shared collectively among all stakeholders if they are to steer organizational behavior. Individuals are not easily swayed from their own values in favor of external ones; they are the basis for our notions of right and wrong, and disagreements arising from conflicting values are not easily resolved. When a facilitator involves as many internal stakeholders as possible while drafting a values statement, it is more likely that individual and organizational values will align (Ebener & Smith, 2015).

Values are best codified and put into practice after a vision and mission have been agreed upon; in fact, activities such as those described in Figure 13.1 (Competency Tree: Creating and Sharing Values) are most effective when large posters of the organizational vision and mission statement are displayed and available for reference, particularly for mid-level management and front-line employees (Orhan et al., 2014).[2] When defining values, the goal is to create a list whose entries are easily aligned with those of the stakeholders. Strategic planning facilitators may want to begin by meeting internal and external stakeholders separately; in my experience, it is best to compile separate lists and compare them to find commonalities. These are written up and presented to a group, which then ranks them according to importance in order to determine a final list of shared values.

2. Orhan et al. is particularly germane to this chapter. Its main thrust is that mid- and lower-level employees, excluded from the processes of creating vision, mission, and values, are not only less vested than the upper-level decision-makers, but also deprived of the opportunity to learn how those things are done. The resulting lack of institutional memory is an unnecessary self-inflicted wound that hampers future prospects.

Once the values have been winnowed, distilled, and agreed upon (I recommend a final roster of three to six entries), there should be a formal organizational response. Ideally, this will not only include the list of values and their definitions, but also thank the stakeholders for their important inputs. It should be published in a prominent, public space. When new organizational tactics are adopted, their announcement should include ways they are tied to the mission statement, are firmly aligned with organizational values, and will help achieve the overall vision.

How to Use Creating and Sharing Vision, Mission, and Values in the Workplace

Why should leaders take sole responsibility for creating a vision? Should they have a monopoly on decisions about the mission? From whom should we import our values? While leadership is often expected to create and disseminate statements about vision, mission, and values, this chapter takes the approach that these things are best done collectively. A vision created in a group endeavor will more likely be seen as aspirational by stakeholders; shared effort toward a collectively written mission leads to greater investment; values are more effective when held communally. High-caliber workplace leadership takes pains to involve others when creating and sharing vision, mission, and values. Nebgen (1991) noted that clear communication was the most critical element at each phase of strategic planning and management; David and David (2016) reinforced this by noting that the most effective way to share a vision is to involve people from all organizational levels in crafting it. The same holds true for mission and values, and all managers should have input during each process; discussion groups are an excellent way to do so.

Competencies in Brief

Simply put, competencies are skills and abilities that pertain to a given task. The term became established in managerial circles after a study by Boyatzis (1982), commissioned by the American Management Association, used competencies to describe underlying characteristics "causally related to effective or superior performance in a job" (p 21). Over the years, leadership competencies have been arranged into functional clusters and behavioral trees for ease of use (Saltsman & Shelton, 2019; Cockerill, 2021). Organizing competencies in such fashion simplifies the process of identifying key requirements for a position, allowing a clear outline of the skills necessary for success. During hiring, this helps organizations provide accurate job descriptions and then determine which candidates have the skills, knowledge, and abilities to perform the required tasks; later, competency clusters can be used to measure employee performance, rewarding achievements and providing guidance for development plans. Good leadership will not only evaluate an employee based on the competencies associated with their job, but will also reevaluate the job itself periodically, to make sure that the actual tasks performed have not changed over time. Similarly, this process ensures that employees are up-to-date with the latest trends and developments in their field and competitive in their roles. Failure to do so can lead to a disjunction between the competencies sought and those needed for success.

As with any other task, crafting and disseminating vision, mission, and values statements requires a specific set of skills. This chapter organizes those necessary competencies into a simple set of competency trees, one for vision and mission and one for values, shown later in Figures 13.1 and 13.2. The following section describes how those skill/ability sets are used in the process of developing a vision, mission, and values.

Workplace Competencies for Creating Vision and Mission

This process should begin with creating and sharing vision first, to give a contextual base on which to develop a collectively agreed-upon mission and shared organizational values. This requires competent

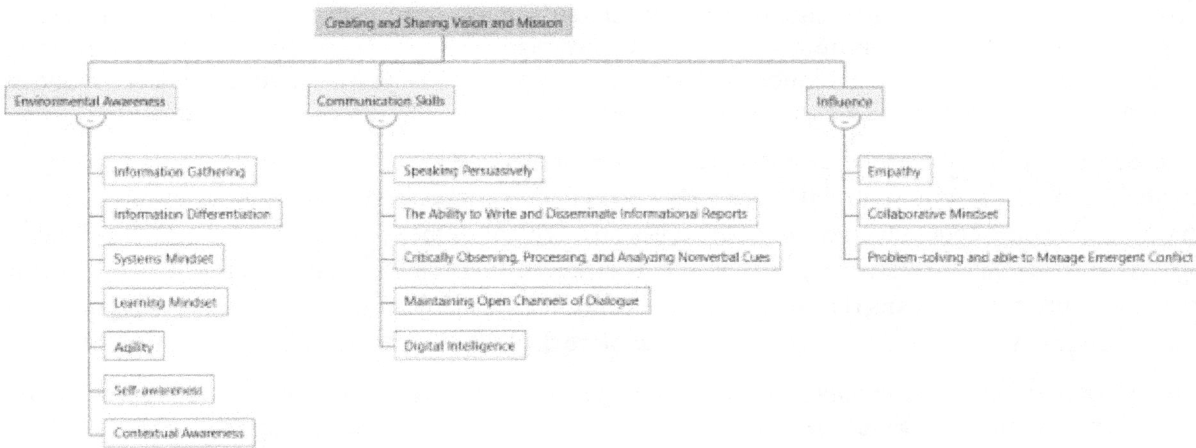

FIGURE 13.1 Competency Tree for Creating and Sharing Vision and Mission

leaders to understand and anticipate environmental factors, to effectively communicate with stakeholders, and to influence others so they stay committed to the vision and adhere to the mission. Each of these three functional competency clusters are essential when creating or developing a vision or mission statement and are illustrated in Figure 13.1.

Environmental Awareness. As Fellini reminded us, we must have a handle on reality before we can evaluate how and why to effect change. As we create a vision, one of the most important tasks is to understand the internal and external environments in which we operate. These factors set the conditions to which we must answer and respond, and recognizing these systems is essential if we want to craft an aspirational vision. Competencies related to environmental awareness include the following, which are necessary for effectively gathering and using information, making assessments, and recognizing the factors that may hinder decision-making or communication.

- *Information gathering* is the first step in any evaluation of the external environment. Understanding the milieu in which we operate is necessary for success and depends on one's ability to source and collect data. This competency requires a degree of communication skills, as knowing how to find information often depends on effectively cultivating and sustaining the professional relationships that give access to relevant and timely data. External sources must be trustworthy and reliable, because we have no direct control over how the data they provide is validated, collected, or housed. Maintaining a mindset valuing exploration, combining curiosity with research skills, must be continually developed to effectively maintain this competency.
- *Information differentiation* is closely related to, but distinct from, *information gathering*. While a leader may be adept at collecting data, that information cannot be utilized effectively without the ability to distinguish between the important and the extraneous. The rapid growth of data analytics as a profession testifies to the increasing recognition that information *quantity* does not equal information *quality*. The information systems and analytical tools available today are capable of handling extravagant amounts of mixed qualitative and quantitative data, and knowing which tool to use—and which types of analyses can demonstrate quantitative impacts versus qualitative influences—requires in-depth knowledge of iterative research design, statistics, qualitative data analysis techniques, and understanding of information-technology software. Translating raw data into digestible, persuasive evidence also requires *communication* competencies, which are addressed in the second tree.
- *A systems mindset* is a way of thinking that involves a holistic view of the world, seeing it as an interconnected system of components, each affecting the others. The relationships between these elements are key to understanding the system as a whole. This approach allows individuals and organizations

to better understand their environment, which leads to a greater ability to predict how changes in one area can affect the entire system. Thus, organizations incorporating a systems mindset can better anticipate and respond to changes and are better prepared to handle any situation, identifying and solving emergent problems quickly and efficiently.

Leaders with this competency are conceptual-framework-oriented and innovatively combine disparate—or even competing—systems into new operating procedures or models. A systems mindset relies heavily on oft-overlooked abductive reasoning, which is also a critical element in design thinking. This kind of logic is based on the understanding that we are making decisions on the *available* information, and that structural uncertainty means that leaders should continuously monitor mediating factors, as changes in data or conditions may remove obstacles that heretofore delimited the best available options.

- A *learning mindset* is an approach that recognizes that there are always areas for improvement and growth. It involves having an open mind and being willing to try new things, despite the risk of failure. People with this mindset learn actively, as a goal in itself, rather than approaching it as the tedious means to an end result. By embracing the often-painful process of learning, they remain open to feedback and criticism, which are then used to improve competencies and results.

A fully realized learning mindset though is not only about acquiring knowledge, but also about understanding and employing it. This means that individuals should be able to take what they have learned, apply it to their current situation, and be open to feedback and criticism about the results, creating a positive loop of continual improvement and growth. This give-and-take means that effective listening is paramount to acquiring a learning mindset, and open-minded people should develop and sustain communication skills to help foster growth in this area. In our research (Nix et al., 2021), *knowledge-seeking* attitudes accounted for up to 27% of the variation in learning attainment for assessed outcomes. This shows that people who are willing to learn—as well as unlearn or relearn—are likely to have better outcomes than those who are not. These individuals are often the quietest people in the room during meetings, but when they share information, it is worth listening to them.

- *Agility*, the ability to quickly and efficiently adapt to changing circumstances, can give individuals and organizations a competitive edge. An agile mindset, like a learning one, is open to change and willing to try new ideas, and requires a certain level of comfort with ambiguity, uncertainty, and failure. However, agility includes creative thinking and the ability to learn fast and make decisions quickly. This competency's main value lies in how it helps avoid the *sunk-cost fallacy*, whereby people who invest time and energy into a strategy or plan of action are reluctant to abandon it because of those expenditures, even when changing course is clearly the more beneficial option. This requires a degree of *self-awareness* (listed next in this cluster) in order to remain both logically invested in and emotionally detached from successes and failures. An agile mindset is essential for organizations that want to stay ahead of rivals and remain competitive in an ever-changing world.
- While *self-awareness* is not especially useful in itself, it is nonetheless arguably the most important competency for a leader to have, as it is essential for the effective deployment of other skills. Knowing our predilections and limitations is the first step in actively, continuously working to mediate them through soft-skills development. Self-aware people try to maintain focus on the reality of a given situation, rather than their internal projections or desires. These leaders want to know about their followers' experiences, even the unpleasant ones; a leader who can separate personal ego from negative feedback makes the difference between an effective workplace and a Dickensian one.
- *Contextual awareness*, a general proficiency in recognizing the environmental factors at work in a given situation, is enhanced by *information gathering* and is a prerequisite for *agility*. Leaders with good contextual awareness tend to be excellent communicators, as they understand how elements in play are affecting their audience.
  - When devising a vision or mission statement though, a specific subset of *contextual awareness* skills is particularly useful: *awareness of cultural context*. While cultural intelligence (Alon &

Higgins, 2005) used to be seen as relevant only in overseas assignments, attitudes are shifting. Today, as organizations increasingly become transnational and global cultural hubs, this skill likely has value in any institutional setting; short courses on language and comparative cultural studies should be on any leader's professional development agenda. Organizational leadership must be proficient at processing contextual cues cutting across cultural boundaries. Failing to do so risks losing an overall awareness of the cultural context in which a leader operates, hindering communication and connection with employees, clients, and outside stakeholders. Note that this competency goes hand-in-hand with many elements of *social perceptivity*, discussed later.

Communication Skills. Mark Twain supposedly said, "the difference between the right word and the almost-right word is the difference between a lightning bolt and a lightning bug." Communication skills are consistently rated as one of the top two critical competency clusters in studies across varied and diverse industries (Cockerill, 2021; Cockerill & Satish, 2021; Saltsman & Shelton, 2019; Shet & Pereira, 2021); while a minor communication miscue might not lead to something as dire as being struck by lightning, the effective transmission of ideas and information is essential if we want others to share our goals. Panel or group activities are typically used to create and disseminate vision, and facilitators of these sessions must have a number of communication-based competencies in order to be effective. Note that as these skills are inherently interpersonal, feedback is essential to developing and practicing them; it behooves us to maintain *self-awareness* and a *learning mindset.*

- *Speaking persuasively* and clearly cannot be overstated. Many firms have recognized the importance of this and hire professional consultants skilled in vision-boarding or communications. An important consideration for effective communicators is language; each tongue spoken in the organization should be incorporated into material, which should also be made as accessible as possible (e.g., using sign language and braille), which can require a degree of *cultural-context awareness.* Delineating expectations around language and accessibility ought to be standard practice for leadership positions at any level.
- The *ability to write and disseminate informational reports* to all constituents is equally important. As with verbal communication efforts, care should be taken to include any necessary translations or accessible versions. Leaders who work with followers who speak multiple languages should realize that their audience may have better comprehension of spoken materials than written ones, or vice versa, and ought to tailor their communications accordingly. Obviously, this competence overlaps significantly with *speaking persuasively* and *cultural awareness*, but ability in any one of those areas does not necessarily translate well to the others. Again, teamwork is key!
- *Critically observing, processing, and analyzing nonverbal cues* has been demonstrated to increase leader effectiveness, while using inappropriate nonverbal cues has been shown to greatly reduce the positive perceptions of followers (Bellou & Gkorezis, 2016). This competency is often used in conjunction with those described in *social perceptivity*, below.
- *Maintaining open channels of dialogue* is essential for ensuring that priorities and expectations are aligned with available resources. One of the most effective ways leaders might dialogue with followers about vision or mission statements is a series of scheduled and ad hoc feedback groups, particularly in the 2–3 months following the creation of those statements. Assessment techniques such as "muddiest-point feedback"[3] are extremely useful to determine whether the aspirational vision was successfully conveyed from leaders to followers.
- A key component to effectively communicating in the modern age is *digital intelligence.* Emerging technologies such as artificial intelligence (AI), robotics and automation, and management systems (among others) have disrupted industries of all shapes and sizes over the last decade, bringing new opportunities, tools, and challenges with them. Digital intelligence is the ability to effectively use these tools to improve the efficiency of decision-making and problem solving; incorporating data and analytics into these processes is a virtual requirement for any organization that wants to remain competitive. Thus, particularly when crafting a mission statement, it is important to approach things

3. "Muddiest points" are the aspects of a task or discussion which were the most difficult to comprehend or master.

from a digital-intelligence mindset which considers how technology can help improve understanding of one's environment, clients, colleagues, and competition. Good leaders will try and forecast how technological improvements may offer new opportunities and plan accordingly. This competency is closely tied in with the first five competencies in the *environmental awareness* cluster; namely, *information gathering* and *differentiation, systems* and *learning mindsets*, and *agility*.

Influence. In brief, influence is the ability to affect other people's internal states and behaviors. This is an obvious prerequisite for marshaling agreement during the creation process for vision, mission, and values statements, and with gaining followers' acceptance of the finished products. Many of the skills described elsewhere in this chapter have application here; in fact, it would not be difficult to argue that *all* of them contribute to building influence! *Maintaining* it, however, is made easier by the following four competencies.

- *Empathy*, the ability to appreciate people's feelings by placing oneself in their positions, plays a central role in how we interpret, evaluate, and reevaluate the mindsets and internal states of others. This competency requires a thorough comprehension of several non-cognitive (affective) constructs, including attitudes, values, beliefs, cultural assumptions, emotions, and emotion-states. Empathy contributes to *influence* because people tend to trust those who demonstrably appreciate them and acknowledge their experiences; furthermore, a grasp of a person's attitudes and emotions can help identify their values and explain their behaviors. This allows for better communication and helps with persuasion. *Self-awareness*, discussed earlier, and *self-control* and *-differentiation*, covered in the next section, are major complementary skills for this competency.
- A *collaborative mindset* builds on each of the previous four *communication* competencies, and reflection on followers' feedback is an absolute foundational requirement. Fundamentally, this mindset requires a shift in attention away from what a leader may want as an individual to what the organization needs as a team. Interestingly, leaders who are good at collaboration are also good at delegation; many people make the mistake of thinking that a delegator is essentially the same as a dictator, but nothing should (or could!) be farther from the truth. Delegating tasks is crucial and is only possible if a leader trusts their followers and believes in their competence; collaboration requires the same faith among team members. *Empathy* and *integrity* help establish the level of trustworthiness required for a collaborative mindset, and this competency is also linked to *self-awareness, self-differentiation*, and being *dialogue-centered*.
- Finally, an influential person often has a reputation for *problem solving and managing emergent conflict*. We naturally look to our leaders to fix what's broken and resolve disputes; when crafting vision, mission, and values statements, this ideally takes the form of facilitating conversations and helping guide consensus. Successfully chairing or moderating those groups draws on the *influence* and *communication* competency clusters, as well as those listed in *social perceptivity* below.

Workplace Competencies for Establishing Values

As the astute reader has no doubt imagined, there is considerable overlap between the competencies used when discussing vision, mission, and values. Still, different sets of activities require different sets of skills, and Figure 13.2 illustrates the three primary competency clusters used while establishing organizational values. The first cluster, environmental awareness, includes a subset of the competencies detailed earlier; these four skills are the environmental ones most relevant to crafting a values statement and are essentially exactly as described before. Thus, this section focuses on the other two competency clusters; do not, however, make the mistake of believing these competencies "belong" to values, any more than earlier ones "belonged" to mission and vision. Every individual skill set is useful for all three tasks discussed here and many other leadership functions as well.

Social Perceptivity. Leaders must remain cognizant of group and individual perceptions, attitudes, and emotions as teams try to achieve consensus during values clarification. The most useful values-establishing activities require panels consisting of workers from all levels of the organization; this ensures that

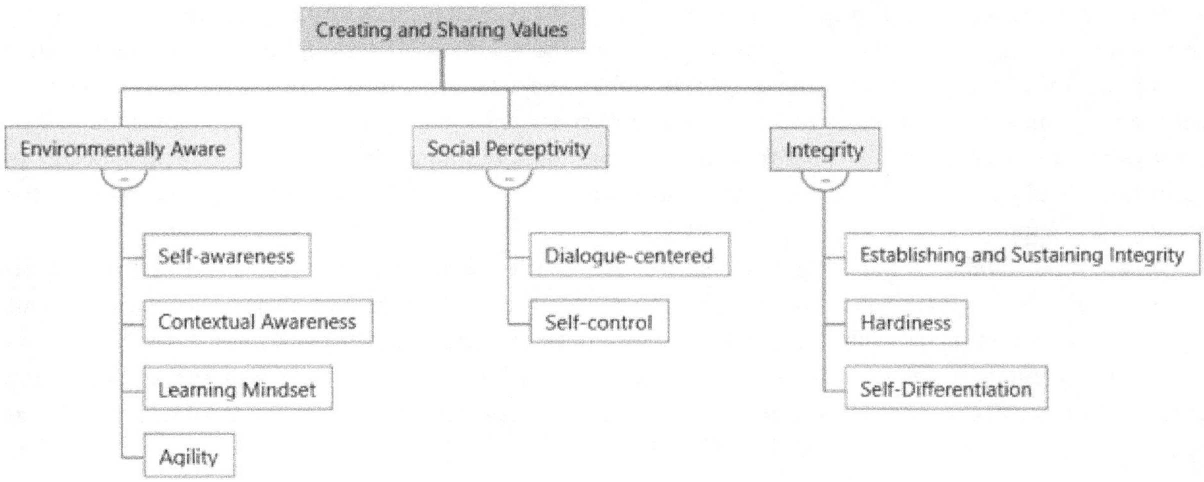

FIGURE 13.2 Competency Tree for Creating and Sharing Values

the resultant values statement accurately reflects principles that will be shared by and inspire everyone. However, this requires a deft touch, as power differentials between levels of participants can hamper communication. Socially perceptive leaders choose to use methods conducive to achieving consensus and are able to shepherd groups toward that end.[4] The following competencies aid in that endeavor.

- Every competency in this cluster is based on keeping a *dialogue-centered* mindset. Shared values are established through consensus, which is often a lengthy process requiring significant back-and-forth communication. While this may seem at first glance to overlap with *maintaining open channels of dialogue* (discussed in the *communication* cluster), there are subtle differences. A dialogue-centered approach is more than just being receptive; it requires the *active* facilitation of communication not only vertically between leaders and their followers, but horizontally among same-tier personnel as well. While *open channels* allow for feedback or problem reporting, it is not enough. When crafting a values statement, leaders must promote dialogue *at every opportunity*, encouraging their followers to speak not only with leadership, but with each other as well. This approach requires putting communication in the forefront, bringing everyone consciously into the work of creating and participating in dialogue. Catalyzing learning and exchanges within a complex milieu of opinions and beliefs, between and within all levels of the organization, is imperative when creating truly shared values.
- *Self-control* is such an important characteristic for a leader that it could well be placed in any of these skill clusters. This competency is focused on managing affect and behavior. Leaders must be aware of their emotional and attitudinal responses, modulating and recalibrating them as needed so that followers receive appropriate feedback and recognize the leader's commitment to the processes. Note that it is easy to fall into the trap of overriding or "bottling up" feelings and reactions in an effort to project an image of self-control. This is not constructive or sustainable; true self-control acknowledges the emotional cues that indicate a problem in need of attention, while conscientiously choosing to respond in ways that will actually help ameliorate the situation or achieve the desired end.

Integrity. Maintaining integrity is essential for success in personal, professional, and organizational life. Being integrity driven means adhering to a set of values and demonstrating a commitment to prioritize

4. I prefer the nominal group technique (NGT). This is a qualitative research methodology used to generate ideas, rank them (as a group) by importance, and use the results to make decisions (Mullen et al., 2021). The NGT is a flexible and powerful tool for group decision-making because anonymity is built into the method, thus encouraging participation from all members, allowing everyone to have a voice while minimizing power differentials.

doing the right thing, even if it has an associated cost. While behaving with integrity may occasionally necessitate making unpopular decisions or pushing back against majority opinion, it also establishes a reputation for being reliable, trustworthy, and fair—especially since a leader with true integrity is willing to admit their mistakes and take responsibility for their actions. Honesty and consistency may not give the answers someone wants to hear in the moment, but nobody wants a leader who lacks those qualities. Ideally, an integrity-driven individual will take risks, model their values, and stand up for others when appropriate.

When creating and disseminating a values statement, it should go without saying that leaders and facilitators should have reputations for integrity and fair dealing. It is much easier to lead conversations about difficult topics when the participants trust their leaders and assume that they will give everyone an equal chance to give input. Finally, as the values statement is distributed, followers will look to their leaders to see if they practice what they preach or disregard those values when convenient. A shared vision and goal cannot be attained unless it truly be shared by all!

- *Establishing and sustaining integrity*, which comes from a combination of honesty and respect for others, is the first step in becoming an effective leader. More than most of these competencies, establishing integrity is an exercise in leading by example. Those who do not understand how to establish integrity will have a hard time gaining a reputation as upright managers; it is not enough to simply *have* integrity internally, but it must be publicly demonstrated in action. When followers see their leaders behaving honorably and honestly, it creates a culture that not only values those things, but makes it easier for everyone to practice them. Holding high ethical standards is imperative, as is maintaining loyalty to the organization, but even consistency in quotidian things such as punctuality and attentiveness in meetings has a significant impact on one's image as a reliable and trustworthy leader. This attention to detail also performatively demonstrates that the topic or task at hand has value; after all, if the boss doesn't seem to think something is important, how can their followers be expected to?
- *Hardiness* is an individual's ability to overcome stress, stay resilient in the face of adversity, and maintain a positive outlook despite difficult circumstances. It is the fortitude to press on and be proactive, seize initiative, and persist in the face of failure. Hardiness is thus complementary to *agility*; while that competency describes the ability to adapt to unforeseen conditions and pivot toward opportunities, it is hardiness which gives one the stamina to carry on until those obstacles can be overcome. For similar reasons, hardiness is also extremely important when trying to maintain a *learning mindset*.

Hardiness is composed of three elements: commitment, control, and challenge. Commitment is the ability to stay focused on a goal or task, regardless of difficulties; control is identifying, assessing, and managing stressors; challenge is the mindset that views objectives and tasks in a positive light, rather than perceiving them as burdensome or negative. Demonstrating hardiness engenders trust by showing followers that their leader is willing to *show up* and put in their best effort, regardless of difficulty.

- Leaders with good *self-differentiation* are able to combine gumption and shrewdness without appearing (or becoming!) Machiavellian in nature. By keeping a sense of self, even when closely working with others, it is easier to maintain perspective and emotional distance from tasks and goals. The ambitions of others are equally important as a leader's ambitions; successes and failures are shared by the team. Self-differentiated leaders will not assign responsibility for one person's experiences to someone else; they strive to create environments that are highly engaging and experientially honest (Bushe & O'Malley, 2013).

Workplace Application: Values Clarification

Clear values are an essential element of teamwork in any group, and teamwork is in turn integral to clarifying values themselves. This process involves discussing, exploring, and understanding individual values and how they relate to collective ones. The process is important because it helps everyone in the group to better understand each other and to work together more effectively. When clarifying values, it is important to create an environment that is open and respectful. Each person should feel comfortable sharing his or her values knowing that those submissions will be evaluated but without fear of judgment or negative criticism. This will help to ensure that the discussion is productive and that all values are respected. One way to begin the process of values clarification is to have each person in the group write down two or three values that are important to him or her. Then, the group can discuss and explore each value, looking for commonalities and differences. This allows everyone to get to know each other better and to gain a deeper understanding of the group's collective values. Another way to clarify values is through an exercise. This can be done either as a group or individually. For example, the group could have an activity that requires each person to identify a set of values and then discuss them. This type of exercise can help everyone in the group to better understand each other's values and to think about how they can work together to achieve their goals. It is important to remember that values clarification is not a one-time process. It should be revisited and discussed regularly, as values and perspectives can change over time. This will help to ensure that the group remains unified and that each person's individual values are respected. Values clarification is an important part of creating a strong team and can help to foster a healthy, productive work environment. In the past, I have used a bidding game activity for values clarification purposes. An underlying challenge inherent in this bidding game exercise is dealing with dwindling resources.

BOX 13.2 **Vision, Mission, and Values: Creation, Clarification, and Definition Exercises**

These exercises are designed to help students get comfortable working with vision, mission, and values statements. Each of the following three activities will dive progressively deeper into the creative processes, culminating in a session where students will collectively determine and define a list of shared values. Facilitators are encouraged to adapt activities to fit the culture of their specific workgroups.

Activity One: How Shared Is Our Vision?

This is an individual activity that takes place outside of class time.

Each person is to interview five classmates or friends, asking them how familiar they are with the vision statements at their respective workplaces (or alternatively, organizations with which they are familiar). Can they describe them from memory, and if so, how clearly? Do they need to refer to a written copy—and if so, do they even know how to access one? Rate their familiarity as low, moderate, or high. What do the results say about shared visions? Present your results to the class and compare them with others. Which vision statements were most memorable? Least? And why? Were the least memorable ones poorly written, poorly disseminated, or both?

Activity Two: Evaluate and Rewrite A Mission Statement

This is a group activity, which should take place outside of class. Time required: 1–2 hours, plus presentation. Participants: Separate class into groups of three or four people.

Each participant should obtain a mission statement from their organization (or one that interests them). As a small group, examine these missions to see if any of the following elements from David and David (2017) are missing: *clients, services, markets, technology, growth and profits, philosophy, organizational self-concept, public image, and employees.* Choose one statement that is lacking several components and rewrite it to include them. Present both versions to the class.

Activity Three: Values Creation, Definition, and Implementation

This is a group activity, best done as an in-class session. Time required: 1–2 hours. Group size: For one facilitator, a group of 5–7 participants is optimal; at nine people, split the groups and have two facilitators.

By taking the time to define their values as a group, teams establish an environment of collaboration and respect wherein everyone feels involved and heard. To this end, it is beneficial to start with an exercise encouraging participants to think about the values that matter to them both individually and collectively. The facilitator begins by asking everyone in the group to think about a challenging situation that is important to them. This could be an ethical dilemma, a personal goal, a work situation, or any other meaningful scenario. Each person should ask themselves questions to help identify the values that are most relevant to their unique circumstances. What motivates them in that situation? What is the desired outcome, and what actions do they feel they need to undertake to achieve it? What elements have the clearest solutions, and which seem most difficult to grapple with? And how would they want to be remembered, once the situation has been resolved? After considering those questions, participants make a list, using a few words to best describe the values they feel are represented in their answers. These can be single-word responses such as "respect" or "justice," or they may be short phrases like "acts with integrity" or "supportive of each other." Once each person has identified their own values, the group will come together to make a shared list of communally held ones. Discuss and refine each item; the team should strive to achieve consensus for each value definition and then rank them in order of importance. Select the top five or six as the organizational values.

Next, the team should consider how they will implement the values they have chosen. For example, they could create an action plan for ways to embody the values in day-to-day work. This could include tangible strategies such as setting expectations for behavior, creating a code of conduct, and establishing rewards and consequences based on compliance. Whatever the mechanisms, the team should ensure that the values are reflected in their decision-making processes and interactions with each other.

As a last step before drafting the final statement, the group should consider the need to revisit the values in the future, reviewing them and making adjustments as needed. This could involve regularly scheduled group reflection sessions or could be informally structured check-ins throughout the year. Whatever its form, the review process should verify that values align with goals and objectives, thus ensuring that the values are communally held and consistently followed.

At this point, the team can write a final value statement. It should incorporate all the above elements, be easy to understand, and take cultural context and accessibility into consideration when deciding how to disseminate the final product.

Concluding Remarks

Vision and mission statements should, respectively, explicitly answer the questions "What do we want to be?" and "How do we want to get there?" Good values promote overall excellence in service to the organization and its activities and should be the basis of decision-making as we undertake the mission, which in turn guides us toward the aspirational vision. An organization that demonstrates faithful adherence to shared, collective values is one which promotes overall excellence in service itself and its goals; when organizational culture professes values but does not demonstrate commitment to them, encouraging general buy-in to a vision and mission is nigh impossible, and commitment is forever out of reach.

Application

Post-Chapter Activities

Consider the following case. After reviewing the scenario, respond to the discussion questions by identifying the competencies described in this chapter, as well as any others you can think of which might have not been illustrated.

BOX 13.3 **Achieving a New Vision**

CJ is the CEO of the oldest freestanding private for-profit winemaking college in the United States, the American Winemaker's Academy (AWA). For the past three evenings, she has lain awake, troubled by declining enrollment at AWA. In 2017, the college's board of trustees created and approved a new vision statement: *Educating and developing winemaking professionals with local opportunities in every corner of the world.* Shortly after adopting this vision, CJ was hired to lead the college in this expansion; the board made it clear she was brought on because of her impressive global mindset. Immediately, CJ and her presidential cabinet crafted a strategic plan which had a primary goal of opening 10 transnational campuses by 2025.

Under CJ's leadership, the next five years saw seven new transnational branches opened, each in a different Asian or African country. Each of those campuses has had a dramatic impact on their local communities and are attracting more students every year. CJ has made a point of visiting each new branch, ensuring that each opened according to established procedures and continues the tradition of excellence on which the college's reputation is built. Despite her efforts though, the exchange rate between the U.S. dollar and local currencies has kept these campuses from generating profits as of yet, despite ever-increasing enrollment.

Worse, expansion into emerging markets seems to have drawn AWA leadership's focus away from its flagship location. For each of the past three years, domestic enrollment at the college has dropped 3–5%; of immediate concern though is the projected enrollment for the new academic year, which forecasts a 27% drop in incoming students. While the program's main strength is its status as the only freestanding winemaking college in the country, several other schools have started and implemented their own winemaking programs. Not only is the top-growth program in the United States one that was established by an alumnus of AWA, but in the last year alone, fully 15 new programs were opened in metro-area colleges, nine of which are led by former AWA faculty members.

CJ knows something has to change. As she reflects back, she realizes that two of the most outspoken and influential board members were the primary authors of the vision emphasizing international expansion; in fact, there was little input from any stakeholders aside from the board of trustees and the international partners running each overseas campus. She will lead a cabinet meeting tomorrow—the first meeting since the abysmal enrollment projections were released.

BOX 13.4 **Questions for Reflection**

- Which competencies led to the college's success overseas?
- How might the global vision have impacted AWA's domestic operations and thus caused the drastic decline in projected enrollment? Which competencies should the team rely on to reverse the trend?
- What are some of the first steps you might recommend to improve domestic enrollment? Which competencies would be most critical for these efforts?
- The cabinet is composed of the president, the chief of staff, and a vice president from each of the college's administrative divisions (Business, Academics, and Student Services). What questions would you ask each of them, and how do you think each member could best contribute to a solution for the school's woes?

References

Alon, I., & Higgins, J. M. (2005). Global leadership success through emotional and cultural intelligences. *Business Horizons*, *48*(6), 501–512. https://doi.org/10.1016/j.bushor.2005.04.003

Bellou, V., & Gkorezis, P. (2016). Unveiling the link between facets of positive nonverbal communication and perceived leader effectiveness: A moderated mediation model. *Human Performance*, *29*(4), 310–330. https://doi.org/10.1080/08959285.2016.1157597

Boyatzis, R. E. (1982). *The competent manager: A model for effective performance.* Wiley.

Bushe, G. R., & O'Malley, J. (2013). Changing organizational culture through Clear Leadership. In L. Carter, R. Sullivan, M. Goldsmith, D. Ulrich, & N. Smallwood (Eds.). *The change champions fieldguide* (2nd ed.) (463–479). Wiley.

Cockerill, A. P. (2021). The leader effect and behavioral complexity. *Journal of Applied Social Psychology*, *51*(12), 1132–1144. https://doi.org/10.1111/jasp.12768

Cockerill, A. P., & Satish, U. (2021). Real-world implications of high-performance competencies and strategic management simulation technology. *Journal of Applied Social Psychology*, *51*(12), 1145–1150. https://doi.org/10.1111/jasp.12777

David, F., & David, F. (2016). *Strategic management: A competitive advantage approach, concepts* (16th ed.). Pearson.

Ebener, D. R., & Smith, F. L. (2015). *Strategic planning: An interactive process for leaders* (D. Crilly, Ed.). Paulist Press.

Federico Fellini. (2023). In *Wikipedia*. https://en.wikipedia.org/w/index.php?title=Federico_Fellini&oldid=1140090959

Mullen, R., Kydd, A., Fleming, A., & McMillan, L. (2021). A practical guide to the systematic application of nominal group technique. *Nurse Researcher*, *29*(1). https://doi.org/10.7748/nr.2021.e1777

Nebgen, M. (1991). The key to success in strategic planning is communication. *Educational Leadership*, *48*(7), 26–28.

Nix, V., Song, M., & Lindbeck, R. (2021). Affective learning outcomes assessment as a path to online dialogic student development. *Journal of Organizational Psychology*, *21*(4), Article 4. https://doi.org/10.33423/jop.v21i4.4548

Orhan, G., Erdoğan, D., & Durmaz, V. (2014). Adopting Mission and Vision Statements by Employees: The Case of TAV Airports. *Procedia—Social and Behavioral Sciences*, *150*, 251–262. https://doi.org/10.1016/j.sbspro.2014.09.051

Saltsman, G., & Shelton, K. (2019). Leadership competencies for global education leaders: A Delphi study of UNESCO delegates and administrators. *Education Leadership Review*, *20*(1), 150–166.

Shet, Sateesh V., and Pereira, V. Proposed managerial competencies for industry 4.0 – implications for social sustainability." *Technological Forecasting and Social Change* 173 (December 1, 2021): 121080. https://doi.org/10.1016/j.techfore.2021.121080.

CHAPTER 14

Creating Strategy

By J. Vincent Nix

If you don't know where you are going, you'll end up someplace else.

—Yogi Berra

Learning Objectives

After reading this chapter, students will be able to:

1. Articulate a definition of strategy
2. Recognize the inherent competitive nature of strategy
3. Understand the critical-competency clusters used in strategic planning
4. Determine their own strengths and weaknesses in these competency areas and plan to develop them accordingly
5. Recognize the use of a common strategic-planning matrix process
6. Create strategies from a case-study activity

Introduction to Strategy

What is strategy? At the base level, it is an intervention intended to increase competitiveness and achieve goals. Originally a military concept, strategic planning was what generals and rulers used to stay competitive with—and eventually crush—their rivals. As businesses adopted the concept, they were just as ruthless; consider the vertical-integration strategy of Standard Oil or Cornelius Vanderbilt's cutthroat railroad and steamship operations. Eventually though the focus on annihilation and absorption waned, and strategy came to include planning for collaboration and cooperation, although competition has always remained at the forefront of strategic concerns.

In most cases, strategy is discussed at the organizational level, but individuals and teams may also use strategic planning and management to improve smaller-scale processes. Regardless of scale, this exercise is inherently forward focused, relying on information and problem solving to take preemptive action and gain a competitive edge. As the ancient Chinese philosopher and military strategist Sun Tzu (2005) wrote, "Victorious warriors win first and then go to war, while defeated warriors go to war first and then seek to win" (p. 72).

Competencies Critical to Creating Strategy

As in Chapter 13, pertinent competencies have been grouped into clusters. While some of these skills will be familiar to readers of the previous chapter, their functions and classifications are different when engaging in strategic planning, as reflected in the groupings shown in Figure 14.1. *Assessment, analysis, and response* is the first step in making a strategic plan, and those competencies are used to gather and process information while laying the groundwork for decision-making. The second cluster is concerned with the *implementation* of those decisions, including how they will be executed long term, while the third group details how *feedback and adaptation* are used to fine-tune a strategic plan and ensure its support among stakeholders. These clusters are illustrated and classified in the tree below.

Assessment, Analysis, and Response. Competencies in this cluster are focused on gathering and interpreting data, and using the results to make informed decisions. The processes below are essential for strategic planning, both in terms of creating the plan itself and in understanding how it can best be effected.

- *Information gathering* is the first step in planning. Before attempting to initiate action, it is necessary to understand the current environment; this in turn means asking the right questions to the right people. Information gathering does not mean simply taking in whatever is available, but also knowing how to separate trustworthy information from conjecture or idle speculation. In order to successfully source and collect data, one should build the *communication skills* that facilitate the professional relationships that give access to useful insights. More than anything, a strategic plan must be founded on accurate information from reliable sources!
- Effective use of gathered information requires *analytical skills.* This competency casts a broad net and includes the suite of abilities needed to collect and analyze data, using the results to inform *decision-making.* People with good analytical skills know how to best interpret data and have a setting-appropriate understanding of which items to include and which tests and software to use. Even

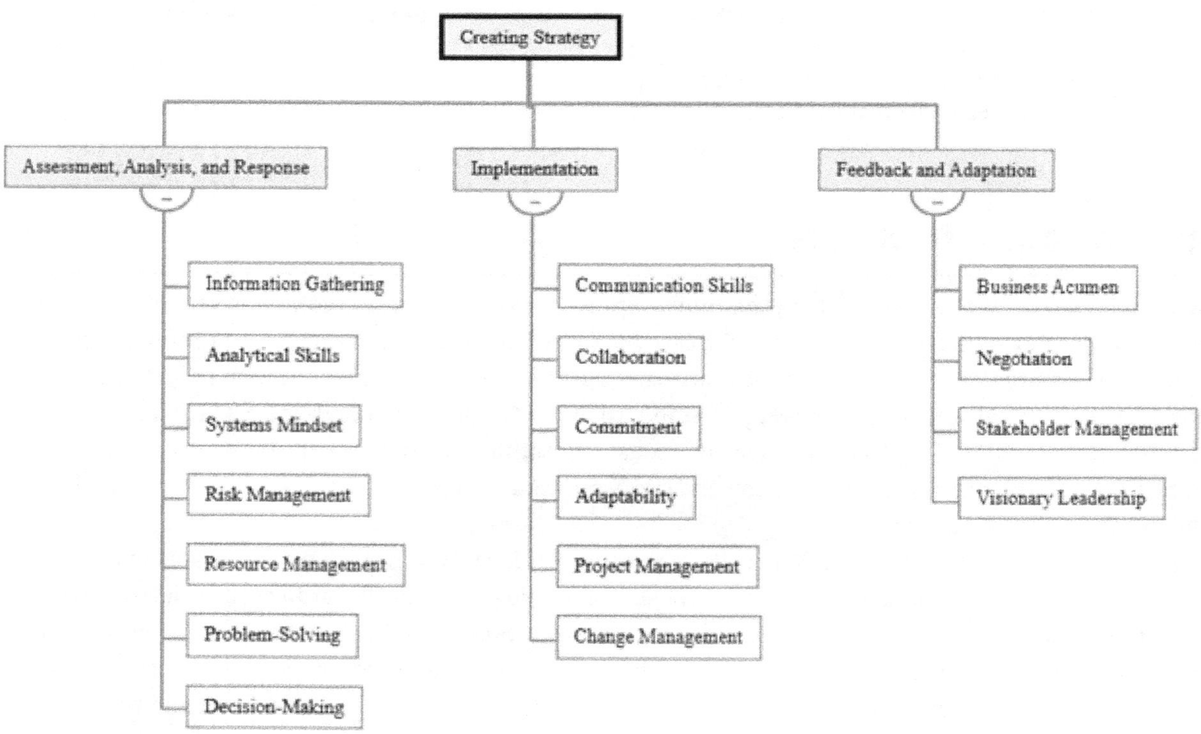

FIGURE 14.1 Competency Tree for Creating Strategy

when hard statistical analysis is not required, someone with this competency will be able to draw meaningful conclusions from the information presented to them. A competent analyst is indispensable when formulating a strategy, as the efficiency and efficacy of a plan is contingent upon how well it reflects actual conditions.

- Having a *systems mindset* means making sense of complex realities by taking a holistic view that uses the relationships between things as the basis for understanding them. What we think of when we say or write "cause and effect" is rarely a simple two-link chain, but should rather be idealized as a great web of interconnected elements; causality is multidimensional and complex. Long gone are the days when consideration of external forces could end with proximate causes; today, global markets, institutions, and ideas require us to take an ever-broadening view of what constitutes the external environment. COVID-19 has illustrated this superbly; by examining the spread of the disease, the effects of lockdowns on supply chains, and social responses, it is easy to see how immediate local effects have global ramifications. Bear in mind that a systems mindset is just as applicable at the intra-organizational level as it is in a global milieu. Internal forces and resources should also be examined as parts of the whole, in order to effectively grasp what an institution's strengths and weaknesses truly are.

Because of this wide-ranging understanding of the internal and external environments, a systems mindset is invaluable when creating strategies. It allows an individual to break free of linear thinking, where a plan progresses stolidly from development, to implementation, to evaluation. Instead, a systems-mindset approach is a circular one, which does not end with evaluation; rather, it takes that data and launches back into a new planning phase. This method of operation is the best way to approach *risk* and *resource management* in a comprehensive and effective way. Despite years of research on systems thinking, it has remained—puzzlingly—largely unremarked (Niño-Zarazúa, 2016) in educational circles. It is my hope that readers of this book are bucking that trend.

- Identifying, assessing, and controlling threats fall under the purview of *risk management*. While organizations must be willing to undertake a reasonable amount of risk in order to achieve their goals, they should almost never take a course of action if it carries significant potential for catastrophe. Good risk management takes a proactive approach, which means not only evaluating the likelihood and impact of negative outcomes, but also creating a "Plan B" to mitigate those effects. Properly executed, this competency involves a periodical review of risk analyses and uses a *systems mindset* to anticipate the knock-on effects of contingency plans.
- *Resource management* is exactly what it sounds like: effectively managing resources in order to achieve desired outcomes. Whether they be personnel, materials, equipment, technology, or financial reserves, this competency is dedicated to using assets in the most effective and efficient manner possible. This includes planning, organizing, monitoring, evaluating, and controlling resources in an ongoing fashion to minimize waste and maximize output. Any strategic plan that fails to take resource needs and availability into account is crippled from the start. Be warned, however: efficiencies for cost, time, or quality are important, but organizational values *must not be overlooked!* It can be tempting to neglect values considerations in favor of dollars-and-cents costs, but remember that an organization's vision, mission, and values are its reason for being.[1]
- After using the above competencies to set the stage, *problem solving* can begin. Identifying the key parts of the issue at hand and determining the best courses of action can be more complex than anticipated. It requires breaking the problem down into discrete items, formulating responses to each, and then resynthesizing them into an effective solution to the whole. The *systems mindset* helps understand that any problem is likely influenced by a number of factors, all of which may need attention. Many of these elements, unfortunately, may well fall outside the problem solver's control; thus, effective problem solving means knowing how to leverage what *can* be changed to effectively counterbalance—or even exert influence over—those externalities that cannot be directly affected.

1. This is why I always say that a budget is the truest form of values-documentation!

- Effective *decision-making* is taking the outputs from *problem solving* and choosing the solutions most likely to be implementable. It is not enough to merely identify effective actions; making the final decision means choosing the option that best meets the needs of the organization given the current situation and larger context. One must think critically, weighing alternatives objectively, before committing to a decision if it is to be well informed, timely, and aligned with organizational goals. If those conditions are met, plans are more likely to succeed.

Implementation. This competency cluster takes over once *decision-making* is complete. The skills below are required for teams and managers to work together to implement the chosen plan of action. In terms of strategic planning, these are the competencies that planners use to interact with stakeholders to get vital inputs while building consensus and acceptance around the new strategy.

- *Communication skills* are needed to convey information effectively and accurately between individuals. This includes both verbal and nonverbal modes of communication, as well as active listening. Without attention to this competency, it is harder to connect with others, build relationships, and work together as a team; *collaboration* is difficult without communication. Not only does this skill set allow effective expression of our ideas, thoughts, and feelings, but it is also the doorway to understanding the perspectives and needs of others—the foundation of empathy, itself a key competency for good leadership.[2]
- *Collaboration*, built upon *communication*, is working with others to achieve a common goal. While it can take many forms, the essence of collaboration is subordinating individual goals and needs to shared ones. Collaborative effort is the best way to marshal support for a project or initiative and by getting more people invested in that effort, more stakeholders are given the chance to improve it through their input and insight.
- *Commitment* is demonstrated by devoting long-term, ongoing effort toward a goal until it has been achieved. It requires a sense of ownership and dedication, which manifest in continual, conscious decisions to remain in pursuit of the desired end. While many people use "buy-in" as a synonym for commitment, there are important distinctions between the two terms. Buy-in is an acknowledgment that an idea, decision, or action is the right course, an agreement that it is worthwhile to put effort in a certain direction. Individuals who buy in can and do make important contributions, and their support is often essential. But for a project to succeed, leaders must demonstrate commitment. Perhaps the best way to illustrate this is through analogy; if a young student professes an interest in playing the guitar, they would be wise to get buy-in from their parents. Lessons and instruments are expensive, and a straightforward way to get financial support is by convincing parents to help. Only the child though can demonstrate commitment, and it is only through that commitment that they will learn to play. Without the student's continued efforts, no amount of cajoling or resources can get them to master the instrument; similarly, if the child does not demonstrate commitment, the parents have no incentive to continue buying in. The learner has to struggle and practice, building calluses despite the pain and persevering through the occasional desire to set the guitar aside, if they are to succeed. Similarly, in any organizational effort, be it strategic planning or some other task, it is the leader's commitment that inspires dedication and evokes effort from their followers.
- *Adaptability* is a vital partner to *commitment*. While the latter keeps us forging ahead, though success be far off or obstacles arise, it is adaptability which allows us to quickly and effectively change course to overcome those hardships. When we embrace this competency, it is easier to adjust to new situations, environments, and conditions, taking advantage of unexpected opportunities and swiftly acting to mitigate new threats. This flexibility also manifests as the ability to rapidly learn new skills and then apply them in novel ways. It would not be too far from the mark to say that adaptability is the soul of strategic planning, for without this competency, change is glacially slow, and it is impossible to anticipate or nimbly react to competitors.

2. See Chapter 13.

- The penultimate competency in this cluster, *project management*, includes the skills needed to plan, organize, and oversee a project from initiation to successful completion. With the possible exception of *data analysis*, which can be delegated, project management requires at least a degree of ability in all the other competencies of both this group and the preceding one. A good project manager *manages resources*, coordinating people, processes, and materials to pursue previously identified goals. They *manage risk*, and use a *systems mindset* to consider internal and external factors affecting the project, identified through *analysis* of *gathered information*. Their *decision-making* is the result of careful *problem solving* and always considers the organization's vision, mission, and values. Once the project is begun, the leader *collaborates* with the team, *communicating* with them and external stakeholders to ensure that effort and progress are appropriately directed, receiving reports detailing unforeseen setbacks or unexpected breakthroughs and *adapting* as needed. Finally, it is their *commitment* that will keep both themselves and their teams consciously pursuing the desired end.
- The final competency in this group is *change management*, shepherding proposed changes through the processes of planning, creation, implementation, and evaluation until they take root within an organization. In a nutshell, change management is taking the final product of a project and ensuring that it survives the transition from plan to reality. In terms of strategic planning, this competency is important because it ensures that proposed strategies are effective, beneficial, and do not simply promote change for its own sake.

Feedback and Adaptation. In terms of strategic planning, this group of competencies are the ones that come into play after the plan has been devised. The strategy was developed in response to a perceived need, with data appropriately *gathered* and *analyzed*, and the *decision-making* process duly followed. It was created *collaboratively*, through the *commitment* of the leader and followers, and now *implementation* is imminent. The only question remaining is how to best ensure the plan is adopted and adhered to.

- *Business acumen* is helpful when promoting a strategic plan. This competency is demonstrated by the ability to understand the financial and operational aspects of an organization. It shows a keen awareness of the competitive landscape and manifests in an intuitive understanding of the salient threats and opportunities. Acumen is a valuable combination of knowledge, skills, experience, and intuition, and stakeholders often defer to those who display it.
- *Negotiation* is the process of advocating for the terms and conditions that achieve desired objectives. It requires *communication skills*, often in conjunction with a *systems mindset*, and both *resource management* and access to good *analyses* are important. Successful negotiations require compromise, which means listening attentively, identifying the interests, and understanding the needs of all parties. Creating strategy usually requires effective and sustained negotiation, as leaders attempt to secure necessary resources and concessions while *managing stakeholders'* disparate needs.
- *Stakeholder management* is closely tied to *negotiation*; the two are so interdependent that it is tempting to consider one a subset of the other. Both skill sets involve looking at the expectations and interests of those affected by a project, plan, or program, understanding their needs and concerns, and developing tactics geared to meet their objectives and ours alike. In a sense, the key relational interaction between these two competencies is that of theory and practice. While a keen *negotiator* can understand what an interested party wants and find a way to reach common ground with them, managing stakeholders requires actually effecting those agreements. Organizational objectives must be merged with these external expectations on an ongoing basis. As most, if not all, strategies require cooperation with outside entities, it is vital to continually evaluate whether they are satisfied with the outcomes of our common efforts.
- The competency which builds on and supports each of the others discussed in this chapter is *visionary leadership*. It is the culmination of all the skills used in strategic planning: the ability to create and communicate a compelling vision of the future that inspires and motivates others to join in and bring it to fruition. Leaders with this quality typically have a strong sense of purpose and a clear idea of what the future might hold, and they use their enthusiasm and passion to motivate others to work toward that image. Being a visionary leader means wholeheartedly striving to further the goals set by organizational values and setting forth the plans to make their achievement possible.

Strategy in the Workplace

Now that we have discussed the competencies that contribute to crafting individual strategies, let us examine how to create strategy in the workplace. The first step is to undertake an environmental scan. As discussed in the *assessment, analysis, and response* cluster, the foundation of any strategy is having a clear picture of existing conditions. Without an accurate assessment of the situation, it is impossible to make effective plans or projections.

While there are several approaches to conducting an environmental scan, each with a different focus, the one that will receive our attention here is the *strength, weakness, opportunity, and threat* (SWOT) analysis procedure. Per David and David (2016), there are two subcomponents of SWOT analyses: external-factor evaluations (EFE) and internal-factor evaluations (IFE).

The external and internal assessments are very similar in form and can be performed in any order, concurrently or sequentially. As an internal stakeholder already familiar with intraorganizational threats and opportunities though, I prefer to begin with an external-factor evaluation. After all, experience has shown that external elements are often more limiting than internal ones because by definition they are outside of our control. For the EFE, factors are categorized as *opportunities* or *threats*, depending on their potential outcomes for the organization.

When preparing to conduct these scans, it is important to recruit knowledgeable participants to provide data. Choose stakeholders who have a good working understanding of the topic of investigation and ask them to do the following:

- Identify the external factors likely to have an impact on the organization's strategic-planning processes and the outcomes it thereby achieves. While a list of factors can include any number of entries, I generally leave room for 10 items to make the next step easier. An inexhaustive list of potential elements would include political, economic, social, technological, and legal factors.
- Examine and weight each of those external environmental elements based on their relative importance to the organization. To do so, distribute 100 points among the identified factors. Points can be assigned as whole integers or fractionally but cannot total more than 100 for *both threats and opportunities combined*. Higher values indicate that an item is more critical to the success of our organization, business, or field.
- Finally, rank the perceived ability of the organization to use that opportunity or minimize that threat, assigning a whole-integer score ranging from one (1) to four (4). A one means the organization is ill prepared for that element, while a four indicates that we believe it to be well equipped to handle the situation.

Note that these assessments are, as mentioned, somewhat subjective. For that reason, it is important to collect data from a diverse group of people when performing an environmental scan in practice. Depending on the situation and size of the organization, it may be appropriate to ask everyone to participate or select a group from those best positioned to give accurate and useful evaluations. The person responsible for the scan distributes worksheets to the participants (remembering to fill out a set as well!). As examples (Figure 14.2, Figure 14.3, and Figure 14.4), these sample EFE matrices[3] are filled out with data from a pilot project in Idaho (Nix et al., 2015), which was designed to transition high-school dropouts into technical college.

The next step is to take the weights from the second sheet and plug them into the following matrix. Then, participants will enter their ratings from 1–4 and multiply those numbers by the weight to get the final weighted score for each factor. Figure 14.5 provides an example.

---

3. Note: All matrices from this point forward were created by using the original template offered with David (2006) during live sessions with staff in 2011. That template has been continuously updated and is publicly available and freely downloadable at www.strategyclub.com

EFE Matrix

Opportunities

Enter up to 10 golden opportunities here.

1.	Walmart Collaboration
2.	College of Technology dedicated grant writer - establish relationship
3.	Counseling Department Clinic - for a doctoral practicum site
4.	Publishing in Refereed Journals
5.	South Eastern Idaho Community Action Association Collaboration
6.	Idaho State University (ISU) Outreach Centers - establish presences
7.	Resource Center Tutoring
8.	Focus on persistence and retention, outcomes-based State funding
9.	Other funding possibilities
10.	ISU College of Technology (additional) funding

Threats

Enter up to 10 critical threats here.

1.	No Tuition dollars
2.	Decreased funding for CND and ABE
3.	100% Grant funded/Constraints of Funder
4.	Often have competing interests within GenEd
5.	Often have competing interests within Community
6.	Lack of Commitment to START from external stakeholders
7.	Political Forces (between and across external stakeholders)
8.	Stigma associated with GED population
9.	CoT/ISU LC Academic relationship stressors
10.	Increased Costs to serve our students/participants

FIGURE 14.2 External Factor Evaluation in Action: Identification of Opportunities and Threats for Idaho Program Pilot

Distribute 100 points by entering a weighted score for each factor that ranges from 0 (not important) to 100 (all important). They must sum to 100. The weight indicates the relative importance of that factor to being successful in the firm's industry.

		Enter the opportunity weights here
1.	Walmart Collaboration	1
2.	College of Technology dedicated grant writer - establish relationship	6
3.	Counseling Department Clinic - for a doctoral practicum site	6
4.	Publishing in Refereed Journals	6
5.	South Eastern Idaho Community Action Association Collaboration	4
6.	Idaho State University (ISU) Outreach Centers - establish presences	3
7.	Resource Center Tutoring	4
8.	Focus on persistence and retention, outcomes-based State funding	8
9.	Other funding possibilities	10
10.	ISU College of Technology (additional) funding	6
		Enter the threat weights here
1.	No Tuition dollars	9
2.	Decreased funding for CND and ABE	4
3.	100% Grant funded/Constraints of Funder	9
4.	Often have competing interests within GenEd	4
5.	Often have competing interests within Community	4
6.	Lack of Commitment to START from external stakeholders	4
7.	Political Forces (between and across external stakeholders)	3
8.	Stigma associated with GED population	2
9.	CoT/ISU LC Academic relationship stressors	1
10.	Increased Costs to serve our students/participants	6
	Total	100.00

FIGURE 14.3. External Factor Evaluation in Action: Weighting the Opportunities and Threats for Idaho Program Pilot

Rate the ability of the firm to effectively respond to each factor from 1 to 4. Where 4 = superior, 3 = above average, 2 = average, 1 = poor.

	Enter opportunity rate here
1. Walmart Collaboration	1
2. College of Technology dedicated grant writer - establish relationship	3
3. Counseling Department Clinic - for a doctoral practicum site	3
4. Publishing in Refereed Journals	1
5. South Eastern Idaho Community Action Association Collaboration	1
6. Idaho State University (ISU) Outreach Centers - establish presences	2
7. Resource Center Tutoring	1
8. Focus on persistence and retention, outcomes-based State funding	3
9. Other funding possibilities	1
10. ISU College of Technology (additional) funding	2

	Enter threat rate here
1. No Tuition dollars	2
2. Decreased funding for CND and ABE	1
3. 100% Grant funded/Constraints of Funder	3
4. Often have competing interests within GenEd	2
5. Often have competing interests within Community	1
6. Lack of Commitment to START from external stakeholders	3
7. Political Forces (between and across external stakeholders)	2
8. Stigma associated with GED population	4
9. CoT/ISU LC Academic relationship stressors	3
10. Increased Costs to serve our students/participants	3

FIGURE 14.4 External Factor Evaluation in Action: Rating the Opportunities and Threats for Idaho Program Pilot

EFE MATRIX FOR Idaho Program Pilot

Critical Success Factors	Weight	Rating	Weighted Score
Opportunities			
Walmart Collaboration	1	1	1
College of Technology dedicated grant writer - establish relationship	6	3	18
Counseling Department Clinic - for a doctoral practicum site	6	3	18
Publishing in Refereed Journals	6	1	6
South Eastern Idaho Community Action Association Collaboration	4	1	4
Idaho State University (ISU) Outreach Centers - establish presences	3	2	6
Resource Center Tutoring	4	1	4
Focus on persistence and retention, outcomes-based State funding	8	3	24
Other funding possibilities	10	1	10
ISU College of Technology (additional) funding	6	2	12
Threats			
No Tuition dollars	9	2	18
Decreased funding for CND and ABE	4	1	4
100% Grant funded/Constraints of Funder	9	3	27
Often have competing interests within GenEd	4	2	8
Often have competing interests within Community	4	1	4
Lack of Commitment to START from external stakeholders	4	3	12
Political Forces (between and across external stakeholders)	3	2	6
Stigma associated with GED population	2	4	8
CoT/ISU LC Academic relationship stressors	1	3	3
Increased Costs to serve our students/participants	6	3	18
TOTAL	100		211

FIGURE 14.5 External Factor Evaluation in Action: EFE Matrix for Idaho Program Pilot

Following the EFE, a similar process is used for the internal-factor evaluation (IFE). In this case, items are categorized as *strengths* and *weaknesses*. These can be related to organizational culture or structure, personnel, or financial or physical resources, among other things. During the IFE, look at each of those strengths and weaknesses, and just as in the external scan, assign each one a weight. Next, the factors are assigned a whole-integer score from one (1) to four (4), with a one representing a minor strength or weakness and a four indicating a very potent one.

With results from the EFE and IFE in hand, we now use the weighted factors to create a SWOT matrix. This provides a visual tool to help translate strengths, weaknesses, opportunities, and threats into actionable tactics during ensuing strategic planning procedures.

Begin by pairing strengths, weaknesses, opportunities, and threats into four categorical types. Strengths are used to take advantage of opportunities in SO strategies and matched with threats to create ST ones. Weaknesses are paired with opportunities, looking for ways these external factors could help overcome or minimize these deficiencies with WO strategies. The final matchup is the WT category, where defensive strategies are devised to protect organizational weaknesses from external threats. WT strategies are generally used as worst-case contingency plans and are designed strictly to minimize harm rather than maximize gain. When planners fail to anticipate and are slow to react, the WT plan could involve *divestiture*, when immediately jettisoning the liability is the most prudent course of action; when a negative outcome was expected and planned for and a profit can still possibly be realized, the strategy is called *harvest*. While SO, ST, and WO strategies are much more common than WT ones, we need to keep divestiture and harvest in mind, lest we incur worse outcomes through inaction or delay. Figure 14.6 displays a set of pre-paired statements as an example and includes one pairing completed in each cell of the SWOT matrix.

When these strategies have been identified, the next step is to look at the combined weighted scores[4] of each. If two factors with high scores are paired, that should be considered a critical strategy (high attractiveness), worth addressing or implementing as soon as possible. Strategies combining lower-weighted factors can be considered less pressing (marked by low attractiveness), implemented over the long term, or even discarded in follow-up executive-level *planning* activities.

The final step in choosing any set of strategies to include in an official *strategic planning document* involves the *total scores* shown at the bottom of the EFE and IFE matrices. The two total scores are combined and used in the *internal-external* (IE) matrix, which can indicate the general strategic stance an organization should likely take. The total score for the sample EFE was 211; let us imagine that the total score for the imaginary IFE was 373. In that case, we would plot the intersection of the two scores (211, 373) on our IE matrix. This places the pilot program in cell IV, which corresponds to a *grow and build* overall strategic direction. The strategic direction recommended by this activity combined with using factors with higher attractiveness scores will be invaluable to the executive team for deciding upon which strategies to pursue over the next business cycle, generally aligned with an organization's fiscal year. See Figure 14.7 for an example.

If the plotted IE score is in cells I, II, or IV, then a *grow and build* strategy is recommended (as is the case in our example here). An IE score nested in cells III, V, or VII indicates that a *hold and maintain* stance, focusing on conserving strength against future environmental changes, is optimal. Finally, if an unfortunate organization's IE matrix score were to fall in cells VI, VIII, or IX, then it is time to consider *harvest or divest* strategies. One hopes against that outcome, but if that's what the matrix shows, it is time to dust off those WT-strategy pairings without delay!

Now that we are properly prepared, let's tackle a hypothetical case.

4. David and David (2016) refer to these as *attractiveness scores*.

SWOT Matrix Template	**Strengths** 1. Commitment of Team to Project's Success 2. Leadership Potential 3. Competent Team 4. Caring Team 5. Dedicated Math Instructor 6. Dedicated Counselor 7. Dedicated Writing Instructor 8. Politically Savvy Coordinator 9. Data-informed Team 10. Three team Members familiar with local culture	**Weaknesses** 1. Have not determined exact recruiting 2. Limited recruitment Budget 3. Limited official linkages to academic 4. Limited Technology Budget 5. No dedicated server for our database 6. Paper-heavy procedures 7. Participants are not "officially enrolled" 8. No dedicated transportation for 9. All participants are "at risk" 10. No budget for hiring additional counselors
Opportunities 1. Walmart Collaboration 2. College of Technology dedicated grant writer - establish relationship 3. Counseling Department Clinic - for a doctoral practicum site 4. Publishing in Refereed Journals 5. South Eastern Idaho Community Action Association Collaboration 6. Idaho State University (ISU) Outreach Centers - establish presences 7. Resource Center Tutoring 8. Focus on persistence and retention, outcomes-based State funding 9. Other funding possibilities 10. ISU College of Technology (additional) funding	**S-O Strategies** 1. Coordinator/College of Technology grant-writer partnership (S#8, O#2)	**W-O Strategies** 1. Recruit through local action agency partnership (W#1, O#5)
Threats 1. No Tuition dollars 2. Decreased funding for CND and ABE 3. 100% Grant funded/Constraints of Funder 4. Often have competing interests within GenEd 5. Often have competing interests within Community 6. Lack of Commitment to START from external stakeholders 7. Political Forces (between and across external stakeholders) 8. Stigma associated with GED population 9. CoT/ISU LC Academic relationship stressors 10. Increased Costs to serve our students/participants	**S-T Strategies** 1. Each team member creates two connections with academic faculty through networking (S#3, T#6)	**W-T Strategies** 1. Ask the doctoral counseling program how we could be classified as a practicum site for their students (W#9, T#6 & T#8)

FIGURE 14.6 SWOT Matrix with Pre-paired Strengths, Weaknesses, Opportunities, and Threats for the Idaho Pilot Project

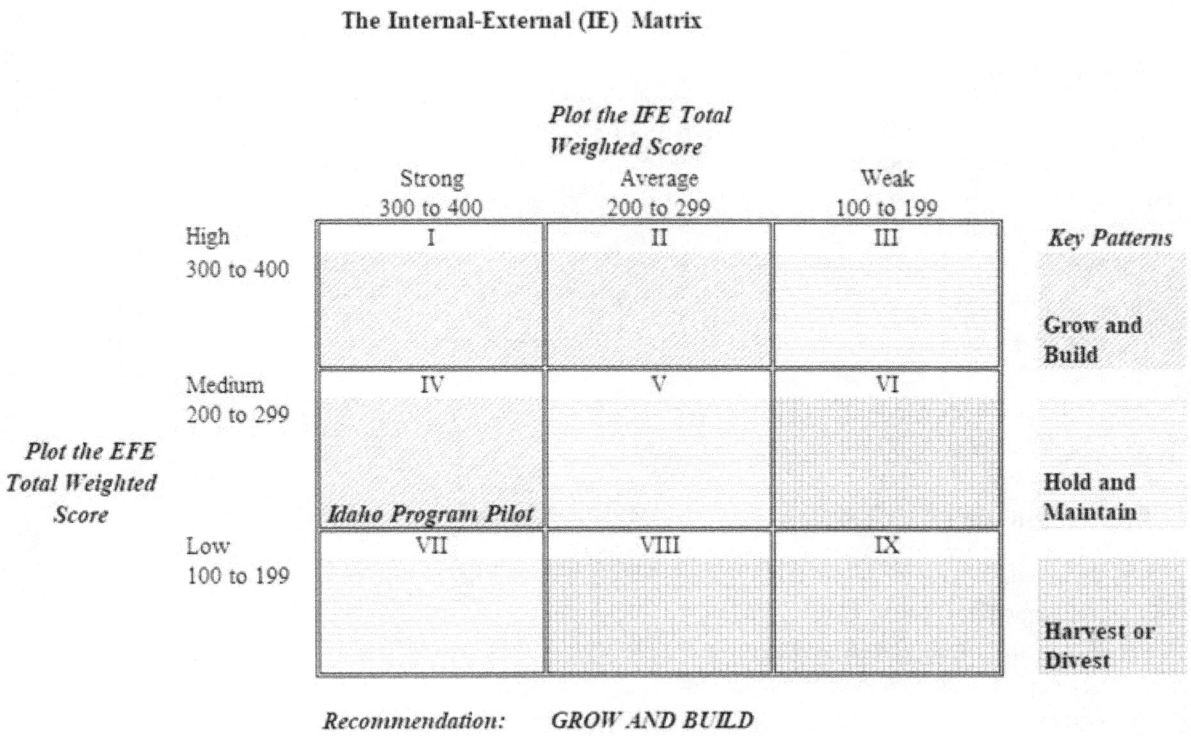

FIGURE 14.7 Strategies in Action: IE Matrix for Idaho Pilot Project

BOX 14.1 **Case Study**

ABC Corporation is a medium-size manufacturer that has been in business for over 10 years. They've seen steady growth in their sales and profits over that time; however, they have recently begun experiencing a decline in their receipts. Management sees the need for a new strategy to turn things around. The stated objective is to create a plan for increasing ABC's sales and profit in a way that also boosts long-term competitiveness. A SWOT analysis completed by selected employees resulted in the following four lists:

Strengths:

1. Experienced management team
2. Established customer base
3. Solid reputation in the industry
4. Well-developed production processes
5. Access to capital and credit lines
6. Good supply-chain relationships
7. Experienced workforce
8. Access to a wide range of raw materials and components
9. Strong financial track record
10. Proven marketing strategies

Weaknesses:

1. Outdated technology and equipment
2. Limited research-and-development resources
3. Lack of innovation in product offerings
4. Lack of investment in marketing or advertising campaigns
5. Weak customer-service reputation
6. Poor pricing strategies
7. Insufficient quality-control measures
8. Excessive overhead costs
9. Lack of diversification across markets, products, and services
10. Insufficient training for employees

Opportunities:

1. Expansion into new markets
2. Developing new products and services
3. Investing in research and development
4. Leveraging digital technologies to enhance customer experience
5. Acquiring new businesses or technologies to expand capabilities
6. Enhancing customer service and support
7. Establishing strategic partnerships with other organizations
8. Exploring alternative financing options
9. Exploring opportunities for cost savings and efficiencies
10. Adopting a more agile business model

Threats:

1. Changing customer needs and preferences
2. Increasing competition from rival firms
3. Potential disruption from emerging technologies
4. Rising labor costs and difficulty finding skilled workers
5. Potential supply-chain disruptions due to global events
6. Government regulations or policies that could impede growth
7. Fluctuations in the economy or currency exchange rates
8. Uncertainty over ongoing trade negotiations
9. Cybersecurity threats from hackers or other malicious actors
10. Rising costs of raw materials or components

BOX 14.2 **Tasks for Practice**

Exercise 1

Combine pairs of SWOT items from the case study into five each of SO, WO, ST, and WT strategies, using internal strengths and weaknesses to address external opportunities and threats.[1] An example of each is included below.

1. *(SO) Enhancing customer service and support offerings to explore opportunities for cost savings and efficiencies.*
2. *(WO) Improving the effectiveness of marketing campaigns to explore alternative financing options.*
3. *(ST) Investing in cutting-edge technology and training for skilled workers to reduce the potential for supply-chain disruptions.*
4. *(WT) Strengthening cybersecurity protocols to mitigate the risks of emerging technologies.*

Now, complete five of each on your own!

Exercise 2

Identify an issue in your work or personal life. Create a SWOT analysis for the issue and identify next steps.

1. Advanced classes (graduate students, for example, or undergrads interested in strategic management) may find it valuable to also assign weights and ratings to the SWOT items, culminating with the creation of an IE matrix.

Concluding Remarks

The four types of strategies, respectively and collectively, explicitly address "How will we accomplish our mission?" The mission, as we remember from Chapter 13, addresses "How do we achieve our vision?" Prioritized SO, WO, ST, and WT statements from every single department should be categorized and ranked by divisional management positions so that they align with budgetary realities. At that point, realistic and sometimes painful decisions need to be based on the organizational values but grounded in financial realism. Transparency regarding the processes through which specific strategies may need to be omitted from the larger set of strategies we collectively term a *strategic plan* is also critical. However, workplace leaders and followers who collectively created the specific strategic statements will have a deeper commitment to the resulting plan than if the entire process were completed without any input.

Application

Post-Chapter Activities

A great homework assignment is to sort all of the WO, SO, ST, and WT strategies by the sums of the weighted factors (attractiveness scores) and combine those into a facsimile of what is generally referred to as a *strategic plan*. Instructors may assign roles (a president along with three to five vice presidents per small group) to groups of students. Each role played should imagine which department (or for smaller organizations, which director) will be tasked with achieving the individual strategies within her or his division. For example, the WO strategy listed in Textbox 14.2 would be assigned to the *director of marketing* position.

For an even deeper dive into *planning* activities, teams could be assigned to create departmental task-outs and timelines; this final sort of group activity was made for an interesting and challenging culminating project in a course specifically focused on *strategic planning*. Each of these sets of role-playing activities may further illuminate how the competencies described in this chapter are put into action, and in many cases will further isolate and identify individual competencies which need to be developed or improved.

References

David, F., & David, F. (2016). Strategic Management: A Competitive Advantage Approach, Concepts (16th ed.). Pearson.

David, F. R. (2006). Strategic management: Concepts and cases (11th ed.). Pearson College Division.

Niño-Zarazúa, M. (2016). Aid, education policy, and development. *International Journal of Educational Development, 48*, 1–8. https://doi.org/10.1016/j.ijedudev.2015.12.002

Nix, J. V., Lion, R. W., Michalak, M., & Christensen, A. (2015). Individualized, purposeful, and persistent: Successful transitions and retention of students at risk. *Journal of Student Affairs Research and Practice, 52*(1), 104–118. https://doi.org/10.1080/19496591.2015.995576

Strategy Club—Strategy Club – The #1 Global Strategic Management Textbook. (n.d.). Retrieved February 25, 2023, from https://www.strategyclub.com/

Tzu, S. (2005). *The art of war: Complete texts and commentaries* (T. Cleary, Trans.). Shambhala.

CHAPTER 15

Leading and Managing Change

By Tracy L. Collum

The only constant in life is change.

—Heraclitus

Learning Objectives

1. Explain why you need to lead change (rather than let the change lead you)
2. Describe at least one common model for and managing leading change
3. Identify steps to create a change plan to enact change
4. Apply change concepts to your own change situation

Introduction to Leading and Managing Change

What is change management? Moran and Brightman define it as (2001) as restoring or updating processes, ideas, and more based on the needs of those within and/or outside an organizational structure. Prosci (2023) defines change management as an "enabling framework for managing the people side of change." Change occurs when needed or wanted to help industry compete, streamline processes, and various other factors. To elaborate, Becker, Lazaric, Nelson, and Winter (2005) stated, "the capabilities of firms to compete depends on their ability to keep introducing new products, or improving their process of manufacture, or both, and such innovating requires continuing change in a range of routines used in a firm" (p. 776).

We all work with and lead change daily. Every decision you make enacts a shift that leads to change. It could be the change in perspective for yourself: your decision-making or your work style. It could be a change in your communication with others, which provides advice on steps to take or gaps to fill work efficiency, projects, and cultural environments. Every little aspect of your day equates to a change as you interact with others.

Why is change important? Van Wart (2013) discusses a leader's role as facilitating an organization into the future; thus, the main objective of leadership is change. Without change, workplaces do not evolve, adapt, or improve—creating a stale environment. Leadership helps to create a dynamic workplace where change is inevitable. Additionally, good leadership allows for change and helps prepare employees for change that inevitably arises. When change occurs, leaders must advocate for resources, as the effectiveness of that leadership may be perceived as low when resources are not available.

The purpose of this chapter is to provide a few guidelines and a rationale for how you can lead and manage the change in your area—no matter your title, salary, or position. This chapter will discuss tips on where to begin and how to keep people involved because "managers are being asked to rapidly respond to changing environments by actively seeking out new opportunities and leading their followers forward to take advantage of them" (Paglis & Green, 2002, p. 215). There will be numerous paths to lead your staff or organization into change. Find the ones that work for your team and create the systems to lead the change positively.

Many areas you have read in this book are also needed to navigate change. Will you need to communicate effectively? Always. Will you need to influence others? Absolutely. Will there be a conflict to manage? Possibly. We could go on and on. Everyone will find the strategy that fits them, but an outline of suggestions below is to help guide you as you work through change. As a leader of your organization, look at the planned (proactive) changes you can make or unplanned (reactive) actions that will come. "The reactive change takes place when internal or external forces pressurize the organization for change while proactive change takes place when the organization itself concludes about change to be desirable" (Hussain, Akram, Haider, Hussain, & Ali, 2018, p. 124).

Leadership Change Models

Navigating change can be a challenge for any leader. Following a change management model with concrete steps can be helpful as you navigate change. Evaluating change at the beginning and throughout the change is necessary for the workplace to remain relevant. As Bekmukhambetova (2021) states, "Change is synonymous with standard business practice, and business needs to change to develop and be competitive" (p. 2). Using an individualized preferred model by the steps provided will guide leaders in having a plan for change rather than not considering important questions. A select few change models and an adaptive personal model are summarized below.

Kotter's 8-Step Model

Kotter (2012) developed an 8-step change model to help corporations lead and implement change. Finding that those leading often skipped necessary areas in implementing change, Kotter's guide details steps to ensure every area supporting the change is intentional and utilized. The 8-step model can be further divided into three overall categories or phases. Bekmukhambetova (2021) describes the phases in a broad sense with the 8 steps over the three phases:

First Phase

1. Establish a sense of urgency.
2. Form a powerful guiding coalition.
3. Create a vision for change.

Second Phase

1. Communicate the vision.
2. Empower others to act on the vision.
3. Plan for and create short-term wins.

Third (Last) Phase

1. Build on change.
2. Commit to the change as the new normal.

ADKAR Model

The ADKAR model, developed by Prosci founder Jeff Hiatt (Prosci, 2023), focuses on people change in addition to process change. The model focuses on five key areas: Awareness, Desire; Knowledge, Ability; and Reinforcement. Bekmukhambetova (2021) describes the ADKAR model as:

1. Brings awareness and understanding of why a change is needed.
2. Gaining support for the change and allowing time for engagement and participation of this support.
3. Getting details and knowledge about the change and how to get there.
4. Includes the ability to implement the change.
5. Maintain and sustain the change.

Wong et al. (2019) call the ADKAR model a user-friendly model that can be integrated easily into various workforces by employees at all levels. Additionally, Wong et al. determined the ADKAR model to be beneficial in the health care field to manage change in their care delivery model on a large scale.

Lewin's Model

Lewin's model involves three steps: unfreezing, moving, and freezing. Lewin's organizational change model is based on planned change. The concept "involves an awareness of the concept of stability" (Bekmukhambetova, 2021, p. 4) to understand then that stability can become unstable. As Hussain et al. (2018) describe, Lewin's first step is the need for change to become apparent to the leader. The second step is for employee involvement to occur to allow the change to occur or move into action. This step is where employees can provide input related to the needed change. The last step in Lewin's change model is freezing or refreezing, which allows planning and commitment to changes.

A 3-Step Model

While change models can provide textbook direction in leadership, leaders also learn and adjust from experience. Being self-aware and flexible while leading change can be helpful in finding one's own leadership approach. One technique I have adapted over years of experience is a simple 3-step approach. Step 1, determine the need(s); Step 2, decide who should be involved; and Step 3, Share the visions. Each step may evolve with the timeline or the projects needed, and a good leader will develop each step as needed.

Simplify the situation with these steps and questions:

Step 1: What is the need?

- Why do we need this?
- How do we get there?
- When do we want this to go live?

Step 2: Dive deep with whom to involve

Who should be involved? senior leaders, employees, other departments, customers? Do not forget to include those in the trenches of the work affected. They will know more than anyone about the implications of the change on the work and the workflow. These employees may be

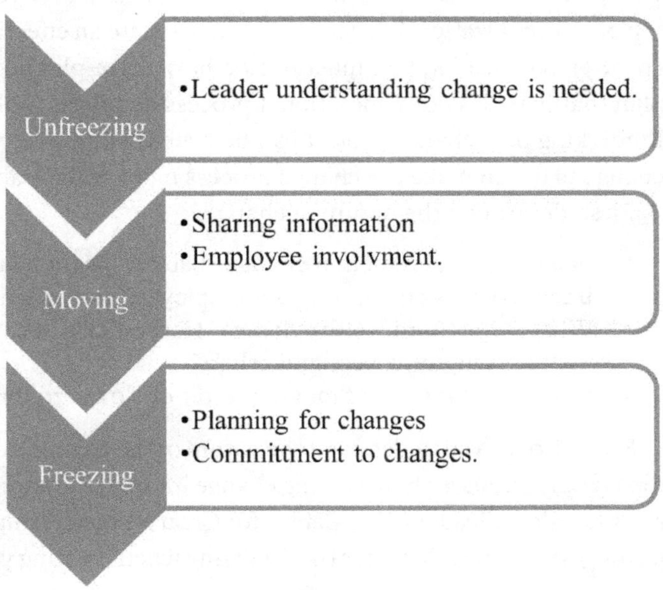

FIGURE 15.1 Summary of Lewin's Change Model

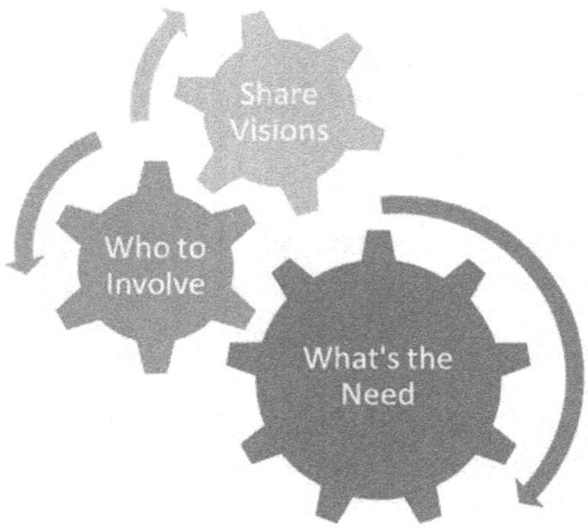

FIGURE 15.2 Evaluating Change

overlooked as not "leaders" or "senior enough," but they offer a useful perspective and credibility for the project.

Step 3: Share vision

- What outcomes does everyone expect?
- When should it be implemented?
- What do you want to see as outcomes?
- Discuss to get consensus and as much agreement as possible.

As you go through these three steps, continue to evaluate and reevaluate each step.

Start these discussions by getting the right people in the room. Keep the initial conversations small and allow a conversation that is open and free of judgment. Remember the expression "no idea is a bad idea." That is the goal when beginning to create the change plan.

When the initial planning is in place, bring in people who can help with implementing the change. Do you need technology developed? Do you need details put together? Do you need people who will test the outcome?

When you know who should be involved, bring them together to help them understand what you need. Be clear about why you need the change and why you have asked them to participate. Regardless of who is involved, share the goal and outcomes of this change initiative, remind them why this change project is important and why *they* are part of this project. Getting buy-in on both why this project needs to happen and why-me provides clarity for everyone to focus on the same goal. Discuss reasonable timelines and be sure from everyone in the group, the implications of the timelines on their constituent group.

How to Lead and Manage Change in the Workplace

As discussed earlier, change happens, whether proactive, reactive, or as part of natural processes in the workplace. Beycioglu and Kondakci state, "Planned change is a kind of change initiative managed from the top of an organization and spread over it to create an effective organization through planned interventions" (p. 789). As a leader, you must decide how these planned changes will take effect and create a change plan that includes both operational/process details as well as the communication needed for this change. Embarking on a change project can be overwhelming for you and your employees. Creating a thoughtful change plan can make the change process more manageable and less disruptive.

First, determine the nature of change:

- Is it a small incremental change (baby steps) or a large disruptive change (giant leap)? What is the impact of this change on your employees and others such as customers?
- What is the timing of the change? How quickly does the change need to occur? How will this timing impact your employees and others?
- What is the impact of moving faster or slower to implement the change?

Second, once you understand the nature of the change, consider how you will implement the change. Uhl-Bien (2021) discusses how moving change into an operational form and navigating resistance to change are a key hurdle for leaders. The Center for Creative Leadership (2020) refers to this as leading the process and leading the people. Consider the following when creating your change operation and communication plan:

- Who are the people who need to be connected to this change to gather their input and perspective?
- Whom do you need to communicate with about the change because it impacts them and their workflow?

- What is the communication message and timing of the message for each of these groups?
- How and how often will you communicate with each of these groups?
- How will you allow for and incorporate questions and feedback from employees and others about this change?
- What resistance to this change do you anticipate from employees or others? What is your plan for surface, acknowledge, and manage this resistance?
- What else do you need to do to keep employees engaged during this change once it is implemented?

Anticipating and planning for employee involvement and engagement is a critical part of your change plan. AlManei, Salonitis, and Tsinopoulos stressed, "A lack of employee engagement in change initiatives is often cited as reason why [change] projects fail" (2018, p. 1162). While communication is critical and "effective communication strategy can build trust and understanding" (Laframboise et al., 2003, p. 309), employees need to be part of the process and have accountability or ownership of change initiatives for these initiatives to succeed. Allowing a genuinely collaborative effort with open communications helps employees connect to the new processes and desired outcomes, as well as the "why" of the change.

Finally, as you refine your change plan:

- Use stages and deadlines to work through the change. Plan enough so that when issues arise (and they will), you will not stress over them—the stress points can be viewed as solvable—not only by you but others involved.
- Collaborate and delegate throughout the change process. Empower your team to think collaboratively and creatively through the change process. This is not *your* change; this change belongs to everyone.
- Create a planning team to work with as you create a plan for the change.
- Create an implementation team to bring the change to fruition.
- Use test groups or gather feedback along the way to ensure you are going in the right direction. Consider who your fans will be and who will be the resisters, and use them to your advantage during the change process by including them and their feedback.
- Which leadership approaches will you use during this change process?
- How will you create "white space" (Funt, 2021) in your schedule to reflect on how the change process is progressing? This is important time to set aside so you can consider the change process, including: progress, feedback, communication and additional resources needed, etc., and make adjustments to your change plan.

Change is not always easy. Go in with a pragmatic, positive lens.

BOX 15.1 **Leading Change in Higher Education**

Chris was associate dean for a division at a university and participated on the university curriculum committee. The curriculum committee decided to make a shift from 3-credit classes to 4-credit classes. This change had potential negative implications for the working adult students in Chris's division, both for scheduling and for qualifying as full-time students for financial aid. Chris explained the change to her team and said, "We need to work together to make this work for our students." Together Chris and her team came up with a pro and con list of how this change would impact students. As they reviewed the list, one of the employees suggested they create scenarios for each of the cons to see if they could more easily identify solutions for the problems. A subgroup created the scenarios, and the entire team was able to identify solutions that would work for the students using the new 4-credit classes. Once the team understood the implications of the change for various student scenarios, they were able to run a report on all students in the division, create a spreadsheet, identify the situation for each student, and how the change would affect each student. As the first two steps of a larger communication plan, Chris sent an email notifying students of the upcoming change and timeline. Her team had individual appointments with students to discuss the implications of the 4-credit class change on their particular situation and create an individual plan for the future. Chris and her team continued communicating with students and gathering their feedback throughout the over-two-years of this change. This change required time, energy, and flexibility from Chris and her team, but the successful student experience through this change made it worth it to them.

Questions:

1. What did Chris (and her team) do well during this change process? What was the impact?
2. What might Chris (and her team) have done differently during this change process? What would be the impact?
3. Which change model might Chris have been following for this change?

Summary

Leading a group through change is never easy. How you lead the group will have a profound impact on the outcome for the change initiative. Remember to communicate, be transparent, be available, and choose the right people to be involved. Evaluate your process, planning, and people often to continue to move forward positively. Not everyone will be on board with the change. Empower those around you. Be flexible and provide grace for yourself, the vision, and the people involved. Change is not easy for everyone, even when the change is understood and wanted. Allowing everyone the space to discuss the challenges and the wins is a healthy way to adjust the vision to make positive improvements.

Application

Exercise 1: Reflecting on the Past

Think of a leader you had in the past that got you through a change (whether you wanted it or not).

1. What was the change?
2. What did the leader do to *help* with the change? (Which of these relate to what was discussed in this chapter?) What was the impact of these things on you, the team, or organization?
3. What did the leader do to *hinder* the change? What was the impact of these things on you, the team, or organization?

Exercise 2: Planning for the Future

Think of a change that is coming up in your professional (or personal) life. Choose one of the change models described in this chapter and plan your change (Kotter, ADKAR, Lewin, 3-Step model). In addition to planning each step of the change, be sure to include *what* you will do, with *whom*, and *why* you will do what you will do.

References

AlManei, M., Salonitis, K., & Tsinopoulos, C. (2018). A conceptual lean implementation framework based on change management theory. *Procedia cirp*, *72*, 1160–1165.

Becker, M. C., Lazaric, N., Nelson, R. R., & Winter, S. G. (2005). Applying organizational routines in understanding organizational change. *Industrial and Corporate Change*, *14*(5), 775–791. doi: 10.1093/icc/dth071

Bekmukhambetova, A. (2021). Comparative analysis of change management models based on an exploratory literature review. http://unipub.lib.uni-corvinus.hu/6443/1/NHBMS_10Bekmukhambetova.pdf doi: 10.14267/978-963-503-867-1_10

Beycioglu, K., & Kondakci, Y. (2020). Organizational change in schools. *ECNU Review of Education, 4*(4). https://doi.org/10.1177/2096531120932177

Funt, J. (2021). *A minute to think: Reclaim creativity, conquer busyness, and do your best work*. Harper Business.

How to Be a Successful Change Leader. (2020, November 24). Center for Creative Leadership. https://www.ccl.org/articles/leading-effectively-articles/successful-change-leader/

Hussain, S. T., Lei, S., Akram, T., Haider, M. J., Hussain, S. H., & Ali, M. (2018). Kurt Lewin's change model: A critical review of the role of leadership and employee involvement in organizational change. *Journal of Innovation & Knowledge, 3*(3), 123–127. https://doi.org/10.1016/j.jik.2016.07.002

Kotter, J. P. (2012). *Leading change*. Harvard Business Review.

Laframboise, D., Nelson, R. L., & Schmaltz, J. (2003). Managing resistance to change in workplace accommodation projects. *Journal of Facilities Management, 1*(4), 306–321.

Moran, J. W., & Brightman, B. K. (2000). Leading organizational change. *Journal of Workplace Learning, 12*(2), 66–74. doi:10.1108/13665620010316226

Nido Qubein, interview by Ron Karr, Velocity Mindset Interview. Karr Associates. 11/1/21. https://fb.watch/e70xlMYTl-/

Paglis, L. L., & Green, S. G. (2002). Leadership self efficacy and managers' motivation for leading change. *Journal of Organizational Behavior: The International Journal of Industrial, Occupational and Organizational Psychology and Behavior, 23*(2), 215–235.

Prosci (2023, May). *What is change management*. https://www.prosci.com/change-management

Prosci (2018). Prosci ADKAR Model: A goal oriented change management model to drive individual and organizational change. Prosci, Inc. https://www.prosci.com/adkar

Rowland, D., Thorley, M., & Brauckmann, N. (2023). *The most successful approaches to leading organizational change*. HBSP. Harvard Business School. https://hbr.org/2023/04/the-most-successful-approaches-to-leading-organizational-change

Steffens, N. K., Wolyniec, N., Okimoto, T. G., Mols, F., Haslam, S. A., & Kay, A. A. (2021). Knowing me, knowing us: Personal and collective self-awareness enhances authentic leadership and leader endorsement. *The Leadership Quarterly, 32*(6), 101498. doi: 10.1016/j.leaqua.2021.101498

Uhl-Bien, M. (2021) Complexity leadership and followership: Changed leadership in a changed world. *Journal of Change Management, 21*(2), 144–162. doi: 10.1080/14697017.2021.1917490

Uhl-Bien, M., & Arena, M. (2018). Leadership for organizational adaptability: A theoretical synthesis and integrative framework. *The Leadership Quarterly, 29*(1), 89–104.

Uhl-Bien, M., Marion, R., & McKelvey, B. (2007). Complexity leadership theory: Shifting leadership from the industrial age to the knowledge era. *The Leadership Quarterly, 18*(4), 298–318. doi: 10.1016/j.leaqua.2007.04.002

van Wart, M. (2013). Lessons from leadership theory and the contemporary challenges of leaders. *Public Administration Review, 73*(4), 553–565.

Wong, Q., Lacombe, M., Keller, R., Joyce, T., & O'Malley, K. (2019). Leading change with ADKAR. *Nursing Management, 50*(4): 28–35. doi: 10.1097/01.NUMA.0000554341.70508.75

Credit

Fig. 15.1: Adapted from Syed Talib Hussain et al., "Kurt Lewin's Change Model: A Critical Review of the Role of Leadership and Employee Involvement in Organizational Change," *Journal of Innovation & Knowledge*, vol. 3, no. 3, pp. 123–127. Copyright © 2018 by Elsevier B.V.

CHAPTER 16

Communications in the Workplace

By Sindy L. Fleming

Dialogue is a process of genuine interaction through which human beings listen to each other deeply enough to be changed by what they learn.

—Harold Saunders

Learning Objectives

After reading this chapter, students will learn to identify:

1. Various types and styles of communication
2. Tenets of the Social Construction Model of communication
3. Tips for using active listening at the base for effective communication in the workplace

Introduction to Communication

Communication is an essential part of the human experience (Ruben & Gigliotti, 2016). It is often used as a tool for conveying information, and we typically think of it as such, but Ruben (2005) explains that it is much more than that and is "the process through which the social fabric of relationships, groups, organization, societies, and world order—and disorder—is created and maintained" (p. 294). It underpins every interaction we have, and words are the vehicle for our thoughts and relationships. Without exaggeration, it can be said that one cannot be a good leader without good communication skills; understanding how we connect through language is the doorway to improving those abilities.

To begin with, it is important to tailor the style of communication to the context. Interpersonal interactions reflect the setting and situation, and understanding the various styles of communication is the key to using them effectively. The basic distinction to make is between formal and informal communication. The formal sort can be seen in the official channels of discourse such as presentations, letters, emails, or speeches. It has a specific structure that adheres to specific rules, employs professional language characterized by formal vocabulary and grammar, and is used in official contexts. Written communications, in particular, are often formal because of the way letters, emails, memos, and the like are used in the workplace. Their structure helps maintain consistency and clarity in the way information is exchanged, and they typically are used as records for future reference or for accountability.

Informal communication, on the other hand, is what most people use outside of meetings, when chatting or checking in with coworkers. It is characterized by casual language and a more relaxed and personal tone. Usually used during casual work gatherings or during breaks, its purpose is to build relationships, exchange personal information, or discuss non-work-related topics. It can be written or oral, depending on place, convenience, and the individuals involved, and may include phone calls, text messages, or interactions on social-media platforms. Understanding the distinction between formal and informal communication is important, as proper use allows one to adapt to different contexts, maintain appropriate professional relationships, and effectively convey messages.

Whether it be formal or informal, a vital component of interaction is nonverbal communication. These elements—gestures, facial expressions, body language, and tone of voice—convey information outside of what is being said and are often influenced by and reflective of our emotions and attitudes. The interpretation of nonverbal cues, which is subconscious and automatic, lets us "read between the lines" to attain a more complete understanding of the intended message. However, individual and cultural backgrounds can influence the interpretation of the verbal and nonverbal message, so it is essential to consider these factors when communicating with others.

Considering the inherent complexity of languages and the wide variety of nonverbal cues, it's no wonder we sometimes stumble in communicating with each other. Particularly in informal settings, misunderstandings are often easily resolved; in the workplace, however, it is much easier to avoid confusion in the first place. By being mindful of what we are saying—and how we are saying it—we can be more successful in conveying our intended message.

To begin with, it helps to have clarity about the purpose and content of communication. What are we trying to accomplish? Are we assigning a task, conveying orders, or initiating a collaboration? Or are we focusing on building relationships? Who is the intended recipient? In particular, understanding the parties involved is key, especially while trying to build relationships. In any case, one should consider how the recipient may react to the information imparted; taking their reactions into account helps one tailor what they convey to make it more effective. By considering the social impact of our interactions, we can be better communicators and achieve better outcomes.

The Social Construction Model of Communication

The Sustained Dialogue Institute (SDI, 2021) says that ideally, good communication involves "each person mak[ing] a serious effort to take others' concerns into their own picture, even when disagreement persists. No participant gives up their identity, but each recognizes enough of the other's valid human claims" that they can foster mutual respect (p. 1). The SDI further notes that to effectively communicate, one needs to engage in active listening, ask clarifying questions, and remember that dialogue does more than just convey information. It requires time, patience, and interaction from both sides, allowing participants to engage in a meaningful way and permitting them to bring forth feelings, emotions, and thoughts. This level of interaction creates a common understanding, enhancing the relationship between the parties.

This approach is taken by W. Barnett Pearce (2007), who devised a new model for communication based on his belief that existing ones focused on the wrong thing. He noted that when learning about communication, most people are taught a paradigm focused on the content of messages, which is primarily concerned with whether content is conveyed in a way that permits reception as intended; this model is a simple back-and-forth channel between participants. He felt this was too superficial and thus created the Social Construction Model of Communication (SCMC), which takes a broader perspective when assessing communications, one which considers the social ramifications when determining whether the desired outcome has been achieved. Later, a coresearcher, Kimberly Pearce (2010), used an expanded model to show

how the "way we talk and ... to whom we talk creates, sustains, and/or destroys relationships, organizations, and communities" (p. 22).

To evaluate one's communications from the SCMC perspective, it is helpful to ask oneself questions such as the following:

- What is my relationship with the other(s) involved?
- What do I hope to achieve through this interaction? What about the other party or parties?
- Do my feelings about the other(s) affect how I perceive what they say?
- Am I able to speak freely, or do I feel the need to self-censor? How about the other(s) involved?
- If we disagree on an outcome, am I willing to risk damaging our relationship(s) to press for the result I want?
- Will this discussion have a broader impact on the way participants are perceived?

Asking questions such as these can help one communicate more thoughtfully, maintaining focus on their long-term goals rather than getting caught up in the immediate interaction. In recognizing how one acts within—and is acted upon by—the world at large, it is easier to take responsibility for how communication is given and received. Doing so increases the likelihood of successfully connecting with others, which in turn gives the communicator greater agency in creating, shaping, and effectively responding to events and outcomes. This requires an understanding of the emotional and rational systems at work when we react to communication.

Emotion and Reasoning: The Automatic and Controlled Response Systems

Emotions are built into every part of being human, including our interactions with one another. They convey important information, have a powerful influence over our thoughts and actions, and arise independently of our conscious desires. Because of their impact, one should be aware of their feelings and consider how they may be affecting our communication. As Kahneman (2013) notes, there are essentially two semi-independent systems driving our thinking: one automatic and one controlled. The first "operates automatically and quickly, with little or no effort and no sense of voluntary control," while the other "allocates attention to the effortful mental activities that demand it, including complex computations ... [and] are often associated with the subjective experience of agency, choice, and concentration" (pp. 20–21).

The automatic process is the more emotional of the two and is intuitive, reactive, and involuntary. The reactions it engenders are based on one's experience, prior knowledge, and memory and functions heuristically. This is what gives rise to "gut reactions," which are intuitive responses reflecting a "most likely" assessment based on experiential data and instinctive reactions. It provides a quick and easy path for us, one which does not require much cognitive effort. This is perfectly appropriate for many situations; it allows rapid responses that would otherwise take time and energy to think through. For example, the automatic process is what lets a driver slow down immediately without having to think when they see a small child toddling next to the road. While it facilitates a tremendous amount of our daily lives, this system (like all extrapolative shortcuts) is prone to certain kinds of error. In particular, it is susceptible to priming, being subtly influenced by associations between things and ideas; to confirmation bias, giving more weight to evidence that supports something one wishes or already believes to be true; and the halo effect, where prior impressions can override current observations. Because of these tendencies, our automatic responses, whether positive or negative, arise from cerebral shortcuts and are not carefully considered. The system itself is biased and unconcerned with our long-term goals or intent. Without taking the time to assess one's emotional state and reflect on their thinking, there is a greater opportunity for communication errors that can have negative impacts on a relationship.

The controlled process, on the other hand, is effortful and based on reasoning. This is what allows us to assess a situation thoughtfully, applying logical analysis of information when making decisions. We often need to mindfully choose to use this system; as Kahneman (2013) remarks, people tend to use automatic processes more often, since it is easier to access, requires less effort, and it is always engaged. So much of what we do is unconscious, and we need to remember to purposefully engage the controlled process when communicating. We have all gone on autopilot during interactions and often do not realize it until it's called to our attention by a disgruntled conversational partner!

Obviously, we want to avoid that situation in the workplace and should put in the effort to activate the controlled process during discussions and meetings. In particular, one should pause when hearing or reading something they do not agree with. It takes a little work, but we can train ourselves to recognize automatic responses and communicate more effectively.

Using Effective Communication in the Workplace

There are several tools one can use for better communication; one in particular, known as active listening, is particularly useful. It involves maintaining focus on what the speaker is saying, asking pertinent questions and reflecting back what they hear to verify they are receiving the message properly. The following scenario will set up an example of how to use the construct.

BOX 16.1 **A Harrowing Affair**

A catered event is being held, and the responsibility for hosting is given to Carla, Karina, and Paula. Guests arrive quickly and line up to get food, and the three employees are working steadily to make sure everything goes smoothly. As the time for dessert draws nigh, Carla and Paula are clearing dinner service and checking in with guests while Karina begins to unbox cakes and pies. She soon realizes that none of the desserts have been precut, and she can only find one clean knife that is suitable for slicing them. Karina starts cutting and quickly begins to feel overwhelmed. There is a variety of cakes and pies; some are sticky, some are bigger than the knife, and some have nuts, which may cause issues with allergies. As she begins cutting, Karina is trying to make sure she doesn't cross-contaminate any of the desserts, frantically slicing, plating, and washing her knife as she does so. As she scrambles to prepare plates in time, Paula comes by to check on the desserts. "Are you about ready for us to start serving?" she asks.

"Just hold on," Karina snaps. "It's gonna take me a minute. I have to focus ... Just come back later!" Paula makes her escape and starts checking on the stragglers who are still eating.

Obviously, Karina was extremely harried, and with tension running high, she was almost certainly operating under the automatic process. Finding herself unable to help, Paula wisely decided to retreat instead of engaging reactively. By doing so, she gave herself an opportunity to activate her controlled process and find a constructive way forward. While there was little she could do in the moment to help with the immediate problem of cakes and knives, Paula wanted to talk with Karina later, hoping both to set up a better system for similar situations in the future and to ensure that their relationship was reinforced.

Before Paula tries to initiate a conversation with Karina, let us explore active listening and see if it can help her initiate a constructive discussion.

Active Listening

Active listening is a powerful tool for effective communication, as it provides not only mechanisms for both speaker and receiver to verify what is being conveyed, but also for soothing the automatic system and tempering emotional response.

1. Be present in the conversation. One's focus should be on the intent of the communication, placing reactions to content or tone secondary. For Paula, this will require her to keep in mind that her intent is to come up with a better system in the future, and more importantly to repair any damage done to her relationship with Karina and reiterate its importance.
2. Acknowledge and thank the other party. Doing so helps disarm their automatic system, allowing them to give more attention to the actual content and process of the communication and less to their emotions surrounding what is being discussed. As the conversation progresses, the remaining elements—summarizing what was shared, asking clarifying questions, being mindful of body language, and focusing on the speaker—will come into play as needed.
3. Use clarifying questions and summarization work together to double-check that the receiver is hearing what's intended. One can—and often should—ask open-ended questions when they are unsure what the speaker meant, prefacing and punctuating them with summaries of what has been received. It is important to avoid injecting one's own opinion, and queries should relate to the topic, eliciting both clarification and the speaker's feelings and reflections. Doing so builds trust, as the listener can feel secure that they are accurately understanding what is intended, and the speaker is given frequent signals that the receiver is engaged. The first verifies information, but the second reinforces respect.
4. Be mindful of everyone's body language. This allows the automatic system to play its part and can spark insightful questions that get to the underlying issues that need communicating. While listening, one should pay attention to the signals they are sending through posture and facial expressions. Avoid sending cues that indicate a closed-off attitude—arms crossed, frowning, looking away from the speaker, and the like. At the same time, let intuition be the guide; if it feels like words and intent do not match, it is probably because body language is indicating a disjunction between what's being said and what's being felt. Those instances provide an excellent chance to ask clarifying questions that can elicit truly meaningful topics.

To illustrate how this might look, let's return to the saga of Paula and Karina. The event has begun winding down, and the time to clean up is approaching. Let's give Paula a chance to apply what she's learned ...

BOX 16.2 **Water Under the Bridge**

As the event starts winding down, Paula watches for an opportunity to reach out to Karina to talk about the hectic scene earlier. Before broaching the subject, she reminds herself to take a moment and get clear about what she wants to achieve. More than anything, she feels it is important to smooth things over, to avoid uncomfortable interactions during the cleanup. Part of that, Paula admits, is feeling stung by the curt tone Karina took before, and part of it is worrying about having come across as unhelpful, since she wasn't able to help with prepping the desserts. "Those are my worries," she says to herself, "but what were Karina's feelings?" Obviously, Karina had felt overwhelmed and unprepared; Paula wants to make sure that they talk about how to avoid or mitigate situations like that in the future, giving everyone an opportunity to step in and share the workload. Before approaching Karina, Paula takes a deep breath and reminds herself to not take anything said personally; Karina may still be feeling harried and might come off brusquer than she intends.

As the guests start to leave, Paula goes over and opens a conversation. "Hey, Karina?" she says. "I'm sorry about earlier; it looked like you were really frazzled, and I wish I could have done more to help." Karina nods and starts to explain how hard it had been. "There were just so many cakes, and pies, and none of them were ready! I don't know who set up the dessert catering, but that really sucked!" As she continues, Karina starts to reactivate her emotional response and raises her voice, pacing and making sharp gestures. Paula, having prepared herself for this, doesn't feel unduly stressed by Karina's tone or posture. Instead, she listens carefully as Karina works through her frustration and starts talking about underlying issues. "It's only my second event like this, you know? I really like this job, and I just don't want to be the weak link, right? It was just ... a lot of pressure. I was afraid I wouldn't get it done in time or would get somebody hospitalized 'cause of some kind of nut allergy."

Paula, remembering to acknowledge and repeat what she's heard, says, "Yeah, that's really hard. I forgot how stressful it is to be the new girl. I'm glad you told me, though. I think you did really well, considering. And yeah, next time, we have to get them to send better-prepared desserts."

They both agree that, hard as it was, they made it through well enough, and the guests seemed happy. "Still," says Paula, "I think we should try and make a plan for next time. You know, have something in place so that if things go sideways, we can at least help each other out a little better. I really didn't like not being able to jump in and make the cake thing easier."

They start to bat some ideas back and forth, and Paula happily notes that Karina seems to be more and more animated as they talk. "She really seems to enjoy being able to contribute," Paula thinks. "I'm glad I asked for ideas!" By the time they begin clearing the last of the dessert service, the two have made a plan, agreeing to meet the day prior to the next event, and run through a checklist to make sure that there wouldn't be any unexpected surprises. Over time, they would be able to make a more and more comprehensive list of things to watch for, and they agree that it's only going to get easier from here.

Paula feels pleased with how the conversation went. By remaining present the whole time, she was able to listen actively and attentively, and she and Karina managed to smooth things over and even come up with a plan for the next event.

As it turns out, Paula was able to use her active-listening techniques to communicate successfully, and she and Karina were able to devise strategies for future events while reinforcing their working relationship. Stepping back during the initial interaction was the right choice because it allowed Paula to take the time to gather her thoughts and get ready to be genuinely receptive to whatever Karina would say. By mindfully practicing active listening, we too can benefit from more fruitful communication in all parts of our lives.

Conclusion

Whether formal or informal, written or verbal, communication is the absolute basis for everything human. Without it, we cannot work together, convey information to each other, or interact socially among our peers. Regardless of the setting or style, the tools laid out in this chapter will help us communicate more effectively, building better relationships and expanding our horizons. Good leaders will know—or learn—when to speak and when to listen and will ensure that everyone leaves a dialogue knowing that they have heard and been heard as intended.

Application: Case Study Exercises in Navigating Workplace Conversations

Case Study One

Brittany is an entry-level staff member in the student affairs division at a college. She has been working in her role for two years and has done well. Her exceptional work has led her to stand out, and her supervisor, Kyle, has increasingly asked her to take on additional duties. Unfortunately, Brittany often does not have enough time to complete her tasks during the workday and has begun taking work home to complete it. She has not been sleeping well and is feeling stressed about meeting deadlines while maintaining the expected high level of quality. One day, Kyle asks Brittany to stop by his office as soon as possible, saying he has something to ask her. She fears that he may ask about progress on her current projects—or worse, that he may ask her to take on another one. When she goes to meet Kyle, Brittany quickly realizes her fears have been realized: Kyle asks her to be the lead for a new assessment project.

Discussion Questions

1. How would you address the situation?
2. If you were Brittany, how would you go about setting up a conversation with Kyle to discuss your concerns about the added project and your bandwidth?
3. What specific strategies could help the two come to an agreement or shared understanding?

Case Study Two

Jorge and Natalie have the same title, work in the same department, and have each been given a few projects to manage. Recently, their supervisor asked Natalie to take the lead on one of Jorge's projects, one that he is passionate about and has grown to identify with over the years. One month after accepting the assignment, Natalie has settled into the leadership role and is beginning to make progress with the project—at which point Jorge comes into her office, looking upset. He asks her why he hasn't been receiving updates and demands to know why he's being left out of the loop.

Discussion Questions

1. What are the relevant issues and concerns here?
2. How do you think Natalie and Jorge are feeling at this time? What are they thinking, and how are they communicating?
3. If you were Natalie, what would you do before responding to Jorge? Reference the practices in this chapter.
4. What specific strategies could be used to sort out the conflict?

References

Kahneman. (2013). *Thinking, fast and slow* (1st ed.). Farrar, Straus and Giroux.

Pearce, K. (2010). *Public engagement and civic maturity: A public dialogue consortium perspective* (3rd ed.). Lulu Press.

Pearce, W. B. (2007). *Making social worlds: A communication perspective*. Blackwell.

Ruben, B. D. (2005). Linking communication scholarship and professional practice in colleges and universities. *Journal of Applied Communication Research, 33*, 294–304.

Ruben, B. D., & Gigliotti, R. A. (2016). Leadership as social influence: An expanded view of leadership communication theory and practice. *Journal of Leadership & Organizational Studies, 23*(4), 467–479. https://doi.org/10.1177/1548051816641876

Sustained Dialogue Institute. (2021). *Sustained dialogue campus network moderator manual 2021–2022*. Sustained Dialogue Institute.

CHAPTER 17

Influencing in Organizations

By Renée Delgado-Riley

People will forget what you said. People will forget what you did. But people will never forget how you made them feel.

—Maya Angelou

Learning Objectives

After reading this chapter, students will be able to:

1. Examine the importance of applying influential skills in the workplace
2. Identify why influence is purposeful and authentic
3. Examine the role of understanding your values, reflection, community, and authenticity in developing an influential skill set
4. Explore an actionable model to develop, practice, and refine an influential skill set
5. Discover ways to infuse influence into everyday practice

Introduction to Influencing Others

The components of leadership and what it takes to create a culture in which others will follow a leader are undoubtedly connected to how they make people feel. Phrased differently, I am referring to any "unseen effect" of consistent intentional acts that shift a person's beliefs, attitudes, dispositions, or actions. This is the impetus behind whether people will feel empowered to support or follow a leader. My agricultural and cultural backgrounds intersecting as a higher education professional always impose a genuine lens on leadership. When I explore, understand, and apply leadership to my work environment, I cannot help but disconnect myself from the way I view Mother Nature, particularly when growing things from seeds. Complementary to when a seed germinates, favorable conditions in the environment are the impetus behind whether the seed will grow or not (see Figure 17.1). My background inevitably biases me to see every leadership experience as one in which supporting optimal conditions to support people's growth is significant. This is an essential skill to harness when helping people and organizations thrive, like the "moment" a seed germinates, is analogous to how we can nurture one another to achieve personal and professional success. This "unseen effect" is referred to as influencing others. This is beyond simply inspiring people to follow; it is influencing shifts in perspectives, values, actions, etc. The ability to influence others is not something one is born with,

FIGURE 17.1 Seed Sprouts

but comparable to learning a new instrument or building a muscle, it requires intentional practice to refine and put into action.

Xinachtli

Xinachtli (sin-a-cha-lee), a Nahuatl word, translates to the "moment a seed germinates." This native Aztec word is an admirable metaphor for what influencing others means in practice. Humans are social creatures and ultimately in the workplace, they are present to support one another and build a community toward a collective vision. The organizational outcomes may be attributed to how they support personal and professional growth in one another. And at the same time, accomplishing their organizational goals and helping one another achieve balance. Influence builds trust and is the real power, which helps foster an organization's success, achieve goals, and helps support the development of team members. This chapter will guide new leaders with practical advice on how they can infuse influential techniques in their professional lives to connect with and empower others. As a bonus, this model can be used in one's personal life. Before we dig into the application of influence in action, we must do our due diligence and explore the science of social influence and its associated literature.

Social Influence

Social influence and its place within the workplace have been a topic of investigation for quite some time. Influence as a social process has a long history of being investigated through research. Such seminal curiosities in psychology have focused on understanding the relationship between personality or unique personal characteristics and their relationship with how these impact others' behavior (Caldwell & Burger, 1997; Higgins, 1990, 2000). Psychologists have found that people with personalities that are high on agreeableness, those who put others' needs before their own, are empathetic along with conscientious, and those who are careful and diligent tend to make use of influential strategies more often (Caldwell & Burger, 1997). The individual benefits of influencing others are linked to supporting belonging, self-esteem, and contributing to one's life purpose (Bourgeois et al., 2009).

Other disciplines such as sociology have explored influence as an aspect of collective interactions and those unique mutual understandings that emerge within those interactions (Persson, 2019). Goffman (1955) and Persson (2019) describe this collective interaction as the "art of managing impressions" (p. 138), leading to the conclusion that influence cannot take place without social interaction (Persson, 2019). Other researchers have found evidence that influential strategies could contribute to work performance (Yukl & Tracey, 1992). Organizations that support transformational leadership styles, those most often associated with inspiring and influencing others, have demonstrated stronger relationships which impact organizational work performance (Gemeda & Lee, 2020; Sonmez Cakir & Adiguzel, 2020). Interpersonal skills and taking initiative are all directly related to influencing workplace productivity (Berg & Chyung, 2008). When influential tactics in the workplace are framed and focused on supporting the best interests of the group, it not only builds social cohesion but also supports decision-making (Henningsen & Henningsen, 2014). Creating influence can affect a healthy balance in the workplace, increase teamwork, and help build stronger relationships (Ross & Boles, 1994; Webber et al., 2015).

Influence Before Power

When many people think of influence, they equate it with power. As some organizational cultures define, "power is the potential to influence someone," and with that emerges the dominance of harnessing that power (Kessler, 2010, p. 138). The balancing act of preserving human relationships during social interactions is one which has been studied. To protect the relationship, influential tactics are superseded over argumentative or demanding approaches to persuade colleagues to change their behavior, those often associated with distributed leadership approaches (Caldwell & Burger, 1997; Gemeda & Lee, 2020). In fact, work environments that foster trust and learning with clear communication are more likely to achieve success (Sonmez Cakir, & Adiguzel, 2020). In Elsevier's *Influencing Others at Work Super Series* (2007), similar tactics associated with transformational leadership, such as active listening and investing in relationship building, are key influential skills in the workplace. A meta-analysis of leadership behaviors that are most associated with perceived organization and team effectiveness revealed that the top items on the list included motivation, consideration, and empowerment. (Burke et al., 2006). Delgado-Riley et al. (2022) identified from a group of leaders that inspiration and influence from institutional leadership was a critical component to improve leadership culture and organizational success (see Figure 17.2).

It is clearly supported in the literature that certain behavior shifts are due to harnessing specific interpersonal skill sets. There are benefits for not only positive shifts in others' behavior, but as well to the individual using influential strategies. Influential strategies within a social context can contribute to improved performance and success. Healthy leadership environments most often include leaders who utilize empowerment or influential strategies toward organizational goals.

How to Use Influencing Others in the Workplace

My guiding principle around the leadership construct is that it is one not based in positionality, but on a set of skills and perspectives that permeates across many roles. Anyone's leadership journey will expectedly be filled with the unpredictable. The world of work culture, especially in the United States, may feel like

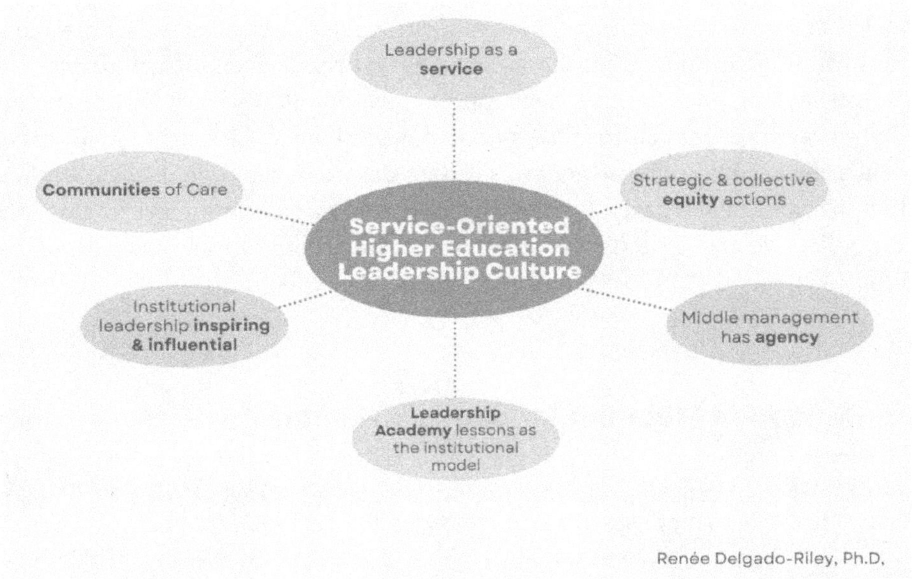

FIGURE 17.2 Service-Oriented Higher Education Leadership Culture

power only materializes from positions of organizational hierarchy and thus influence can only be present in these instances. There is a misconception that one must be in a position of authority to inspire and get people to do things. However, influencing others can happen at all levels of an organization and in our personal lives.

BOX 17.1 **Reflection Moment: Feelings of Influence**

Can you remember a time when you felt excited and you were ready and motivated to do something based on hearing someone speak? Do you recall the senses you felt? How did you feel about this level of excitement? Did it activate you to do the work or follow the person that inspired you?

This sense was likely *empowerment* due to being influenced to do something that one felt passionate about or which was morally aligned with one's needs. Leading with influence allows that sense of empowerment to be embodied within an organization. People gravitate toward passion and want to find fulfillment in their work. Therefore, influencing others in the workplace not only allows people to be excited about the work collectively, but to be more productive in achieving their organizational goals. The surprising fact is that anyone can avail themselves of an influential skill set to empower others in the workplace. We should be able to make people feel empowered, inspired, and willing to follow us or resonate with our ideas, no matter what our roles are in the organization.

Developing an influential skill set is often overlooked. I know during my time in higher education, I inculcated the perception that I could only have influence if I was in a position of power. I was young and naive and as a first-generation student, I was just happy to have a job. I was encouraged to keep my head low and do my job. The phrase around my organization was "get to work," anytime someone even wanted to speak up. Breaking down these barriers of organization hierarchy is not a part of the practical application of influencing others that I am describing. However, it is critical to contextualize that not every work environment fosters influence outside of positional or organizational hierarchy. I would even go as far as to say that sometimes positional or organizational hierarchy can in fact discourage influence. As a result, I am framing "influence" and not equating to organizational authority or hierarchy. The accepted frame is that influence can permeate and be present at any level within the organizational structure. If one's organizational culture does not infuse influence currently, it only takes one person to begin to change the system with the goal to saturate others in the organization. Influence does not just exist within positions of authority. It sometimes helps to think of influence as this sense of moving people toward a collective and shared mission by connecting them to their passions and shifting their values, beliefs, actions, etc.

BOX 17.2 **Reflection Moment: Influence in Action**

Beyond hierarchy or organizational power, will people be influenced to follow you without any positional authority, but rather because they believe in your messages and trust you?

And regardless of organizational structures, one can easily build an influential skill set with intentional practice. Positional or organizational hierarchy is not a necessary component of the skill set it takes to influence others; however, if one is in a position of authority, this model can amplify their success. In fact, at times the culture of work may have the appearance that positional authority is necessary for influence, but the formula discussed here can happen from any position in the organization to include those with authority. Enacted fully and practiced strategically, in no time anyone will be able to hone their influential skill set in the workplace (see Figure 17.3).

I believe that developing and applying four key principles will allow anyone to harness the power of influence.

1. **K**now your *why*
2. **E**mbrace reflection
3. **B**uild community
4. **A**uthentically engage

By keeping it simple and poignant, it is about empowering others to live and breathe a shared passion, connecting or engaging, and supporting the growth and development of those involved in what I classify as a "community of care." The KEBA model of influence is meant to be developmental, with each step integrating lessons from the previous, so that by the time you get to Step 4, you will be able to implement this model of influence in the workplace in its entirety. Influence can be sharpened from each step of the model, but moving toward the final step will provide you with a set of valuable influential resources to utilize in the workplace.

Know Your *Why*

Simon Sinek's "Golden Circle" (2019) has been a framework of inspiration in my work as a higher education assessment professional. It is not an empty platitude of simply understanding your *why*, but contextualized

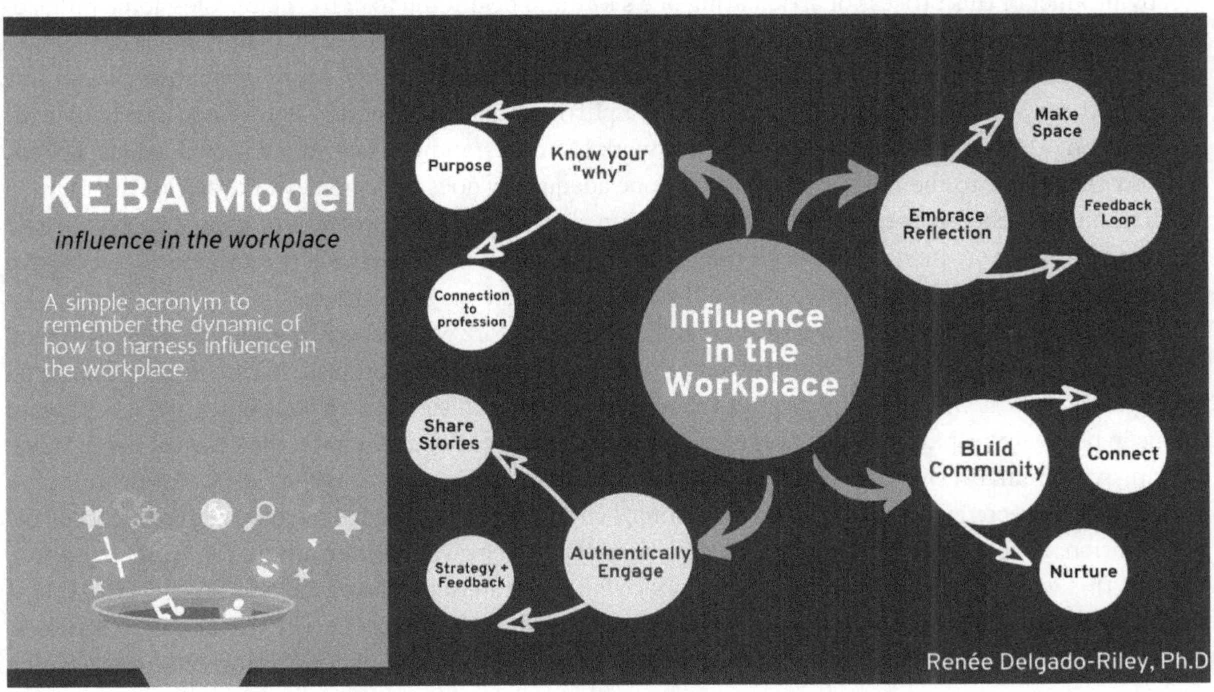

FIGURE 17.3 KEBA Model of Influence

and applied, it can really help one lead with intentionality and authenticity. As George and Sims (2007) mentioned, finding one's "True North" is about finding those deep inspirations and passions to engage and embed within one's work. It is often easy to tell people what one does within an organization, but how often does one share with people *why* they do the work they do? This forces one back to reflect on why they do the work they do. This is the rationale for why they continue to work hard for their organization, is it not? Knowing one's *why* is fundamental for multiple reasons. First, it helps one remember their inner passions for their position in the organization. Second, it helps one ground their work and ensure it is aligned with their overall personal goals. Finally, it becomes the core for their professional philosophy. Acknowledging and making time to be explicit about their *why* creates the foundation for crafting a professional philosophy. A professional philosophy articulates one's guiding beliefs regarding their role and incorporates elements of how they view these beliefs intersecting with their work in the organization. To craft a professional philosophy, one must remind themselves of this *why*. I challenge everyone to take 2 minutes to write down their *why*.

BOX 17.3 **Crafting a Why Exercise**

Take 5–10 minutes to reflect on the following questions:

1. What is important to you?
2. What is your life's purpose?
3. Why do you want to be in your chosen profession?
4. Is there a significant life event that inspired you to be in this chosen profession?
5. How will you measure your success in your profession?

A by-product of this process of articulating one's *why* and beginning to craft their professional philosophy is that it allows one to look at it often, then revisit and update it as needed. This statement is meant to be dynamic and evolve with one's professional experiences. Also, when self-doubt or imposter syndrome creep in, these statements can, on their own, be uplifting and motivational. Before one can maneuver influence on others, they must do the reflective work of understanding their foundational values, beliefs, and how they relate to their professional role. If one adequately does their homework, this assists them in understanding their values more fully, where they are currently in their profession, and where they would like to go. This is a strategic framework that one can use to better understand their motivations. It is an imperative step in building an influential skill set that they can use with others.

By embodying this process, this will aid in one's ability to work with others by allowing them to extend this *why* exercise to almost any work project, program, or organizational task. Investing the time to go through this process will almost guarantee that clarity in communication with colleagues in the workplace will be in place. By keeping it simple, it is empowering others to easily understand the vision at hand. When working with humans, they are incredibly dynamic, and it is important to make this process meaningful, useful, and connected with them in a way that aligns with their own passions for *why* they are a part of the organization. People do not just want to be told what to do—they want a connection, they want a passion. More of this will come later in this chapter under "build community"; however, this is an essential first step in working with others. Begin with one's *why* and then help facilitate the *why* exercise with others in the workplace. Recentering people with their *whys* begins the first phase of connecting with others in the workplace. Once time is spent on those, moving toward applying *why* to the organization will begin helping others ideate the overall vision in context of any project, task, program, etc.

BOX 17.4 **Applying the *Why* to the Organization**

Take 10–20 minutes to reflect on the following questions collectively:

1. How is this project, task, program, etc., aligned with the overall vision and mission of the organization?
2. Why are you engaging in this project, task, program, etc.?
3. What do you hope this project, task, program, etc., will accomplish?
4. Who should be present in helping bring this project, task, program, etc., to fruition?
5. How will you measure that you are successful when implementing this project, task, program, etc.?

Embrace Reflection

Reflection is a concept that is heard frequently in education and frankly is something I have heard time and time again. It is encouraged in a lot of contexts. We may have even been encouraged to use reflection. However, life easily gets in the way of the opportunities to have the space to reflect. Life is fast paced, and often the workplace is so focused on productivity and getting the work done that making time to reflect becomes a lower priority. Nonetheless, reflection is a process, not an action, that must be prioritized in building an influential skill set for the workplace. In Delgado-Riley et al. (2022), research focused on understanding ways to improve inclusive leadership cultures in higher education from a group of leaders in their voices; leaders overwhelmingly acknowledged the importance of taking time to reflect as one of the most helpful experiences in their journey of leadership. Reflecting with intentionality is not just having a fleeting thought or making some time to think more in depth about something. Instead, it is making the space to have thorough reflection time. Some people may have preconceived notions about what reflection may look like in practice. In fact, there is no universal reflection model because this will manifest differently for everyone. The process of reflection is not just simply about recalling experiences, analyzing, and understanding them, but identifying how values impact our lenses of reflection. One's unique experiences and background ultimately influence how they reflect on these experiences. The power of this deep thinking is where transformation can occur. Before an influential skill set can be entirely implemented in the workplace, it has to be individualized and internalized, much like the first concept of *knowing your why*: to embrace reflection fully, it must be an individual experience first. Deep thinking is not prioritized in our modern work culture, and it is helpful to schedule time for weekly reflection. For me, I like to spend time doing deep reflecting at the end of a long week, rather than at the beginning of the week. People will need to identify what time of the day and week work best for their mind, but it is important that they schedule the time to engage with this process.

BOX 17.5 **Embracing Reflection**

Take 10 minutes to reflect on the following questions weekly:

1. What is going well for you right now?
2. What is not going well for you right now?
3. How are your values influencing the way you are understanding this experience?
4. If you could do things differently, what would you do and why?
5. What have you learned because of this experience?

It is about asking oneself to spend time looking back, understanding the context, values, lessons learned, and identifying ways to continually improve both personally and professionally. Reflective questions can be used to guide one's reflection and are conducive to writing in a journal, taking notes on a phone, etc. The goal is to create intentional space to go through this process of deep thinking. This process can even be done in a car, train, airplane, or while doing a task that does not require full cognitive attention (e.g., folding laundry, and so forth). Another powerful way to reflect is with a trusted friend, partner, family member, or coworker. Having another lens can help walk one through lessons learned and help brainstorm ways to further grow and develop. Once reflection becomes a part of a weekly routine, the next advanced step of practicing this method should occur within the workplace. It is powerful and helpful enough to incorporate these deep-thinking activities into practice, but it is even more critical to model these in the workplace. This is when influence begins to come into play in the workplace. By encouraging the process of deep thinking and modeling this behavior for others in the workplace, this is beginning to strengthen the ways that one can interact with others in the workplace.

Embodying this reflection process and facilitating it in the workplace provides a bird's-eye view of knowing how people are feeling about the organization and can provide leaders with informational feedback on how to engage with them in the future. Understanding will make one privy to people's reflections in addition to their own and thus will help them influence others around a shared mission or goal. Additionally, this exercise provides space for vulnerability and creates a connection with the people in the organization. It essentially builds trust. If people in the organization have not bought in, engaged, or do not feel as if there is a collective mission, modeling this organizational reflection process will aid in improving employee engagement.

BOX 17.6 **Reflection with Others**

Take 30 minutes to reflect on the following questions with colleagues

1. What is our organization doing well right now?
2. What is not going well for our organization?
3. How well are we communicating?
4. Were our goals met? Why or why not?
5. How can we better support our colleagues?
6. If we could do things differently, what would we do and why?
7. What have we learned because of this experience?

The above activity is best conducted first with individual reflection, then partner and group sharing. Some learners need more time to process before sharing in a group context. It is important as the facilitator to set ground rules for ensuring that respect towards one another is in place. Contextualizing these questions to a specific task, project, program, etc. makes this process more relevant and meaningful. *Xinachtli (sin-a-cha-lee)*, the 'moment a seed germinates', in context of when people are provided the inspiration to shift their perspectives and actions in the workplace, becomes apparent during the process of embracing reflection (see Figure 17.4).

Build Community

FIGURE 17.4 Leaf with Dew

It is only natural in a work environment that people desire connections while working toward a common goal. Context matters in all organizations, and anytime we are thinking about influencing others, we need to ask ourselves if we have the right people present. Whose voices are present? Whose are not? I think people underestimate the power of these questions. We need to ensure we are making these connections both in employees' hearts and minds. It is about shaping the organization by building with these connections in mind and forging forward with a clear message, vision, and having the courage to move the organization forward. This is hard. People can mobilize the organization and its employees, but they will fall short of the mission and burn out if they are not thoughtful about navigating the organizational culture. One can have the most robust work plan for accomplishing one's organizational goals, but if they are not thoughtful about culture within the organization, trouble emerges, and one can spin their wheels and go nowhere. In terms of the KEBA model of influence, by knowing one's *why* and making space to reflect, this helps recenter others to the vision of the organization when building community. When beginning to foster a sense of community in the workplace, it is important to consider the people who make up an organizational culture. Building community is set on helping connect people to the collective vision. People want to know how their work in the organization fits into the bigger picture. People want to feel like they belong, and by building community with clear goals, embodying reflection, and ensuring that all voices are present, they can foster a more efficient organization.

Building a community is much more than just having people together in the same space. It is creating an infrastructure to support intentional connections with its members. These connections then can foster the sharing of experiences and thus deeper connections. Within this environment, once sharing of experiences between its members becomes more commonplace, the sense of trust, safety, and openness becomes a norm within this community. This act of sharing experiences can be profoundly empowering and inspiring for its members. If members of a community feel safe sharing, this can serve as a basis for collective growth and learning. When humans feel safe enough in a community to share, they are demonstrating their values, and thus this can permeate and empower others in the community to also feel safe. Together, through multiple perspectives, backgrounds, the sharing of experiences, and the unique voices can be provided a space for improved mutual understanding of one another. Once this community is built and nurtured, one in which its members feel free to be their authentic selves and feel safe, is when influence among its members begins to take root. When supporting many minds, souls, and hearts of humans in this type of supportive space, innovative solutions come to light. Exploring solutions and brainstorming ideas from various perspectives can be a valuable experience, one that challenges us to rethink and relearn from our peers. Ultimately, the power of building community in any goal or mission can be amplified by its members through their shared purpose.

Inclusion

Including members' voices who only align with leaders' voices is not the goal of building community. The goal is to include all voices, even the ones that may not align with one another. It is important to challenge one's traditional ways of thinking and working to connect with their peers. As the facilitator, to use influential tactics within the community is where this work takes time and effort. It does not have to be daunting, but instead focus on what small acts of empathy and compassion can each day be integrated into the workplace. Having a community of peers who get together, meet, and discuss the organization is purely transactional. Real community is when dialogue is integrated and collaborative. It is about working through challenges with one another with a heart of compassion and a lens of inclusion. Strong communities thrive through adapting to challenges, working to improve to be more equitable with their members, innovating and embracing conflict and diversity. It is often common in higher education leadership environments to surround oneself with like-minded people who agree, rather than include representatives of all members of the broader community in a way that is inclusive. Although most people roll their eyes with icebreakers in the workplace, these are small intentional acts that foster sharing. Members will be empowered to share pieces of their human experience that can provide a more holistic perspective beyond the organizational role they hold. These simple questions can evolve into helping build trust and thus a thriving community. Taking just 5–8 minutes at the beginning of a meeting to do a quick icebreaker activity to foster building a strong community—one that is safe—can harbor trust. These moments of vulnerability create an environment of sharing. I strategically chose some of my favorites, which I share at the beginning of meetings with my peers. I also preface each instance with, "I value the humans behind our jobs and am going to spend 5 to 8 minutes just focusing on building community." I have yet to have someone not engaged in the process and have noticed since the onset of the pandemic that people are much more excited to engage in this type of activity.

BOX 17.7 **Fostering Community Engagement**

- Children today will never understand the struggle of what?
- What's a passion of yours you have yet to act on?
- What is something that represents where you are from, and why is it representative?
- What were some wins from your weekend?
- What are your forthcoming goals this season?
- Name your favorite children's story, and why it is your favorite?
- If you could rid the world of one thing, what would it be?

We must build relationships in our community before influence can take root. Sharing a story with others in the workplace will allow people to connect on a deeper level. Connecting with one another is imperative in supporting one's community, as well as aiding organizational strategic goals. If people are prioritized, tasks will inevitably follow, with guidance and leadership emerging as a tactic from a group (Delgado-Riley et al., 2022). Influence is about the inspiration to encourage people to be the best version of themselves. It is focused on mentoring them, connecting them to untap their potential. We are also here to support one another as we grow and prosper in our profession. It is important to not forget that through building a community and network of fellow colleagues, we are nurturing seeds to grow, and eventually, *Xinachtli*, the "moment a seed germinates," will come to fruition. Building a community and navigating challenges is one that deserves to be celebrated. *Xinachtli* emulates the development and growth of a thriving community (see Figure 17.5). This is what I believe we are here to do for one another by supporting our community growth. This work invariably takes more effort than facilitating a few icebreakers at meetings, but this is the beginning of creating intentional efforts to support a community that is integrated rather than just hosting a series of member meetings in a transactional way.

Authentically Engage

FIGURE 17.5 Seed Sprouts

The final step in the KEBA model of influence focuses on combining all the above steps and thus aligning one's true self to their behaviors in the workplace. This consists of being self-aware of mistakes and centering relationships in this process. To move to this step of the model understanding one's *why* fully, the ability to practice embracing reflection into one's life, and already have grasped building community are necessary. This final step of the model includes combining all the previous steps and fosters the ability to be authentic in the workplace and support one's colleagues. Supporting a work environment where people feel safe to share their experiences, concerns, and feedback even when not aligned with leadership requires an investment in the relationships among colleagues. Therefore, this step comes last in the KEBA model of influence because building community takes effort and is a necessary ingredient to move toward authentically engaging. To influence others, normalizing the human experience, which includes acknowledging mistakes and learning from them are critical in supporting one another. Authentic leaders can positively impact attitudes and behaviors within their organizations (Avolio et al., 2004). I am sure many people have experiences with organizations that do not allow the free sharing of feedback, which results in colleagues feeling disconnected and then prioritizing protecting themselves instead of engaging in dialogue. Organizations with authentic leaders have higher productivity and their employees are more motivated (Vrapca, 2015). So, when people authentically engage, how different would these organizations look? Enacting this model and emerging to this final step will allow one to practice a full set of influential skills in the workplace. What exactly does it mean to authentically engage?

BOX 17.8 **What It Means to Authentically Engage**

- Model your authentic self
- Create an environment of bidirectional and informational feedback
- Normalize mistakes
- Honor commitments
- Celebrate colleagues when they can be their authentic selves

Feedback, Mistakes, and Commitments

How does one create the infrastructure to authentically engage? Creating a feedback loop for bidirectional information is not only important for embracing reflection, but it is important in providing for all voices in the workplace to be heard. It promotes self-agency among colleagues and is a component of ensuring that if things do not go as planned, or if there are opportunities to celebrate, a supportive infrastructure for productive discussions exists. Inclusion of colleagues' voices and experiences in this process allows one to be continuously challenged with the focus on improvement, but also concentrates on validating what is working. This infrastructure that harnesses intentional listening with the goal to dig deeper is how coworkers can authentically engage with one another. Supporting this type of environment alone allows one to model authenticity and appreciate feedback. However, to fully implement this final step, actions and behaviors need to also go further. Focusing on what matters to colleagues and organizations will allow one the opportunity to be better, reframe when things are not going well, grow, adapt, and be flexible. With this strategic process one can successfully honor commitments to one's colleagues. This does not mean that every colleague's request will be supported; however, this will create a process for discerning if this request is aligned with organizational values as well as those shared values within the work community. The process of honoring commitments essentially allows one to stay focused on what matters. What can be done to ensure that supporting the process of feedback in one's organization becomes part of everyday practice?

Practicing Authenticity

This type of action is more than just a simple task accomplishment or checking something off of a to-do list. This is a process that requires intentionality and planning. With effort, enacting a process to solicit feedback can allow people to own up to their mistakes and honor commitments. However, authentically engaging is much more than going through the motions. Having the actions behind this process is the heart to ensuring that this becomes part of the organizational culture. This is about conceptualizing one's values and how those values manifest in the workplace with others through their behavior. It's about questioning, observing, and reflecting through embracing reflection. It is about cultivating this inclusive mindset within their organizational community. And it is known that sometimes one must question assumptions and unpack existing habits that are not helpful in that organization. This process alone can stir up many different emotions and issues with colleagues. Remember to stay focused on one's *why*, act with integrity, and cater communications and relations with colleagues that are centered with care. When people demonstrate appreciation in the workplace, it should not be obligatory, but genuine. I think the best analogy I have heard was at the 2015 Escaleras Institute focused on developing Latina/o/x leaders in Student Affairs was, "Lift as you climb." This to me encapsulates what it means to authentically engage. It is about working with your colleagues and celebrating them when they can be their authentic selves and supporting their professional growth. It is working together toward a shared vision (*knowing your why*), using reflection to refine one's values and actions, building up and supporting those in your community, and authentically engaging (see Figure 17.6).

FIGURE 17.6 Cucumber Harvest

BOX 17.9 **Authenticity and Observation**

Have you been fortunate enough to be in an organization that supports the questioning, observing, and reflecting to move toward a more authentic organization?

Application

Previously I described the conceptual framework of the KEBA model of influence and its attributes; the real work can now happen through application of the model. Capturing this process and implementing it in the workplace takes intentionality. This section is designed to share how to use this model in everyday practice. For those new to an organization, creating influence is completely possible because any individual can impact colleagues' behavior, attitudes, and the workplace culture. Any role in an organization or company requires the employee to hit the ground running and achieve the required responsibilities. Although the critical factor in any job is to achieve organizational outcomes with respect to the roles and responsibilities, the prioritization of connections with colleagues should be elevated if one wants to create influence. The KEBA model of influence is not just for institutional or culture change but can be used by any person and applied in their everyday jobs. Influence in everyday work need not be grand but small, intentional acts that promote people's dispositional shifts. These can be as simple as how workflows are determined, organization of customer service desks, or how daily tasks are completed.

The KEBA model of influence can be used to discover new ways to see your job responsibility and roles. When becoming invested in a new organization and learning a new job and its associated responsibilities, it is critical to connect with colleagues. Otherwise, when moving up in the organization and when trying to accomplish tasks that require collaboration, one might end up with burned bridges and people who are not invested in the organization. This section will guide new professionals along with seasoned ones with ideas how they can support their colleagues, connect with them, create influence every day while working, and how the KEBA model of influence can manifest in everyday practice. The following case studies, examples, and tips focus on how influence might manifest in the workplace. At the end of each case study is a series of reflection questions, with the goal to make these stories relevant and applicable to one's experiences along with some tips to infuse this model into everyday practice. Influence in the workplace is an evolving process. To empower others in the workplace with influence, it is vital that each step is explored and considered.

Examples in Action: Knowing Your *Why*

Beginning with one's *why* is an essential first step in practicing influence in the workplace. Below is an example of how Joshua Ackgard uses his *why* to influence program development in his community.

BOX 17.10 **Case Study #1: Passions in Action**

Joshua Ackgard, a program coordinator in the Division of Student Affairs at a large urban university, was clear about his values to support closing historic achievement gaps and supporting college access for traditionally underserved students. Joshua is an alumnus of this university and was fortunate to participate in programs focused on supporting low-income students around community engagement and leadership. Because of his experiences in these programs and the positive impact it had on his personal, academic, and professional life, he was always volunteering his time to speak to students and mentor them. His boss, the associate vice president, was working with another large university and a private donor to create a statewide program focused on college access, affordability, and youth leadership and engagement. Because Joshua was well known for his motivational energy with students, his boss began including him in meetings to plan this new program. Joshua made his *why* known in the workplace and was acting on these passions through engaging students via motivational talks. This display of his passions was directly tied to why he was asked to be involved in the planning for this program. Joshua was excited to be involved because he was at the heart of creating a novel program that had never existed before. This new program would provide fully paid scholarships to high school students to attend the university; meanwhile, they would engage in leadership in their communities. Joshua made sure to articulate his values in planning meetings around his dedication to closing historic achievement gaps. No matter how complicated the program development work was, he was able to embed his own values in the program's values as well as influence the program's curriculum and processes. Once the logistics of the program were set, applications poured in from across the state. Joshua was at the forefront of creating an inclusive scoring rubric and interviewing schedule to select students. After the inaugural group of students were selected, Joshua got to personally inform each one via phone. In those one-on-one conversations, Joshua made sure to express why this program exists and share how his passions align with the program. By knowing his *why* and living this out in the workplace, Joshua was able to influence this new program from the logistics, curriculum, and ultimately influence the students' lives.

Case Study Reflection

Learning about how Joshua shared his *why* and influenced the leadership program, below are questions that can guide reflections in Table 17.1.

TABLE 17.1 **Case Study Reflection: "Passions in Action"**

What were the benefits of Joshua explicitly sharing his *why* in the workplace?
Describe any drawbacks you foresee because of sharing your *why* in the workplace.
How will you plan to share your *why* in the workplace?

Everyday Practical Tips

When entering a new position, knowing what you want to accomplish is often described in the position description or there may be supplemental details from one's supervisor. However, waiting for the organization to provide what they define as success in this professional role will not create influence immediately. Of course, allowing one's leadership to set expectations is a given, but I am talking about spending a little time doing research on this organization, which will orient new employees to the values and options available. Essentially studying everything about the organization, its mission/vision and what was shared during the interview process is a step in the right direction. Finding a purpose within the new organization will provide an outline for doing the job well. Plus, it will begin a process of documenting the organizational culture and possible ideas that can be shared with leadership. Delivering results early will help employees identify their goals and help them align with their purpose. Finding their purpose and *why* allows the new employee to recognize they are part of something bigger. The method in which the employee goes about finding their passion and sharing ideas, resources, etc., while finding that passion can also create and establish influence. Employees that are clear about their goals as they relate to their roles and responsibilities will undoubtedly create influence more quickly.

BOX 17.11 **Reflection Moment: Beginning to Harness Influence**

Are you clear on your own professional short-term and long-term goals? How do these goals fit into your organization? Do you have what you need to bring these goals to fruition?

Examples in Action: Embrace Reflection

Making the space and time to reflect is not often a priority in the workplace. Below is an example of how Josefina Lopez influenced the Food Security Taskforce (FST) on a college campus to engage in reflection and develop a strategy.

BOX 17.12 **Case Study #2: Reflection Strategy**

Josefina Lopez, a director of assessment in the Division of Student Life at a liberal arts university in the Pacific Northwest honed her skills as a strategic assessment planner. Josefina was asked by the novel Food Security Taskforce (FST) to support their assessment and evaluation needs. During a preliminary meeting with the FST chair, it became very apparent that there was a conglomerate of programs across the university targeting food insecurity under this umbrella, but there lacked a unified strategy. Any good assessment practice needs to begin with the reasons the program exists and help evaluate its strategic objectives. Realizing the FST did not have strategic objectives, Josefina made time to reflect on appropriate next steps for facilitating this process and supporting the FST. Josefina, after careful reflection post the preliminary meeting, decided that the FST would benefit from a strategic planning process and space to reflect on why they do the work along with creating a clear plan for executing this work collaboratively. By understanding the value of reflection in this process and the need to make the space for the FST to do this work, Josefina brought this to the group. The group was hesitant at first because often reflection and strategic planning get a bad reputation for being time consuming and lacking actions behind the words. After a year of monthly meetings, Josefina worked diligently with FST on reflection questions, both at the individual and group levels. Questions focused on "what are we currently doing well?" Other questions included "what are the needs of those we serve?" and "what are the major activities required for meeting these goals?" After each reflection session, Josefina summarized the themes and moved on to the next phase of the process. Using the data from these reflection questions, Josefina was able to draft a vision, mission values, and strategic objectives for the FST. Once proposed to the FST, Josefina continued with validation reflection questions focused on "where are we in realizing our vision for those we serve?" and "what are the essential steps that need to take place for us to realize our vision?" After these sessions, a visual and narrative of a unified strategy for the FST was presented. Josefina realized the importance of embracing reflection and applied her influence to encourage this same behavior within the FST. By embracing reflection, Josefina made sure to influence this process with the FST and ultimately helped them work more collaboratively with one another through this process. By embracing reflection in the workplace, Josefina was able to influence how the FST functions and allowed her to understand their collective vision and goals more fully to support its assessment and evaluation needs.

Case Study Reflection

Josefina exerted her influence to encourage strategic planning for the Food Security Taskforce (FST). Spending time on the questions outlined in Table 17.2 can promote a more in-depth reflection.

TABLE 17.2 **Case Study Reflection: "Reflection Strategy"**

What were the advantages of Josefina proposing that the FST use reflection to develop a strategy rather than jump right into the assessment process?
What if the FST did not embrace reflection as a strategy?
What type of self-reflection will you make time for when things in the workplace do not go as planned?
Describe any opportunities you noticed in your workplace to infuse reflection.

Everyday Practical Tips

Creating influence every day is about developing a skill set within the "embrace reflection" step of the KEBA model of influence. When people create influence, there are associated benefits. People will seek influential employees out to gather their perspectives, include them in conversations. These influential employees do not need to be in high-level positions of authority to influence others. Any role in the workplace can utilize influential tactics to inspire and get people to change their behavior, attitudes, or perspectives. One of the reasons this step of the model is foundational is that the employee who can use reflection well has a strategic understanding of the workplace and how processes work. This type of information is powerful for helping to understand how to navigate one's roles and responsibilities, but key to gaining insight in how to make decisions and shift the culture. Crucial to empowering others, having a strong understanding of how various systems within the organization function will support helping everyone know how their job supports the overall success. Having a reflective mindset is such a powerful tool to fundamentally understand where the organization has been, how it fits into the overall structure, how the systems work, and supports planning for the future. Thus, being a strategic thinker with the ability to reflect and look ahead supports culture change, resource allocation and alignment of activities. Even if the employee is not in a position of authority, fostering this reflective thinking will support workplace discussions and be a viable asset to improving the overall culture.

Examples in Action: Build Community

People in organizations are the integral foundation for their success. Damien prioritizes people over tasks to improve the culture of assessment. Below is an example of the role of community in ensuring care is modeled.

BOX 17.13 **Case Study #3: Assessment Community**

Damien Arnold, who oversees assessment efforts at a large urban university on the West Coast, was asked by the vice president of Student Life to create a culture of assessment in the division. To not just apply best practices from previous universities, Damien spent six months meeting with colleagues on his new campus about their assessment needs and what type of support they desired. In these conversations, Damien began by framing his approach to assessment, why it is important, and asking reflective questions. After these sessions with colleagues, Damien realized there were many silos among colleagues on campus already tasked with coordinating assessment. Across these various silos emerged many different perspectives and experiences with assessment. Unfortunately, most of those experiences were not positive. There was a breakdown in why people were doing assessment and its utility. A lot of information was being collected, not being shared, and often not meaningful for employees. Most of his colleagues were doing assessments because they were told to do so, rather than feeling empowered to do assessment that could improve and validate their programs. Damien recognized the need for community building around this effort. He implemented a community-focused model under each unit to develop assessment skills, frameworks, and used as a basis for planning assessment efforts a model, named Community Assessment Knowledge Experts (CAKEs). Through this process, Damien used team-building techniques to create cohesion within the newly formed assessment communities. He also made sure to include all members and encourage storytelling around their assessment experiences and discuss what they would like to learn. Damien fostered this in a collective way and never superseded his knowledge over others, but instead was a peer in helping facilitate community building around assessment within the respective units. Damien made sure to influence the process of creating an assessment culture through building community first. Prioritizing the people in the assessment process was critical in his workplace by making sure his colleagues felt heard, validated, and could contribute to a culture that was meaningful to their work. Building this type of community in the workplace allowed Damien to influence how assessment was conducted, improve its usefulness and application, and get people excited about the assessment process that improved the way they worked with students.

Case Study Reflection

Damien used his influence to foster a community around assessment. There are reflection questions outlined in Table 17.3 guiding how this may be applied to one's workplace.

TABLE 17.3 **Case Study Reflection: "Assessment Community"**

Why do you think Damien prioritized community?
Describe when an initiative or project was impeded by a lack of community in your workplace.
What are some things to observe to ensure that a community is forming in the workplace?
Think about all your workplace tasks, etc., and describe something right now that would benefit from stronger group cohesion and a sense of community.

Everyday Practical Tips

Since the onset of COVID-19, the whole meaning of "get out of your office" may take on a different meaning in some instances, but the intended message is to build connections with others. To build community in the workplace, employees will have to become more familiar with the organizational context and its people. Getting out of the office (virtually or in person) is fundamental to forging partnerships and collaborations. Familiarity is critical and important. Relationships in the workplace are directly related to attitudes; thus we need to listen more and adapt our messaging to the appropriate audience when connecting with colleagues (Ross & Boles, 1994). Forming these connections will begin the process of building trust. Employees demonstrating empathy, focusing on listening, learning, and connecting will ultimately increase agency to becoming a known influencer. Embedding this skill set in every workplace conversation should be common practice, but using it to engage in difficult discussions is even more important. Only then will others in the organization begin to trust and follow them regardless of their positionality.

BOX 17.14 **Influence and Difficult Conversations**

To foster trust, when discussing difficult conversations with colleagues, ask, "Have you considered the impact of *X issue*?" "What do you think of our approach?" "Do you think there is another way to do this better?"

Examples in Action: Authentically Engage

Authenticity in the workplace allows for deeper engagement and opportunities to improve workplace culture and employee engagement. Ramos uses influence to authentically engage with colleagues, leadership, and enact a cultural shift in how certain behaviors are rewarded.

BOX 17.15 **Case Study #4: Authenticity in Action**

Mary Ramos, Staff Council leader at a top southwestern university, an organization that supports a positive workplace experience for staff on campus, was working on establishing herself as an influential leader. Mary had just conducted focus groups across campus with staff to learn about how to better support their workplace experiences. The focus groups provided staff a free lunch and time to meet with other staff members to discuss how they would like to see the campus improve. This nonthreatening environment allowed Mary to meet with staff and share the mission of the Staff Council, establish rapport, reflect on strengths and opportunities of the workplace, and to understand what was important to them. Mary made sure that she was clear about the Staff Council's goals and ultimately wanted to make it a better university. These sessions were beneficial toward helping employees understand how the Staff Council was committed to supporting them, while at the same time building community and helping employees feel like their voices mattered. The common quote from the sessions was, "Thank you for including us and caring about what we have to say." After writing up the focus group report, during her tenure as president of the Staff Council, Mary met with several university leaders for informal one-on-one meetings to share the results, customizing these differently for the president, provost, chief financial officer, and HR director. Mary made sure to listen and convey that she wanted not only to make it a better workplace for employees but wanted to help support each of the university leaders in accomplishing their goals. Mary was authentically engaging not only with staff through focus groups, but with university leaders. These meetings proved fruitful because the number one recommendation from focus group sessions was to reward good supervisory behavior more intentionally. Mary recommended that an annual supervisor award for staff be created, and all the university leaders agreed to pay for the cost of a celebration, awards, and stipends for recipients. Mary was able to hone her influential skill set to make a programmatic change for campus that would benefit not just employees but university leaders, and ultimately she shifted the culture of reward behavior that mattered.

Case Study Reflection

Mary practiced authenticity in the form of engagement to advocate for change. Her influential skills were mature, in the sense that she used clarity around Staff Council's *why* facilitated reflection sessions, built community around support, and shared these with leadership to change the campus culture. Using the questions outlined in Table 17.4 can serve as a model of applying authenticity in one's workplace.

TABLE 17.4 **Case Study Reflection: "Authenticity in Action"**

Why do you think the feedback sessions were beneficial?
How does authenticity show up in your workplace? If it does not, how would you want it to show up?
Describe something in your workplace that could benefit from authentically engaging with colleagues and leadership.

Everyday Practical Tips

Within the workplace, how people create influence will manifest in how they *show up*. Leading by being authentic and doing one's job is the process for creating influence. Doing a good job expresses to others that the employee feels confident and comfortable. It also shows their level of commitment to the organization. It demonstrates that the employee can follow through on their responsibilities and is a core component to building one's reputation in the workplace. The essential elements for influence to grow and develop in the workplace begin with focusing on what can be controlled. The simplest form is the everyday ability to deliver on promises, make decisions, and collaborate with others when necessary in the context of one's job. Focusing on what one can control is the beginning of the process to create influence in the workplace. By following through on employment obligations, one will ultimately gain confidence and be regarded by others as influential. As this confidence builds, humility must grow as well. Working to authentically engage in the workplace means showing up and doing your work as one's whole self but remaining humble through the process.

BOX 17.16 **Influence and Relevance**

Being in a position with authority may provide power and formal influence in the workplace, but creating and maintaining influence will undoubtedly be possible by focusing on doing your job passionately and well. How do you currently perform your job as it relates to passion?

Operationalizing the KEBA Model of Influence

Since influence and the KEBA model comprise of skills, this can easily manifest in any job. When we think of our job, we often gravitate toward tasks and the specific roles and responsibilities it entails. When using the KEBA model of influence in the workplace, it is important to focus on how through one's work, encouraging peers to succeed can be accomplished. The foundation for harnessing influence and using the KEBA model entails understanding one's goals and what success looks like in one's job. Realizing that one's roles and responsibilities are a part of something bigger and aligned with organizational goals will improve not only employee success but be the conduit to fostering healthy workplace relationships. The core of understanding how one's work is tied into overall organizational success is a critical component to harnessing influence in everyday practice. To forge workplace relationships and infuse influence with others, the premise of understanding oneself will only foster trust and authenticity in the future. The forming of these connections produces a solid framework for using the KEBA models every day.

This model will take practice to refine and apply it to one's life, workplace style, and values. Following each step and giving oneself grace in this process are keys to success. Focusing on what one can control and not allowing extraneous factors one cannot control impact one's attitude and application of this model are key. Centering humans when one operationalizes the KEBA model of influencing others in the workplace is where emphasizing a community of "care" manifests. With the influential skill set, one is responsible for the groundwork of the "moment a seed germinates" in their organizations. Influence is about making these human connections and moving things forward with clarity and courage and will be on the right track for supporting a culture of influence and inspiration. People want to feel connected and have their passions aligned in the workplace. Humans like what they know and sometimes change can be uncomfortable when applying the KEBA model.

Time must be spent observing how the systems within the organization are interacting to have a breakthrough idea—this takes space, not necessarily time. If one feels stuck at any step in the model, return to Step Two, *embrace reflection*. And if one feels at any point there is a misalignment of one's values, return to Step One, *know why*. This process can be difficult and discouraging, and I too have been there. It is normal to question one's reasons for remaining in the organization and for working hard for change. People will have to make the best decision given the information and evidence within their reach. Honing one's influential skills in the workplace takes practice and courage. By keeping this model simple, I hope that you will have the confidence and capacity to help your current or future organization achieve a shared vision through exercising an influential skill set.

References

Avolio, B. J., Gardner, W. L., Walumbwa, F., Luthans, F., & May, D. R. (2004). Unlocking the mask: A look at the process by which authentic leaders impact follower attitudes and behaviors. *The Leadership Quarterly, 15*(6), 801–823.

Berg, S. A., & Chyung, S. Y. (2008). Factors that influence informal learning in the workplace. *Journal of Workplace Learning, 20*(4), 229–244. https://doi.org/10.1908/13665620810871097

Bourgeois, M. J., Sommer, K. L., & Bruno, S. (2009). What do we get out of influencing others? *Social Influence, 4*(2), 96–121. https://doi.org/10.1080/15534510802465360

Burke, C. S., Stagl, K. C., Klein, C., Goodwin, G. F., Salas, E., & Halpin, M. (2006). What type of leadership behaviors are functional in teams? A meta-analysis. *The Leadership Quarterly, 17*, 288–307. doi:10.1016/j.leaqua.2006.02.007

Caldwell, D. F., & Burger, J. M. (1997). Personality and social influence strategies in the workplace. *Personality and Social Psychology Bulletin, 23*(10), 1003–1012. https://doi.org/10.1977/01461672972310001

Delgado-Riley, R., Simnitt, E., & Hocker, A. (2022). *Moving from a performative to service-oriented higher education leadership culture.* Unpublished manuscript.

Gemeda, H. K., & Lee, J. (2020). Leadership styles, work engagement and outcomes among information and Communications Technology Professionals: A cross-national study. *Heliyon, 6*(4). https://doi.org/10.1016/j.heliyon.2020.e03699

George, W. O., & Sims, P. (2007). *True north: Discover your authentic leadership.* Wiley.

Goffman, E. (1955). On face-work. *Psychiatry, 18*(3), 213–231. https://doi.org/10.1080/00332747.1955.19023008

Henningsen, D. D., & Henningsen, M. L. (2014). A preliminary examination of perceptions of social influence in group decision making in the workplace. *International Journal of Business Communication, 52*(2), 188–204. https://doi.org/10.1977/2329488414525448

Higgins, E. T. (1990). Personality, social psychology, and person-situation relations: Standards and knowledge activation as a common language. In L. A. Pervin (Ed.), *Handbook of personality: Theory and research* (pp. 301–338). Guilford.

Higgins, E. T. (2000). Does personality provide unique explanations for behaviour? Personality as cross-person variability in general principles. *European Journal of Personality, 14*(5), 391–406. https://doi.org/10.1002/1099-0984(200009/10)14:5<391::aid-per394>3.0.co;2-6

Influencing others at work super series (5th ed.). (2007). Elsevier.

Kessler, E. H. (2010). Gaining power and influencing others. *Management Theory in Action*, 137–155. https://doi.org/10.1057/9780230106024_8

Persson, A. (2019). *Framing social interaction: Continuities and cracks in Goffman's frame analysis.* Routledge.

Ross, L. E., & Boles, J. S. (1994). Exploring the influence of workplace relationships on work-related attitudes and behaviors in the hospitality work environment. *International Journal of Hospitality Management, 13*(2), 155–171. https://doi.org/10.1016/0278-4319(94)90036-1

Sinek, S. (2019). *Start with why: How great leaders inspire everyone to take action.* Penguin Business.

Sonmez Cakir, F., & Adiguzel, Z. (2020). Analysis of leader effectiveness in organization and knowledge sharing behavior on employees and organization. *SAGE Open, 10*(1), 215824402091463. https://doi.org/10.1977/2158244020914634

Vrapca, A. (2015). *The analysis of authentic leadership in the case of the small medium company Settegusti in Kosovo.* [Master's Thesis, University of Ljubljana]. Official Gazette of the Republic of Slovenia.

Webber, J. K., Ser, E. M., & Goussak, G. W. (2015). Work habits as positive and negative influence on workplace productivity. *Global Conference on Business and Finance Proceedings 10*(1), 182–191.

Yukl, G., & Tracey, J. B. (1992). Consequences of influence tactics used with subordinates, peers, and the boss. *Journal of Applied Psychology, 77*(4), 525–535. https://doi.org/10.1037/0021-9010.77.4.525

Credits

Fig. 17.1: Copyright © 2020 Depositphotos/david_ioa.
Fig. 17.4: Copyright © 2022 Depositphotos/photowrzesien.
Fig. 17.5: Copyright © 2020 Depositphotos/NewAfrica.
Fig. 17.6: Copyright © 2018 Unsplash/Markus Spiske.

CHAPTER 18

Drive for Results

By Joseph D. Levy

Evidence does not "speak for itself". Instead, it requires interpretation, integration, and reflection in the search for holistic understanding and implications for action.

—Kuh et al., 2015

Learning Objectives

After completing this chapter, the reader will be able to:

1. Describe results-informed leadership
2. Summarize how to set targets for program or area results
3. Determine a measurement approach for a target
4. List at least two considerations for reporting target results
5. Identify at least two relevant audiences for whom to engage with results
6. Reflect on how to drive for results in their role at their organization
7. Articulate a plan to act on results as part of continuous improvement efforts

Introduction to Results-Informed Leadership

People in leadership positions should have results in mind with respect to their organization's purpose, mission, and strategies (Kuh et al., 2015). Values and operational procedures are not enough. How would one know if or to what extent actions are moving an organization in the right direction? Targeted results can serve as guideposts to help make sure alignment with initiatives and strategies are maintained. This chapter reminds leaders about the necessity of driving for results in order to use that information to influence actions and decisions.

Typically, I differentiate being informed versus driven by results. Considering data as results, one who is *data-driven* may make decisions and operate exclusively based on what the results reveal. Alternatively, one who is *data-informed* will consider the results in addition to experience, intuition, and feedback from multiple perspectives before making a decision or taking action. I have encountered other leaders and organizations who interpret these terms differently: *data-informed* may be episodic in nature or a checklist item, whereas *data-driven* describes an aspect of their leadership—a hunger to consume and use data. In this chapter, I combine these mindsets to encourage *data* or *results-informed* leaders who are driven to use data and create spaces for multiple stakeholders to engage with or interpret results that help inform decisions.

In leading results-informed work, one should recognize the bias inherent with results. Measures are constructed and data collected by people whose positionality and biases can—positively or negatively—influence the results and their interpretation (Heiser et al., 2017). Data are without meaning on their own; interpretation, connotation, and sentiment are provided by the people involved (Kuh et al., 2015). In other words, results are not inherently good or bad; people provide such labels based on their perspectives. Encouraging and including multiple perspectives and identities in the interpretation processes can minimize and balance bias, helping determine the best and most equitable course of action.

A results-informed leader should be concerned with equity (Montenegro & Jankowski, 2017). Their behavior and value alignment can create scenarios where calculated risks or investments are made to encourage improvements over time for minoritized or marginalized populations, as opposed to abandoning pilots based on early results not meeting expectations or discontinuing efforts due to the small size of the populations impacted. Those latter situations raise issues worth investigating: which people, perspectives, and identities are setting expectations? Are they the same people and identities as the populations being studied or served? Is it as easy to dismiss results if decision-makers had to face and hear the voices of respondents instead of just seeing numbers? Leaders must challenge conventional narratives and be intentional as to which perspectives are included as part of continuous improvement efforts (Heiser et al., 2017; Montenegro & Jankowski, 2017). After all, leaders should be concerned about results and betterment for all, not just the majority.

Whether closing equity gaps or measuring overall success, one should conceptualize results in relation to organizational progress. Wehlburg (2007) described results as a three-dimensional spiral in relation to continuous quality improvement. A typical evaluative cycle, moving from planning as a start to reporting and taking action as the end, is like a two-dimensional circle. With the completion of each cycle, progress is made with competencies of people involved, changes to services and interventions, and measures adapted. Such progress collectively contributes to continuous improvement and creates a wider, larger, cyclical layer atop the previous circle. No longer two-dimensional evaluation, the continuous improvement process can be conceptualized as a spiral. Inspired by Wehlburg (2007), the Commonwealth for Learning (2010) created a visual image of this quality spiral, illustrated below in Figure 18.1.

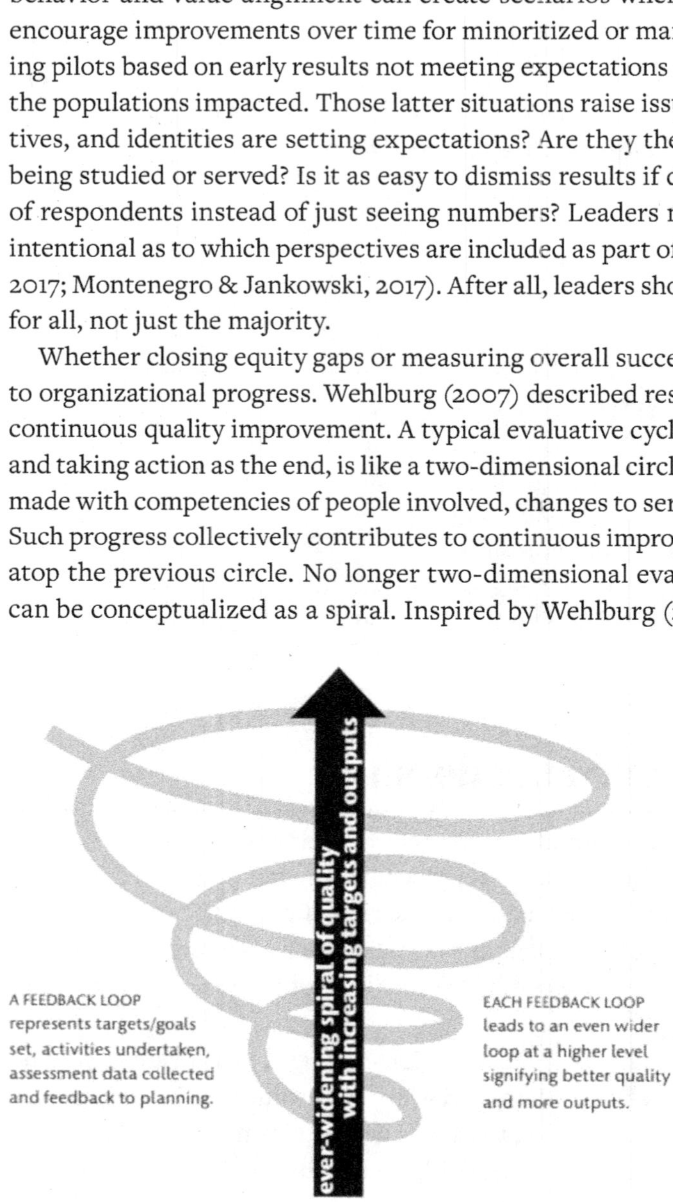

FIGURE 18.1 Quality Spiral (Commonwealth for Learning, 2010, p. 197)

A drive for results encourages leaders to hold outcomes and results in mind for organizational strategies. Results should inform and encourage collaboration with multiple perspectives to interpret and discuss best courses of action for maximizing benefits. Results are obtained through formal, structured measurement processes that create an ever-expanding and ongoing spiral for continuous quality improvement.

This chapter will provide context and exemplify specific elements of an environment conducive to results-informed leadership. These elements include setting targets, measuring targets, reporting, and taking action. Next, the chapter will provide specific examples of results-informed leadership in practice at multiple levels: project, office or department, and division or organization levels. The chapter concludes with reflection questions to encourage leaders and promote intentionality in efforts to drive for results in their respective organizations.

Elements of Results-Informed Leadership

To best enact results-informed leadership, there are environmental conditions and process elements to have in place for leaders to engage and influence. This section will detail setting targets for performance or strategic goals. Considerations are provided with respect to measuring targets and then for reporting and taking action on those results. The reader should consider this information when generating results-informed practices for themselves and when engaging and leading others in this work.

Setting Targets

When I use the term target, I am referring to a desired or expected level of performance. I am describing what would be an indicator of whether or not an outcome, process, or strategy was achieved. The reader may consider this by another name—goal, outcome, success criteria—but I will use the term *target* for consistency. This section will describe what targets are—in context to planning and alignment of operations—types of targets and how targets relate to reports.

Targets exist to ease reporting and interpretation of results with respect to success for learning, production, usage, or achievement (Levy, 2021). Without a target, determining success or achievement can be an extremely subjective activity. For example, a workshop resulting in 75% of attendees being able to articulate their leadership philosophy may sound like a positive result until one is informed last year's workshop attendees had a success rate of 90%. Having a set target value to compare results against makes reporting easier and more meaningful (Kuh et al., 2015).

An operational strategy or assessment plan helps situate interventions and measures in relation to larger initiatives, resources, and environmental factors (Commonwealth for Learning, 2010; Levy, 2013). Targets are the explicitly stated expectations of planned interventions as revealed through measures. Knowing the scrutiny or scale at which to be setting targets can depend on environmental factors, resources, and initiatives at play for an organization. Including timeframes (monthly, quarterly, annually, etc.) for processes and reporting cadence are also relevant. Familiarity with operational strategy can offer guidance for articulating targets, just as understanding the levels of organization involved can help determine when to create sub-targets beneath a larger target's umbrella.

When articulating targets, consider different forms which may be required:

- **Expectation**—this target is the result one would expect to see based on historical data or performance. It is ideal when there is no expected action or effort needed for achievement. As an example expected target: the organization meets external quality assurance standards (as it has the previous three years).
- **Aspirational**—this is a target which may require some operational changes in order to be achieved. Based on inconsistent or slightly lower past performance, leaders will take action for improvement with processes or interventions in order to achieve this level of result. As an aspirational example: the organization not only meets but exceeds external quality assurance standards in at least two areas.
- **Stretch**—this is a target for which one needs to exert a major effort to align operations and consistently deliver excellence in order to achieve. As a stretch example: the organization exceeds external quality assurance standards in at least five out of eight areas.

Regardless of the type of target one is using, language and intention are key. Whether qualitative or quantitative in nature, targets should be explicitly aligned to initiatives, operations, or services. This alignment helps determine specificity of language and what would be a realistic result given the scope or nature of the intervention. The target should be written in a way that it is clear and easy to determine achievement as *yes* or *no*.

Measuring Targets

In determining measures for targets, it is important to consider existing efforts. Because targets may relate to new initiatives, it can be equally effective to create one's starting point. This section will describe how to do both, as well as considerations for matching any target with intended data type for reporting.

Where current programs and initiatives exist, leaders should reflect on targets and measures which may already be established (Levy, 2021). Consider key performance indicators, internal benchmarks compared to past data, external benchmarks compared to peer organizations, or external standards for which one is called upon to meet. Look to past and existing reports for trends or insights; perform document analysis to identify metrics in relation to interventions and departments. All of these examples could prove fitting as measures for targets given the proper alignment.

BOX 18.1 **Example Targets**

Targets related to means:

At least 80% of students will cite tutoring as a major influence for their grade improvement

The average customer will indicate quality of services as 4 out of 5 stars

Targets related to rubric scores:

Score of 17 or higher for the rubric overall

Averaging a score of 3.0 or higher on rubric criteria #4 and #5

Targets related to proportions:

75% or more of employees perform at the Proficient or Outstanding level overall

Fewer than 20% of students will have to use emergency academic counseling for course add/drops

Where alignment or metrics do not already exist, it is more than appropriate to create a starting point from which to measure (Levy, 2021). One's hypothesis for target results can be informed by reflecting on possible categorical outcomes which are *lower than expected or disappointing, higher than expected or exciting*, and an outcome *on par with expectations and not very surprising*. When creating from scratch, do not fret about getting the target and measure perfect. One can always justify the target-setting approach when interpreting results and reporting, then demonstrating results-informed leadership by taking action to adjust targets and measures accordingly for the next evaluative cycle.

Whether one has existing measures to work with or not, *do not engage in this work alone* (Commonwealth for Learning, 2010; Heiser et al., 2017; Kuh et al., 2015; Levy, 2021). Check with colleagues for sharing of existing instruments, related data, or offering feedback on new instruments and targets. Engage students or clients to consider what they believe to be reasonable or appropriate measures and expectations. These target populations of respondents can also assist with piloting instruments as measures to offer feedback on design and help preview the resulting data as it would be captured. Finally, consider external resources or support; reach out to partners with organizational or quality assurance standards, as well as colleagues at other organizations regarding their practices.

As measures are finalized, it can be necessary to revisit target language (Kuh et al., 2015; Levy, 2021; Wehlburg, 2007). In addition to targets aligning with operations and strategy, agreed-upon targets should match with available data types. If needing to report on the percent of programs accomplishing a milestone, phrase the target for the percent of programs versus a count of programs or average program behavior. Use the focus on measures and results to ensure targets are not vague statements like "employees will be proficient in performance." Are *all* employees expected to be proficient? Is proficiency expected in *all* areas of performance? A more specific and report-oriented target could be, "80% or more employees will score proficient or higher on performance rubric dimensions associated with task and project completion." Including the specificity of an emphasized competency for a given year (i.e., cultural competence, project management, navigating in uncertain or ever-changing environments) helps reiterate the necessary and relevant data to analyze and report. Be intentional with target language and measure selection to achieve results that will remain relevant when reported and shared with stakeholders.

Reporting and Taking Action

Arguably the most important steps in results-informed leadership—reporting and taking action—are necessary given the abundance of data collected and decisions to be made in the best interest of the organization and its community (Kuh et al., 2015). Effective leaders should strive to operate in environments with relevant reporting shared at a frequency to equip decision-makers with necessary information as needed, while also keeping the larger organizational community aware and informed (Levy, 2013). This section will define reporting in practice, offer recommendations for reporting, and provide considerations with respect to taking action based on results.

When I think about reporting as a concept or process, a report is synonymous with a story. An effective report describes one's process to plan and collect data, selection of measurements and analysis methods for data, interpretation of results in relation to historical trends or contexts, and detail for intended or recommended actions. Similar to what is depicted in Figure 18.2, a report should describe what was done, what was found, what it means, and what is going to be done because of the results. Like any story, depending on the intended audience and purpose, the detail, length, and medium can vary to best meet circumstances.

Because reporting—in general or with specific data—may not be an area of formal experience or competence for all individuals (Commonwealth for Learning, 2010; Kuh et al., 2015), I want to offer a few practical tips to help encourage effective efforts. First, remember that results should be kept in context and acted upon accordingly. With operational data and decisions, it can be more art than science, so one should not discredit results simply because the data set or sample size is small. Remember, data points often represent people and their experiences; while it can be easy to push aside a spreadsheet, it can be far more difficult to tell people their experiences are not relevant because their voices were not abundant or loud enough. Conversely, one should also not necessarily revamp an entire program or initiative due to a single data point. Triangulation of data and inclusion of multiple perspectives can go a long way in helping navigate what can be gray territories of data-informed decision-making.

With respect to analysis and results interpretation, be ready to disaggregate data by pertinent demographics or operational factors (locations, departments, etc.).

Process

Analysis

Interpretation

\+ Intended Actions

Report

FIGURE 18.2 Report Elements

Disaggregating data can surface equity issues or outliers that might otherwise be masked in the meaty middle of means and medians (Heiser et al., 2017; Montenegro & Jankowski, 2017). For example, the overall average from a college's student population may report a strong sense of belonging, but disaggregation could reveal lack of belonging reported by transgender students. Interpretation is less about the target achieved for one population versus another, but instead a story focused on what sense of belonging reported by student populations looked like in relation to a target and how specific actions and initiatives are being encouraged for implementation to address students who do not feel like they belong.

Reporting underscores the importance of targets remaining relevant and meaningful over time (Kuh et al., 2015; Levy, 2021). If a particular department or initiative is always meeting targets, at some point they should consider if their targets are appropriate. Where appropriate, they should be sure to disaggregate results to make sure the target is being achieved across populations or operational elements like locations. Likewise, if measuring the same things and consistently achieving targets, consider raising the expectations and adjusting the targets to better meet the trending reality. Finally, consider measuring targets in new or multiple ways. Methodological diversity can be good for surfacing potential equity concerns, triangulating data points for increased understanding, and helping validate success or achievement of targets from multiple perspectives (Heiser et al., 2017).

The operational story does not end with reports, however; taking action is a crucial step and presents key opportunities for results-informed leaders to lead by example (Kuh et al., 2015). When results are shared, leaders can push back against claims that data is good or bad, positive or negative: data is data. With data being neutral, one may need reminding that it is people who ascribe meaning to data, making positionality, biases, and perspectives all the more relevant in the interpretation and storytelling processes with results (Heiser et al., 2017; Kuh et al., 2015). Leaders can help keep people focused on continuous improvement and overall betterment. The report is not bad, negative, and should never be shelved just because targets were not met. As long as there is a plan to address known issues or to better understand why targets were not met, that part of the report should be driving conversations and carrying momentum into future planning and measurement efforts.

Since reporting can be more art than science, let taking action be a powerful, concrete, and inspirational part of the process. Demonstrate results-informed leadership by triangulating relevant data from multiple sources to encourage future action (Heiser et al., 2017; Montenegro & Jankowski, 2017; Wehlburg, 2007). While there could be a small data set calling for a specific operational change, if the change requires few resources and it is known that the same population expressed similar concerns in other avenues, why not make the change to increase satisfaction within that population, demonstrate being data informed, and model being responsive to results? Likewise, reserve judgment and offer support to the voices with concerns which are not able to be addressed at this time. Validate those voices, perspectives, and experiences because circumstances could change, trend-data could accumulate, and there could be enough momentum to bring about these changes in the future (Heiser et al., 2017).

Leaders can help hold people accountable to take action with reports (Kuh et al., 2015; Levy, 2013). Far too many reporting processes lack an accountability or follow-up mechanism for the outcomes of documented or encouraged actions. Use templates of plans or future reports to ask authors to recall and report outcomes of actions, or create space in area or cross-departmental meetings to discuss actions taken based on previous reports and results. Regardless of whether targets were met or not, one action which can (and should) always be taken is sharing results.

Results should be shared with multiple audiences in the format and with the level of detail appropriate to them (Kuh et al., 2015). Sharing is more than just forwarding a report or spreadsheet; isolate important and necessary details from the results and pair with contextual information to illustrate relevance to the audience (Levy, 2013). After all, sharing department initiative results should look different to engage the CEO versus front-line staff within the department. Realize, too, sharing efforts can be leveraged for beneficial by-products: share past results to encourage future survey completion, announce departmental improvements by crediting the data that informed the change, or promote achievements and pride points for the organization through target achievement or initiative progress reporting. Leadership includes effective communication; results-informed leadership should include sharing results in multiple ways to various audiences.

How to Use Results-Informed Leadership in the Workplace

While some examples have been provided throughout the chapter to help illustrate specific concepts, this section will provide use-cases of results-informed leadership to compile and present content as it could come together in practice. Use-cases are provided at the division or organization-wide level, the office or department level, and the project level. Each use-case will outline possible targets, measures, reports, and actions that a results-informed leader could employ contextually.

Division/Organization Level

As an organization, Disruptive Development has made a commitment to advancing diversity, equity, and inclusion (DEI) efforts throughout the company. To make sure the company is living their values, leadership set a target which could quantify scope and success of DEI-related activity. As a result, Disruptive Development determined the following as a course of action:

<u>Target:</u> 80% or more of DEI-related targets throughout the company will be met or exceeded.

> Attention and concern for DEI is a company value, which means there should be efforts across the organization which align or contribute to enhancing the culture for DEI. Knowing the company value and current societal climate, there are high expectations for targets to be met. That said, unlearning ideas and dismantling structures can be difficult work, so 80% might be a high but realistic achievement across the organization/company.

<u>Measures:</u> Review existing targets across departments to identify DEI-related projects or aligned efforts to DEI-related initiatives.

> This measure at the company level can leverage reporting at a departmental level. Leadership can review reported departmental target information to identify which are DEI related in order to isolate those data for this company-level measure. While retaining department source of each DEI-related target for area-specific insights later, target achievement is aggregated in order to determine if 80% or more of overall company DEI targets were achieved or not.

<u>Reports:</u> Aggregate existing target achievement results submitted across the company; share at the company-wide level with overall results and contributions per department called out.

> The company can report overall DEI-related target achievement as a progress metric and demonstration of company activity related to their value of DEI. These collected targets are reviewed for themes associated with their nature: policy, procedure, professional development, or client-related efforts. Beyond reporting overall and departmental target achievement, results are shared in relation to target themes in order to add more texture to the kind of DEI-related efforts and improvements taking place at Disruptive Development.

<u>Actions:</u> Determine overarching themes to refine strategies or propose actions for change based on company-wide results; departments can identify area-specific actions given the organization-wide context for their DEI-related target achievement; subsequent reporting can celebrate and share about DEI-related progress and achievements to the broader community.

With results of company-wide and departmental target achievement related to DEI, leadership can engage in collaborative discussions for emerging themes, issues, or priorities in order to refine strategies and actions going forward. Departments can then revisit their respective action plans—and goals for change to consider any additions or enhancements—in light of organization-level insights around DEI. Actions for change aside, it is important that Disruptive Development celebrates and contextualizes their individual and collective achievements vis-à-vis living out their values with respect to DEI. The company shares internally and externally about the progress occurring in hopes of inspiring similar change with other organizations and communities.

Office/Department Level

The Implementation Department is responsible for helping clients integrate and use technology to meet their needs. Because implementation is just one part of this company's processes (including marketing, sales, and consulting), onboarding and orientation are important for new employees in the Implementation Department to understand the roles they play in relation to the larger organization. The director of the Implementation Department determined the following to measure the efficacy of onboarding:

Target: By 60 days with the company, all new Implementation Department employees will be able to describe how their individual work contributes to organizational strategies.

The onboarding process for the Implementation team takes a solid month of passive and active training, digestion of materials, and familiarization with policies and processes. Employees shadow existing employees and meet with key collaborators across the company to learn more about its operations. Expected to be fully functional in their role, the additional 30 days incorporated into the target allows the new employees time to acclimate to their role and experience-related operations in their work. Given the intentionality of the onboarding process and time to independently operate in their roles, the director of the Implementation team believes it is fair to expect all employees to know how their work fits with larger company operations and goals.

Measures: Onboarding process survey (quantitative and qualitative data) and qualitative data from interviews with Implementation Department colleagues and supervisor.

Aligned with Human Resources (HR) recommending a 60 day check-in with new employees, the Implementation team administers HR's standard onboarding survey for new employees. In addition to the self-reporting from the new employee, the Implementation team also interviews fellow team members to collect peer and supervisor feedback as validation. With quarterly onboarding cycles, there is a beneficial by-product of this process reorienting existing employees to the onboarding experience, as well as constructive scrutiny for the spirit and nature of operating procedures.

Reports: Download of compiled survey results; summary report of themes surfaced from interviews; share all results with Implementation team, while only sharing pertinent results with HR regarding onboarding efforts and company leadership regarding organizational strategies.

The company's survey technology automatically analyzes survey responses and provides aggregate reporting with visuals, as well as individual response results. The director of the Implementation, or designee, reviews notes captured from peer and supervisor interviews about new employees to identify themes. While overall strengths and areas for improvement are drawn from the survey and interview results are useful to the Implementation team, results for onboarding efforts are shared quarterly with HR to consider for support or process change with the Implementation team and beyond. Additionally, results specific to organizational strategy are shared quarterly with company leadership to gauge awareness and departmental ability to see alignment with higher-order operations. By doing this, leadership can consider clarity, frequency of communication, and accessibility of organizational strategy information.

Actions: Work individually with new Implementation team members who were unable to achieve the target to understand issues, concerns, gaps with onboarding, and their efforts in relation to larger organizational strategies; develop action plans to help those employees achieve the target; make adjustments to onboarding process as needed.

Given the nature and timing of the Implementation team's work in relation to organizational processes, it is important to work with new team members to address any barriers preventing them from being able to describe how they individually contribute to organizational strategies. In collaboration and with the support of their supervisors, new Implementation employees will develop individual action plans for this specific competency development. The Implementation Department will collaborate with HR and other departments quarterly to consider actions to address gaps or issues with the department (and possibly company) onboarding process, as well as collaborate with company leadership to ensure effective sharing of organizational strategy information with Implementation team members. Even if the target is met, an annual reflection still occurs since onboarding efforts can always be more resourceful, efficient, and balanced for work style.

Project Level

Among other responsibilities, the Quality Assurance Department is responsible for fielding and resolving technical issues related to a variety of organizational webforms and other public website functions. Service excellence is an important goal for this department and the organization as a whole and can impact regulatory or accreditation-related external entities. Because the technology team within the Quality Assurance Department had never been asked to report on their efficacy before, the technology team leader reflected upon past experience, the varying complexity of their work, and teammate feedback to help determine the following:

Target: 90% or more of technical issues logged by phone or email will be resolved within three business days.

In alignment with the department and organizational value of service excellence, care was taken in determining numerical values in this target. While some technical issues can (and should) be resolved in less than a business day, aspects of the website may need to be confirmed by other departments and approved by marketing before various changes can be implemented. Three business days may seem like a long time for fixing a broken link or typo on a form, but can be considered as efficient if multiple departments are needed to collaborate or contribute to a possible fix. Reflection on past volume and types of requests helped determine percent and timeframe for the target; having data collected and reported this year can help refine a future target here, if necessary.

Measures: Issue-tracking software (qualitative and quantitative data) and qualitative data from team discussion and interpretation of data.

While not asked to report in relation to targets historically, it helps that the Quality Assurance Department already has issue-tracking software in place. With this software, it will be easy to capture time stamps of logged issues, notes about the nature of the issue, active or resolved status, and timestamps for changes in ticket information. Aside from the quantitative and qualitative data output from the issue-tracking software, there will also be qualitative data from the Quality Assurance technology team reviewing those data and offering their thoughts, interpretations, and feedback.

Reports: Automated monthly report form issue-tracking software and monthly summary report from the Quality Assurance technology team.

> Although the target is concerned with cases being resolved within three business days, it is important to look at trends and results across cases. Automating a report from the issue-tracking software to share results each month provides a regular cadence for formal review and sharing of results. The Quality Assurance technology team can codify their feedback with results from automated reports into executive summaries determining if the target was met for the given month and any insights regarding issue trends or noteworthy aspects of cases that took longer than three business days to resolve. Any executive summary report is shared with the rest of the Quality Assurance Department, as well as related departments or internal leadership, who may be impacted by topical issues or advancements. Annual reports drawing highlights from the monthly executive summary reports are shared externally with customers, clients, or pertinent community members as a signal of quality assurance.

Actions: Engage stakeholders within and beyond the department to identify frequently occurring issues and preventing ticket resolution from happening within three business days; determine and execute system changes to limit or overcome challenges with technical elements or issue resolution; adjust target as needed.

> While the Quality Assurance technology team may be the first people to see and make meanings of results, it is important that the report is shared and considered by the rest of the Quality Assurance Department, as well as other website users (broader staff, clients/customers, et al.). The technology team leaders leverage those perspectives with respect to identified issues and barriers, as well as possible changes in processes, practices, or content. Other complementary data (budget, resources, initiative progress across the organization) are considered to strategize and plan to execute on the respective action items. Finally, since the initial target was based on anecdotal feedback and past experience, the technology team uses the results from the monthly (and ultimately annual) reporting to raise the target if well over 90% or within three business days; there may also be a need to adjust what is measured to approximate something more meaningful and relevant.

Application

This chapter provided context and exemplified specific elements of an environment conductive to results-informed leadership. After describing how to set targets, measure targets, and reporting and taking action, the chapter offered use-cases of results-informed leadership in practice at multiple levels: project, office or department, and division or organization level.

These elements have applications to any level of work and any organization. Consider applying these questions to being a part-time employee at a grocery store. Regardless of role (cashier, grocery clerk [stocking], etc.), one can consider to what extent their department or the organization as a whole is role modeling results-informed leadership. To what extent are data talked about? Are numbers shared with respect to time on task for employees in relation to productivity or effectiveness? What about busy times of day when work may be especially stressful? Are any results shared with respect to customer satisfaction or feedback about service?

As a conclusion and encouragement to promote results-informed leaders to act with intention as they drive for results in their organizations, consider the following reflection questions for application:

1. To what extent does results-informed leadership align with project, office/department, or division/organizational practice?
2. Given existing project, office, or organizational strategies and initiatives, what targets need to be set for this year given results from past measurement or performance?

3. Who should be involved in determining measures for priority targets for the organization?
4. What changes might be made to enhance the reporting process in the organization?
5. What can be done to better engage key or neglected audiences with results?
6. How can organizational leaders be held accountable for following through on action plans for improvement?

In each of the aforementioned cases, the grocery store management should have past data as a reference. When onboarding, hiring, or encouraging employees in relation to store strategies or initiatives, targets should be set to help employees understand the extent to which their work is maintaining the status quo versus requiring a considerable amount of effort to meet a stretch goal. To encourage result sharing and support target setting, employees can ask questions and make requests for data.

Collaboration is paramount. If it does not come about organically, one could make requests to listen in or be part of conversations and decision-making processes. Involving multiple perspectives can benefit store leadership and the employees; employees gain knowledge, awareness, and factors considered in the business of the store, while store leadership gains direct feedback and insight from fresh perspectives or different vantage points of operations. Such invitations for engagement can make it clear where leadership's attempts at communication or transparency are not effectively reaching employees or the greater store community.

Leadership should create (and employees take advantage of) spaces and opportunities for feedback. The store's leadership can invite commentary on goals and strategies, sharing past results and current initiatives. Employees and customers of the store can offer praise for what is going well or they appreciate their experience with the store, as well as critical commentary of where to make improvements. This process may even surface the reality of key populations or stakeholders being prioritized and neglected. The store's leadership and employees can reflect and consider how to help ensure equity and agency for members of the greater store community.

Through all of this work, the store should role model accountability. With data sharing, target setting, employee motivation and strategizing, and promoting collaboration—even through feedback gathering—the store's leadership can promote a data-informed culture for which they are striving. Employees can demonstrate the role they play in this environment, both offering feedback to leadership and carrying out their roles to best serve customers. In both cases, the store can encourage transparency and integrity with respect to actions taken for improvement. Store leadership can regularly report on results and updates with respect to larger strategies to help hold themselves accountable, the same as employees committing to deliver on promises made to customers to answer questions, provide services, or offer support and assistance to best meet customer needs.

Beyond the grocery store example, organizational and individual responses to the reflection questions above coupled with their efforts to promote data-informed leadership ought not to be exhaustive in their approaches or perfect from the outset. This work is iterative in nature, requiring steadfast commitment, continuous improvement, and accountability to do the right things well. It is okay to start small, especially when trying to make changes to an existing or well-established culture. Pick one area to improve and set about to make change, evaluating and reporting on progress while inviting collaborative perspectives to support the initiative along the way. Successful efforts, no matter how small, can inspire and create momentum to bring about larger, improvement-focused change across the organization.

References

Commonwealth for Learning. (2010). Quality assurance toolkit for open schools. Author.

Heiser, C. A., Prince, K., & Levy, J. D. (2017). Examining critical theory as a framework to advance equity through student affairs assessment. *The Journal of Student Affairs Inquiry, 3*(1).

Kuh, G. D., Ikenberry, S. O., Jankowski, N. A., Cain, T. R., Hutchings, P., & Kinzie, J. (2015). Using evidence of student learning to improve higher education. Jossey-Bass.

Levy, J. D. (2013). ABCs of ineffective assessment cultures: Spelling out the wrongs to make right. *Journal of Student Affairs*, 22, 35–40.

Levy, J. D. (2021). Why and how you should set learning targets for every program [Blog]. Modern Campus.

Montenegro, E., & Jankowski, N. A. (2017, January). Equity and assessment: Moving towards culturally responsive assessment (Occasional Paper No. 29). University of Illinois and Indiana University, National Institute for Learning Outcomes Assessment (NILOA).

Wehlburg, C. M. (2007). Closing the feedback loop is not enough: The assessment spiral. *Assessment Update*, *19*(2), 1–15.

Credit

Fig. 18.1: Copyright © by Commonwealth for Learning and Joe Levy (CC BY-SA 3.0) at https://open.saide.ngo/repository/opensaide/pubQAOSToolkit.pdf.

CHAPTER 19

Political Savviness

By J. Vincent Nix and L. Misty Song

You can observe a lot just by watching.

—Yogi Berra

Learning Objectives

After reading this chapter, students will be able to:

1. Articulate a definition of political savviness
2. Recognize how political savviness can help shape the work environment
3. Understand the competency clusters underpinning political savviness

Introduction

In my callow youth, a wise mentor once remarked, "Vince, you say you don't want to get involved because you hate politics. Well, *everything* is politics, so if you say you don't want to get involved in *anything*, I don't know what you're good for." While he may have been overstating my degree of disengagement, he was right about the central role politics[1] plays in most human endeavors. It is essential that leaders are politically savvy, a complex social construct which encompasses recognizing and understanding the interpersonal dynamics at play in a given situation, including the power relationships, unwritten rules, and informal networks involved. Its foundation rests upon a strong knowledge of the laws, norms, and conventions of the political environment, a deep comprehension of human behavior and social structure, and familiarity with the language and style of political discourse. A degree of political savviness helps one to understand an organization's hierarchy and the roles and motivations of actors therein, as well as the strategies and tactics used by different groups and individuals in the political arena. It is the ability to read between the lines, to infer the goals and concerns of those involved, and anticipate their decisions and the outcomes thereof in diverse contextual situations.

1. When most people hear "politics," they think "government," but the word applies to the activities, actions, and strategies involved in gaining and exercising influence in any social power structure or organization. Here, political savviness refers to the ability to understand the dynamic relationships in a given organization and successfully navigate the political landscape to pursue one's goals.

This competency is indispensable for those in positions of power, for leaders must constantly read the current social situation, concurrently evaluating the interactions and relationships of different institutions and individuals while assessing how to best influence them. It involves a thorough understanding of workplace culture, including the values, beliefs, and norms that drive behavior and decisions. Understanding the perspectives, opinions, and interests of different players will enable one to make more informed strategic decisions, avoiding pitfalls and gaining access to the information and resources which can help you reach your goals.

Political savviness—in contrast to my earlier Chapters 13 and 14, which deal with relatively concrete constructs—is quite nebulous. It is frankly a hard nut to crack, so to speak—particularly in regard to devising a how-to curriculum! The concept is hard to quantify and difficult to teach, and it was hard to approach the topic without a degree of trepidation. How does one teach something that is easiest to describe in the negative, when it is easier to point out someone's lack of political finesse than it is to label what makes another so remarkably savvy?

In the end, the key was to stop treating political savviness like an element of management—focused on quantitative constructs and measurable outputs—and to begin thinking of it like leadership, which encompasses a much broader philosophical lens and includes inherently qualitative concepts that are much more difficult to quantify. From that perspective, becoming politically savvy vividly illustrates the process of leadership emerging from management. All theories (including ones about leadership) typically seek to explain (and eventually predict) phenomena, while management practices are focused on cataloging data as observational evidence (Bogen & Woodward, 1988). As Haig (2005) points out, "the methodological importance of data lies in the fact that they serve as evidence for the phenomena under investigation" (p. 374). Effective management then is generative—and in best-case scenarios—produces leadership as a phenomenon.

Unfortunately, we have no magic juice to offer, no miraculous shortcut that will guide you unerringly to a politically savvy future. As we stated, it is difficult to quantify or reliably teach ... but we *can* point you toward the competencies that in our experiences are characteristic of those who embody the construct. As you learn about those components, you will find your strengths and weaknesses, telling you what to practice, where you are most effective—and whom to put on your leadership team so that their abilities can enhance and balance your own. While political savviness comes to some more easily than others, understanding and practicing the individual competencies incorporated into the construct will benefit anyone who wishes to be a more effective leader. The next section identifies the core elements of political savviness and delineates the skills inherent to each.

Competencies

It could be said that political savviness is the ability to read the political tea leaves and understand the motivations behind the decisions of organizational characters, leaders, and managers. Why do they want to do what they're proposing? What might be the unintended and unforeseen impacts their actions have on interpersonal and interorganizational relationships?

Answering these questions requires an understanding of three critical processes: affective intelligence,[2] compromise, and coalition maintenance, each with a unique set of competencies.[3] The first group includes the skills needed to recognize one's own values and emotional states, which are a prerequisite for the other two clusters. Affective intelligence is what allows for effective communication because it gives us

2. *Affect* (the root of affective) is a term used to describe our emotional system, mindset, and feeling-states and will be discussed in detail in the following section.

3. Readers are invited to refer back to Chapter 13 for a scholarly overview of competency clustering.

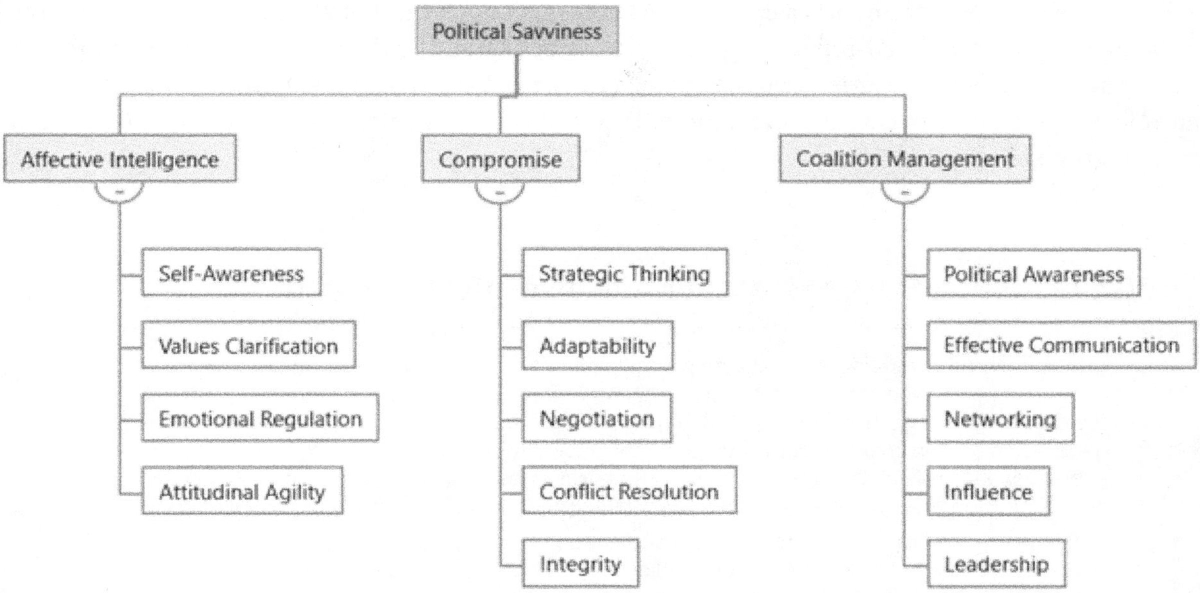

FIGURE 19.1 Competency Tree—Political Savviness

an awareness of how our internal states impact our interactions with others and helps identify our most important priorities. Compromise, of course, includes the competencies that come into play during negotiations or strategic planning; it does not simply refer to compromising with another party but can also apply to making compromises with ourselves, as we decide which of our goals must take priority over others. The last cluster, coalition management, is where political savviness brings all the elements together to create leadership. Humans work together because they can achieve more when they do so; a leader who creates a coalition, bringing teams together in pursuit of common aims and values, is the very heart of an organization.

Affective Intelligence

Affective intelligence is the ability to understand, use, and manage the dispositions (i.e., values, emotions, attitudes) or mindsets of oneself and others in healthy and productive ways. This is important in all relationships, as it allows empathy and understanding and thus is a valuable asset in professional roles. Effectively managing[4] our own emotions facilitates better decision-making in our workplaces, reducing the frequency or impact of contentious interactions. Recognizing the affect of others—which includes an awareness of their values and cultural beliefs—facilitates communication, allowing for more persuasive arguments and greater mutual benefit from cooperative projects.

People can develop and improve their affective intelligence, practicing it so they can better recognize and understand the emotions, attitudes, and beliefs of themselves and others. In our experiences, the most effective ways to improve, develop, and sustain affective intelligence are by practicing mindfulness

4. This is a fraught word when discussing emotions; please note that "managing" does not here signify "controlling" or "restricting." Appropriately managing emotions requires identifying and recognizing the feeling, determining how and why the emotion has arisen, and understanding how it impacts thinking and decision-making. Only then can appropriate action be taken to manage the emotional response, whether that be revisiting a plan of action, communicating with another party, or initiating an institutional or personal change.

and self-reflection. Mindfulness is a conscious awareness of our own thoughts, feelings, and emotions in the present moment.[5] Self-reflection is the process of examining those internal states in order to better understand how they arise, and the impacts they may have had on prior events. By reexamining our role in events, we can better understand how our internal state manifests in our decision-making or interactions.

BOX 19.1 **Reflective Exercises for Affective Intelligence**

1. Journaling is a powerful tool for reflecting and building affective intelligence. Set aside some time each evening to write your feelings, emotions, and attitudes about specific interactions throughout the day. Wiltshire and Ronkainen (2021) suggest categorizing such constructs into themes to aid understanding. Experiential themes describe the subjective intersection of beliefs, values, and events; inferential ones reflect on reframing situations to explain personal contexts; dispositional themes would focus on the elements that came together to produce the phenomenon observed.
2. Reflection questions are ways to delve deeper into our affective intelligence. Examples might include "How did that experience align with or conflict with my core values?" or "What attitudinal or emotional responses did I exhibit in the face of alignment or conflict?"

Self-Awareness

By examining oneself, a person gains a better understanding of how they influence—and are influenced by—the world around them. In the context of political savviness, self-awareness is key to recognizing their own biases and how those prejudices may be influencing their views and actions. This is important for making sure that one's decisions are based on accurate information and not on preconceived notions or groupthink. In addition to understanding our own political views and biases, self-awareness is also useful for understanding the larger political landscape. As individuals become more aware of their own political beliefs, they can also begin to engage in meaningful dialogue and discourse with those who might have different views. This can help to foster understanding, collaboration, and (most importantly!) compromise, which is essential for a healthy and functioning political system.

Values Clarification

Values clarification, which builds on *self-awareness*, is the process of exploring and defining one's own beliefs and values, which requires asking and discussing fundamental questions such as: What is important to me? What do I believe in? What do I stand for? By doing so, people can come to better understand their own values and develop the hierarchy of goals and desires that serves as a roadmap for compromise and negotiation.

This should be explored individually at first before attempting to articulate them in group activities; if values are not well defined, individuals tend to follow the crowd, leading to groupthink. They can use these values to inform their decision-making, such as which candidates and policies to support. Values clarification can also help people to possess better-informed biases and better assess the facts and arguments in political discourse. In this way, values clarification can help to equip people with the tools to become more politically engaged, informed, and develop into civic-minded individuals. Overall, values clarification is

5. For an overview of the *mindfulness* construct that includes research on the efficacy of mindfulness training, see Sauer, 2018.

an important part of developing political savviness. It helps people to identify their core values, articulate them in a political context, and better assess the facts and arguments in political discourse.[6]

Emotional Regulation

Emotional regulation refers to managing and controlling one's emotions in order to facilitate a desired outcome or goal. We do this all the time, taking stock of our affective state and addressing what it is communicating to our rationality. You can see emotional regulation in everything from a card player keeping a "poker face," to a parent managing anger by counting to 10 instead of lashing out at their child, to a first-time bungee jumper taking deep breaths to manage their fear before leaping off of the platform. This competency requires *self-awareness* and *clear values* and involves acknowledging what message our feeling-states are sending us, and addressing them by disregarding or incorporating them appropriately so that we can make good decisions that move us closer to what we want.

It follows, then, that politically savvy people must be able to regulate their emotions in ways that allow clear thinking, decisiveness, and a calm demeanor. Doing so allows one to remain analytical and *act* on the message an emotion conveys, rather than *reacting* to the feeling itself. Doing so is the foundation of diplomacy and tact; remaining calm, collected, and communicative in heated situations allows disagreement without being disagreeable. It helps one read the room to know when to back down and when to stand one's ground.

Attitudinal Agility

The final competency in this cluster, *attitudinal agility*, is a synthesis of all the ones that came before. It encompasses the ability to think and act with a flexible attitude, as required by different situations, individuals, and cultural contexts. People with this trait are able to anticipate problems, recognize (theirs and others') mindsets, and adjust their approaches to respond to situations quickly and effectively. Rather than approaching a person, issue, or situation with a fixed attitude, they recognize how their feelings and expectations color their responses and recalibrate as necessary. By doing so, they maintain good relationships with their colleagues and superiors and are more open to understanding the motivations of those around them. Attitudinal agility can be developed and improved through practice and observation and by practicing consciously choosing an attitude when responding to different types of situations.

Compromise

At its core, compromise is not about "giving things up," but about finding practical ways to achieve one's goals and effect one's values. It requires a tactical approach, prioritizing goals and keeping foremost in mind what ends are the most important. The politically savvy understand that they may not be able to achieve everything they want in a single negotiation or round of arbitration. Instead, they are willing to make concessions on certain issues in order to secure victories over others. This pragmatic approach allows them to move consistently toward their larger objectives. While some desired outcomes may have to be deferred, steady progress can build momentum and create a sense of accomplishment. More importantly, compromise fosters a sense of collaboration and cooperation as individuals work together to find solutions that address multiple concerns. In the process, not only do we often get some of what we want, all parties better understand one another and may find common ground on which to build effective and fruitful relationships.

6. The reader is encouraged to refer back to Chapter 13, this volume, for reflective values-clarification exercises.

Strategic Thinking

Political savviness also requires *strategic thinking.* As readers will recall from Chapter 14, this is the process of developing and applying a plan of action to achieve a desired goal, which involves gathering and analyzing data, formulating hypotheses, testing, and developing effective solutions. Strategic thinking requires an understanding of the available resources, the timeline, and the organizational structure, along with a well-defined goal. This competency draws heavily on *values clarification*, as it is predicated upon having a clear idea of one's own priorities and vital aims. A degree of *political awareness* (described later) is also a must, as it factors into considerations about the potential risks and rewards associated with the proposed plan of action. Strategic thinking is not a one-time process but rather an ongoing series of processes that require constant evaluation and adaptation.

Adaptability

Compromise often involves responding to changing circumstances and quickly re-prioritizing desired outcomes. Thus, *adaptability* is a core competency, which uses *attitudinal agility* and *strategic thinking* to recognize when it is necessary to modify our tactics and keep flexible enough to adjust plans accordingly. When faced with new challenges, it is essential to be able to change one's methods and strategies as appropriate or risk losing one's competitive edge. The ability to think on one's feet can be the difference between success and failure, and this adaptability is an absolute prerequisite for successful *negotiation*. One who cannot adapt their approach often has a difficult time finding ways to achieve their goals when the situation changes; as the saying goes, "adapt or die!" Organizations that fail to do so cannot long stay relevant in a changing world.

Negotiation

Politically savvy individuals with strong *negotiation* skills are well situated for leadership roles. This competency draws from every branch of the tree; one can easily argue that none of the skills grouped into *coalition management* are effective without a good negotiator to back them up! Successful negotiation requires one to have *clear values* and good *emotional regulation*, so that one can rationally choose between competing priorities and stick to the *strategic plan*. *Effective communication* is a must so that all parties understand exactly what is being offered and accepted, and *influence* both gives an advantageous position from which to negotiate and makes it easier to convince others to accept the final compromise. And having *integrity* makes others more comfortable negotiating in the first place, when they can be confident that the terms of any agreement will be adhered to.

Good negotiators are able to identify the interests of all parties involved and know how to craft solutions that are mutually beneficial. It requires thinking on one's feet, the ability to read people and anticipate their needs, while still clearly articulating one's own position and desires. Strong negotiation skills significantly increase the likelihood of achieving one's goals, both personally and professionally.

Conflict Resolution

Going hand-in-hand with *negotiation* is *conflict resolution*. Politically savvy individuals have the skills needed to navigate conflict successfully, drawing on their *emotional regulation* and *communication* abilities to approach problems rationally and with clear understanding. It benefits too from *political awareness* because understanding the dynamics at play in any given dispute is central to weighing the potential outcomes against risks and rewards. Listening, understanding, and respecting others' perspectives are key elements of resolving conflicts, and doing so is fundamental to creating a safe and productive environment. Practicing conflict-resolution techniques helps to build strong, healthy relationships—both inside of the workplace and out.

Integrity

Chapter 13 devotes considerable discussion to the benefits of cultivating a reputation for *integrity* and they are worth reiterating here. More than anything else, it is worth remembering that while people may not like hearing the honest answer sometimes, and honorable decisions may be unpopular or face opposition from the majority, no one wants to follow a person who lacks reliability, consistency, and candor. Knowing that their leader is fair and trustworthy is a powerful motivator for any member of a team. Of all the competencies in this chapter, integrity is the one easiest to learn and practice. Be dependable and accountable, follow through on promises and decisions, and uphold the norms and expectations of your organization. Even something as basic as punctuality is important, as it demonstrates respect for others and a willingness to "play by the rules." Ultimately, integrity is a fundamental component of success in any professional setting.

Coalition Management

As noted earlier, it is impossible to achieve alone what we can easily accomplish working with others. Building a coalition is an important step in realizing our dreams, but it also requires careful consideration of the wants and needs of all its members. One must identify a common goal or objective that everyone can rally around; this shared purpose helps to create a sense of unity and cohesion within the coalition. Keeping open lines of communication and creating an environment where all voices are heard and respected allows for constructive dialogue and gives opportunities to address any differences or conflicts that may arise.

This does, however, require ongoing effort and attention. It is important to have a strategic plan and to regularly assess whether progress is being made toward fulfilling it, making adjustments as needed. This may involve revisiting or revising the coalition's objectives or reevaluating the roles and responsibilities of individual members. Effective leaders are vital to maintaining a coalition, as they must continually inspire others to stay committed to the cause. By fostering a strong sense of teamwork and collective responsibility, leaders can create and sustain cohesion within the coalition, keeping the majority of members motivated and engaged most of the time.

Political Awareness

As the name implies, *political awareness* is fairly foundational to the whole construct of political savviness. We have to be conscious of the power structures and culture in an organization, understanding the various systems, events, and ideologies that shape the social and economic landscape of that institution before we can begin to harness them usefully. At its core, political awareness is knowing the various interests of different political players and how they interact with each other in order to create a cohesive organizational management framework.

Effective Communication

Politically savvy individuals must be able to *communicate effectively*, knowing when to speak and when to stay silent, recognizing how their words and actions may be interpreted or misinterpreted by others. It requires all the competencies of *affective intelligence* and is essential for *conflict resolution*, *networking*, and *leadership*. While one may be able to devise a sound *strategic plan* without good communication skills, it will be tremendously difficult to implement, as it will be nearly impossible to ensure that everyone understands one another and is on the same page about what to do next. Effective communicators often use the techniques described in Chapters 7 and 16 (this volume): actively listening to others, watching for nonverbal cues, and speaking clearly while checking to ensure that content is accurately conveyed. These practices permit one to express ideas and feelings while maintaining an awareness of their audience, adjusting their communication styles to match the needs and attention of peers, superiors, and customers. Giving honest and appropriate feedback and receiving constructive criticism are key components of this competency!

Networking

Networking is what we do when we use our *political awareness* to *communicate* with the *influential* people around us. Knowing who is who, the roles they play, and the resources they command and challenges they face is the heart of networking. The most politically savvy individuals in an organization are adept at building relationships with key stakeholders; the more people you are connected with, the more likely you are to have access to valuable resources such as industry news, trends, and information that can be used to our advantage or be available to help someone out when they need it. The importance of reciprocal beneficial relationships with a strong network of contacts cannot be overstated, and leveraging those connections is the fastest and most efficient way to achieve organizational goals. Professional networking can help us connect with people who provide us with career-advancing opportunities, while social networking can help us build relationships with those who share our interests, cultures, and beliefs. By reaching out to and maintaining meaningful connections to others, we can open up a world of possibilities that can help us to grow and succeed.

Influence

Successful *networking* is an effective way to accrue the currency of political savviness: *influence*. Being able to effectively persuade and motivate coworkers is key to creating a successful team. Through *effective communication*, *leadership*, and a healthy dose of *integrity*, a leader solidifies their reputation as someone worth following. With the right approach, a leader can push their team in a positive direction, establishing a culture of trust, respect, and understanding that encourages growth and innovation in a cooperative and collaborative environment. Influence ensures that everyone is working together toward common goals effectively and facilitates favorable outcomes while *negotiating*.

Leadership

If affective intelligence is the cornerstone upon which political savviness is built, then leadership is the capstone. It both supports the other competencies and derives from them, and it is difficult to pin down exactly what qualities make up a "born leader." Unquestionably, effective leaders are inspiring and know how to develop and manage a team. Furthermore, they demonstrate the ability to take the initiative and act decisively but also guide and collaborate with people from diverse backgrounds. Great leaders set the pace, provide clear direction, and create a culture of accountability while also being able to foster an environment of creativity and innovation. In the end, being a leader requires continual improvement through practice and self-reflection, relying on solid communication skills and strong affective intelligence.

Political Savviness in the Workplace

Now that we have identified the elements of political savviness, we can hopefully better understand the many ways it contributes to success in the workplace. More than anything, the strategic advantage that comes from being savvy leads to better decisions and stronger connections and greatly facilitates career advancement. Reciprocally advantageous relationships with influential people give access to valuable information, resources, and advice that bring one's goals within reach. A deep knowledge of organizational culture—and how to leverage it in your favor—can help you build a reputation as a leader and influencer in the workplace. Ultimately, developing political savviness is how we can understand others and use that understanding to achieve our own aims.

That may sound manipulative and Machiavellian, but it does not have to be. Politically savvy leaders with self-awareness, concrete values, and the ability to regulate their emotional responses know how to strive to realize their goals while still respecting others and encouraging their growth and innovation as well.

After all, one of the main pillars of political savviness is compromise. Building consensus through authentic negotiation benefits *everyone*, and those advantages compound over time. As we and our comrades reach our own goals, we are all better situated to help one another go even further. By understanding the needs and interests of different people in the workplace and finding ways to meet them, we garner trust and build a reputation for fair dealing and reliability, expanding our influence and establishing our leadership. You could do far worse than use your political savviness to create a positive work environment, where goals are clearly defined and often met, needs are considered and respected, and people have faith in their leaders.

How to Develop Political Savviness

As noted earlier, it is fiendishly difficult to develop an effective training course for enhancing political savviness. Nevertheless, there are a few general ways one can advance their capabilities in this regard. Here are some tips for developing political savviness in the workplace:

- *Listen* more than you talk. Pay particular attention to the perspectives of different people and try to be mindful of and how they intersect.
- *Observe* the dynamics between the various individuals and groups, and take note of how decisions are made. Obviously, the higher-ups will have more say in what happens, but look for people who seem to wield outsize influence. Try to suss out why that may be the case.
- *Ask* questions to understand the perspectives, values, and beliefs of different people in the workplace. Don't be shy about asking why someone does what they do or what they hope to achieve; more often than not, they will be happy to share.
- *Practice networking.* Whenever possible, meet and interact with new people and learn whatever you can from them. Keep their abilities and needs in mind and tap or fulfill them, respectively, whenever feasible.
- And *more than anything, practice.* Use your burgeoning skills in different situations in the workplace, learning from your mistakes and building on your successes.

As you develop your political savviness, don't forget to practice those skills not only in the workplace but in the wider world as well. Get involved! Participate in community events and volunteer for local organizations. Every group you take part in gives another set of opportunities to use these competencies, as well as opportunities to get more invested in civic life. That involvement will help you grow personally and professionally, getting savvier in the process. As your political sense develops, you will find it easier and easier to apply what you have learned at the workplace. That in turn translates into better organizational roles and further professional advancement. Political savviness increases opportunity—and conversely, its lack will derail careers quicker than anything else we have seen.

Ideally, political-savviness training would be included in the professional learning plan for any aspiring workplace leader. Managers need to know how to develop and maintain relationships with key stakeholders, including workplace supervisors, direct reports, and lateral coworkers, all of whom influence and are influenced by one another. It is impossible to muster support for projects or initiatives without understanding their effect on various individuals and groups. Leaders must develop strategies to navigate the complexities of their political environment in ways that further their goals.

Application

As noted earlier, political savviness is difficult to teach but easier to recognize. The following reflections may help you identify elements of the construct in yourself and others. It may provide ideas on how to cultivate them further.

Reflection One

Think about a time you looked at someone and were struck by how well that person navigates politics. Pick out two or three characteristics and behaviors that particularly stood out, and deconstruct those traits. How would you define them? Do they match one or more of the competencies in this chapter? If not, do your best at writing and defining a newly suggested competency that covers what you've observed!

Reflection Two

Now, consider a time you observed a colleague's behavior and wondered how they could possibly be so naive, politically speaking. Again, pick two or three behaviors or attributes that contributed to that impression. Which of the above competencies were missing? How would you recommend developing and sustaining those missing elements? Write a brief training plan to do so.

Reflection Three

Finally, take a moment to reflect on times when people seem to unexpectedly tap into sources of influence that may not have been immediately apparent or even run counter to the organization's traditional hierarchy. Can you think of many cases? Are there any similarities between them? Discuss with classmates the types of positions and people that seem to accrue unexpected political clout. Are there common characteristics among them such as length of service, "having someone's ear," or personal connections outside the workplace? Do those characteristics fit into any of the competencies described earlier, or do they need new ones written for them? When discussing, consider ways in which these less obvious power structures can be cultivated and maintained.

Having completed these reflections, what did you learn that you can apply to your own political savviness? What will be the impact for you and others?

References

Bogen, J., & Woodward, J. (1988). Saving the phenomena. *The Philosophical Review, 97*(3), 303–352. https://doi.org/10.2307/2185445

Haig, B. D. (2005). An abductive theory of scientific method. *Psychological Methods, 10*(4), 371–388. https://doi.org/10.1037/1082-989X.10.4.371

Sauer, S. (2018). Observation oriented modeling revised from a statistical point of view. *Behavior Research Methods, 50*(4), 1749–1761. https://doi.org/10.3758/s13428-017-0949-8

Wiltshire, G., & Ronkainen, N. (2021). A realist approach to thematic analysis: Making sense of qualitative data through experiential, inferential and dispositional themes. *Journal of Critical Realism, 20*(2), 159–180. https://doi.org/10.1080/14767430.2021.1894909

Conclusion

By Vince Nix

The real beginning of influence comes as others sense you are being influenced by them—when they feel understood by you—that you have listened deeply and sincerely, and that you are open.

—Stephen R. Covey

Lessons from Workplace Leadership

Organizations are realizing they must prioritize the development of effective leaders to achieve their goals. Executives across a dazzling array of industries agree that one of their top challenges is finding the right people to fill mission-critical roles; competent, talented individuals are in high demand, and organizations must not only recruit but *develop* the next generation of leaders.

And how should one select a candidate for leadership? The preceding chapters have a common thread, in that the authors all believe that doing leadership in workplaces is about being *influential*. Skills, intelligence, organizational talent, managerial competence. These elements are important in their own right, but influence is key in convincing others to commit to your objectives and vision. The consensus is that effective leaders identify and leverage their influence through mindful self-management, by understanding how to lead and motivate others, and by knowing how to steer an organization, division, or department.

Workplace Leadership Coda

As a coeditor of this volume, what struck me was an unexpected apparent departure from the notion of "leadership style" as a central concept. While our theoretical chapter used the term (specifically, to define past scholarly approaches to the formal study of leadership as a phenomenon), only four other authors across three chapters chose to include the phrase. Instead of focusing on an individual's approach to leadership, authors instead examined specific roles, discrete leadership functions, and the importance of "reading the room" to ascertain others' readiness to follow. Workplace leadership is not about settling on a particular style but rather requires frequent recalibrations and flexible approaches to sometimes abrupt situational or strategic changes. Good leaders are ones who have—and inspire—genuine attachment to the fiscal, ethical, and emotional health of their organizations and are committed to improving and sustaining excellence and success. Real workplace leadership requires clarity of roles and vision—almost entirely dependent on effective communication—and leaders who deploy contextually appropriate competencies, assessing needs, understanding context, and subsequently building capacity.

Workplace Leadership: The Functional Tome

This text provides a comprehensive guide to essential leadership proficiencies and abilities, and we believe *each chapter* in this book will be useful for three groups of people: first and foremost, students who are newly minted leaders or who are aspiring to become leaders; second, scholars (or emerging intellectuals) who are researching the nuances and complexities of leadership; and third, those who are building leadership-development programs based on core leadership competencies. Part I defines and examines leadership as a construct, introducing classic and emerging theories while presenting ethical leadership as the recommended approach; this establishes a foundation for understanding leadership as a goal. Parts II, III, and IV then focus on the competencies or competency clusters that are critical for workplace leadership success. These later chapters illustrate how those skills and abilities could be employed in the workplace, giving practical ways to buff the specific competencies needed to influence workplaces. We hope that offering practical suggestions and real-life examples through applied exercises will assist academics and leaders alike as they seek to understand and implement leadership competencies.

Summation of Workplace Leadership

Organizations that prioritize effective leadership in order to achieve goals and foster constructive work environments should place particular importance on developing future leaders. The text examines several leadership theories, touching on ethics, courage, emotional intelligence, and communication. We combine these elements into a number of functional competency clusters which address coaching and motivation, conflict resolution, and navigating the political landscape in and around an organization. Discussion of the various roles and skills employed by leaders is accompanied by chapters discussing tactical and strategic goals, as well as the formulation and articulation of vision, mission, and values. Taken as a whole, the volume intends to clarify and explain the elements that both allow organizations to identify potential leaders and then help those individuals learn how to best exercise their influence and direct others to achieve success.

Printed in the USA
CPSIA information can be obtained
at www.ICGtesting.com
CBHW082104290824
13581CB00111B/1045

9 781793 568861